Hints and Guesses

Hints and Guesses

William Gaddis's Fiction of Longing

Christopher J. Knight

The University of Wisconsin Press

The University of Wisconsin Press
2537 Daniels Street
Madison, Wisconsin 53718

3 Henrietta Street
London WC2E 8LU England

Library of Congress Cataloging-in-Publications Data
    Knight, Christopher J. 1952–
        Hints and guesses: William Gaddis's fiction of longing/
    Christopher J. Knight
        320 pp.   cm.
        Includes bibliographical references (p. 285) and index
        ISBN 0-299-15300-2 (cloth: alk. paper)
    ISBN 0-299-15304-5 (paper: alk. paper)
            1. Gaddis, William, 1922–   —Criticism and interpretation
            2. Satire, American—History and criticism. 3. Social problems in literature
    I. Title
    PS3557.A28Z75   1997
        813'.54—DC20   96-42512

In memory of Fred Asnes, friend and poet

For most of us, there is only the unattended
Moment, the moment in and out of time,
The distraction fit, lost in a shaft of sunlight,
The wild thyme unseen, or the winter lightning
Or the waterfall, or music heard so deeply
That it is not heard at all, but you are the music
While the music lasts. These are only hints and guesses,
Hints followed by guesses. . .
                    —T. S. Eliot, "The Dry Salvages"

If calculation and judgment are to answer the question
Which way?, perfectionist thinking is a response to the
way's being lost. So thinking may present itself as a
stopping, and as finding a *way back*, as if thinking is
remembering something.
    —Stanley Cavell, *Conditions Handsome and Unhandsome*

CONTENTS

Acknowledgments

There are a number of people whom I would like to thank for their support and assistance with regard to the writing of *Hints and Guesses*. For their unstinting encouragement, I would like to express my warmest appreciation to Charissa Jones, Candice Mancini, James Reiss, James Sosnoski, my parents, Robert and Rosemary Knight, and to my sisters—Barbara, Suzanne, and Jayne—and brother, Robert, and their families. For readings portions of the manuscript, I would like to thank Michael Holquist, Walter Reed, and Keith Tuma. At the University at Albany, I would like to thank both Bonnie Merrill and Suzanne Lance for their invaluable technical assistance. Among those associated with the University of Wisconsin Press, I would especially like to thank Dale Bauer, Mary Elizabeth Braun, Raphael Kadushin, Shelia Leary, Carol Olsen, and Susan Tarcov. Among those scholars who have taken a genuine interest in the fiction of William Gaddis, I would especially like to thank Warsaw University's Zbigniew Lewicki, who, along with Jerzy Welna, offered me the opportunity to teach a year-long seminar on Gaddis's work, and Tomasz Basiuk, whose participation in the seminar made it, for me, such a worthy event. Also among Gaddis scholars, I would like to thank Patrick O'Donnell and Steven Moore for their expert advice, and John Kuehl, for first introducing me to the fiction. On a somewhat more personal note, I would like to extend my profound gratitude to Sarah Hapner and John Cassidy, the first for her day-to-day friendship and support during the composition of this book, and the second not only for all the work he put into copyediting and typesetting the manuscript but also for his long years of friendship. Finally, I wish to thank William Gaddis for writing some of the most beautiful prose fiction that we, in the United States, have had the blessed fortune to be offered to us.

The correspondence between William Gaddis and Keith Botsford in the collection of Keith Botsford papers is quoted courtesy of the Yale Collection of American Literature, Beinecke Rare Book and Manuscript Library, Yale University.

Abbreviations

CG	*Carpenter's Gothic*
IR	John Kuehl and Steven Moore's *In Recognition of William Gaddis*
J R	*J R*
PR	*Paris Review* interview with William Gaddis
R	*The Recognitions*
RG	Steven Moore's *A Reader's Guide to William Gaddis's* The Recognitions

Hints and Guesses

Introduction

My title, *Hints and Guesses*, is taken from T. S. Eliot's *Four Quartets*, a poem that William Gaddis in the early stages of his work on *The Recognitions* intended to weave into the novel's fabric.[1] In the end, he chose not to do this, but a number of the poem's lines do surface throughout Gaddis's fiction, as for instance in *The Recognitions:* "Tragedy was foresworn, in ritual denial of the ripe knowledge that we are drawing away from one another, that we share only one thing, share the fear of belonging to another, or to others, or to God" (103), and in *Carpenter's Gothic:* "as though to recover what had been lost and found and lost again and again" (155).[2] The mood of the passages—which is in large part the mood of Gaddis's fiction—is one of mourning, reflective of the sense that an unnameable something has vacated the stage of our existence. "There is something missing, [. . .] if I knew what it is then it wouldn't be so missing," says Han in *The Recognitions* (95). This could be said by any number of Gaddis's characters, so pervasive appears the sentiment. Gaddis's fiction itself can largely be said to constitute a meditation on, or a response to, this felt vacancy—to the sense that twentieth-century material culture provides all the means necessary for survival except the reason why we should seek it.

The age is, or thinks of itself as being, posttheological, but it has not found a raison d'être to replace that which it has rejected, and so we find ourselves, Gaddis suggests, with "that sense of loss overreaching any of fulfillment" (*IR*, 8). This said, it seems doubtful that Gaddis believes that this same sense of loss can be undone by an embrace of theology. While not uninterested in religious questions, Gaddis nevertheless tends to identify theologies with the absolutizing of these same questions. Not atypical in this respect is his remark, when contrasting *The Recognitions*' Wyatt Gwyon to the early

3

Renaissance painters he would emulate, that the earlier painters were "from Giotto on, very safely encased in a frame of reference, working in a frame of Absolutes for their talents or their genius, in works largely for the Church. And this is exactly what Wyatt does not have around him. So he is really taking refuge in that framework of belief" (*PR*, 63).

In *The Recognitions*, this seeking of refuge in a prior age's beliefs may be preferable to what the other characters do, or do not do, with regard to finding mooring, yet still seem inadequate. Granted, it may be possible for an individual to find solace in the past, but the gesture will eventually founder unless the prior system can be revitalized to the point where it functions as a living set of beliefs. I do not say that it cannot, for clearly millions continue to believe what Giotto and others believed. But within the milieu inhabited by artists and other intellectuals, there is much less optimism this way, even noticeably less than in this century's first decades, when artists either made specific avowals of religious faith, in the manner of an Eliot, Moore, or Hemingway, or else felt comfortable in thinking of their artistry as a substitute for religious belief. Modernism itself often seemed to be about the substitution of an aesthetic for a religious practice, though given the essential differences between the two, it is not surprising that the gesture was relatively short-lived. While not unpriestlike, Gaddis does not make the mistake of wishing to substitute his work for religion, yet this makes his sense of loss all that much more overwhelming. He longs for what should give meaning to his life, but finds himself most attentive to its absence, and to the sense of having inherited a paper trail that may lead nowhere: "Though I weep for order I live still in a world of scrawled notes on the backs of envelops" (*IR*, 14). Here, the accumulation of knowledge and experience proves not a solution to the problem but an encumbrance, impeding the path forward as well as sapping the resolve. Or as Geoffrey Hartman, in another context, writes, "the growth of the historical consciousness, its multiplying of disparate models all of which press their claim, amounts to a peculiarly modern burden," leaving one such as Gaddis "surrounded by abstract potentialities, imperatives that cannot all be heeded, options exhausting the power of choice" (103–4).

Given the mood of Gaddis's work, it should be tempting to describe it under the rubric of modernism or, as has been more commonly the case, postmodernism. Though both these categories entail all kinds of reductions (and individually fail to do justice to the full tenor of Gaddis's fiction), it does seem that Gaddis's achievement represents the efforts of an artist who has imbibed the lessons of Eliot and the modernists and who, in thinking through their solutions, has explored the trail that later, more committed postmodernists should call their own. There is, for one, no doubt that Gaddis has a kinship with those modernists like Flaubert, Eliot, Pound, and Musil who, in Frank Kermode's words, sought "to produce encyclopedias for the fallen modern world." Referring to texts such as *Madame Bovary, The Waste Land, The Cantos,* and *The Man Without Qualities,* Kermode comments that

> These are the encyclopedias of exile, the great and hopeless attempts to get a world into a book, not a world or a book like Dante's, to be bound up in one volume of exactly one hundred cantos, but a world of heresies and exile, as seen by a privileged and tormented minority and got into books of strange fragmentary shapes, dreams of an order hardly to be apprehended. To be avant-garde, to be elite (and Eliot very strongly believed in elites) is to be in opposition to whatever simply *is,* whether you are exiled in Paris or London, Rapallo or Trieste.
>
> It is moreover to confront the corrupt world with messages, mostly about its corruption, which it will not, of its own will, even try to decipher. (*Appetite for Poetry,* 114–15)[3]

The difference between the modernists and Gaddis, however, is that whereas a Pound or an Eliot possessed a certain confidence in his solution to civilization's disarray, Gaddis, living at a later moment, even more diffuse, must feel as if the difficulty has been impossibly compounded. Every solution to the problem of order—be it aesthetic, philosophical, or theological—seems to carry within its own undoing, to the point that *différance,* with its habit of suspending ultimate questions, becomes something like a ruling paradigm. This helps to explain why there are so many failed priests and artists in Gaddis's fiction. They are simply too overwhelmed with the difficulty of holding the pieces together, of making sense of the world, the way, for instance, Jack Gibbs, a prisoner of his own encyclopedic project to interweave the turn-of-the-century realms of "government, invention, art, industry, and religion" (*J R,* 576) into a single narrative, discovers, after sixteen years, that he cannot carry it through, that he lacks the faith—both in the book and, more important, in the world—to see it through.

This said, it would be a mistake not to note the difference between the frequent failings of the novels' artists and the extraordinary success of Gaddis's own accomplishment. If many of the said artists' knees buckle at the prospect of trying to wrest order from the fabric of a multitudinous world, Gaddis's work testifies to the fact that the effort, postmodern skepticism notwithstanding, remains worthwhile. "[C]areless or predisposed readers," he notes, "see these books as chronicles of the dedicated artist crushed by commerce, which is, of course, to miss, or misread, or simply disregard all the evidence of *their own* appetite for destruction, their frequently eager embrace of the forces to be blamed for their failure to pursue the difficult task for which their talents have equipped them, failure to pursue their destiny if you like, taking art at the center, as you say, as redemption in, and of and from, a world of material values, overwhelmed by the material demands it imposes" (*PR*, 71). It is true, as Frederick Karl has observed, that in Gaddis there are no "hackneyed plea[s] for the superiority of the artist over life" (*IR*, 178), and yet the work of the artist remains of prime importance. Gaddis neither substitutes art for theology nor thinks less of it for not fulfilling all our needs. Still, art is very much part of the larger effort to glimpse the secret at the heart of things, and in this sense, it bears a kinship with religion. Or as Gaddis writes, they manifest a common "criterion": "that which constitutes poetic faith for the writer in Coleridge's familiar 'willing suspension of disbelief,' and for the religionist the leap of faith enshrined in Augustine's misquotation of Tertullian, 'Credo quia absurdum'" ("Old Foes," 1–2).[4] Here, then, the artist's project remains one not of skepticism and despair but of hope, however frustrated and embattled. This is why Gaddis, referring to Edward Bast's effort to introduce J R to the realm of the sublime, speaks of it (a gesture tied up with the composer's identity as an artist) as "that *real* note of hope in *J R*" (*PR*, 72).

Heidegger once said, "One cannot lose God as one loses his pocket knife." Gadamer puts a friendly twist on the remark: "in fact one cannot simply lose his pocket knife in such a fashion that it is no longer present. When one has lost a long familiar implement such as a pocket knife, it demonstrates its existence by the fact that one continually misses it" (*Philosophical Hermeneutics*, 234–35). Here, the object, even in its absence, continues to assert its presence, much in the way that "Hölderlin's 'Fehl der Götter' or Eliot's silence of the Chinese vase are not nonexistence, but 'being' in the most poetic sense because they are silent" (235). This is also true, to take an example from *Carpenter's Gothic*, of the way in which the house's "petit musée" interior testifies to Irene's presence, even though she has been gone for some time. In each instance, "[t]he breach that is made by what is missing is not a place remaining empty within what is present-to-hand; rather, it belongs to the being-there of that to which it is missing, and is 'present' in it" (*Philosophical Hermeneutics*, 235). It is a key point in relation to Gaddis's fiction, for even when it seems to be offering evidence of the contemporary world's disorder, there remains the sense that such disorder cannot be understood apart from the context of an implied order, or metaphysics. Gaddis works as much via apophaticism as direct statement. This is also why categorizations that seek to designate his work as either modernist or postmodernist are bound to fail, for while attempts to situate his work historically are not to be discouraged, these two specific categorizations are themselves notably incomplete without one another. Which is Gaddis, a modernist or a postmodernist? Neither and both, especially if by the latter is meant something akin to what Kermode calls "a permanent state of affairs," wherein it is acknowledged that "a tension between history and modern value (or between Modern and Postmodern) is constitutive of all literature" (*History and Value*, 133).

It is because I think the theme "something's missing" and the method of apophaticism are both intrinsic to Gaddis's work that I am sympathetic to those descriptions (and there have been several) that ascribe a religious dimension to the fiction. Religion, as defined by Carl Jung (whom Gaddis quotes), "designates the attitude peculiar to a consciousness which has been altered by the experience of the numinosum" (Gaddis, "Old Foes," 2), or as Rudolf Bultmann writes, it "is the human longing for something beyond the world, the discovery of another sphere where only the soul can abide, freed from everything worldly" (13). As used here, religion is the dimension that caters to the urge, spoken of by Gaddis, "to escape whole the limitations of my own mind" (*IR*, 3). It is not a dimension identified with any particular religious order per se,[5] but rather speaks to the felt presence of "the supernatural, that which is mysterious, spiritually inhabited, impossible to describe or to understand" (Gaddis, "Old Foes," 2). Thus, while both sympathetic (e.g., Wyatt, Stanley, Gibbs) and unsympathetic (e.g., Reverends Ude and Bobby Joe) characters are, at one time or another, identified with particular theologies (e.g., Calvinism, Roman Catholicism, Protestant Fundamentalism), the novels convey a mood of skepticism toward institutional religion, even as they, in a manner somewhat akin both to Kant's method of negative presentation and to Emerson's universalism, suggest that the quotidian is best understood sub specie aeternitatis. Just as Emerson felt that institutional Christianity left its communicants short of "where the sublime is, where are the resources of astonishment and power," Gaddis's sense of the religious, of what is valuable, appears identifiable with those moments when men and women find their lives intersecting with an order larger than themselves. Sometimes the circumstances of this intersection are, on the surface, quite ordinary, as when, in *Carpenter's Gothic*, Elizabeth's doings in the kitchen and the bedroom appear, in a reworking of the second section of "Burnt Norton," illustrative of that "still point" Eliot spoke of as "neither arrest nor movement":

> Movement brought her eyes up, arrested by the clock; all that moved was the dapple of the leaf-filtered sun on the kitchen's white wall, still as breathing till she turned for the radio which promptly informed her that Milwaukee had toppled the Indians four to one, but not of what game they were playing, and she turned it off, poured a glass of milk to carry up the stairs where she turned on the television and slipped off her blouse, sunk against the pillows. [. . .]
>
> —A que hora . . . Even here, where the leaf-broken sun climbed from bared shoulder over her parted lips, the movement continued on the lids closed against it, penetrated in diffuse chiaroscuro where the movement composed the stillness and herself sealed up, time adrift as the sun reached further, shattered by the telephone. (32)

At other times, the transcendent is more familiarly evoked, as in Wyatt Gwyon's anamnestic experience when seeing Picasso's *Night Fishing in*

Antibes, in Amy Joubert's response to the night sky, and in Christina Lutz's similar response to the ocean-fronting pond. The pond in *A Frolic of His Own* is often evoked as a timeless counter to a frenetic reality measurable in billable hours. When looked out upon one winter morning following a snow-fall, it is discovered as a "frozen pond [. . .] gone in an unblemished expanse of white under a leaden sky undisturbed by the flight of a single bird in the gelid stillness that had descended to seize every detail of reed and branch as though time itself were frozen out there threatening the clatter of teacups and silver and the siege of telephoning that had already begun" (439). The whiteness here recalls Melville's use in *Moby-Dick* of this noncolor to evoke that mystery demanding acknowledgment, and offers further evidence that Gaddis's work can be conceived as in that tradition which includes not only Emerson, Eliot, and Melville, but also Hawthorne, Thoreau, and Henry James. Here, I am thinking of the James whose work bends in the direction of those "things that, with all the facilities in the world, all the wealth and all the courage and all the wit and all the adventure, we never *can* directly know; the things that can reach us only through the beautiful circuit of belief and desire."

What these "things" are always remains somewhat mysterious in James, as they do in Gaddis. David Plante, a fine novelist in his own right, has commented upon this mystery that refuses dissection,

> To say what, in Henry James, the devotion is *to* is impossible. It is vague, and the vagueness gives it, amazingly, its brightness. Reading a long, long passage in one of his books, one from time to time forgets—one is, by the very language, detached from—what the repeated word "it" refers to, so "it" becomes the impression, an atmosphere, a sense, "a harmony without parts." This "it" was, I imagine, the secret that englobed his life and writing. (99)

Of course, to speak this way, of a secret that invokes something like the Kantian sublime, may be to go against the grain of the historical, or critical, moment. New Americanist critics like Rob Wilson, in *American Sublime: The Genealogy of a Poetic Genre*, and Donald Pease, in "Sublime Politics," argue the essential romanticism of the Kantian or European sublime, and suggest that this tradition, in traversing the ocean, was significantly transmuted. For Wilson, the appeal to the sublime in the United States cannot be separated from the "American will to national power" (925) and its symbolic technology. He argues that the Kantian sublime, "as dialogue between man and God within the discourse of the will-to-power over the manifest landscape, has been superseded in American poetics by an implied dialogue between man and various technologies. Such sublimity takes place within the bliss-and-dread discourse of submission to a naturalized system—Capital—which has become the 'always-already-given' of global vastness that the ego must now contend with" (32–33). Pease argues, in the ideological American rendition, the sublime was not man's but Nature's discourse. And Nature, through rude scenes eloquent with signs of prior dramatic conflict, some order *beyond Nature*, seemed to command man to get in touch with Nature's higher will and obey the implicit command to move beyond Nature. Of course the actual source of this will emanated neither from the natural landscape nor from some higher will but from man's future power over the landscape expressed in the policy of western expansionism. Through the subtle turns of the American sublime, the liberal taking axe and hammer to the virgin land could, with childlike innocence, proclaim that only through destruction of Nature's bounty could he feel by doing what nature commanded as if he were truly in touch with nature's will. (46)

Both Wilson and Pease wish to root the sublime in specific historical formations. This is an understandable ambition, for like any concept, including that of the Deity, the sublime entails the values of the epoch. And the way in which even the most abstract concept assumes historical coloring must be thought worthy of examination. It is, for instance, probably fair to say that the Kantian sublime itself represents something like an attempt to talk about God without talking about God, an attempt that begins to make sense only in the historical context of the Enlightenment and its stress on material explanation. Here, the Kantian sublime might be considered a form of apophaticism, a *via negativa*. And yet the question remains whether we can invoke a sense of the world—the *uni*-verse even—in its most numinous aspect, as something unframed by our material histories, even as we ourselves can only guess, not say, what this is. And in doing so, can we still refer to this as a worthy interest, and as invoking the sublime mood? I think we can, and that Gaddis, in fact, does so.

In speaking of the sublime in relation to Gaddis, then, my inclination is to follow the contemporary lead less of Wilson and Pease than of Rodolphe Gasché, "an advocatus Kantii" ("On Mere Sight," 111), who, in his essay "On Mere Sight," thinks it imperative that a space be kept open not only for the imagination but for its object, even when the latter escapes human representation. It is important to remember, he writes in reference to Kant's *Third Critique*, that "[c]ontrary to the beautiful, which must be understood as the direct presentation of the possibility of schematizing presentable concepts, the sublime takes upon itself the presentation of what is unpresentable. Thus, the task in question is a variation of what Kant calls (in paragraph 59) 'symbolic hypotyposis,' a variation because, as Kant contends, there are only two sorts of hypotyposes. Indeed, like symbolic presentation, the sublime renders the intelligible only indirectly, and does so in what I would call a *negative hypotyposis*" (113). Gasché is responding specifically to Paul de Man's critique (in "Phenomenality and Materiality in Kant") of Kant's notion of the sublime, a critique which, like that of Wilson and Pease, seeks to reinscribe the argument back into its material conditions.[6] Yet Gasché's point is that the material realm offers to thought not only itself but also what is not-itself, most notably when every attempt to map this realm ends in failure: "the endeavor to present the intelligible totality as the totality of nature is impossible, not only because that totality is unpresentable, but also because no totalization of nature can be achieved. The *Augenschein*, however, though failing to present the intelligible, offers it to thought" (115).

How does this connect to Gaddis's work? Gaddis is a novelist who gives every evidence of perfectionist thinking, which is dependent upon an enlarged notion of reality, whereby *what is* asks to be understood in the light of what the materialist should say is but imagined. Such thought is utopian, of course, and would appear at odds with the scenario of *différance*, though perhaps this latter suggestion is premature. Gasché argues that it is. For him, the notion of *différance* makes sense only within the context of "universally shareable generality and ideality." Or as he, in *Inventions of Difference*, explains the relation: "to problematize difference from the perspective of its invention is, first and foremost, to account for its specificity or singularity against the horizon of intelligibility with respect to, and within which, difference, even in its most extreme form, must be consecrated. For a difference to make a difference, and hence to be one in the first place, its uniqueness must be wrenched from and negotiated within a system of conventions. The question concerning the invention of difference, therefore, refers especially to the irruption into the world of that difference which, according to a long tradition, initially institutes universally shareable generality and ideality" (21). This notion, which Gasché himself locates in Derrida's own concept of *différance*, is thereby at odds with the more postmodern notion of *mise en abîme*. For Gasché (and, I believe, for Gaddis as well) this latter notion constitutes something like a "spurious infinity" (as opposed to a "true infinity": "the idea of true infinity is a philosophical *must*" [136]).[7] The spurious infinity begins and ends in the realm of the material. That is, it begins with the particular and then either enlarges it exponentially or moves away from it in an endless process of playful difference. In the first instance, it creates an Abstraction with its genesis in the concrete material; in the second instance, it creates a labyrinth of semiological difference. In both instances, the notion of a Totality, like that of the unrepresentational itself, remains suspect, even as it remains essential to any satisfying explanation of experience. Or as Gasché writes:

> But the concept of spurious infinity, with all its intra-philosophical shortcomings is, for that matter, a semantic concept too. The endless continuum that it refers to is one of semes reeling along in an infinite perspective. But also within the horizon, present in its absence, is the hope of achieving a sum total. If the Derridean concept of the infinite is to be distinguished from the concepts of

potential and spurious infinity, and it is supposed to radically breach the possibility of totalization of the true infinite, of the semantic in general, it can no
longer be of the order of a semantic concept. It must be a nonsemantic concept
if it is to achieve at all what it purports to do, and if it is not to fall prey to the
philosophical verdict that disposes of spurious infinity. (*Inventions*, 139)[8]

I pursue the point as far as I do because I think it necessary to reclaim
Gaddis's work from postmodernism's exclusive realm,[9] where much recent
criticism has consigned it. I say this not because this realm, or methodology,
has nothing to teach us (it does) but because when pursued at the large-scale
expense of other descriptions, it too can be limiting. In any event, included in
this criticism are not only essays and chapters by some of Gaddis's finest
readers (e.g., LeClair, O'Donnell, Strehle, Weisenburger, et al.) but also two
of the three monographs devoted to Gaddis: John Johnston's *Carnival of
Repetition: Gaddis's The Recognitions and Postmodern Theory* and Gregory
Comnes's *The Ethics of Indeterminacy in the Novels of William Gaddis*.
Johnston's is certainly the most challenging book on Gaddis's work (even as
I find Steven Moore's *William Gaddis* the most useful and least distortive).
Here the discussion is often brilliant, but Johnston's ambition to read
Gaddis's novels (and by extension all novels) as a poorer cousin to, and sub-
set of, literary theory strikes me as misguided. I am not against theory, quite
the contrary. However, I want to resist Johnston's too insistent suggestion
that the creative artist is paralytic until he or she is enabled by theory: "But
now, thanks to structuralist theory, we can see that it is precisely this disequilibrium between an excess in the signifying series and a lack in the signified
series that defines the novel's [*The Recognitions'*] structure" (124). In
Carnival of Repetition, Johnston portrays Gaddis as too much like Mikhail
Bakhtin, Gilles Deleuze, and Julia Kristeva's best student: "the important
point is that Bakhtin's theory accounts for the distinctive features and formal
unity . . . of *The Recognitions*" (4). This would, I imagine, bother me less if
Johnston did not also bring in Baudrillard, with his gleeful conflation of
Disneyland and the United States, to help explain matters: "America itself is
the *real* Disneyland, just as modern prisons conceal the fact that the social
fabric itself . . . has become carceral" (195). It is postmodern "discriminations" like these—which might better be described as the refusal to discriminate—that encourage Johnston willfully to misread Wyatt's "Thank God
there was the gold to forge" speech and to embrace the view that "'meaning'
does not originate in the individual's intentional act but is always produced
out of nonsense and its perpetual displacement in a preexistent and underly-
ing system or structure" (185).[10]
Gregory Comnes's commitment to a postmodern axiology also makes for
some rather wrenched readings of the Gaddis novels. Or so I judge his claim
that Gaddis's work constitutes a subversion of Thoreau's: "Gaddis calls into

question what Thoreau simply assumed, the very possibility of living 'deliberately' as an act of discovery" (*Ethics of Indeterminacy*, 4). And his claim that Gaddis "acknowledges the endurance of the bureaucratic good and recognizes that any offsetting moral principle of loving one's neighbor must include its successful execution in the bureaucratic world to have meaning" (8–9). The latter is an odd thing to say about the author of *J R*, a novel that savagely satirizes bureaucracy and its pigeonholing, countinghouse ethic. The point, of course, is not that goodness should stop at the company door, but that when a company places greater value upon its corporate, or bureaucratic, structure than upon its own workers, then something has seriously gone awry. It is a simple enough point, but seems to get misplaced in Comnes's struggle to identify Gaddis's fiction with an "ethics of indeterminacy," a scheme fraught with confusions of the critic's own making. Nor are Comnes's arguments strengthened by his professed doubts in "textual reference" (10) and his belief that Gaddis's novels do not require close, patient readings: "My concern is not to read exhaustively each of Gaddis's novel: Steven Moore has already engaged in the Herculean task of plowing through the thickets of Gaddis's prose" (15). Comnes prefers to tag Gaddis with a position—"[a]s postmodern texts, Gaddis's novels are ideologically sound" (2)—than to read the texts for what they claim to be, novels, or part of a long tradition of achievement that includes (aside from the American efforts alluded to above) *Crime and Punishment*, *The Brothers Karamazov*, *Jane Eyre*, *Bleak House*, *Middlemarch*, *Heart of Darkness*, *Nostromo*, *Sons and Lovers*, *Remembrance of Things Past*, *Ulysses*, *Finnegans Wake*, *The Counterfeiters*, *A Handful of Dust*, and *The Waves*. It is a tradition which, when it is more broadly considered as literature, includes the works of Plato, Aristotle, Augustine, Shakespeare, Montaigne, Pascal, Goethe, Rousseau, Keats, Hopkins, Rilke, and Yeats. As Gaddis himself notes, "Speaking of influences, I think mine are more likely to be found going from Eliot *back* rather than forward to my contemporaries" (*PR*, 68). But this is not the kind of thing the postmodern critic wishes to hear.

Unsettling as Comnes's remark about "Gaddis's prose" may be, it does suggest the difficulty of these novels, a difficulty that has not disappeared even with the arrival of three monographs, one reader's guide (Moore's on *The Recognitions*), and scores of scholarly essays devoted to the explanation of the work. *Hints and Guesses* will not radically alter this situation, but it represents an attempt, like most prior scholarship, not only to come to some better understanding of this writer's "careful obscurity,"[11] but also to trumpet the importance of Gaddis's fiction. I do not share Johnston's view, based in "the theory of post-modernist writing as a self-reproducing 'text'" (172), that the reader is as responsible, say, for *The Recognitions* as Gaddis himself: "in *The Recognitions* we are led to participate in a transformation from a literary 'work' conceived as unique, organic, autotelic, and authored, in the sense of filiated to the writer as father and creator, to an 'already written' and constructed 'text,' endlessly open and produced by the reader" (157). The claim borders on immodesty and ingratitude, and while it is unnecessary to revere every novelist or poet, I agree with Valentine Cunningham that in the most notable instances—and what is Gaddis's fiction but a most notable instance—"imaginative writers and their writings matter more than mere critics [or readers] and their theories about writing" (60).[12] No critic of Gaddis's work has yet approached his genius, and it is best to admit this from the start. It is, in part, this conviction that explains and justifies my methodology, a "practical criticism (in the widest sense)."[13] I began my initial study with no prior thesis about the fiction except that it is important, a conclusion reached from having read and reread the work over time. This is not to say that *Hints and Guesses* does not focus on certain themes, motifs, and techniques. Readers would be unforgiving if it did not. However, I wish to emphasize that my response began in an intuition with regard to the fiction's importance, followed by a search for the source of this intuition, including most notably the details of the artistry.

"God is in the details," Aby Warburg used to say, a statement that, like Nabokov's "Fondle the details," suggests that if we are insensitive to the details, the elements of difference, we will most likely be insensitive to the larger things as well. This is an important point with regard to Gaddis, whose fiction gives every evidence that its author has gone through a painstaking effort to get the details right, be they those of Flemish painting, Wall Street finance, sub-Saharan colonial politics, or the Rules of Federal Civil Procedure. It is this same concern that prompted Gaddis, responding to an interviewer's question about *J R*'s financial details, to say that he "wanted them right, thinking *if* someone who is well-versed and familiar with the world of finance, with what goes on in the market and so forth, read *J R*," he or she would not be disappointed, for "even though it's a quite improbable story, it is still possible" (*PR*, 69–70). Yet if Gaddis is noticeably careful regarding details, he is also sensitive to the way in which these same details, or facts, often find their truth transmuted into something quite different via the agencies of distance, time, and interpretation. As McCandless in *Carpenter's Gothic* puts the matter, there is "a very fine line between the truth and what really happens" (130). Something *does* happen, but what it is is sometimes impossible to say. So many things get in the way of the event and its recall, much in the manner of the emblematic story that Wyatt, in *The Recognitions*, tells about Mary Stuart's death:

That's why most writing now, if you read it they go on one two three four and tell you what happened like newspaper accounts, no adjectives, no long sentences, no tricks they pretend, and they finally believe that they really that the

way they saw it is the way it is, when really . . . why, what happened when
they opened Mary Stuart's coffin? They found she'd taken two strokes of the
blade, one slashed the nape of her neck and the second one took the head. But
did any one of the eye-witness accounts mention two strokes? No . . . it never
takes your breath away, telling things you already know, laying everything out
flat, as though the terms and the time, and the nature and the movement of
everything were secrets of the same magnitude. (113)

Secrecy resides in the very heart of the visible, and each attempt to resay
what happened risks introducing us to all that we did not see, all that
remained invisible while we, on hands and knees, worked in the putative
realm of fact. It is a situation reminiscent of that which gives impetus to
Frank Kermode's fine book *The Genesis of Secrecy*, the sense that mystery is
itself inescapable, that it is part and parcel of all that appears otherwise: "We
are most unwilling to accept mystery, what cannot be reduced to other and
more intelligible forms. Yet that is what we find here: something irreducible,
therefore perpetually to be interpreted; not secrets to be found out one by
one, but Secrecy" (143).

The fact that, in Emerson's words, "Everything is made of hidden stuff"
does not deter us from interpretation. Instead, it probably only goads us on the
more. We know that every text will in one way or another deceive us, that, in
Nietzsche's words, there are no facts, only interpretations. Still, the desire to
get at the heart of a text's meaning, its secret, remains strong, and reconciles
us to the inevitable embarrassments. Here, we are moved not only by the
inevitability of failure but also by the possibility of truth. "We are," says
Kermode, "all fulfillment men, *pleromatists*, we all seek the center that will
allow the senses to rest, at any rate for one interpreter, at any rate for one
moment" (*Genesis of Secrecy*, 72). The Gaddis novels, by reason of their
artistry and difficulty, invite interpretation, motivated less by a theory than by
a desire to glimpse the secrecy of things, texts included. Engaged by the novels' details, one sets out to find where they lead, to what larger meaning or
truth. Of course, some might think the effort futile, that Gaddis's novels invite
readings not hermeneutics. I wish, however, to resist the suggestion, prefer-
ring to respond to the novels less as a modernist or a postmodernist than as
someone who, taken by the novels' surfaces, also intuits that these surfaces
are bound to one another in a relation, or relations, that are not obvious or
apparent, but that may nevertheless be important and meaningful, and that
may be as determinant of the surfaces, or details, as these are of it, or them.

In *Hints and Guesses*, my first ambition is to attend to the novels themselves, knowing that their complexity should acquit me of the charge that my
interests are too formal. It is not that I am uninterested in questions of formal-
ism—I am interested, especially if others are prepared to grant that form
might, as Ernst Bloch argued, be understood as "ideological surplus," the con-

sequence of a utopian function that esteems Brecht's phrase "something's missing" as a way of understanding all the things that remain before us (Bloch, 15). Yet even as no serious study of Gaddis's work can truly avoid the interest of form, my first and fullest attention in *Hints and Guesses* is toward those matters (e.g., cultural, ethical, and political) that reach beyond this interest. For instance, in the discussion of *The Recognitions*, I am particularly attentive to the motifs of forgery and Flemish painting and the way in which the two influence a third: the role of the aesthetic. And I am also very much interested in the novel's depiction of the late 1940s and early 1950s Greenwich Village art scene, the novel's main locale. For a long time we thought of that scene, identified as it was with the Abstract Expressionist movement, as the Golden Age of American painting. Gaddis's novel does not take this view. Instead, we find many of the criticisms that more recent art historians and cultural critics (e.g., Diana Crane and Serge Guilbaut) have begun to make about the paintings' relation to market forces and even Cold War politics. In the first chapter I try to bring some of these criticisms forward.

Then, in the second chapter, on *J R*, I enlist the help of classic and contemporary economic theory (i.e., Marx, Simmel, Schumpeter, Weber, and Heilbroner) to critique Gaddis's portrait of a post-Vietnam American capitalism, wherein Wall Street has "conjured up such a mighty means of production and exchange," to borrow from Marx and Engels, that it is "like the sorcerer who can no longer control the powers of the underworld that he had called up by his spirits." I follow this by addressing a central question raised by the novel: "what [exactly] is worth doing" in the late twentieth century? The question is a very real one in Gaddis's work, and nowhere more so than in *J R*. Like Plato, who pithily put the matter, "It is no chance matter we are discussing, but how one should live," Gaddis is a writer keenly focused on the question of the examined life. He may be a postmodern writer, but he is also something more than this (particularly given postmodernism's cool acceptance of our historical belatedness). Hence one aim of this study is to critique Gaddis's work in light of both Kant's *Third Critique* and Adorno's *Aesthetic Theory*, the first for what he has to say about originality, design, perfection, and the sublime; and the latter for his attention to the way that the mid-century artist exemplifies an ethic of resistance, especially to mainstream culture.

More briefly, the chapter on *Carpenter's Gothic* attends to such matters as cultural conspiracies, the religious right, domestic violence, and postcolonial politics. Most of these are charged topics, yet Gaddis's treatment of them is less that of the polemicist than that of the novelist sensitive to nuance, and I try to discuss them in this vein. Finally, the last chapter, a discussion of *A Frolic of His Own*, examines Gaddis's theme of justice according to the terms manifest in the novel. These terms are complicated by the fact that the novel makes so much specific reference to state and federal law. Actually, says Gaddis, there was a point when he planned to make the fourth novel "all lawsuits, no narrative at all," a plan he dropped only when "I began to realize I can't get every law case in America in this novel," and things had to be "cut down" (D. Smith, 36). Thus, my own response to the novel tries to answer what are basically two questions: first, what are the legal questions at issue and how might these best be understood? And second, how does justice, concretely and abstractly, find itself imagined? In the first instance, I find the novel particularly attentive to the issues of copyright and procedural law, and I have done my best to get on top of these matters. In the second instance, I find that justice is imagined less as aligned with one concept or another and more as something found (and lost again and again) in the interstices of these various concepts, which in the present instance include natural law, legal right, political right, an ethic of care, and the transcendent. The first four of these concepts are each identifiable with one of the novel's main characters, whereas the last concept—the transcendent—is less identified with one specific character than encapsulated in the narrative's events, making its presence palpably felt only on occasion, but then to great effect.

As must be evident from this foreshadowing, my study focuses more on those matters that might be described as extramural. I do not deny that the fullest study of Gaddis's work demands an attention to the intramural, to the textuality that has oriented so many postmodern readings. But like the latter readings, my own reading is a partial one, starting from the assumption that the work's encyclopedic range and complexity make definitive readings impossible. The future may offer more comprehensive readings, but for now it seems best to proceed somewhat more circumscriptively. In the present case, my attention is decidedly directed toward Gaddis the social satirist. Of course, it has been argued that the twentieth century, with its vaunting of *différance*, is no longer hospitable to satire, for the genre often masks a utopian project.[14] I think the latter true, but I do not, as should be clear, think this a reason for placing a pox on satire. Such action is, and always will be, premature, and if carried out will leave no one to answer, in the present instance, Johnston's question, "But what are we to make of the novel's [*The Recognitions*'] obvious satire, which takes up a good portion of its content?" (173). Johnston is not the best person to answer this question, for as he notes, "satire generally depends upon pre-existent values and directs our attention toward the activities represented" (173), whereas his own interest in the fiction is much more attentive to its element of parody: "In general, his [Gaddis's] attitude recalls Swift's credo that everything spiritual and valuable has a gross and revolting parody, very similar to it, with the same name, but with the proviso that the 'parody' has now become the reality" (150). It is only partially true, and contra Johnston I would argue that the novels' value very much resides in the fact that their parody has a limit, especially if we believe, with Nabokov, that "Satire is a lesson, parody is a game" (*Strong*

Opinions, 75). My point, as made above (see note 10), is that whereas it has become commonplace to view postwar novelists as full-fledged parodists and black humorists,[15] it is better perhaps to discuss Gaddis's own use of the carnivalesque as tied in with a utopian project, as a suspension of the law—with the purpose of correction and renewal—rather than a rejection of it. Like Bakhtin's notion of the carnival as regenerative—"We must stress . . . that the carnival is far distant from the negative and formal parody of modern times. Folk humor denies, but it revives and renews at the same time" (*Rabelais*, 11)—Gaddis's own use of parody appears essentially reformist, to the point that we might say that the parody is seldom separate from, and usually subordinate to, satiric purposes. This is not to say that Gaddis employs satire with the same self-confidence as a Swift or Waugh, for the epistemological avenues are clearly more debris ridden. Still, as I read him, Gaddis's project is much less akin to fabulation than to *parodia sacra*, wherein the parody finds its own license and legitimacy in the very thing it parodies. (Of course, not all parodies are scornful and derisive. Linda Hutcheon remarks that Joyce "uses parody as much to resacralize as to desacralize" [14], and the same can be said of Gaddis.)

In Gaddis's fiction, there exists an apparent, albeit invisible, relation between individual characters and a numinous, sacred realm, the latter of which speaks of all that requires knowing and compliance, even as it is unknowable and its demand asymmetrical. Here, though, the "individual" can be understood in at least two opposing forms: first, as the resident of a democratic and materially advanced society who values autonomy and spatial privacy, and feels no obligation toward any truth larger than self-interest; and second, as one who, intuiting an absence, makes a concerted effort to return to the primacy of felt being, to that rare moment wherein being true to the Other is, paradoxically, synonymous with being true to oneself. Or as Derrida (in his discussion of Jan Patočka) puts it, "[t]he individualism of technological civilization relies precisely on a misunderstanding of the unique self. It is an individualism relating to a *role* and not a *person*. In other words it might be called the individualism of a masque or *persona*, a character [*personage*] and not a person" (*Gift of Death*, 36). But there is also the individualism that, predicated on an ethic of responsion, seeks its truest self in the recesses of what remains occulted. Here, we do well "to speak . . . of mystery or secrecy in the constitution of a *psychē* or of an individual and responsible self. For it is thus that the soul separates itself in recalling itself to itself, and so it becomes individualized, interiorized, becomes its very invisibility" (*Gift of Death*, 15). The distinction is an important one, and seems also relevant to Gaddis's own understanding of individual character. Throughout his novels, we repeatedly meet with two divergent types of characters. There are first those who, caricaturelike, are the products of their environments and whose understanding of individuality is strictly circumscribed by the expectations of the visible. Then, there are those who, in the mode of Dostoevsky's Alyosha, are almost "honest by nature, demanding the truth, seeking it and believing in it, and in that belief demanding an immediate deed, with an unfailing desire to sacrifice everything for this deed, even life." Of course, only the exceptional few satisfy this description, yet if we cast our net wide to include those who would, if countervailing forces were not so prevalent, orient their lives this way, we might include not only the more diligent artists such as Wyatt Gwyon, Stanley, and Edward Bast, but also some of the less diligent artists—Jack Gibbs, Tom Eigen, Schepperman, Schramm, McCandless, and Oscar Crease—and those who are artists less in fact than in spirit: Esme, Amy Joubert, Elizabeth Booth, Harry and Christina Lutz, Judge Crease, et al. The predominance of artists among those who realize something like personhood in Gaddis's fiction should lead us to the conclusion not that all artists are attentive to the demands of the spirit so much as that all those who are attentive to these demands have a touch of the poet about them. But this is close to being a tautology, for the point is that the artists who truly merit our respect in Gaddis's fiction are those who resist the demands of the material culture and press it toward an alignment with a world elsewhere, a religious dimension not necessarily churchly.

In short, then, when I speak of my first interest as locatable in the novels themselves, I do not mean to suggest that my practice does not move toward conclusions. It obviously does, and these same conclusions also have a way of influencing what is seen and valued. The conclusions I draw tend, as noted, to picture Gaddis as a social critic, as an artist and intellectual who judges experience via the measure of an enlarged culture or perspective. Granted, he is first and foremost a novelist, and his novels possess that quality of virtuality which is the essence of art. But the novel has traditionally maintained a crucial, dialogical tension between itself and "reality." Lionel Trilling addressed this tradition when, in *The Liberal Imagination*, he wrote: "The novel has had a long dream of virtue in which the will, while never abating its strength and activity, learns to refuse to exercise itself upon the unworthy objects with which the social world tempts it, and either conceives its own right objects or becomes content with its own sense of its potential force—which is why so many novels give us, before their end, some representation, often crude enough, of the will unbroken but in stasis" (260).[16]

Gaddis's novels are part of this tradition, even as in their postmodern aspect they might be said to complicate it. Others, as noted, have dwelled on the postmodernism, but it is the former aspect that truly interests me, the sense in which Gaddis's novels imply a realm (in Trilling's memorable phrase) "beyond culture." Thus, while I acknowledge that Gaddis's novels are as interesting for their technique as for their themes and longings, it is the latter that interest me more. I do not assume that these are discrete or unrelated interests, but while I have little to add, say, to Johnston's excellent discussion of character mirroring in *The Recognitions* or Patrick O'Donnell's equally fine discussion of the play of unidentified voices in *J R*, I find that not enough has been said yet about the way these novels not only critique society but do so from a perspective that stands apart from it. Here, it is a matter not of escaping culture so much as of refusing its official versions and judging it by an alternative reality, or ideal, that may exist as something only imagined, or may exist as something more than this, i.e., as a truth possess-ing metaphysical dimension.[17] In the end, this may entail less a question of will, as Trilling would have it, than a question of imagination, and even of faith. Still, in Gaddis's fiction, will has something to do with the matter as well. The novels themselves—the fact that they got written at all—are the reflection of an extraordinary assertion of will, of the desire not only to do more than one could but also to do it regardless of whether the novels should find acceptance or not. In such circumstances, the will does not operate alone, however. Gaddis could not have written these novels if he had not also been compelled by an imagination that refused to find rest in things as they are, and if he had not the faith to believe that what is not (materially) may be as real as what is.

Gaddis's novels, then, are as much about a rupturing of the status quo as about a rewriting of it. But it is the second scenario to which postmodern criticism wishes to attend, not the first. It is, paradoxically, a conservative gesture, as is apparent, for instance, in Comnes's readiness to hold the dis-cussion of ethics hostage to the forces of American capitalism, fearful of countenancing any notion of reality that calls into question its manifest mate-riality. Still, if we are to give these novels their due, we will have to approach them with a greater openness regarding our notions of the real. Gaddis is very much in the mold of what Giles Gunn calls a "strong poet: someone whose redescriptions are predicated on the human ability through language to avail us of possibilities for understanding that language itself cannot name" (*Thinking Across*, 115). As readers, we need to be responsive to this aspect of his work. Otherwise, we risk reading it in the light of what it would critique, of reading its ethos as "naturalistic and pragmatic" (Comnes, 18). Of course, to suggest that we read Gaddis's work in the context of a world elsewhere is to rely as much on an intuition as on a fact or a revela-tion, and implies no wish to claim a greater knowingness, as opposed to a greater openness, vis-à-vis the world.[18] Here, as Gunn says, this intuition might be a response to "the ineffable, the unthinkable, the undecidable, or simply the vague" (*Thinking Across*, 115). My hope is that it is more like the former than the latter (though even vagueness has its value).[19] Thus, while it is not surprising that some critics might choose to read Gaddis's fiction almost solely in terms of its textuality, there is also good reason for reading it in relation to, or in tension with, one, a social reality extant outside the nov-els' borders, and, two, a world elsewhere, which, for lack of material definition, we might speak of as the realm of the numinosum. These two modes of reading need not be thought of as antithetical, though in practice they often appear this way. Here, in *Hints and Guesses*, I wish to acknowledge the importance of both methods, albeit imagining the first relation as a subset of the second.

I have already previewed what I wish to discuss, but before beginning I would also like to say a word or two regarding the basic principles at work. There are at least three, including (1) an attention to novelistic details; (2) a readiness to see the novels as critiquing a real social world and raising real ethical (i.e., human) issues; and (3) the sense that both the details and the critique must be understood in the light of an enlarged perspective or realm, in which ostensibly disparate things are found to hold together and assume meaning. In the first instance, I proceed with the assumption that these are, in fact, novels that need to be read closely, and that if we ignore the details, we will miss the meanings. Experience suggests that it is best to move from the details to the meaning, though the movement is probably more pendulum-like, with details hinting at meaning, and meaning suggesting how we should read the details. Whatever the case, I read Gaddis's novels with the sense that details are pregnant with meaning and not to be glossed over. In the second instance, I am inclined to read Gaddis's fiction, despite its penchant for cartoon, as largely a comment and satire on the world outside its covers. I am not sure that I would, like Louis Auchincloss, call the author a "novelist of manners," but I believe, along with M. D. Carnegie, that "[w]hen the history of 20th century American letters is written, William Gaddis will occupy a prominent place as the most devastating satirist of American postwar society."[20] Hence, I am not of the opinion that there are no "real" characters in these novels, even as I acknowledge that the plethora of caricatures makes us more suspicious of even those characters—e.g., Wyatt Gwyon, Amy Joubert, McCandless, and Christiana Lutz—whose realness, or three-dimensionality, would otherwise seem self-apparent. Here, the inclination of the postmodern critic is to attend to the caricatures and to conclude that Gaddis's intention is a thinking beyond bourgeois subjectivity. I attend to the three-dimensional characters and conclude that the caricatures themselves are the consequence less of a deliberate posthumanistic ideology than of a satiric wit, set in motion by an enlarged conception of human possibility. Gaddis, in an interview, has given credence to this notion, saying that "Some of them ['the academics, critics and reviewers'] call my work postmodern, but I really don't have any interest in this. If they want to call it postmodern, fine. I'm sure they would be amazed if they knew that I think *J R* is in many ways a traditional novel" (Logan and Mirkowicz). Along these same lines, he has also said that he "can never resist" "the temptation of satire or parody" (Bradbury, *Writers in Conversation*, 5).[21] Still, it is the fiction itself that strengthens the conviction that we do well to think of this novelist's efforts as something like a reformer's desire to change the world, to make it more like something it is not. This desire is, as I have said, predicated on a third thing, and this is an intuition of the world as a place that masks its purposes, its meanings, even as these latter things are those that we must take cognizance of if we are to live rightly in the world. Like anything else in Gaddis's fiction, this intuition is not above being ironized or parodied, but if we attend only to this and not to the way in which it also demands respect, we shall badly misread the fiction. The point is, this intuition takes us into the realm of the numinous, which is also the realm of the religious. It is not a realm easily recognized or read, but not to make the effort represents the ultimate failing.

Finally, I would like to say a word about the present state of Gaddis criticism. As recently as 1993, Malcolm Bradbury and William Gass, friendly critics both, could be found speaking of the attention that Gaddis's novels have garnered as cultlike. In *The Modern American Novel*, Bradbury writes of *The Recognitions* and *J R* that "[t]hese two novels make it clear that Gaddis is one of the remarkable figures of the recent American novel, though, unlike Pynchon's, his work seems largely to have remained the interest of a narrow readership, perhaps even a cult" (251). And in his rather eccentric introduction to *The Recognitions*, Gass writes that the novel, which "remains widely heard about, reverently spoke of, yet narrowly read," "needed devotees who would keep its existence known until such time as it could be accepted as a classic; but a cult following is not the finest one to have, suggesting something, at best, beloved only by special tastes—in this case, the worry was, a wacko book with wacko fans" (vi). Fortunately, Gass redeems the insult by going further, pointing out that while "a cult did form," it was "a cult in the best old sense, for it was made of readers whose consciousness had been altered by their encounter with this book" (vi).

In truth, though the initial responses to *The Recognitions* constitute an outrage,[22] since the publication of *J R* in 1975 Gaddis has not been that badly served by critics. For starters, he has been altogether fortunate to have among his admirers Steven Moore, whose first book, *A Reader's Guide to William Gaddis's* The Recognitions, is an indispensable reference tool, and whose subsequent efforts, *In Recognition of William Gaddis* (a collection of essays that Moore, along with John Kuehl, edited) and *William Gaddis*, have also been much welcomed. In addition to Moore's work and the committed postmodern readings found in John Johnston's *Carnival of Repetition* and Gregory Comnes's *The Ethics of Indeterminacy in the Novels of William Gaddis*, Gaddis's work has received prominent attention in the major histories of postwar fiction—Bradbury's *The Modern American Novel*, Karl's *American Fictions: 1940-1980*, Kuehl's *Alternate Worlds*, and Tanner's *City of Words*—and has been the subject of scores of essays, many of first-rate quality, including Dominick LaCapra's "William Gaddis's *The Recognitions*," Steven Weisenburger's "Paper Currencies: Reading William

Gaddis," Susan Strehle's chapter, "*J R* and the Matter of Energy," in *Fiction in the Quantum Universe*, and Patrick O'Donnell's chapter, "His Master's Voice," in *Echo Chambers: Figuring Voice in Modern Narrative*. The response has, more times than not, been highly flattering. Tanner has called *The Recognitions* "one of the most important novels written since the last war";[23] LaCapra, like Tanner, has argued that the first novel has only "acquired increasingly broader relevance since" its 1955 publication (34); Karl has spoken of *The Recognitions* and *J R* as "sequential histories of our time" (*American Fictions*, 302); Bradbury has called Gaddis "one of the best of contemporary novelists" (*Modern American Novel*, 254); a *New Yorker* reviewer has placed the work "in the tradition of Joyce, Beckett, and Pynchon" (31 January 1994: 89); and William Gass has claimed that "no one who loves literature can follow these motions, these sentences, half sentences, of William Gaddis, very far without halting and holding up their arms and outcrying hallelujah there is something good in this gosh awful god empty world" (ix–x).

As one can see, Gaddis criticism has, to this point, been often characterized by a tone of advocacy, with the critics thinking it their first responsibility to enlarge his circle of readers. In *Hints and Guesses*, I too think of myself as an advocate, but I also write mindful of another, somewhat newer, obligation, and that is as a critic responding to a writer assumed to be canonical. It is an important shift, with definite consequences regarding one's reading practices. Or as Kermode writes, the "control of interpretation is intimately connected with the valuations set upon texts. The decision as to canonicity depends upon a consensus that a book has the requisite qualities, the determination of which is, in part, a work of interpretation. And once a work becomes canonical the work of the interpreter begins again" (*Art of Telling*, 174). It takes a long while for a writer to become canonical, but it is more than forty years since the publication of *The Recognitions*, one of this century's most important American novels, and since then, through the publication of *J R*, *Carpenter's Gothic* and *A Frolic of His Own*, Gaddis has made it clear that the first novel was no fluke, that this is a body of work that demands the most serious attention. It demands, in effect, exegesis. I say this mindful of the fact that we are currently urged not to revere literary texts as quasi-sacred. Often, the admonition comes not from those who would caution us against the conflation of different spheres, but from those who would see all spheres as one: the material. I myself am more respectful of the first claim than the second. Still, to the degree that a text becomes canonical, to the degree that it suggests irreducible meanings, it continues to bear a resemblance to sacred texts, a resemblance that makes the obligation of interpretation only that much more pressing.[24] It is, in any event, in this vein, as novels demanding interpretation, and therefore as a variant of the sacred, without exactly being this, that I propose, here in *Hints and Guesses*, to read the four

Gaddis novels. I do so in the trust that there exists a cult ("in the best old sense") of readers, both present and future, who will also deem the effort worthwhile.

1

The Recognitions and Wyatt Gwyon's Role as Artist/Forger/Artist

> Hast thou betrayed my credulous innocence
> With vizor'd falsehood and base forgery?
> —John Milton, *Comus*

Wyatt's Rejection of Mid-Century Abstraction

Among Gaddis's novels, *The Recognitions* (1955), his first, has received the greatest amount of scholarly attention. Steven Moore published *A Reader's Guide* to the novel, John Johnston's *Carnival of Repetition* is itself largely a study of this one novel, and there have been several dozen articles devoted to it. Here, then, I do not set out to discuss the novel in anything like its fullness, for the reason that, one, the novel has already provoked a wide range of discussion; and, two, the novel is so encyclopedic and complex that it makes, in the space of a chapter, a full-scale analysis all but impossible. I propose to limit my own discussion to the novel's protagonist, Wyatt Gwyon, in relation to his role as a mid-century painter who, disenchanted with the aesthetic zeitgeist of his time, turns to the forging of Flemish masterworks. I have discussed some of these matters in an earlier essay, "Flemish Art and Wyatt's Quest for Redemption." Since then, I have thought a great deal more about the novel and would like to pursue the discussion further.

The artist is a stock character in Gaddis's fiction, of course, and in *The Recognitions* artists are everywhere, a situation that undercuts their distinctiveness. This does not necessarily translate into a dismissal of the artist per se. In fact, Gaddis's investment in the possibilities of the artist is considerable. Nevertheless, the artist manqué is the prime subject of Gaddis's satire and rebuke. For a satire of this sort, he chooses (as is his knack) his time and place well, for the time is mid-century and the predominate place is New York's Greenwich Village. It is the Village at the height of its bohemian confidence—cocksure that the only person worthy enough to take the measure of existence is the artist, especially when impoverished and exiled. Matters of aesthetics, economics, geography, and morality all seem to find themselves rolled up into a single cause, an attitude that Clement Greenberg, the culture's mythographer, noticed and celebrated. Or as he wrote at the time: "The morale of that section of New York's Bohemia which is inhabited by striving young artists has declined in the last twenty years, but the level of its intelligence has risen, and it is still downtown, below 34th Street, that the fate of American art is being decided—by young people, few of them over forty, who live in cold-water flats and exist from hand to mouth. Now they all paint in the abstract vein, show rarely on 57th Street, and have no reputations that extend beyond a small circle of fanatics, art-fixated misfits who are as isolated in the United States as if they were living in Paleolithic Europe" (Crane, 47).

The Village did, in fact, host impressive achievement, notably in the work of Barnett Newman, Arshile Gorky, Robert Motherwell, Franz Kline, Hans Hofmann, Willem de Kooning, Jackson Pollock, and, most significantly, Mark Rothko. But for every painter who managed to wrest an individual idiom, there were scores, if not hundreds, of artists who lost their way in an abstractionist idiom that could be, perhaps paradoxically, not only challenging but also surprisingly banal. Nor were these always separate instances. Witness, for instance, the promptings, or lack thereof, motivating Kline's "painting experiences," wherein he did not, he said, "decide in advance that I'm going to paint a definite experience, but in the act of painting it becomes a definite experience." Or Motherwell's statement that *Doodling is not a style but a process*, a process in which *one's own being is revealed*, willingly or not, *which is precisely originality*, that burden of modern individualism" (Arnason, 228). Here, the impulse was, in Harold Rosenberg's words, "Just *TO PAINT*" (Doss, 386), in the belief that if the artist did this with gusto, he or she might even rival the Creator. Thus, Greenberg wrote that "[t]he avant-garde . . . artist tries in effect to imitate God by creating something valid solely on its own terms . . . ; something *given*, increate, independent of meanings, similars or originals. Content is to be dissolved so completely into form that the work of art . . . cannot be reduced in whole or part to anything not itself" (5–6). And so also wrote Newman, in the 1948 rallying cry "The Sublime Is Now": "We are freeing ourselves of the impediments of memory, association, nostalgia, legend, myth, or what have you, that have been the devices of Western European painting. Instead of making *cathedrals* out of

Christ, man, or 'life,' we are making it out of ourselves, out of our own feelings" (Chipp, 553). It was, then, an art-for-art's-sake aesthetic, and while
artists in others periods (the present included) have often judged this aesthetic harshly, the mid-century abstractionists were, in fact, proud of it. Hence
Greenberg's remark: "'Art for art's sake' and 'pure poetry' appear, and subject matter or content becomes something to be avoided like the plague" (5).

In *The Recognitions*, most of the artists also embrace an art-for-art's-sake
aesthetic. However, Wyatt Gwyon, a thirty-three-year-old painter, does not,
for he cannot escape the thought that there is here something missing, most
notably a sense of necessity. Too much of what he sees justifies itself as individual self-expression, predicated on the conceit that the artists are themselves so important that the world has no other choice but to take notice. For
Wyatt, purpose, including aesthetic purpose, is better sought apart from personal ambitions and appetites. But looking around him, in the late 1940s, he
finds these in fact dominate, that the personal urge-cum-aesthetic "just to
paint" is perceived not as the empty gesture it is but as something profound
and revelatory. Or as Wyatt says to the art dealer and purchaser of souls
Recktall Brown:

> It's a question of . . . it's being surrounded by people who don't have any sense
> of . . . no sense that what they're doing means anything. Don't you understand
> that? That there's any sense of necessity about their work, that it has to be
> done, that it's theirs. And if they feel that way how can they see anything nec-
> essary in anyone's else's? And it . . . every work of art is a work of perfect
> necessity.
> —Where'd you read that?
> —I didn't read it. That's what it . . . has to be, that's all. And if everybody
> else's life, everyone else's work around you can be interchanged and nobody
> can stop and say, This is mine, this is what I must do, this is my work . . . then
> how can they see it in mine, this sense of inevitableness, that this is the way it
> must be. In the middle of all this how can I feel that . . . damn it, when you
> paint you don't just paint, you don't just put lines down where you want to,
> you have to know, you have to know that every line you put down couldn't go
> any other place, couldn't be any different . . . But in the midst of all this . . .
> rootlessness, how can you . . . (144)

"All of our highest goals are inhuman ones" (589), Wyatt believes, but in
The Recognitions this is an atypical conviction. In fact, the Village community has every appearance of being an Eliotian wasteland. So many characters
are hangers-on of one sort or another, people of no special talent beyond that
of attaching themselves to those more gifted. Most nights they can be found
at the Viareggio, "a small Italian bar of nepotistic honesty before it was dis-

covered by exotics," the same "people for whom Dante had rejuvenated Hell six centuries before" (305). Like those whom de Kooning described as "want[ing] to take the talking out of painting," but who seem to "do nothing else but talk about it" (Chipp, 556), characters are often found talking for the sake of talking: "Someone said, —Picasso . . . Someone else said, —Kafka. . . . A girl said, —You deliberately try to misunderstand me. Of course I like art. Ask anybody" (65).

Still, not all the Villagers are the same, and some stand out more than others. Included among the latter are Stanley, a composer whose influences are Bach, Corelli, Gabrieli, and Palestrina; Otto, a playwright, whose work never rises above unconscious parody; Max, a modish abstractionist; Hannah, whose infrequent still lifes and landscapes possess, says Stanley, "integrity of purpose" (187); Agnes Deigh, a literary agent; Anselm, whose work includes, says Stanley, "a beautiful poem [. . .] about Averroes, the Arab thinker in the Middle Ages" (458); and Esme, who, in addition to being a poet and drug addict, functions as Wyatt's "Solveig" (550). Of these, Max is the one whose work is most antithetical to Wyatt's own, representing a sort of misfired avant-gardism. Max is known also for his plagiarism from Rilke, but his most mentioned work is *L'Ame d'un Chantier*, or *The Workman's Soul*. A canvas of some pretension, there is even a party, in a Sullivan Street apartment, to celebrate its unveiling. Here, the painting, hanging above a gray chipped mantel, hardly solicits attention:

> No one was looking at it. The unframed canvas was tan. Across the middle a few bright spots of red lead had been spattered. The spots in the lower left-hand corner were rust, above them long streaks of green paint, and to the upper right a large smudge of what appeared to be black grease. It looked as though the back of an honest workman's shirt had been mounted for exhibition, that the sleeves, collar, and tails might be found among the rubble in the fireplace. (176)

If the painting looks like a "workman's shirt," this is because that is exactly what it is, albeit cut up and framed by Max (623). Technically, then, *L'Ame d'un Chantier* presents no real achievement, the originality, if it exists, attaching itself less to the execution than to the thought. The guests nevertheless participate in the pretense, and good-heartedly attempt to recognize its aesthetic value. Talking about the canvas, or shirt, Hannah makes more of an attempt than Otto, however, who, at a loss for what to say, cannot avoid pilfering from a prior conversation with Wyatt:

> —What do you think of the painting? she said, looking above the mantel.
> —The colors are good. Very bright.
> —Bright?
> —Well, I mean the orange and the green. Of course, a painter is limited by

his materials, isn't he. I mean, there are pigments you can't just mix together in certain mediums and expect them to bind. There are certain pigments you can't lay over others and expect them to hold, I mean of course they break up, you have to know your materials and respect them, but modern painting . . .
—I think it's the saddest thing Max has ever done. It's an epitaph.
—Léger, I mean Chagall . . .
—The emptiness it shows, it hurts to look at it. It's so real, so *real.*
—Soutine, of course, Chagall and Soutine, Otto continued, —there won't be one of them in sight anywhere in a hundred years, they'll break up and fall to pieces right on the canvas. Inherent vice, I believe they call it. There are certain pigments . . .
—I think it's the saddest thing Max has ever done. (181–82)

As Peter Campbell writes, "Abstract painting is a game played with our interpretative faculties. It makes them work harder and gives them rest; it exploits and teases them" (19). Here, unless the possibility that the canvas can resist meaning is granted—that it might, in fact, be meaningless—one is likely to lose at this game. In one sense, Max's canvas might be compared to those texts that since Mallarmé, says Rodolphe Gasché, "sweep away the possibility of decision, of mastering their meaning as unity, that is, of mastering their meaning at all" (*Tain of the Mirror*, 266). Gasché believes that all texts resist interpretation to one degree or another. Thus, there should be something to gain by continuing to ask the meaning of, for instance, a Stein portrait (e.g., "Picasso") or even a Max canvas: "But the fact that these texts cannot be thematically exhausted in terms of content or form does not at all imply . . . that one ought to abandon the search for their meaning. Such a conclusion would amount to an aestheticizing and obscurantist reaction by the *hermeneuein*, that is, by understanding. This search for meaning should not be abandoned but rather intensified, and in such a manner as to account for the ultimate possibility of these texts' meaninglessness" (*Tain of the Mirror*, 266). Perhaps, though such an investigation seems to make more sense, or to be more meaningful, when the text is a Mallarmé poem or a Stein portrait, if only for the reason that if attention is restricted to canonical artists, there are, at least, implied boundaries. But if there be an obligation to attend to every Max canvas and its like, we will inevitably find ourselves adrift in a hermeneutical Sargasso Sea. Nevertheless, being good sports, Max's party guests valiantly try to find meaning in *L'Ame d'un Chantier.* After all, if "[t]hinking it out" is, as Max tells Otto, what takes the greatest amount of time, it is only right that the latter should be able to repeat, when pressed by the artist, that "[t]he colors are good" (189).

The repetition points to another difficulty with mid-century abstraction. While a handful of painters were able to forge a stylistic identity (e.g., Pollock's drip paintings, Motherwell's *Spanish Elegies*, and Kline's black-on-white motif), most were not so successful. Often, abstraction as concept overwhelmed abstraction as practice, even though the concept was comparatively simple. The consequences this had not only for painting but also for criticism were, as we now realize, too circumscriptive. Or as Campbell writes: "The simple graphic vocabularies which Abstract Expressionism supported set a limit on the number of critical explanations it could sustain. Most could be reduced to an investigation of the viewer's relationship to a painting seen as an object rather than as representation, and the relationship between the painter's personality and intentions and the kind of marks made. Without problems of representation, technique, social purpose or iconography to deal with criticism became deep, serious and impoverished" (20). This impoverishment is evident in the responses to Max's canvas, which in addition to those offered include Hannah's judgment that "[t]he composition's good. Max is good with composition, he's successful with it, but he still works like painting was having an orgasm, he has to learn that it isn't just having the experience that counts, it's knowing how to handle the experience" (184); and an unnamed youth's judgment that "Max seems to have a good sense of spatial values [. . .] but his solids can't compare, say, with the solids in Uccello. And where is abstract without solids, I ask you?" (306). More caustic is the response, offered by one unnamed soul to another: "Did you see his paintings? Crap, all of them, even if he has got a sense of form" (577).

Whatever people think of his work, Max still remains assured of receiving good reviews for he knows how to work the system. Unlike Wyatt, who refuses the offer of a good review in return for a percentage of the profits, Max is unprincipled. In fact, he relishes the critic's request, for this saves him the publicist's 10 percent commission (940). For Max, art and salesmanship go together, and if a public is not buying one style, he will shift to the one that it is. The aim is less to explore or work through a style than to be identified with one, especially one on the cusp. This explains Max's turn from doing abstract homages to the proletariat to abstract "fragments lifted right out of Constable canvases" (623), and, in a gesture reminiscent of Pollock's drip paintings, to that style wherein "[h]e climbs up a ladder with a piece of string soaked in ink, and [. . .] drops it from the ceiling onto a canvas on the floor" (940).

Meanwhile, regarding *L'Ame d'un Chantier*, it is an interesting title but there is little evidence that Max and his crowd feel any genuine allegiance to working people. Stanley (who, like Wyatt, resists the reigning aesthetic) speaks rightly of "the gulf between people and modern art" (632). This gulf is symbolized by the way that the "[n]eighborhood folk" who, "in small vanquished numbers," still patronize the Viareggio give their space away in late afternoon to the artists, their quiet way of asking that they be left alone. By evening, the bar is "taken over by the educated classes, an ill-dressed, underfed, overdrunken group of squatters with minds so highly developed that they were excused from good manners, tastes so refined in one direction that they were excused for having none in any other, emotions so cultivated that the only aberration was normality, all afloat here on sodden pools of depravity calculated only to manifest the pricelessness of what they were throwing away" (305). The older residents appear suspicious of, and somewhat timid before, the newcomers; and the newcomers, when not patronizing them, are contemptuous of their aesthetics (or lack thereof) and servility to the dollar. Basil Valentine is too much an aristocrat and a European aesthete to be thought a representative of this crowd (though he has his links to it), but his hatred, predicated on aesthetic grounds, for the culture's ordinary people is not that different from the crowd's own contempt. "There is their shrine," he tells Wyatt at one point, directing his attention to the Empire State Building, "their notion of magnificence, their damned Hercules of Lysippus that Fabius brought back to Rome from Tarentum, not because it was art, but because it was big. S P Q R, they all admired it for the same reason, the people, whose idea of necessity is paying the gas bill, the masses who as their radios assure them, are under no obligation. Under no obligation whatsoever, but to stretch out their thick clumsy hands, breaking, demanding, defiling everything they touch" (386).

Esther's Christmas party offers a more particular example of the bad feelings alive between the artists and the community. I refer to the story of Benny, the designer who once contracted out his own work to Wyatt, but who was fired once it became evident that the work was not his. Now, having moved into television work, Benny finds himself the recipient of the green-shirted critic's snide accusations about what he does for a living: "So tell me the truth [. . .]. —Do you guys really give this same crap to each other you're giving to me, pretending it's a cultural medium? or do you just admit you're all only in it for the money, that you've sold out" (602). This comes after the critic has asked if Benny might quietly pass some scriptwriting work his way. In return, Benny, who has had too much to drink, explodes, letting out all his indignation against not only an individual but a class that has made no secret of its disdain for who he is and what he does:

> I know you, I know you. You're the only serious person in the room, aren't you, the only one who *understands*, and you can prove it by the fact that you've never finished a single thing in your life. You're the only well-educated person, because you never went to college, and you resent education, you resent social ease, you resent good manners, you resent success, you resent any kind of success, you resent God, you resent Christ, you resent thousand-dollar bills, you resent Christmas, by God, you resent happiness, you resent happiness itself, because none of that's *real*. What is real, then? Nothing's real to you that isn't part of your own past, *real life*, a swamp of failures, of social, sexual, financial, personal, . . . spiritual failure. Real life. You poor bastard. You don't know what real life is, you've never been near it. (602–3)

Benny has his own misgivings about what he does, but does not need to be accused by this critic, who, as Stanley notes, "looks like an Inquisitor" (600). In fact, before this eruption, Benny has asked Esther about Wyatt: "Is he doing what he wanted to do now? or like me, is he doing what he can do, what he has to do . . ." (596). Or as he tells Mr. Feddle, "I got into this [television] and I found everybody believed what they were doing. They all believe it, and after awhile you believe it too" (605). Benny himself does not believe it, at least not all of it. Still, he refuses the suggestion that it is the critic's right to rebuke him. He is simply doing what he can, what his talents permit, all the while knowing that something is missing.[1]

This sense of something missing is also relevant to the artists' own work. In the space long occupied by religion, they have substituted art, yet without offering proof of how it might work as a transcendent judgment. "[E]ven Voltaire," says Stanley, "could see that some transcendent judgment is necessary, because nothing is self-sufficient, even art, and when art isn't an expression of something higher, when it isn't invested you might even say, it breaks up into fragments that don't have any meaning" (617).[2] To make art self-contained, autonomous, something that relates to nothing else, except if that relation be one of opposition, is the error of the age. "When art tries to be a religion in itself," says Stanley, "a religion of perfect form and beauty," it ends up finding itself "all alone, not uniting people, not . . ." offering them a way out of their malaise (632). Once unmoored, art, its pretensions notwithstanding, too quickly begins to seem like just another indeterminate thing. Forms begin to proliferate, and the more they seek definition in self-reflexivity, the less impressive is their claim of necessity. For Stanley, it is as if his colleagues "have set out to kill art," and if it once seemed desirable, in the words of Henry James, whom he quotes, "to work successfully beneath a few grave, rigid rules," the pressure of the present is directed toward the discovery of "new mediums and new forms," leaving the artists without "time to work in one that's already established" (186). Here, Anselm interrupts Stanley, suggesting that "to write music like Gabrieli" is not exactly an answer either (186). The point is fair enough, but does not, in itself, discredit Stanley's argument on behalf of disciplinarity. The purpose of disciplinarity is to focus questions, to make them responsive to a larger understanding or system of belief. Without this responsiveness, Stanley says, everything will be marked by separateness, the fragments of a lost or forgotten whole:

> —This self-sufficiency of fragments, that's where the curse is, fragments that don't belong to anything. Separately they don't mean anything, but it's almost impossible to pull them together into a whole. And now it's impossible to accomplish a body of work without a continuous sense of time, so instead you try to get all the parts together into one work that will stand by itself and serve the same thing a lifetime of separate works does, something higher than itself [. . .]. (616)

Stanley does well to point out the trouble with an aesthetic that is too self-involved and, as a consequence, fragmentary. But his solution is also problematic, for in the place of an art that is too attentive to the particular and the contingent, he would substitute an art that is perhaps too attentive to the absolute and timeless. He seeks to complete a composition that will "be finished to a thorough perfection," with "every note and every bar, every transition and movement in the pattern over and against itself and within itself proof against time" (323). Stanley's perfectionism is not to be dismissed, for perfectionism itself is crucial not only to each of the serious artists in the fiction but also to Gaddis himself. Still, there is a way in which Stanley's ambition constitutes less a solution than an attempt to impose closure. Here, art is imagined too much like a monument, forgetful of the need to enter into a conversation with the world. Thus we find Stanley's work "always unfinished," likened to "the tomb he knew it to be, as every piece of created work is the tomb of its creator" (323).

Stanley shares qualities with those whom he criticizes for making art "a religion of perfect form and beauty." He speaks of how modern art fosters a divide between its creators and ordinary people, though his own quest for perfection fosters a similar divide, cutting him off from those people most interested in his welfare. He would, of course, distinguish himself from his fellow artists in terms of where they each locate their love. The others seem to place their love in the art objects themselves, whereas Stanley places his in something apart from, even "higher" than, the object: "It isn't for love of the thing itself that an artist works, but so that through it he's expressing love for something higher, because that's the only place art is really free, serving something higher than itself" (632). Here, however, we might recall Adorno's warning that "[e]very step that art works take in the direction of perfection is one towards self-alienation" (250). The sentiment is especially applicable to Stanley, who at one point, seeking distance from his own self, attempts suicide (849). The distance, though, is not only from himself but also from others. Despite Stanley's conviction that art must strive to be obedient to the dual, yet singular, demands of love and necessity, he fails to understand how much these demands originate from below as well as from above. The narrator, mocking Stanley's longing, accents its almost masturbatory aspect: "Fenestrula! If ever he should get to Italy, it was in that cathedral that he wanted to play the organ; a lonely ambition, solitary epiphany" (319). Meantime, Anselm, upset with Stanley and his "God-damned sanctimonious attitude," charges him with shutting everyone out of his life: "Stanley, by Christ Stanley that's what it is, and you go around accusing people of refusing to humble themselves and submit to the love of Christ and you're the one, you're the one who refuses love, you're the one all the time who can't face it, who can't face loving, and being loved right here, right in this lousy world, this God-damned world where you are right now, right . . . right now" (635).

Later, Father Martin says much the same, albeit less bluntly, after Stanley has confessed to him all his doubts about his actions, even while remaining obsessed with his work: "We live in a world where first-hand experience is daily more difficult to reach, and if you reach it through your work, perhaps you are not fortunate the way most people would be fortunate. But there are things I shall not try to tell you. You will learn them for yourself if you go on" (952). In a sense, Stanley does, at the very end, learn the lesson hinted at by Father Martin. With the work completed and about to be played on the Fenestrula organ, the emotion that most holds him is one of loss, of all that he has sacrificed on behalf of the work:

> And it was those he thought of, and not the work he thought of, as he stood alone in his room and looked at the work, which was all that was left. He looked at it with sudden malignity, as though in that moment it had come through at the expense of everything, and everyone else, and most terribly, of each of those three souls: but there was this about him, standing, running a hand through his short hair, pulling up his belt, and staring at that work, which since it was done, he could no longer call his own: even now, it was the expense of those three he thought of, and not of his own. (955)

I am not quite sure which three souls Stanley has in mind, though I suspect they are his mother, Agnes Deigh, and Esme, two of whom have died by this point. What is clear is that Stanley's art has entailed an element of betrayal, not only of his time, working as he does in the mode of Bach, Corelli, Gabrieli, and Palestrina, but also of those people whom he might have loved more. In the end, wringing out augmented fourths (the discordant "devil's interval") on the Fenestrula organ, Stanley brings the cathedral, unable to withstand the vibration, down upon him. He dies, but the work is rescued, albeit only to be spoken of, from time to time, "with high regard, though seldom played" (956). Stanley's end and the fate of his work clearly bespeak a moral lesson. But while this denouement is a harsh one, it looks better than what awaits some of the other Villagers and their work. In fact, Stanley is one of the more attractive characters in the book. Granted, he may sacrifice too much, yet at least the music's composition stands forward as an act of love.

Earlier, when walking the Village streets with Max and Otto, Stanley says that "[a]rt is the work of love" (465). Again, it seems true. However, it also seems true that most of the artists here are motivated less by love than by fear. They particularly fear for their identities, that they may fail to prove to others, as well as to themselves, that they are real. As Wyatt says, "there's no ruse at all that people will disdain, to prove their own existences" (800). Among the Village crowd, the efforts include Mr. Feddle's autographing other people's books (533); Esther's penchant for meeting painters and poets "as though you could sop up something from them in a handshake" (613); Otto's ceaseless plagiarism of other people's words and gestures; Max's taking as his mistress the wife of a famous painter (940); Ludy's adventure in a Spanish monastery; the multiple suicide attempts; and the wholesale exchange of "the things worth being for the things worth having" (499). Fear drives these people. They congregate together in a small geographical space, attending the same exhibitions and parties, reading the same journals and books, praising one another's work in public and denigrating it in private, largely as a consequence of their own insecurities and the longing to have their existence validated in some way, particularly as there is so much about modern life—e.g., the city's anonymity, the population explosion, the Darwinian competition, and so on—that squelches individual identity. No longer convinced that they have souls to save, the majority live lives of expediency and quiet desperation.

That Wyatt is able to resist the pressure to conform testifies to an atypical strength of character. Crémer's review of his Paris show, employing the critic's patented condemnation ("Archaïque, dur comme la pierre, dérivé sans coeur, sans sympathie, sans vie, enfin, un esprit de la mort sans l'espoir de la Résurrection" [74; also 665]), is just one of the factors that make Wyatt rethink his future. More important than the review, or the prior request for a bribe, is Wyatt's sense that the historical moment is unpropitious. True, the moment is always this way, especially for the adventurous artist. Still, Wyatt's uneasiness seems a testimony to something more than personal doubts or a conservative aesthetic. Rather, what he sees is an art world wherein style has become an end in itself. Artists do not live and breathe in a style so much as relate to styles as if they were garments. From this, there follows the sense that the artist, fearing to be caught in last year's fashion, must pay continuous heed to what others are doing. Artists, thinks Wyatt, have stopped thinking of beginnings and ends, and have become entrapped in reactive gestures: "People react. That's all they do now, react, they've reacted until it's the only thing they can do, and it's . . . finally there's no room for anyone to do anything but react" (143).

Wyatt's disdain for his contemporaries is, to a degree, justified. Granted, at mid-century, three of the finest painters in the Western tradition—Picasso, Bacon, and Rothko—were all working hard and doing important work.[3] Add the names of Avery, Hofmann, de Kooning, Pollock, Newman, Reinhardt, et al., and it seems, in fact, an unusually attractive time. So, certainly we need to qualify Wyatt's statement that "there's no direction to act in now," a statement that he makes in response to Recktall Brown's that "[a]rt today is spelled with an f" (143). Still, Wyatt has a point. For one, Abstract Expressionism quickly developed an imperious dimension, one that began to manifest itself at the Kootz Gallery show, "The Intrasubjectives," from which such well-respected painters as Carl Holty, Romare Bearden, and

Byron Browne were ostracized. Serge Guilbaut writes: "Though surprising to many people in the art community, the rejection of these three famous artists from the best avant-garde gallery was nevertheless read as a signal: after 1948, to be an ambitious painter meant to be an 'abstract expressionist.' The style becamé tyrannical" (178). There was little support for a range of aesthetic values, Greenberg going so far as to say that independence "should be counteracted, even at the risk of dogmatism and intolerance" (Ashton, *New York School*, 158). The situation was made worse by the fact that there were so few galleries for an artist to exhibit in and even fewer critics to judge the work. Diana Crane writes that in the 1940s, "the number of galleries specializing in the sale of contemporary American art was probably around twenty" (3); and that given the shortage of genuine critics, it was possible for a few critics almost to dictate the way an artist should work, as Greenberg did with Pollock. Crane writes: "Despite claims to the contrary, the mainstream art of the 1940's and 1950's remains a critic's art rather than an art of rebellion" (51).

At one point, Wyatt complains to Valentine, "Criticism is the art we need most today" (335). It seems to have been true. But more than the lack of galleries and critics, what most deters Wyatt is his conviction that aesthetic purposes have become more arbitrary, more market driven, and less responsive to painting's tradition and that upon which this tradition, in the best cases, predicates itself. Saying exactly what this antecedent is, however, remains difficult, if not impossible. For Wyatt, this does not mean that the quest to search out and to know more about the source of being is given up. Nor does it mean that anamnesis has no part to play in the search. Quite the opposite; and here anamnesis, or remembrance, is imagined as twofold: it speaks of a recall of painting's tradition; it also speaks of a Platonic recall, i.e., of remembering laws of being. Or as Esme writes: "Rooted within us, basic laws, forgotten gladly, as an undesirable appointment made under embarrassing pressures, are a difficult work to find. The painter, speaking without tongue, is quite absurdly mad in his attempt to do so, yet he is inescapably bound toward this" (472). It is particularly this latter sense that recalls to us the rule of necessity, entailing as it does an element of obligation to work mindful of a pattern eternally discoverable within the fabric of being. Painting, for Wyatt, is a matter of gradual recall, never quite finished, but wherein the sketch and the completed canvas represent two completely different stages in the attempt to reach a perfection that hides itself amidst imperfection's realm.[4] It is a conception quite at odds, say, with Harold Rosenberg's concept of the sketch as the painting's equal. Rosenberg mentions an artist who claimed that a second artist was not, in fact, modern because "[h]e works from sketches" and that this, perforce, "makes him Renaissance." Rosenberg continues, saying that here, unfortunately, "the principle, and the difference from the old painting, is made into a formula. A sketch is the preliminary form of an image the *mind* is trying to grasp. To work from sketches arouses the suspicion that the artist still regards the canvas as a place where the mind records its contents—rather than itself the 'mind' through which the painter thinks by changing a surface with paint" (Chipp, 570). It is the latter stance that identifies the true modern, at least for Rosenberg. The painting as expressive "act is thought more worthy, here in the postwar period, than the painting as an act of bringing to consciousness something hidden, removed, distant, or even lost.

Anamnesis remains a crucial element in Wyatt's aesthetic. Somewhat by way of explanation, he tells Esther about how he was in a sense forced, when viewing Picasso's *Night Fishing in Antibes* (91), into a recognition of a reality altogether at odds with the quotidian:

> —Yes but, when I saw it, it was one of those moments of reality, of near-recognition of reality. I'd been . . . I've been worn out in this piece of work, and when I finished it I was free, free all of a sudden out in the world. In the street everything was unfamiliar, everything I saw was unreal. I felt like I was going to lose my balance out there, this feeling was getting all knotted up inside me and I went in there just to stop for a minute. And then I saw this thing. When I saw it all of a sudden everything was freed into one recognition, really freed into reality that we never see, you never see it. You don't see it in paintings because most of the time you can't see beyond a painting. Most paintings, the instant you see them they become familiar, and then it's too late. (91–92)

For Wyatt, there exist paintings, albeit few, whose compositions so hint of another reality—a reality that, while encompassing our own, transcends it—that they function somewhat like doorways. So elusive is this second reality that its recognition gives way almost immediately to its opposite. Hence, says Wyatt, the frequency with which people laugh at the Picasso canvases, for one cannot "see them anytime," as they are meant to be seen. No, "you can't see freely very often, hardly ever, maybe seven times in a life" (92). Here, the key word is "freely," meaning to see something outside the realm of circumstance, "to come to know something," in Gadamer's words, "more authentically than we were able to do when caught up in our first encounter with it" (*Relevance*, 47). Or as Gadamer, at greater length, comments:

> [W]hat is recognition? It does not mean simply seeing something that we have already seen before. I cannot say that I recognize something if I see it once again without realizing that I have already seen it. Recognizing something means rather that I now cognize something *as* something that I have already seen. The enigma here lies entirely in the "as." I am not thinking of the miracle of memory, but of the miracle of knowledge that it implies. When I recognize someone or something, what I see is freed from the contingency of this or that

moment of time. It is part of the process of recognition that we see things in terms of what is permanent and essential in them, unencumbered by the contingent circumstances in which they were seen before and are seen again. This is what constitutes recognition and contributes to the joy we take in imitation. For what imitation reveals is precisely the real essence of the thing. (*Relevance*, 99)

The "real essence of the thing," "freed from the contingency of this or that moment of time," is, as Gadamer argues and Wyatt believes, precisely what eludes cognition at the same time that it determines what is, and is not, authentic. It is a contentious point, for there is currently great skepticism regarding those investigations that imply a belief in the noncontingent or metaphysical. In a recent review essay, Richard Rorty tweaks the nose of Charles Taylor for so much as raising the issue of authenticity, saying that he himself and "other post-Nietzschean philosophers . . . no longer take seriously any of the various projects which Derrida calls 'metaphysical'" (3). But Wyatt is obsessed with the sense "of something irretrievably lost," "the sense of recalling something, of almost reaching it, and holding it," the it being, as he tells Esther, "[r]eality" itself (119). He believes (or so Otto recounts his conversation) that as one cannot invent the shape of a stone, the patterns of reality are already present, independent of our invention (123).[5] Believing this, Wyatt also evinces an interest in quiddity, or "what the thing is, the thing itself" (125), even as, with Kant (125), he understands that such knowledge shall always be beyond our cognition. We find ourselves, thinks Wyatt, "all trying to see in the dark" (125).

Yet if the quotidian leaves us in the dark, Wyatt initially believes that the artist, at his or her best, is something like a seer and that painting is a potential avenue by which a more authentic reality might be glimpsed. By novel's end, he will reach the conclusion that, as he says in retrospect, "[a]rt couldn't explain it" (870), an understanding earlier reached by Esme: "Paintings are metaphors for reality, but instead of being an aid to realization obscure the reality which is far more profound" (473). Wyatt's conclusion does not deny art's power to shed light on things as they are. However, it does suggest that (1) things are more complicated than this (i.e., art as luminescent); and (2) to imagine that art's power this way is unique is hubris on the part of the artist. There is, then, a sense in which it is fitting that the sculptor Praxiteles, who, says Cicero, was able, after removing all the excess marble, "to reach the real form that was there all the time underneath," should reveal only the "high-class whore" Phryne, the model for the sculptor's Cnidian Venus (185). But if the truth were only this, a whore rather than a goddess, it would be no less simple. Better to err on the side of hope than of despair.

For Wyatt, art remains a crucial effort to recall shapes and forms rather than to invent them. He is, as Luke, the patron saint of artists, admonishes one to be, the perfect disciple of his own teacher, Herr Koppel. (Luke 6.40: "The disciple is not above his master: but every one that is perfect shall be as his master.") From Herr Koppel, he has learned that it is not by seeking to be original that the artist achieves an understanding of origin:

> That romantic disease, originality, all around we see originality of incompetent idiots, they could draw nothing, paint nothing, just so the mess they make is original . . . Even two hundred years ago who wanted to be original, to be original was to admit that you could not do a thing the right way, so you could only do it your own way. When you paint you do not try to be original, only you think about your work, how to make it better, so you copy masters, only masters, for with each copy of a copy the form degenerates . . . you do not invent shapes, you know them, auswendig wissen Sie, by heart . . . (89)

How is the artist to know these shapes? The answer, it seems, is through a respect for the discipline and a respect for what discipline, if it be authentic, predicates itself upon: origin. Can we say what constitutes this origin? Not exactly. Does this, then, mean that origin does not exist? No, it does not mean that, even as it does not preclude that. Still, though Herr Koppel conceives of painting as a branch of ontology, and hence fideistically, the sense is that the experience that he speaks of—that of the painter who is able, intuitively, to recall nonquotidian forms—is, in somewhat Kantian manner, available to all; and that what distinguishes the genuine artist is a certain obedience to this same intuitive knowledge. In *The Critique of Judgment*, Kant writes, "The aesthetic judgement . . . refers the representation, by which an Object is given, solely to the Subject, and brings to our notice no quality of the object, but only the final form in the determination of the powers of representation engaged upon it. The judgement is called aesthetic for the very reason that its determining ground cannot be a concept, but is rather the feeling (of the internal sense) of the concert in the play of the mental powers as a thing only capable of being felt" (I.71). Herr Koppel's aesthetic seems to depend on this "feeling," derived from "the internal sense." The predication does not preclude it from question begging, but its question begging is of a hopeful sort.

"To paint," says Esme, "is to intensify, to remember" (472). It entails consciousness and craftsmanship, but it also entails something else: the painter's willingness to play the role of a medium. The painter's truest inventions do not originate with him or her, but in a sense appear already extant. We see this when Wyatt, using Esme as a model, appears to draw on a knowledge not his own. Still, even as he for a time shares in this knowledge, it also ends up excluding him. Once completed, the painting begins to divorce itself from the painter and to assume something like an objective existence. The painter is reduced to another onlooker. This is why, says Wyatt, "the work of genius"—genius representing that ability to tap into a truth larger than one-self—is always more interesting than genius itself (81). Meanwhile, there is Wyatt's painting, wherein the tracing out of the form seems to bespeak a knowledge not bound by accidents:

> She was silent, beyond the outlines which she fitted perfectly enough to have cast them there in a quick reflection done without intent, without knowing. Some time passed. With each motion of his hand the form under it assumed a reality to exclude them both, to empty their words of content if they spoke, or, breathing, their breath of that transitory detail of living measured to one end; but left them, his motions only affirmations of this presence which projected her there in a form it imposed, in lines it dictated and colors it assumed, and the accidents of flesh which it disdained. (274)

For Wyatt, painting entails the question of perfection. Even when perfection is not present in the canvas, which is most of the time, it makes itself known by its absence. It is that which constitutes itself as the something missing, the something lost. It is that to which all art aspires, as "[a]ll music . . . aspires," thinks Lyotard, to a state of "grace" "in which the differentiation of the one and the multiple would not have place or time" (163). Like "the perfection of Mozart, work of genius without an instant of hesitation or struggle" (*R*, 81),[6] perfection, in general, reconciles the opposition between movement and stillness, speaks of an order that transcends the quotidian even as it includes it. It is, in architectural terms, symbolized by "the arch [that] never sleeps" (607), just as it resides in the perfect tension found in the bridges designed, in Benny's name, by Wyatt. "[E]very tension," says Benny, "was perfect, the balance was perfect, you can look at those bridges [. . .] and see them leap out to meet themselves, see them move in perfect stillness, see perfect delicate tension of movement in stillness, see tenderness in suspense" (606). It does not surprise that Benny, looking at Wyatt's designs, should feel that it was "like a part of me working, like the part of myself working there" (606). The designs bespeak an intuitive order that is essentially available to all, even though all do not acknowledge it. Still, this order acts as its own bridge, making it possible for Benny to imagine that Wyatt's designs were something that he himself might have produced had he been more assiduous. This, then, is why Stanley defends Mr. Feddle from those who would see only the ludicrousness of his putting his name to other people's work:

> But if Mister Feddle saw a copy of a play by Ibsen, if he loves *The Wild Duck* and wishes he had written it, he wants to be Ibsen for just that moment, and dedicate his play to someone who's been kind to him, is that lying? It isn't as bad as people doing work they have no respect for at all. Everybody has that

feeling when they look at a work of art and it's right, that sudden familiarity, a
sort of . . . recognition, as though they were creating it themselves, as though it
were being created through them while they look at it or listen to it and, it
shouldn't be sinful to want to have created beauty? (534–35)

In a sense, the work of genius requires that if we do not, like Mr. Feddle,
put our name to it, we quote it in one way or another. Something like this
happens when we read, hear, or write about such work (e.g., *The
Recognitions*); but beyond this, there is the sense that we are required to live
the work. It is what Kant seems to mean when he draws the distinction
between imitating and following the example of genius. The first is too
servile, whereas the second, taking more chances, learns from the example
and then goes further. "The rule," Kant writes, must "be gathered from the
performance, i.e. from the product, which others may use to put their own
talent to the test, so as to let it serve as model, not for *imitation*, but for *following*" (II.171). Here, works of genius incarnate origin, even as origin
always escapes this incarnation. So while works of genius cannot surpass origin—Kant: "genius reaches a point at which art must make a halt, as there is
a limit imposed upon it which it cannot transcend" (II.170)—they can
embody it in new and different ways. Before they function as examples to
subsequent efforts, they too "follow" what has come before, not by the repe-
titions of details, but by returning to the source of the prior artist's creativity:
"*Following* which has reference to a precedent, and not imitation, is the
proper expression for all influence which the products of an exemplary
author may exert upon others—and this means no more than going to the
same sources for a creative work as those to which he went for his creations,
and learning from one's predecessors no more than the mode of availing oneself of such sources" (II.138–39).

Creative work that returns to the source of creativity, or origin, is itself
always original, where originality refers not to the brand new—the fulgurant
object whose momentary flash appears without cause—but to the work
attuned to the world's immanence. Such work entails both *gravitas* and
pietas, to the point that, as George Steiner notes, we cannot help but take note
of its tie to the religious and the metaphysical: "The encounter with the aesthetic is, together with certain modes of religious and of metaphysical experience, the most 'ingressive,' transformative summons available to human
experiencing. . . . [T]he shorthand image is that of an Annunciation, of 'a terrible beauty' or gravity breaking into the small house of our cautionary
being" (*Real Presences*, 143).[7]

Meanwhile, it is because Wyatt works mindful of the obligation to make
his painting bear witness to origin that he finds it so difficult to finish so
many canvases, including the portrait of his mother. Or as he tells his father:
"There's something about a . . . an unfinished piece of work, a . . . a thing

like this where . . . do you see? Where perfection is still possible? Because it's there, it's there all the time, all the time you work trying to uncover it" (57). An artist grows to accept that perfection is elusive, but remains committed to the task, knowing that if the work falls short, it nevertheless allows the artist to gauge the distance between what he or she has done and what remains to be done. In Bloch's words, such work constitutes an "anticipatory illumination" (153), and participates in the desired perfection even as it is not that. Yet for some artists, overwhelmed by the sense of perfection, it seems almost preferable to abandon the work before its completion, for fear that the gap between the conception and the object should prove too dispiriting.[8] Wyatt is, in this respect, somewhat like Michelangelo, who, says Vasari, "had such a distinctive and perfect imagination and the works he envisioned were of such a nature that he found it impossible to express such grandiose and awesome conceptions . . . , and he often abandoned his works, or rather ruined many of them" (472). Perfection may prove too much, and rather than setting the unfinished in motion, keeps it at bay. Even as a boy, Wyatt found the idea of perfection debilitating. During his illness, when the paintings and sketches began to pile up, copies seemed easier to do than originals for they did not raise the problem of perfection: "Of these fragments of intricate work most were copies. Only those which were copies were finished. The original works left off at that moment where the pattern is conceived but not executed, the forms known to the author but their place daunted, still unfound in the dignity of the design" (52).

Beyond the sense of how far short the work falls in relation to perfection, the ambition to participate in origin remains debilitating for another reason. This has to do with both the Platonic and the religious (e.g., Jewish, Puritan) notion that the artist's work blasphemes what it professes to honor. It is a rival creation that would usurp the role of the Creator, substituting in the place of creation a false reality. Aunt May early on forcefully impresses on Wyatt the difference between true creativity, the Lord's, and false, the artist's: "Our Lord is the only true creator, and only sinful people try to emulate Him" (34). There is Origin, or what is, and originality, or the attempt by others, Lucifer included, to place themselves in the space of the Lord, of Origin:

—Lucifer was the archangel who refused to serve our Lord. To sin is to falsify something in the Divine Order, and that is what Lucifer did. His name means Bringer of Light but he was not satisfied to bring the light of Our Lord to man, he tried to steal the power of Our Lord and to bring his own light to man. He tried to become original, she pronounced malignantly, shaping that word round the whole structure of damnation, repeating it, crumpling the drawing of the robin in her hand, —original, to steal Our Lord's authority, to command his own destiny, to bear his own light! That is why Satan is the Fallen Angel, for he rebelled when he tried to emulate Our Lord Jesus. And he won his own domain, didn't he. (34)

Aunt May's rhetoric is of hell and brimstone. Yet her point is not without its merit. We need only think back to Greenberg's claim that the avant-garde "artist tries to imitate God by creating something valid solely on its own terms" (6) to become mindful of the dangers inherent in originality, of what is lost when a group of artists, the New York School included, demand its "own domain." The difficulty, perhaps, resides less in the work than in the claim (i.e., that the picture "is aesthetically valid; something *given*, increate, independent of meanings, similars or originals" [Greenberg, 6]). It takes only a single spectator, seeing the picture otherwise, to force it into new meanings, for the picture's meaning is never completely self-defined, and possesses such qualities only for those for whom meaning is itself meaningful. In any event, claims such as Greenberg's propose a self-contained primacy for the picture, a gesture that deliberately obscures its relations to things. Yet, of course, the tendency to obscure is not singular to the pictures of the Abstract Expressionists. It is in the general nature of pictures, no matter how much they intensify our sense of reality, also to obscure it. That is why Kant feels that "there is no more sublime passage in the Jewish Law than the commandment: Thou shalt not make unto thee any graven images, or any likeness of any thing that is in heaven or on earth, or under the earth, &c" (I.127).

For Kant, the sublime speaks of that which is unpresentable. God is the most notable example, for any image here will prove insufficient and, in its circumscription, false. Like other "childish devices," the image appears to help people understand the Deity, but it in fact "deprive[s] them . . . of the ability, required for expanding their spiritual powers beyond the limits arbitrarily laid down for them, and which facilitate their being treated as though they were merely passive" (I.127–28). A more appropriate representation would shun the image in favor of a more "negative presentation," which allows the imagination to rise "to enthusiasm" (I.127). This enthusiasm (the opposite of fanaticism) makes clear how wrongful is "[t]he fear that, if we divest this representation of everything that can commend it to the senses, it will thereupon be attended only with a cold and lifeless approbation and not with any moving force or emotion" (I.127). The point seems debatable, for it is not clear how representation should divest itself of all images (something different than replacing one sort of image [e.g., sensuous and concrete] with another [e.g., abstract]). It would seem that we are fated to conceive things in terms of images, or representations, and that while such objects will always escape complete determination, what is lost will always need to be measured against what is gained. Still, in *The Recognitions*, sympathy seems to be expressed for the Kantian view, as evidenced in the exchange between Wyatt and Brown's servant, Fuller, a character who, like Esme, often speaks wisely:

—It seem a very general inclination to contemplate God as an old mahn until
the mahn become old himself, he [Fuller] said to the moving figure.

—I suppose it does, was all the answer Fuller got; nevertheless he went on,
—Seem like the foreign people find a comfort makin these pictures.
—And you find them unnecessary, do you?
—If it give them comfort and sustain them . . .
—No, but for you. For you.
—No sar, it make itself an obstacle for me.
—And you just believe God is there.

Fuller answered, —We don't see him, sar, but we got to believe he there. And
Fuller made wild anxious motions with his white hands in the space between
them, like someone waving farewell to a friend on a departing ship, a friend constantly obscured by the waving arms and figures of other people. (347–48)

Wyatt's own discomfort with the artist's role, particularly with imitation,
stems in large part from his having been raised in a tradition wherein the
image is thought almost sacrilegious. In his youth, "[e]very week or so he
would begin something original. It would last for a few days, but before any
lines of completion had been drawn he abandoned it" (55). If, as an adult, he
no longer works under the prohibitions imposed by his aunt, he still has difficulty in finishing original work. This is most evident with the portrait of his
mother, the unfinished state of which leads Esther to complain that she wishes he would finish the portrait so that "there might be room for me" (88).
Wyatt responds that, unlike his mother, Esther is alive and present, the suggestion being that one of the painting's purposes is to make absent things
present, or approximately so. Hurt by Wyatt's failure to understand her sense
of exclusion, Esther adds a second request—that he "finish something original" (89). This leads to Wyatt's recounting Herr Koppel's admonition against
the cult of originality, a lesson he never forgets. Imperfection may be
unescapable, yet to work in a mode wherein perfection's possibility is not
even acknowledged constitutes a failing of another dimension. This partly
explains why Wyatt feels more comfortable painting copies than original
work. In the first, an end, the place of perfection, is discernible even if the
artist, lacking genius, pursues the lesser option of imitation (as opposed to
following). Hence, it is noted that as a boy, Wyatt's "copies continued to perfection, that perfection to which only counterfeit can attain, reproducing
every aspect of inadequacy, every blemish on Perfection in the original"
(55). This is not a happy solution, but it seems preferable to the third option,
originality, defined by Valentine as "a device that untalented people use to
impress other untalented people, and protect themselves from talented people" (252). When the artist denies perfection's measure and makes newness
or "the individual creative expression" (Guilbaut, 181) a quintessential value,
art loses its imagined mooring and necessity. For Wyatt the latter plays a crucial role in what he does, to the point that he appears to work in accord with
Steiner's contention that

meaningful art, music, literature are not new. . . . Originality is antithetical to
novelty. The etymology of the word alerts us. It tells of "inception" and of
"instauration," of a return, in substance and form, to beginnings. In exact relation to their originality, to their spiritual-formal force of innovation, aesthetic
inventions are "archaic." They carry in them the pulse of the distant source.
(*Real Presences*, 27–28)[9]

How does one return "to beginnings," to "the pulse of the distant source"?
Perhaps via a respect for the long, unbroken history of aesthetic achievement
which, in a vital sense, constitutes the artist's patrimony. Here, respect is
demonstrated not from a distance, but through participation. In the painter's
case, there is the need to learn the craft, the mechanical rules that govern
matters of design, color, genre, and materials, rules that are no less requisite
for the fact that they appear mechanical. The rules have been learned over
time, and they speak of a formalizing of nature's truths, which the artist, like
the mathematician or physician, does well to acknowledge.[10] Now and then,
individual rules will prove insufficient, generally because better rules have
been discovered, so that while the particulars may change, the principle (i.e.,
of rules) remains constant. It is only the most recalcitrant artist, then, who
would wish totally to reject tradition and its rules. Or as Kant writes:

> there is still no fine art in which something mechanical, capable of being at
> once comprehended and followed in obedience to rules, and consequently
> something *academic* does not constitute the essential condition of the art. For
> the thought of something as end must be present, or else its product would not
> be ascribed to an art at all, but would be a mere product of chance. But the
> effectuation of an end necessitates determinate rules which we cannot venture
> to dispense with. Now, seeing that originality of talent is one (though not the
> sole) essential factor that goes to make up the character of genius, shallow
> minds fancy that the best evidence they can give of their being full-blown
> geniuses is by emancipating themselves from all academic constraint of rules,
> in the belief that one cuts a finer figure on the back of an ill-tempered than of a
> trained horse. Genius can do no more than furnish rich *material* for products of
> fine art; its elaboration and its *form* require a talent academically trained, so
> that it may be employed in such a way as to stand the test of judgement.
> (II.171–72)

Wyatt would, I think, agree with Kant, especially regarding the point
about genius's dependence on formal training. That is, despite the romantic
notion that genius and training are somehow antithetical, the capacity to discern nature's laws needs to be augmented. This helps explain why Wyatt
goes to study in Europe. There, the tradition of painting is older, and if a tradition carries forward with it an accumulated learning, it is best to move in it.

As Eliot ventured, tradition is not simply something inherited: "if you want it you must obtain it by great labour" (*Selected Prose*, 38). There are no short-cuts, and while the American art community was, in the 1930s and 1940s, the beneficiary of Europe's tragedy, resulting in the exodus to the United States of some of the continent's most prominent artists (e.g., Hofmann, Ernst, Tanguy, Masson, Seligmann, Mondrian, Léger, Glarner, Lipchitz, Zadkine, et al.),[11] this migration did not obviate the need for American painters to school themselves in the European tradition. Hence, Wyatt goes to Munich to study under Herr Koppel, and then to Paris, to practice in what was recognized at the time as art's capital. In addition to working with and among recognized masters, Wyatt steeps himself in the history of European painting, especially the achievements of the Flemish and Italian Renaissance masters. So enthralled is he with the work of the former that once he commits himself to forgery, he starts to think of himself as "a master painter in the Guild, in Flanders" (250). He is mistaken, but the fact that he has any success at all as a forger has everything to do with his European training. Noting that few Americans have been successful in forging European masterworks, Lawrence Jeppson writes:

> It is significant that, whereas [David] Stein and [Fernand] Legros, both born in Egypt, and [Elmyr] de Hory, a Hungarian, achieved their greatest commercial success on our shores, our country has never turned out a really first-class art forger. But it will. In the past art forgery demanded great technical skill, and many of the best forgers spent long years doing picture restoration. This was simply not an American vocation. The future American art-fraud genius will not need these long painful years of apprenticeship, for he will not be faking Rembrandts or Goyas, not even Monets or Rouaults. Instead he will be doing American Minimal Painting and Pop Art and international Op Art. (312)

I wish to hold off discussion of Wyatt's forgeries to a later section. At present, I simply wish to accent Wyatt's belief in disciplinarity, his belief, in Eliot's words, "that not only the best, but the most individual part of his work may be those in which the dead . . . [artists], his ancestors, assert their immortality most vigorously" (*Selected Prose*, 38). Wyatt schools himself not only in the Flemish masters, but also in such important painters as Titian and El Greco. Or as he says to Ludy toward the novel's end, "we all studied . . . with Titian" (873), the "we" here including El Greco and Juan Fernández Navarette. By study, Wyatt seems to mean not only an actual pupil-teacher relation (the kind El Greco had with Titian in Venice), but also an immersion in the other's work to the point that it begins to inform one's own. This, says Wyatt, is what happened with Navarette, working in the presence of the Escorial's Titians.

The artist learns from other artists, past and present. He or she also critiques them. This is how tradition works. It is not simply a past shaping the present; it is also a present shaping—or reshaping—the past. So the work of Milton Avery shapes that of Mark Rothko, just as the latter's makes us rethink the former's in a whole new light, and this is true of, among others, Velázquez and Bacon, and de Kooning and Pollock. The list could go on ad infinitum. In *The Recognitions*, all sorts of aesthetic reevaluations occur as emphases shift from one domain to another. Wyatt's Flemish period represents a keen critique of the New York School, yet just as this critique starts to register, the introduction of Titian and El Greco forces us to rethink the appeal of the Flemish aesthetic and, in turn, that of the New York School. In theory, the process never ends, as each artist or school makes an attempt to put all the puzzle's pieces together only, in time, to see the proffered solution undermined by all the possibilities not considered. Or as Wyatt, sensitive to both contingency and the need to imagine an order equal to, if not greater than, contingency, puts the matter:

> How . . . fragile situations are. But not tenuous. Delicate, but not flimsy, not indulgent. Delicate, that's why they keep breaking, they must break and you must get the pieces together and show it before it breaks again, or put them aside for a moment when something else breaks and turn to that, and all this keeps going on. (113)

Still, the suggestion is that despite the delicacy of situations, there is a need to go on and to make sense of them, even if the solutions are never more than quasi-permanent. It is with this sense of things that I would like, in the next section, to suggest the relation of the Flemish masters to the New York School and then of the colorists Titian and El Greco to them both.

Flemish Painting as an Alternative Aesthetic

Even before Wyatt's Faustian pact with Recktall Brown, we find him painting in the manner of the early Flemish masters. For instance, Wyatt tells Crémer, when the critic makes a visit to his Paris studio, that he works in "the style of the early Flemish . . . [painters]" (70), a remark that elicits not so much surprise as a query as to which Flemish painters he means. Crémer suggests van Eyck, but Wyatt says no, his work is "less" stern. Then Crémer suggests Roger de la Pasture (also known as Roger van der Weyden). Wyatt does not answer yes or no, but instead names Memling and Gheerardt David. He says that he "did one picture in the manner of Memling," but that Herr Koppel, responding more to the subject matter (the flaying of the Emperor Valerian), compared it to David's *The Flaying of the Unjust Judge*. At this point, as far as Wyatt is aware, the picture has been lost, when in fact it has been stolen, and later surfaces as an original Memling (74–75). Why should Wyatt, in the mid-twentieth century, wish not only to paint in the style of the Flemish masters, but also think it viable? The answer has much to do with his low opinion of contemporary work.

In his manuscript notes, Gaddis writes that "[m]odern art and music are not comments on current values, soul-lessness, spiritual failure as they pretend to be even to themselves. But they are simply products of it. Painting has no place, most of it [is] more static than Egyptian two-dimensionals" (Koenig, 113). Gaddis is not Wyatt. Still, their doubts about the prevailing aesthetic appear of a piece. Meanwhile, I would mention one other point before explaining the attraction of the Flemish work for Wyatt, and this has to do with his being drawn to the competing roles of the artist and priest. He has been raised, less by his father than by Aunt May, to enter the priesthood, like several generations of Gwyon men before him. He does study for the priesthood, though he leaves the seminary before taking orders. The reason for his departure is not clear, though it appears connected with his own religious doubts, doubts that later (after his disengagement from Brown, Valentine, and the others) he asks his father to help him put to rest. His father cannot do this, for he has so disengaged his own person from both the church and the world that, after his Mithraic Christmas service, he is institutionalized. With no one then to help Wyatt to answer his question, *"Am I the man for whom Christ died?"* (440), he is thrust back into his search. Wyatt's doubts are never allayed, which is not to say that his question does not continue to act as a determinant. It does, as it has all along. To return to his interest in the Flemish masters, I would argue that it is itself consequent upon his desire to have this same question answered.

As a painter in the twentieth century, Wyatt meets with a difficulty. The roles of priest and artist are no longer so companionable, a problem highlighted in an exchange between Valentine and Wyatt:

You have something of the priest in you yourself, you know.
    —Damned little.
    —Far more of that than the renegade painter.
    —Are they so separate then?
    —My dear fellow, the priest is the guardian of mysteries. The artist is driven to expose them.
    —A fatal likeness, then.
    —A fatal dissension, and a fatal attraction. (261)[12]

There are a number of things to comment on here. One, despite Wyatt's denial, people are struck by his priestly character. Valentine sees it; Esther has seen it ("You are a priest!" [116]); and Wyatt himself will come around, as noted, once more to think of his vocation as that of the priest: "I'll be a

minister, I'll know what I'm doing . . . I'll out-preach Saint Bernard" (430).
Another point is that the relation of art and religion is never static, but
changes from one epoch to another. Valentine speaks of a time, following the
collapse of the Roman Republic, when religion replaced art as a primary
avenue of value and understanding (245). More recently, art seems to have
replaced religion, something that has occurred, as Eliot points out, over a period of stages. Among the Victorians, Eliot says, "The decay of religion, and
the attrition of political institutions, left dubious frontiers upon which the poet
encroached; and the annexations of the poet were legitimised by the critic. For
a long time the poet is priest: there are still, I believe, people who imagine that
they draw religious aliment from Browning or Meredith" (*Use of Poetry*, 16).

Wyatt is drawn to this scenario, wherein the artist almost operates as a superior priest, interested in spiritual or religious questions but not encumbered with
the institutional baggage that makes the priest's life appear almost a compromise. This helps explain his decision to work in the Flemish style, for it allows
him to explore those religious questions that still remain important to him, even
as his doubts prevent him from attending to them with the priest's commitment.
Eventually, Wyatt sees the fallacy in all this: art is not religion; and the artist is
not a priest. Their interests may, and often do, intersect, but their differences can
never be entirely discounted. Because Wyatt has somehow known this all along,
he knows well enough to resist this movement's later stage, wherein "art tries to
be a religion in itself" (632). Or as Eliot, identifying this phase's origins with
Arnold, writes: "he discovered a new formula: poetry is not religion, but is a
capital substitute for religion—not invalid port, which may lend itself to
hypocrisy, but coffee without caffeine, and tea without tannin. The doctrine of
Arnold was extended, if also somewhat travestied, in the doctrine of 'art for
art's sake.' This creed might seem a reversion to the simpler faith of an earlier
time, in which the poet was like a dentist, a man with a definite job. But it was
really a hopeless admission of irresponsibility" (*Use of Poetry*, 17).

Valentine seems right: the contemporary relation between religion and art
speaks both of a "fatal dissension" and a "fatal attraction" (261). Where the
priest may be assumed to be "the guardian of mysteries," the modern artist
has often sought to be the exposer of these same mysteries, the way Barnett
Newman claimed that the Expressionists were jettisoning "outmoded" myths
and religions, and replacing them with the cathedrals of their own feelings.
In this view, art is the Supreme Fiction, a cathedral unto itself and to that
"feeling" which Newman felt all should find compelling. It is possible to
wonder, however, what sort of bargain Newman, Motherwell, and the others
thought they were making. They throw off so much (i.e., memories, legends,
myths, political and religious beliefs and their institutions) and seem to offer
such piffling things (e.g., Motherwell's mysticism, Newman's feeling,
Rosenberg's event, and Greenberg's increations) in their place. It is this kind
of trade-off that provokes Adorno's statement about how "[h]aving dissociat-

ed itself from the religion and its redemptive truths, art was able to flourish. Once secularized, however, art was condemned, for lack of any hope for a real alternative, to offer to the existing world a kind of solace that reinforced the fetters autonomous art had wanted to shake off" (2). When art is project-ed as an end, it is anticipated that it will offer consolation to those overtaken by ill fortune. However, art seemed ill prepared for this new role, and its insistence on "a religion of perfect form and beauty" (632) was not quite consolation enough, or not the sort most people desire. This, in part, explains Wyatt's disenchantment with the contemporary aesthetic and his conviction regarding its "irresponsibility."

Is Wyatt's decision to work in the style of the Flemish masters, then, more responsible? Maybe not. But if it be a mistake—and I think it is—it is diffi-cult to fault Wyatt for rejecting the claim that art must be its own end. The claim severs art's relations to so many things, from the trivial to the pro-found. This separation proves too much for Wyatt, and he chooses not to go along with it. Like Gaddis, in his conviction that "[t]he process of art is the artist's working out of his own redemption" (Koenig, 90), Wyatt believes the artist's work crucially important, especially as it serves as a means to a larger understanding. Saint Paul, he recalls in Brown's company, tells us to redeem time, to which Wyatt adds, "A work of art redeems time" (90). Working in the Flemish style allows Wyatt to combine the ambitions of both the priest and the artist. Rather than blocking his desire for a more encompassing understanding, the Flemish style appears to facilitate it. As with Picasso's *Night Fishing in Antibes*, Flemish paintings appear to promote a sense of recognition, a recall of a pattern already there. They press the viewer "to see beyond" them (92), a concept the narrator comes back to, at novel's end, say-ing that while Wyatt's eyes were "directed at the painting, [they] were focused far beyond it" (871). For Wyatt, paintings work best when they afford us something like a metaphysical glimpse of the world. Certainly, for him, the Flemish pictures work this way, making it apparent that our "recog-nitions go much deeper, much further back" (250). These recognitions, how-ever, are available only to those, like Wyatt, who "look with memories that . . . go beyond themselves" (250).

"All good art," writes Steiner, "begin[s] in immanence" (*Real Presences*, 227), and the Flemish paintings proceed no differently. What is most fine about them, notes Valentine, is "that sense of projecting illumination, instead of receiving it from outside" (239). This luminism is mostly a matter of tech-nique—particularly reflective of van Eyck's inventiveness with oils[13]—but technique always has consequences in terms of the way something is under-stood. The Flemish paintings' luminosity suggests that all things are inspirit-ed, that divinity has not fled the world. This suggestion also follows from the Flemish masters' use of multiple perspectives, for this multiplicity adds to the sense that God is not in one place, viewing Creation as from a distance, but omnipresent. The Flemish masters, says Wyatt,

> found God everywhere. There was nothing God did not watch over, nothing,
> and so this . . . and so in the painting every detail reflects . . . God's concern
> with the most insignificant objects in life, with everything, because God did
> not relax for an instant then, and neither could the painter then. Do you get the
> perspective in this? [. . .] —There isn't any. There isn't any single perspec-
> tive, like the camera eye, the one we all look through now and call it realism,
> there . . . I take five or six or ten . . . the Flemish painter took twenty perspec-
> tives if he wished, and even in a small painting you can't include it all in your
> single vision, your one miserable pair of eyes, like you can a photograph, like
> you can painting when it . . . when it degenerates, and becomes conscious of
> being looked at. (251)

Perspective is a crucial concept, both in Flemish paintings and in *The Recognitions*, for the latter also works via a method of multiple perspectives, never letting us rest too long in any one angle of vision.[14] Single perspective puts a distance between the percipient and what is seen, and suggests that the latter can be mastered and cognized as a solitary, noncontradictory thing. Multiple perspectives, by contrast, force one to inhabit multiple locations, each of which is likely to call into question that which counts as truth else- where. Of course, as singular human beings we cannot be in more than one place at a time, and this makes the single perspective attractive. It is some- thing that we almost fall into. Still, we can try to imagine what others might see from their angles; and if as human beings we are destined to see things more vigorously from one angle, we can conceive of how the Deity should not experience the same limitation. By definition, God is all-seeing, or capa- ble of seeing things from all angles at once. The Flemish paintings, mean- while, reinforce the sense that things are, in fact, seen from several angles at once, as if God were watching.

The Flemish painters' employment of multiple perspectives nicely fits with their belief that Divinity was everywhere. Still, this employment was a reflection less of a choice than of the fact that they had not yet mastered the art of single perspective. As Panofsky points out, perspective, "a mathemati- cal theory of vision" (3), was at this time a recent invention, originating in the work of the Italian trecento artists Giotto and Duccio. Later, the German artist Albrecht Dürer wrote, "*Perspectiva* is a Latin word and means a 'Durchsehung'" or a view through something (Panofsky, 3). While not an accurate translation, Dürer's definition typifies the way the early Renaissance painters conceived of the technique. With perspective, Leone Battista Alberti said, the canvas became a "kind of window" opening onto a three-dimensional space. The consequence of perspective, writes Panofsky, is "that the pictorial space is subject to the rules that govern empirical space,

[so] that there must be no obvious contradiction between what we do see in a picture and what we might see in reality—excepting, of course, the symbolic representation of spiritual events as in Roger van der Weyden's 'Seven Sacraments' and those supernatural phenomena which defy the laws of nature by definition as is the case with angels, devils, visions, and miracles" (141).

As Panofsky explains, the point is not that the Flemish artists did not try to introduce perspectivism into their work. They did. However, theirs was less a "correct" perspectivism than something more empirically worked out, the product of "subjecting shop traditions and direct visual experience to draftsmanlike schematization" (5).[15] Thus, even as Flemish painting, especially after van Eyck, moves in the direction of naturalism, it still holds onto some medieval elements, notably multiple perspectives and the other-world iconography. To illustrate this point, Panofsky compares van Eyck's portrait of Giovanni Arnolfini and Jeanne Cenami with the *Death of St. Ambrose* in San Clemente. The Italian master "conceives of light as quantitative and isolating rather than a qualitative and connective principle, and . . . he places us before rather than within the picture plane" (7). In contrast, van Eyck

> studies and uses light . . . in terms of diffraction, reflection and diffused reflection. He stresses its action upon surfaces as well as its modification by solids and thereby works that magic so ardently admired throughout the centuries. . . . And where the death chamber of St. Ambrose is a complete and closed unit, entirely contained within the limits of the frame and not communicating with the outside world, the nuptial chamber of the Arnolfinis is, in spite of its cozy narrowness, a slice of infinity. Its walls, floor and ceiling are artfully cut on all sides so as to transcend not only the frame but also the picture plane so that the beholder feels included in the very room; yet the half-open window, disclosing the thin brick wall of the house and tiniest strip of garden and sky, creates a kind of osmosis between indoors and outdoors, secluded cell and universal space. (7)

The Flemish work seems suspended between two worlds: the medieval and the modern. It does not belong entirely in either, even as it carries with it spiritual memories of the former and anticipates the naturalistic truths of the latter. The tension eventually becomes a problem for Wyatt, but for a long time he thinks of himself as a quasi-member of the Flanders Guild, obligated to work only with the best materials and mindful of God's presence: "I'm a master painter in the Guild, in Flanders, do you [Valentine and Brown] see? And if they come in and find that I'm not using the . . . gold, they destroy the bad materials I'm using and fine me, and I . . . they demand that . . . and this exquisite color of ultramarine, Venice ultramarine I have to take to them for approval, and the red pigment, this brick-red Flanders pigment . . . because I've taken the Guild oath, [. . .] to use pure materials, to work in the sight of

God . . ." (250).[16] Wyatt has had a little too much brandy when he offers this
defense, and he is, at this point, in Brown's corrupt employ. Still, the speech
helps to explain his identification with the Flemish masters. As Wyatt sees
the matter, their work evinces an integrity and a piety that have been undermined by the modern perspective, especially as it celebrates originality and
scientific explanation. Like Stanley, who believes that scientific explanations
of religious matters seem befuddled because "science doesn't even understand the question" (600), Wyatt is dismissive of science's refusal to let enig-
mas be, as in the instance of the Mona Lisa's smile: "Science explains it to us
now. The man who painted her picture couldn't see what he was doing. She
didn't really have an enigmatic smile, that woman. But he couldn't see what
he was doing. Leonardo had eye trouble" (870). Science, like reason, makes
"means [. . .] ends in themselves" (290), and, in a self-justifying logic,
begins to defend itself by recourse to its own reasons. Reasons give way to
further reasons. Yet for Wyatt there comes a point when one simply wishes
to escape reason's rules: "Reason! but, good God, haven't we had enough . . .
reason" (86).

If we can trust Otto's recall of his conversation with Wyatt, the latter is
particularly drawn to the Flemish painters' attention to what Panofsky (referring to van Eyck) speaks of as "the simultaneous realization, and, in a sense,
reconciliation, of the 'two infinites,' the infinitesimally small and the
infinitely large" (3). Thus there is from Wyatt praise for "the discipline, the
attention to detail, the separate consciousnesses, in those paintings," as well
as "the thoroughness with which they recreate the atmosphere," as in the
instance of Memling, who "piles up perfection layer by layer," much "like a
writer who can't help devoting as much care to a moment as to an hour"
(124). The Flemish paintings exhibit a belief in perfection, as something that
one can aspire to, outside the reign of reason and superior to it. However,
perfection does not exist simply beyond the realm of the quotidian, but infus-
es it. Accordingly, the painter keen to perfection's call must devote as much
attention to the drawing of a single thread of hair as to the larger design.
Wyatt is such a painter, as indicated by the exchange between
Brown—"They looked like every hair was painted on separately [in Wyatt's
van der Goes forgery]"—and Valentine: "It was, of course" (233). Here, the
whole depends on the particular, as the particular depends on the whole. We
may try to speak of each as if it possessed independent existence, yet neither
can exist without the other. What Wyatt, then, most values in the Flemish
masters, with their belief that "God dwells in the details," is their devotion to
both the quotidian and the divine. To paint this way, however, requires more
than skill; it requires faith. "When Hubert van Eyck painted" the *Steenken
Madonna*, Wyatt tells Brown, "it wasn't just a man, painting a picture, of a
woman"; it was an expression of both feeling and belief (363). It is what

Cennini, as Wyatt reads in the *Libro dell' arte*, posited as the prerequisite of the superior artist, wise enough to know that "even if you were not adequately paid, God and Our Lady will reward you for it, body and soul" (146).

Wyatt lives in a skeptical age, divorced from the faith of a Fra Angelico, whose piety would not allow him, while painting a Christ on the Cross, to rise off his knees. Or as Wyatt says when asked to paint a Fra Angelico: "Do you know why I could never paint one, paint a Fra Angelico? Do you know why? Do you know how he painted? Fra Angelico painted down on his knees, he was on his knees and his eyes full of tears when he painted Christ on the Cross. And do you think I . . . do you think I . . ." (242). Yet if Wyatt cannot paint a Fra Angelico, he does manage to paint works by Memling, Dierick Bouts, Roger van der Weyden, and Hugo van der Goes. The Memling work, done while still a student, was something he did in the style of Memling, as opposed to actually trying to pass it off as a genuine Memling.[17] Still, stolen from Wyatt, it is later passed off as an authentic Memling, the account of which gets reported in *Die Fleischflaute* (The Flesh Flute), an art publication which Wyatt finds in a Parisian café. Here, the reporter not only offers the narrative of the painting's discovery, but goes on to comment, somewhat surprisingly, that it was Memling "who had brought the weak beginnings of Flemish art to the peak of their perfection, and crystallized the minor talents of the Van Eycks, Bouts, Van der Weyden, in the masterpieces of his own German genius" (75). It is an opinion at odds with those expressed by such scholars as Conway, Friedländer, and Panofsky,[18] and whatever reason there might be to take the opinion seriously is here undermined by the publication's name and the failure to suspect that the "[c]rude overpainting" that originally hid Wyatt's Memling might not itself be a trick to offset questions regarding the picture's authenticity (75). We might, then, do better to understand the *Fleischflaute* opinion as more akin to that of the Romantics and Victorians who, says Panofsky, considered Memling in his "sweetness the very summit of medieval art" rather than like a Felix Mendelssohn, who "occasionally enchants, never offends and never overwhelms" (347).[19]

The Memling canvas is an apprentice's work and might be thought of as validating the opinion that Wyatt lacks the talent necessary to make a true contribution to painting. And when this canvas is put alongside Wyatt's later choice to forge Flemish masterworks, the judgment seems more secure. Still, I myself would not go this far, for a young artist's work is never a perfect measure of future success, and Wyatt has been confronted with an unusual set of obstacles. Meanwhile, if the Memling painting is understood as that of an apprentice and Wyatt's talent as deficient, there still remain ways in which his work is quite extraordinary. He starts to demonstrate his capabilities in the Dierick Bouts and Hugo van der Goes forgeries. For one, these painters were more talented than Memling and thereby more difficult to emulate; and for another, Wyatt's work has matured to the point where it possesses an expressive quality not associated with forgeries. It is this quality, and not his ability to mimic the gestures of dead artists, that moves Valentine, on first seeing the Bouts and van der Goes in *Collectors Quarterly*, to say: "I am impatient to meet anyone capable of such work. Not an instant of the anxiety one always comes upon in . . . such work. To be able to move from the painstaking, meticulous strokes of Bouts to the boldness of van der Goes" (229–30).

There appear to be three Wyatt forgeries in the *Collectors Quarterly:* two smaller Boutses and the van der Goes, the subject of which is the descent from the Cross. A Roger van der Weyden also appears—it is remarked upon and dismissed as "rather saccharine" by Max (460)—but this may not be one of Wyatt's forgeries, for he never refers to it, nor does Brown or Valentine, though Crémer had earlier asked if Wyatt worked under Roger's influence and there are magnified reproductions of Roger's work, along with those of Bouts and van der Goes, in the Horatio Street studio (70, 271). Perhaps the Roger is genuine, which would make for a nice irony, given Max's high praise for the fake Bouts and van der Goes. Still, it is reasonable to wonder whether the Roger picture might be Wyatt's, for, unlike with Memling, there is a temperamental affinity between the two artists. In fact, Roger is noted for the rigidity of his lines, as well as an emotional constraint that, in its most severe form, suggests an "algebra of suffering" (459), qualities that Max, paraphrasing the *Collectors Quarterly* captions (written by Valentine), also finds in Wyatt's Bouts. So it should make sense that Wyatt, who finds himself drawn to flamenco for its sense of privacy, pity ("but refusing pity"), and "precision of suffering" (112), should also appreciate Roger, an artist so constitutionally different, as Panofsky points out, from the far less private Jan van Eyck: "Roger's world is at once physically barer and spiritually richer than Jan van Eyck's. Where Jan observed things that no painter had ever observed, Roger felt and expressed emotions and sensations—mostly of a bitter or bittersweet nature—that no painter had ever recaptured. The smile of his Madonnas is at once evocative of motherly affection and full of sad foreboding. The expression of his donors is not merely collected but deeply pious. Even his design is expressive rather than descriptive" (249).

Bouts is not the painter that Roger is. Roger, along with Jan van Eyck and van der Goes, is one of the most accomplished of Flemish artists. But Bouts, whose style shows the influences of Roger, also remains respected, and there is, again, a logic in Wyatt's choice here. Panofsky writes of his mature style (and it is this with which Wyatt's forgeries are identified: "The finest painting, and perhaps the culminating achievement of the fifteenth-century genius Dierick Bouts" [363]) that it shows "Western art at its maximum distance from classical antiquity, the figures seem to move reluctantly and give the impression that the body is too alien and extraneous to the soul to interact with it at all" (317). He also notes how "the congenital stiffness of Dirc Bouts' figures . . . serve to divert our attention from the bodies to the carefully individualized faces and make us aware of the complexities that lurk beneath their taciturn mouths and heavy-lidded eyes" (318). These are qualities that might crop up in Wyatt's work, for he also experiences a split between his body and his soul, hiding his deepest emotions behind an unreadable visage. This said, the Bouts forgeries remain somewhat anonymous pictures in the Gaddis novel. Neither their titles nor their themes are ever mentioned; and the most we can learn about them (apart from Wyatt's detailed discussion as to how he faked their age [248]) comes from the *Collectors Quarterly* caption and from Valentine's brief appraisal: "Much more apparent [are the details, e.g., the hair] in the Bouts he did, of course. Exquisite control of brilliant colors, the ascetic restraints in the hands and the feet" (233).[20] From this, one gathers the sense that the Bouts pictures are less landscapes than portraits of some sort. (Actually Valentine observes that Wyatt, through the use of mirrors, has modeled for the small Bouts picture.) This, despite the fact that Bouts himself is perhaps best know for introducing a greater attentiveness to landscape. Again Panofsky: "If Roger van der Weyden may be described as a figure painter as little interested in scenery as was possible for a Netherlander, Dirc Bouts may be described as a landscapist as little interested in figure problems as was possible for a man of the fifteenth century" (318).

One other thing we might note with respect to Wyatt's Bouts is the repeated mention that at least one of the pictures is small (231, 240). Since Gaddis probably used Friedländer as a source, it might be that the picture's size connects with some critics' contention that, in Friedländer's words, certain "small-size devotional pictures in the style of Bouts have been associated with the Munich triptych [composed of the *Adoration of the Kings* in the center, and *St. John the Baptist* and *St. Christopher* on the wings] and a special master, a follower of Bouts, constructed." Friedländer himself is not convinced that such another master exists: "As far as I can see, this attempt to create an independent personality capable of existing next to Bouts has not been successful." He argues that the small pictures, while different from the triptych in some respects, remain more akin to it than not: "The small size in itself conveys an impression of daintiness. The composition seems lighter and more pleasing, the figures move with greater freedom. The intensive and fiery local colours press closer together over small areas, which produce a vivid interplay of colour. For the rest, form, colour, conception, types and everything else are in complete accord with the Bouts style which can best be verified in Munich itself where the triptych and the *Sacrament* altarpiece hang side by side" (31). Here, part of the excitement of discovering a new, yet small, Bouts canvas should relate to its possible influence on the said controversy. If the canvas is identifiable in style with the Munich triptych, it would offer further confirmation to Friedländer's argument and help corral this same triptych into the circle of legitimated Bouts masterworks, from which it threatens to be pulled: "for this work one is trying to retain the old-fashioned name 'Pearl of Brabant.' In recent art literature we find frequent attempts to remove the 'Pearl' from the Louvain master's 'jewels'" (31). As Valentine knows, whether critics will judge it an authentic Bouts or not will depend quite a bit on their own previous allegiances. Or as Valentine, anticipating the likely scenario when a signed Hubert van Eyck canvas should appear, observes:

> —There are authorities who still insist that Hubert van Eyck is a legend, that he never lived at all, that Jan van Eyck never had an older brother. As a matter of fact, I'm one of them myself, but, wait. [. . .] —Now don't you understand? If a painting appears, a signed, fully documented painting by Hubert van Eyck, they'll be proved wrong. The others, the . . . experts and art historians who have been insisting that there was a Hubert van Eyck will pounce on this new picture. They won't question it for a moment, because it will prove their point, and that's all they care about. It will prove that they've been right all the time, and that's all they care about. The painting itself doesn't matter to them, their authority is all that's important. (255)

Actually, the authenticity of the small Bouts is questioned. Experts at the Dalner Gallery judge it "a palpable fake" (231). Why they should do so is not clear, even to Valentine, though he has his guess: "what made them say that I cannot imagine, unless they wanted to discredit it and bring down the price. Dalner has done that before" (231). It could also have something to do with the Friedländer debate, though I suspect Valentine's own suspicion more likely. In any event, through Valentine's apparent offices, Dalner is instructed in the price of his honesty, for when a subsequent picture, one by Lorenzo di Credi, is questioned by the gallery (probably for good reason, for to judge by Wyatt's earlier cryptic response to it [128], there appears to be something wrong with the picture), the gallery is sued for slander, forcing an expensive settlement. As Valentine cynically comments, "These vulgar attempts at honesty [can] prove too expensive" (231), and "[s]o long as people are afraid of being found out, you have them in the palm of your hand" (231). The upshot is that the Dalner Gallery's doubts about the authenticity of the di Credi as well as the Bouts are neutralized, and the canvases now enter the realm of museum-quality masterworks, distorting the history that spawned them.

Meanwhile, as Dierick Bouts canvases begin popping up in Hell's Kitchen pawnshops (288), Wyatt's attention has shifted more to the forging of Hugo van der Goes masterworks. Of all the Flemish artists who capture Wyatt's attention, van der Goes seems the most like him. A native of Ghent, famous for the Portinari altarpiece, and said by a contemporary to be "equaled by none this side of the Alps" (Panofsky, 330), van der Goes is famous as well for the acuteness of his emotional state—for "a struggling soul" and a melancholia that was, at times, suicidal (Friedländer, 40). Then there is also the singularness of his retreat from the world when, in the autumn of 1475, he entered the Roode Kloster as a lay brother, and remained there until his death in 1482. While in the cloister, he continued to paint, to see outsiders, and even, on occasion, to travel. In fact, it was during a return journey from Cologne that, according to the monk Gaspar Ofhuys, van der Goes had his most serious breakdown. Ofhuys's account is hardly a sympathetic one—Panofksy labels it "a masterpiece of clinical accuracy and sanctimonious malice" (331)—yet I think it worth quoting, at least in part:

> I was a novice when Van der Goes entered the convent. He was so famous as a painter that men said his like was not to be found this side of the Alps. . . . He was often cast down by attacks of melancholy, especially when he thought of the number of works which he still had to finish; his love of wine, however, was his greatest enemy, and for that at the strangers' table there was no restraint. In the fifth or sixth year after he had taken the habit, he undertook a journey to Köln with his brother Nicholas and others. On his return journey he had such an attack of melancholy that he would have laid violent hands on himself had he not been forcibly restrained by his friends. They brought him under restraint to Brussels, and so back to the Convent. The Prior was called in, and he sought by the sounds of music to lessen Hugo's passion. For a long time all was useless; he suffered under the dread that he was the son of damnation. At length his condition improved. Thenceforward of his own will he gave up the habit of visiting the guest-chamber and took his meals with the lay-brothers. (Conway, *Early Flemish Artists*, 184–85)

There is much in van der Goes's character here that resembles Wyatt's: the problems with alcohol, the fear concerning his soul, the retreat to a monastery, and the anxiety over his art. (Panofsky writes, "Rumor . . . traced the cause of his derangement to his inability to rival the perfection of the Ghent altarpiece. And in this explanation, insufficient though it may be, there may be a grain of truth" [331].) Valentine draws the connection between Wyatt and van der Goes when he takes note of how *The Descent from the Cross*, a van der Goes forgery, betrays the "slight uncertainty of a tremendous passion, aiming at just a fraction more than he could ever accomplish" (230), a statement meant to apply first to Wyatt and then to van der Goes.[21] Or as Valentine, completing the bridge, tells Brown: "Van der Goes. He died mad, you know. Settled down in a convent, working and drinking. He believed himself eternally damned, finally ran about telling everyone about it" (230). Beyond the fact that Wyatt has already painted three van der Goes

pictures, other events linking the two artists include Valentine's reference to
the Horatio Street studio as the "Rouge Cloître"; Esme's offer to play the lute
for Wyatt, as "they did for him" (van der Goes) (272); and Wyatt's entry, at
the point of madness, into the Real Monasterio de Nuestra Señora de la Otra
Vez. In a sense, Wyatt looks back to van der Goes, as the latter looks forward
to him. Or, as Panofsky writes, "Hugo van der Goes . . . is perhaps the first
artist to live up to a concept unknown to the Middle Ages but cherished by
the European mind ever after, the concept of a genius both blessed and
cursed with his diversity from ordinary human beings, . . . subject to alternate states of creative exultation and black despair, walking on dizzy heights
above the abyss of insanity, and tumbling into it as soon as he loses his pre-
carious balance" (330). The state of mind is, of course, familiar to Wyatt,
memorably evidenced in his New Year's Eve restaurant conversation with
Esther:

> —Suffering . . . suffering? Why . . . don't you think about happiness, ever?
> —Yes, did you hear what that woman said? . . . I think it's the artist is the
> only person who is really given the capability of being *happy*, maybe not *all*
> the time, but *some*times. Don't you *think* so? Don't *you* think so? . . .
> —And what did you say?
> He put down his empty glass. —I said, there are moments of exaltation.
> —Exaltation?
> —Completely consumed moments, when you're working and lose all con-
> sciousness of yourself . . . (112)

"The exemplary modern artist," writes Susan Sontag, displays a willingness to "venture into the far reaches of consciousness," even at the risk of
sanity. A "free-lance explorer of spiritual dangers," he or she becomes something like "a broker of madness" (212–13), taking the chances that other people, perhaps wisely, refuse. Wyatt is such an artist, and this helps to explain
the attraction, for him, of van der Goes s late period. Here, the Flemish
artist's work begins, says Friedländer, to speak of a "dangerous passion"
(39). Wyatt has always worked somewhat at the edge of normative experience, but when he meets Valentine, his work has also begun to speak of this
same "dangerous passion." Prior to this point, as noted, Wyatt had completed
three van der Goes paintings, including *The Descent from the Cross*.[22] This
last painting is spoken of by Valentine as "magnificent. It is, almost perfect.
Perfect van der Goes" (239). Valentine also observes how Wyatt's work
draws its inspiration from van der Goes's late period: "the flesh tones in this
are incredible, even in reproduction. This ashen whiteness, and the other
large masses of color, a marvelously subdued canvas. This is the sort of thing
he painted late in his life. When his mind was beginning to go" (233).
Valentine's reference to van der Goes's mental state anticipates, of course,
Wyatt's own breakdown.

Meanwhile, Wyatt has almost finished a fourth van der Goes painting: *The Death of the Virgin*. Only the necessary damage has been left undone. Originally, Wyatt tells Valentine, he intended to paint an altogether different picture, an *Annunciation*—"because they're . . . well have you ever seen a bad one?" (241). Then, his thoughts shifted to the present theme. This surprises Valentine, for as he says to Wyatt: "But there is one, you know, a splendid one of van der Goes, it's in Brussels" (241). Wyatt does know this, but he has, he says, decided to finish one that "is later, painted later in his life, when the shapes . . ." (242). Things remain somewhat unclear, nevertheless. That is, the Bruges *Death of the Virgin* is not only an extraordinary painting, unlikely to encourage duplication, but also generally credited as being among van der Goes's last works. Hence, it is hard to imagine that van der Goes should have painted a second *Death of the Virgin* in the space between the completion of the Bruges painting and his own death in 1482. It might be that Gaddis simply wishes to make a connection between Wyatt's state of mind and that of van der Goes while working on *The Death of the Virgin*, this picture wherein "the shapes . . . ," as Wyatt begins to say, seem to waver toward a state of metastability. Panofsky himself notes the element of dissonance about the work's colors and shapes: "the indistinct bleakness of the light that comes from the left foreground is shattered by the glare of the miraculous apparition while the desaturated blues, reds, mauves, pinks, and browns, some of them *as dissonant as unresolved seconds*, weirdly contrast with the chalk-white of the Virgin's kerchief and St. Peter's alb and with the green-fringed yellow of the big glory" (338; italics added).[23] Furthermore, says Panofsky, "the intensity of simple-hearted devotion, prophetic ecstasy and muted sorrow have reached a point at which emotion blots out consciousness and threatens to break down the barrier that protects reason from both the subhuman and the superhuman" (338). Can Wyatt still imagine, then, a space wherein to paint a later version?[24]

There is another reason, however, why Gaddis should wish Wyatt to paint this subject matter: it plays into the theme of forgery as a dishonoring of the past and the dead. The theme is particularly picked up by Esme and Valentine. Esme, Wyatt's model for the Virgin, is keenly aware of how she is asked to play a counterfeit, both to be and not to be the woman in the painting: "Not to be of her at all, —but my bones and my shadows those of someone so long since dead, dead if she ever lived at all" (270). A "counterfeit creature," Esme allows Wyatt "to search with clinical coldness the "austere perfection" of her face, and yet not to discover her, searching as he does with "academic disinterest" but "not the eyes of a lover" (270). Esme also picks up on something else, that for the Flemish artist and populace, death meant something completely different from what it has come to mean. Death was understood as a departure, yes, but with the sense that a destination, heaven, awaited. This is made clear in van der Goes's picture, wherein we find hov-

ering above the Virgin's death chamber Christ and the angels, waiting to
greet the Blessed Mother upon her arrival in heaven. But in the interim,
death itself, Esme believes, has been "defamed." That is, in having betrayed
the belief in Divinity that reconciles life with death, we have yet to acknowledge that without this belief, death makes all our lives absurd. Or as Esme, in
some of the novel's most poignant lines, says:

> —Dead before death was defamed [. . .] —as it is by those who die around us
> now, dying absurdly, for no reason, in embarrassment that the secret, the dirty
> secret kept so long, is being exposed, and they cannot help it, cannot hide it any
> longer, nor pretend as they have spent their life in doing, that it does not exist.
> Yes, the blue, the beautiful blue of Her mantle there. How abashed they are to
> leave us, making up excuses and apologies with every last breath, so ashamed
> are we to die alone. How shocking it will be to see the day come again, out
> where they are, where the law does not permit him to sell lilies. (275)

The culture defames both the past and death—turning its back on them,
not taking them seriously—and Wyatt participates in this failure when he
both forges the Flemish paintings and damages the Virgin's face, the latter of
which still retains an element of truth about it even if it be a lie. Or as Esme,
"watching his hand move" the knife across "the face laid with closed eyes,"
tells Wyatt, the picture speaks of a reality "[b]efore death was dishonored,
[. . .] as you are dishonoring it now" (275). Valentine (as mentioned) also
takes note of this, though his judgments, unlike Esme's, reflect a coldness
that is itself a problem. Still, when viewing the same painting, Wyatt's *Death
of the Virgin*, he likewise comments on how the picture speaks of "[d]eath
before it became vulgar" (334). But then he goes further, making it clear that
he never imagined death as anything but vulgar except for the privileged
few: "when a certain few died with dignity" (334). The others died, as they
still die, going "to earth quietly like dung" (334). The difference is that now
death makes no exceptions. Again, it is a cold view, and while Valentine is
somewhat appreciative of Wyatt's ambition to recall a time when death was
not completely vulgar, he has no delusions about the work's essential dishonesty. It represents, as he, viewing the forgery, tells Wyatt, "a perfect lie"
reflective of "a pitifully selfish career!" (335).

At this point, Wyatt is beginning to think the same thing. Hitherto, the
forgeries have satisfied certain values that he, against the grain, has continued to esteem. These include tradition and craftsmanship; an originality that
roots itself in origin; lucency and a multiple consciousness; a refusal to denigrate the moment at the expense of the hour; and a sense of perfection, in
which all things move toward God. But he begins to wonder whether his
forgeries are not a betrayal of these same values and of the past itself.
Thinking of the damaged Virgin's face, he confesses to Brown that it may be

possible "to dictate to the past" in terms of what it has created, "but to impose one's will upon what it has destroyed takes a steady hand and rank presumption" (358–59). It does, as does the initial forgery.

Another matter of importance is the Flemish masterworks' quality of disguised symbolism. Here, everything has symbolic import, even when the naturalistic drawing suggests otherwise. Thus the lily symbolizes purity; the columbine "the Sorrows of the Virgin"; fruit "the *gaudia Paradisi*"; the candle light "the ascendancy of the Light Divine over the light of nature"; and so on (Panofsky, 146, 144, 126). But the symbolism often remains disguised out of respect for the artist's growing obedience to the laws of perspective and to naturalism in general, a respect that their medieval predecessors, whose symbols were bolder, did not share. Again, the Flemish painters work between the medieval and modern worlds. Their work entails an increasing naturalism, but does not altogether leave behind the sense that things are infused with the spiritual. For them, the world seems pregnant with meaning, even though their increasing naturalism would, in time, undermine this conviction. Panofsky writes:

> In Early Flemish painting . . . the method of disguised symbolism was applied to each and every object, man-made or natural. It was employed as a general principle instead of only occasionally just as was the case with the method of naturalism. In fact, these two methods were genuine correlates. The more the painters rejoiced in the discovery and reproduction of the visible world, the more intensely did they feel the need to saturate all of its elements with meaning. Conversely, the harder they strove to express new subtleties and complexities of thought and imagination, the more eagerly did they explore new areas of reality.
>
> In the end, the whole universe "shone[,]" as Suger would say, "with the radiance of delightful allegories"; and it has justly been said of the "Annunciation" in the Mérode altarpiece that God, no longer present as a visible figure, seems to be diffused in all the visible objects. The naturalism of the Master of Flémalle and his fellow painters was not as yet wholly secular. It was still rooted in the conviction that physical objects are, to quote St. Thomas Aquinas . . . , "corporeal metaphors of things spiritual" . . . ; and it was not until much, much later that this conviction was rejected or forgotten. (142)

Why does this matter of disguised symbolism warrant discussion in connection to Wyatt's project? Well, the difficulty, as Valentine will argue, is that the Flemish masters' naturalism might be conceived of as not simply a technical advance over their medieval predecessors, but as actually calling into question their devotion to the spiritual project itself. In *The Recognitions*, there is much comment about how contemporary art is mired in a realm of fragments that aspire to self-sufficiency. It is, Stanley says, the "modern disease" (615), wherein "we live among palimpsests," everyone and thing refusing to "fit into one whole, and express an entire perfect action" (616). We are left with "the breakage," with "pieces everywhere" (616). Perhaps things once were whole, but it is important not to romanticize the past out of our frustration with the present. The present is different from the past, and it is a mistake for the former to impose its rule upon the latter. Still, there are ways in which the past and the present are similar, and it is unlikely that things were ever as integrative as Stanley and Wyatt imagine. Can we really believe that the Flemish never experienced spiritual doubts, never mixed aesthetics with commerce, never succumbed to fear and self-interest? These are among the questions Valentine poses to Wyatt:

> —Yes, I remember your little talk, your insane upside-down apology for these pictures, every figure and every object with its own presence, its own consciousness because it was being looked at by God! Do you know what it was? What it really was? that everything was so afraid, so uncertain God saw it, that it insisted its vanity on His eyes? Fear, fear, pessimism and fear and depression everywhere, the way it is today, that's why your pictures are so cluttered with detail, this terror of emptiness, this absolute terror of space. Because maybe God isn't watching. Maybe he doesn't see. Oh, this pious cult of the Middle Ages! Being looked at by God! Is there a moment of faith in any of their work, in one centimeter of canvas? or is it vanity and fear, the same decadence that surrounds us now. A profound mistrust in God, and they need every idea out where they can see it, where they can get their hands on it. [. . .] —all of it cluttered with separation, everything in its own vain shell, everything separate, withdrawn from everything else. Being looked at by God! Is there separation in God? (690)

Valentine does well to disabuse Wyatt of his cultish regard for the Flemish painters, of his naive faith that fifteenth-century Flanders "was all like the Adoration of the Mystic Lamb" (689), and of his credulity with regard to the ambitions of Chancellor Rolin and the other patrons: "These fine altarpieces, do you think they glorified anyone but the vulgar men who commissioned them? Do you think a van Eyck didn't curse having to whore away his genius, to waste his talents on all sorts of vulgar celebrations, at the mercy of people he hated?" (690). Still, Valentine's own profound mistrust and dislike of people color everything he says. Earlier he accused Wyatt of profound innocence, much like his classmate, Father Martin: "You and Martin. The ones who wake up late. You suddenly realize what is happening around you, the desperate attempts on all sides to reconcile the ideal with reality, you call it corruption and think it new. Some of us have always known it, the others never know" (383). It is, he goes on to say, people like Wyatt and Martin who cause all the world's trouble, waking up to find corruption where they thought it did not exist, and then frightening the world with their crusades. There is some truth in Valentine's complaint, but even misdirected idealism seems preferable to his resolute cynicism. And to say, as Valentine does, that the Flemish painters display not "a moment of faith in any of their work" (690) is, corrective value aside, a lie, reflective of the sort of person who, under the guise of honest self-examination, says to Wyatt, "Why I know that I hate them [ordinary people], where you wish you could love them" (386).

Wyatt lacks Valentine's self-knowledge—lacks, in a sense, a formula. He is still too busy trying to sort things out, trying to discover what meanings might be validated by the world, and what are his own obligations. It is a process likely to have no definitive end, which is not the same thing as saying that it lacks direction or that it is unmindful of telos. Meanwhile, Valentine's cynicism helps Wyatt by forcing him to see forgery's inescapable "calumny" and the fallacy of locating divinity so entirely in the past. The Flemish masterworks are not only about piety, but also about uncertainty and skepticism, evinced by a naturalistic technique that begins to trust in things more than in God. Faith wrestles with its opposite, as it does in any age. The "tendency to assume a simple historical development from the 'sacred' to the 'profane,' from the 'spiritual' to the 'secular'" has been, writes Kenneth Burke, quite common, but it remains "so simple a dialectic" that it seems odd how readily we fall for it (35). Wyatt does fall for it. Yet, disabused of his mistake by a series of events, including the exchange with Valentine (which ends with Wyatt stabbing Valentine with a penknife and leaving him, so far as he knows, for dead), Wyatt embarks on yet another journey, one that takes him to North Africa and eventually to the Real Monasterio de Nuestra Señora de la Otra Vez.

Wyatt enters the monastery in a state somewhat akin to that of van der Goes entering the Rouge Cloître, which is to say one verging on madness. But madness and its approximation are two different states, and there is something almost feigned about Wyatt's behavior, as if he, like Hamlet, were using madness as a disguise to protect himself from a world that has become too much his adversary. In any event, he has not stopped thinking about painting, and about the best way to front the world. Painting, or living "in a world of shapes and smells," still seems important. Thus, he tells Ludy, "The things that were real to other people weren't real to me, but the things that were real to me, they . . . yes they still are" (893). Not in quite the same way, however, for what he comes to see is that his own work has entailed too much an element of refusal and of the schematic, with things kept noticeably separate. "Separateness, that's what went wrong," he says, "[e]verything withholding itself from everything else" (874). He realizes now the need to reach beyond the goal of "crowding the work," of cloistering himself alone with the work, "until it becomes a gessoed surface, all prepared, clean and smooth as ivory" (896). Things should not be so programmed, for the world

itself is more spontaneous, articulative more of possibility than of adaman-
tine rule. The perfection that Wyatt sought in his Flemish canvases was itself
the prisoner of rule, the slave to a perfection not resident in the world so
much as the product of other men's artistry, working a half millennium ago.
Or as Valentine, taking note of how fast he works, earlier commented: "You
do work fast, don't you. Yes, van der Goes was a fast painter himself [. . .].
But after all this is rather different isn't it, you know where you're going all
the time. None of that feeling of, what was Valéry's line, that one can never
finish a work of art? one only abandons it? But here there's none of that
problem, is there. Eh?" (334).

If Wyatt adopts Valentine's line—and he does—that the Flemish painters
were too "afraid of spaces," too ready to assert "every vain detail," and too
attentive to "gilding the pieces, [. . .] for fear there was no God" (875), then
he needs to work out an alternative aesthetic. He does so, and if we do not
see him put it into practice, we do get a good sense of what its main painterly
values should be. In fact, his new aesthetic is precisely this, a celebration of
the painterly over the formal elements of line and contour. Of course, part of
Wyatt's success in working in the Flemish manner has been tied to his skills
as a draftsman. It is not a coincidence that he designed bridges for Benny at
the same time that he painted in the Flemish style. The two skills, while different, are also analogous. There is a draftsmanlike skill at play in the
Flemish paintings, particularly as they attempt to master the skills of perspectivism. This is evident in a painter like Roger van der Weyden (a clear
influence on Wyatt), who, as Friedländer writes, "composes like a sculptor, a
carver in relief, by isolating the figure groups in his mind and adding the
landscape backgrounds; he disposes the plastically conceived figures on the
surface like a draughtsman by emphasizing the contours" (4).

Wyatt's decision to distance himself from the Flemish almost entails a
comitative distancing from the values of drawing. Almost, but not quite, for
we need only think of Jan van Eyck's painterly effects to realize that line and
color are seldom separate affairs. Still, Wyatt, in wishing to break his
bondage to the Flemish mode, places a new emphasis on the value of color.
This shift leads him to think more seriously about the work of such colorists
as Titian and El Greco, artists whom he has not previously mentioned. The
choice here is not surprising. We may believe, with Merleau-Ponty, that
"there is no one master key of the visible, and color alone is no closer to
being such a key than space is" (181). Yet, to enter into this discussion—i.e.,
drawing versus color—is, perforce, to call up the example of Titian, if not of
El Greco. The reason has to do with Michelangelo's comment to Vasari,
wherein he lamented that while he liked Titian's "colouring and style very
much, . . . it was a pity artisans in Venice did not learn to draw well from the
beginning and that Venetian painters did not have a better method of study."
To which he added, "If Titian . . . had been assisted by art and design as

greatly as he had been by Nature, especially in imitating live subjects, no artist could achieve more or paint better, for he possesses a splendid spirit and a most charming and lively style" (Vasari, 501).

Vasari registers his agreement, and goes on to speak of the difficulties that confront any artist "who has not drawn a great deal" (501). However, as Charles Hope points out, the difference here was not simply between Tuscan and Venetian artists, with the former extolling the value of *disegno* and the latter the process of painting. It was also between the present and the future. That is, despite the greatness of a Michelangelo or a Raphael, the future of painting would follow more in the footsteps of the Venetian model. Western painting, in a sense, found itself making an extraordinary decision with regard to its future painterly values. Or as Hope writes:

> The shift in emphasis from conception to execution, which first occurred in Venice, is one of the decisive developments in European art. All those painters, from Velázquez and Rubens to the Impressionists and beyond, who exploited the particular characteristics of oil pigment to create a distinctive personal manner were in this respect heirs to the Venetian tradition, however much they may have owed in their figure-style and compositions to central Italian artists like Michelangelo and Raphael. In this development Titian played a crucial rôle, both because of his exceptional fame and because of the wide diffusion of his pictures at an early date. (8)

Wyatt's acknowledgment of this leads him to say, more than once, that "We all study with Titian" (872). Titian, says Wyatt, taught El Greco (who spent, after Greece and before Toledo, at least three, and perhaps as many as six, years in Venice) the virtue of simplicity, of spaces, and of color—in short, of plasticity: "Yes, he studied with Titian. That's where El Greco learned, that's where he learned to simplify, [. . .] —that's where he learned not to be afraid of spaces, not to get lost in details and clutter, and separate everything . . ." (872). El Greco studied directly under Titian, but Wyatt's initial remark also speaks of all those artists who learned not from direct tutelage but from seeing, from having the example of Titian's canvases before them, the way, for instance, the Spanish painter Juan Fernández Navarette learned from seeing Titian's paintings in the Escorial: "He studied with Titian. [. . .] —Titian's paintings in the Escorial, he saw them when he went there to paint for the king, and his whole style changed. He learned from Titian. That's the way we learn, you understand" (870). It is an important point for Wyatt, and I suspect for Gaddis. The artist learns from other artists, from seeing and thinking about their work. For an artist to make a contribution, there needs to be an appreciation of art as a discipline. Individual paintings inevitably entail a multitude of values—e.g., economic, political, ethical, cultural, and religious—but if there is no acknowledgment of past achievement, then the work, thinks Wyatt, must suffer. This is not to denigrate extradisciplinary values, or to suggest that disciplines can really refuse to be interdisciplinary. Such values are crucial—even to defining aesthetic value itself[25]—and it should almost go without saying that today disciplines define themselves in relation to other disciplines and are, perforce, interdisciplinary. Still, a discipline also speaks of a tradition, a set of core practices and values established over time. Disciplines may prove fragile and temporary or they may (e.g., philosophy, music, painting, literature, and physics) prove sturdy and long lasting. When they prove the latter, however, it is imperative for those who would work in them not simply to demonstrate a familiarity with the tradition but to live it. If the aspirant does not, the work will likely appear marginal, addressing questions that either have admitted of past solutions or are more complicated than supposed. If the aspirant does, the hope is that the work will build on the tradition and advance its element of promise. Traditions are not only coercive and circumscriptive, and we should be mistaken to think so. In the best instances, they are less about fettering than about freedom. For proof, we need only look to the example of El Greco working in the tradition of Titian.

For El Greco, as José Gudiol notes, Titian represented "a starting-point" (22). From Titian and the other Venetians, El Greco learned much about color values and, for a time, was attracted "by that exuberance of flesh that was so much to the taste of Titian, Tintoretto and Veronese" (22). But as a native of Crete and as one who would eventually find a second home in Spain, El Greco also knew another reality, one "that was predominantly dark, spare and nervous, [and] . . . prone to lyrical exaltation in its attitude to religion" (927). This reality made it possible, when he moved to Toledo, to "play . . . with the chaotic without ever letting it overcome him" (27). This is likewise suggested by Wyatt's remark to Ludy about El Greco's instrumental role in our own feelings for the Spanish sky ("The sky. If no one ever painted it until El Greco did? Look at it, the Spanish sky" [892]) and by Ludy's almost panicked response to its ever evolving possibilities and spaciousness:

> And glad of an opportunity to escape the strained face and the eyes, Ludy stared out at the sky. He stared; and found himself trying to find something to fix his eyes upon, but every line led him to another, every shape gave way to some even more transient possibility. And he stood there trapped, between the vast spaces before him and the intricate response behind to which he almost turned, seeking some detail for refuge, when the voice in strained calm over his shoulder stopped him, gave him, at any rate, separate fragments to hang one sense upon while he suspended the torment of loss through the other. (892)

Ludy's response helps to elucidate another matter—that of the bird— though to explain this we need to backtrack to El Greco. In this chapter, despite the several references to El Greco, there is mention of but a single painting: *The Descent of the Holy Spirit*. According to Moore (*RG*, 280), the picture described is actually *The Annunciation* (ca. 1597–1600), the main interest of which, says Gudiol, is located "in the ascending movement of light that goes from the figure of the Virgin to the central area of the upper part, passing through the intense white of the dove of the Holy Ghost" (181). It is, in fact, a picture in which the Virgin and the Angel Gabriel appear separated by a dive-bombing dove, or Holy Spirit. That Gaddis should choose to change the picture's name so as accentuate this motif does not seem surprising. However, it is a significant gesture, for it suggests how much Gaddis wishes to cement the link between the Paraclete and the bird that darts through this chapter's final pages. It also seems significant that Ludy, panicked by the Spanish sky and its refusal to offer him anything to hold onto, should also feel threatened by the bird.

The bird first disturbs Ludy's too-reasoned existence when he sits inside his room, trying to work his thoughts about Easter, as spent in the monastery, into an inspiring prose: "One felt, at that glorious moment, that their faith lit the way before them, escorting the Eucherist to their beloved Superior, who lay now hovering between life and death" (889). It is ironic that at the very moment that, as Ludy writes, his "heart ~~started~~ sprang up in my breast," filled with "the true meaning ~~in of~~ in the message ~~brought~~ held forth ~~for~~ to all mankind, of all faiths, and creeds, and color, in this symbol of life eternal," the handsome symbol of the bird strikes and flutters against his window pane, yet "he saw nothing and heard nothing" (890). Then, when he wakes up the next morning, he looks "out at the dawn with eyes as clear as the early sky itself, and features as reasonably detailed and separate as the illuminated composure of the landscape before him, where the world had emerged from that dangerously throbbing undelineated mass of the unconscious, to where everything was satisfactorily separated, out where it could all be treated reasonably" (891). The point is, Ludy is a man of reason, wishing to have everything out where he can see it, separate and graspable. The bird, or what it symbolizes, is not this, and it frightens him, making his "blood run cold" (897). It also cuts him with its talons, so that he pleads with Wyatt to "[j]ust take it away" (898). After Wyatt has gone off, Ludy returns to his room, hopelessly puzzled by the Latin quotation—Augustine's "Dilige et quod vis fac" (Love and do what you will)—offered by Wyatt, only to find the bird "sitting on one of the framed pictures" (900). Frantically he tries to shoo it out of the room, and as the bird flies back and forth, fluttering "from one picture to the other," Ludy passes back and forth before the mirror, where, it is said, "he might have glimpsed the face of a man having, or about to have, or at the very least valiantly fighting off, a religious experience" (900). So it seems.

The Titian and El Greco motif at novel's end has much to do with the larger theme of fragmentation and unity. Over the course of the narrative, the

Flemish pictures, initially identified with spirituality, come to be identified otherwise: as signaling fear. Like the anxious person who, alone in a very quiet space, shouts out as a way to front the silence, to make it seem less threatening and real, the Flemish painters, from this perspective, noisily paint over the silence—over Divinity. Their paintings seem too detailed and busy, directing our attention away from what they ostensibly ask us to experience. All art is, in Sontag's words, "cursed with mediacy" (182). Still, if the Flemish paintings obscure a more profound reality, it would be a mistake to see them only this way. Wyatt struggles to replace one understanding (the Flemish paintings as saturated emblems of Divinity) with another (the Flemish paintings as emblems of separation), though we ourselves might do better to avoid this antithesis. In any event, Wyatt comes to see the colorists as getting closer to the truth of the matter. He speaks of them as "painters who weren't afraid of spaces of . . . cluttering up every space with detail everything vain and separate affirming itself for fear that [. . .] there was no God" (875). If he should ever work again as a painter, I suspect that he would work as a colorist, a tradition that was itself very much alive in his day.

It would not be inconceivable for Wyatt, embracing the colorist tradition (or at least its early manifestation) to move to a point whereby the works of, say, a Hofmann or a Rothko would begin to assume new, more pregnant meanings. They certainly are major colorists, and we can easily think of them as working in the line of Titian and El Greco. They saw themselves this way, as working within the tradition of Western painting. Hofmann himself refers to Cézanne's declaration that "[w]hen color is richest, form is fullest" as a "guide for painters" (67), for those who believe that "a line concept is scarcely more than illustration" (65) and that "color is the real building medium" (67). And Rothko, the supreme colorist, looks back to the work of Fra Angelico and thinks that he himself might be better conceived as a Renaissance painter. In a sense, then, Wyatt, had he looked more carefully, might have found contemporaries who shared not only his estimation of color but also his desire for transcendence. Hofmann, for instance, felt that a painting was finished only "when feeling and perception have resulted in a spiritual synthesis" (Chipp, 541); and Rothko thought of his paintings as beginning in "an unknown adventure in an unknown space," yet moving toward a completion signaled "in a flash of recognition," hinting that the end is already present in the beginning. Or as Rothko writes, "Ideas and plans that existed in the mind at the start were simply the doorway through which one left the world in which they occur" (Chipp, 548).

Still, while there might be advantages to conceiving of color in opposition to line, and to investing it with rich metaphorical meaning, we should be skeptical of those claims that place color beyond the realm of mediacy. I like what Merleau-Ponty has to say here: "The return to color has the merit of getting somewhat nearer to 'the heart of things,' but this heart is beyond the color envelope just as it is beyond the space envelope" (181). In short, the problems of drawing and color are neither necessarily separate nor antithetical. Line (the essence of drawing) can, as in Merleau-Ponty's example from Matisse, speak of "a certain disequilibrium kept up within the indifference of the white paper; it is a certain process of gouging within the in-itself, a certain constitutive emptiness—an emptiness which . . . upholds the pretended positivity of the things" (184). Like color, then, line not only can but must speak of something not itself, something absent, by which it achieves its sense of materiality and presence. And if line achieves its definition vis-à-vis what is not line, included among the latter is color. Line and color, while different, are bound in a relation that does not encourage separate solutions. Or as Merleau-Ponty writes: "Because depth, color, form, line, movement, contour, physiognomy are all branches of Being and because each one can sway all the rest, there are no separated, distinct 'problems' in painting, no really opposed paths, no partial 'solutions,' no cumulative progress, no irretrievable options" (188).

To come back, then, to the question of whether we might conceive of Wyatt as modifying his aesthetic allegiances to the point that he would work alongside a Hofmann or a Rothko, I think that though we might answer with a "maybe," there is also the sense that Wyatt, rightly or wrongly, wishes to reach beyond art's circle. At the novel's end, he has, as noted, reached the conviction that art itself cannot "explain it" (870), cannot sufficiently elucidate the profounder questions concerning Being. It is not clear that any discipline, science included, can. Still, Wyatt seems not only to have undergone a shift in his aesthetic allegiance, but also to have reached a point where the aesthetic project itself appears suspect. If so, this might help us to understand the significance of his "restoration" work. That is, when Ludy first comes upon Wyatt, now called Stephen, he is restoring a Navarette canvas depicting St. Dominic "kneeling before a crucifix suspended in midair" (867). He has previously restored a canvas by Valdés Leal, and he plans on restoring another by El Greco. However, to Ludy, as he stands nearby, it appears as if Wyatt is not so much restoring as destroying the Navarette painting. As Ludy finally says, "the foot here, it's almost gone. You . . . why are you taking it away, it . . . this whole part of the picture here, it's not damaged" (872).

Is Wyatt actually destroying the canvases? Ludy seems to think so, protesting not only that there is nothing wrong with the section of the Navarette canvas that Wyatt works with the knife, but also that there is nothing wrong with the next restoration project, the El Greco: "But you . . . there's nothing wrong with it at all, it's . . . it's in fine condition, that painting" (872). In addition, we might note that Wyatt's scraping is described in terms similar to those depicting his earlier damaging of the *Death of the Virgin* (275). Still, this said, it seems impossible to make any final determination.[26] Wyatt could simply be scraping off a later painter's overpainting.

Whatever the case, there is a strong suggestion that Wyatt wishes to move beyond art. He feels the need to act, but the aesthetic project in the twentieth century, with its vaunted claims, must for him be more broadly conceived. Hence, in his manic state, preparing to embark on a life lived deliberately, he seems to leave art behind, perhaps in a manner not so emotionally unlike Rothko's own taking leave of art, when he came to see his own late work as inadequate: "They are not paintings" (Ashton, *About Rothko*, 197). Yet whereas Rothko, finding that art was not enough, decided (like Pollock and Gorky before him) to end his life, Wyatt chooses to go on, to see not if art by itself can "explain it," but whether in the company of other connections and values, art might make more sense.[27]

Forgery, the Substitution of the False for the Real

In her essay on Han van Meegeren (1889–1947), famous for his successful forgeries of Vermeer canvases, Hope B. Werness speculates that in addition to the Dutch artist's hostility "to experts, progressive artists, and art critics," the motivation for his forgeries included "financial motives pure and simple . . . ; proof of the lasting importance and beauty of seventeenth-century art as opposed to the despised decadence of modern art; proof of his genius as an artist; proof of the venality of the experts—art historians, dealers, and critics who look at signatures and not the merit of the work" (22). In other words, his motivations were rather ordinary, and do little to alter our sense that his work was also a crime. Yet when we turn to Wyatt, whose story clearly owes much (especially in technique) to the van Meegeren episode, our sympathies are engaged. The reason, I think, has much to do with motivation. Wyatt may be misguided, but his ambition—to facilitate his sense of recall—seems worthy. The motivations attached to money, personal hurt, and envy do not seem, as they did for van Meegeren, to count for very much.[28] Wyatt finds himself manipulated by people, Brown in particular, for whom such motivations have appeal, but his own motivations are, however naive, more idealistic. Brown thinks that he can persuade Wyatt by an appeal to both his vanity and his wallet. He tries, that is, to seduce Wyatt with the offer of an arena in which his "genius" will be given credit (142), and then offers a business deal, only to have Wyatt question its pertinence to the things that most matter:

> —We're talking business, Recktall Brown said calmly.
> —But . . .
> —People work for money, my boy.
> —But I . . .
> —Money gives significance to anything.
> —Yes. People believe that, don't they. People believe that.

Recktall Brown watched patiently, like someone waiting for a child to solve a simple problem to which there was only one answer. The cigarette, lit across from him, knit them together in the different textures of their smoke.

—You know . . . Saint Paul tells us to redeem time.

—Does he? Recktall Brown's tone was gentle, encouraging.

—A work of art redeems time.

—And buying it redeems money, Recktall Brown said. (144)

In the end, Wyatt does accept Brown's offer, and it would be a mistake to say that he is not at all swayed by matters of vanity or income. Still, it is his pursuit of that which lies beyond the painting—the pattern awaiting discovery—that most motivates him. Or as he tells Brown, frustrated by the latter's failure to understand his motives: "Damn it, am I the only one who feels this way? Have I made this all up alone?" (143). He has not made it up alone; there are others, even in the novel (e.g., Stanley and Esme), who feel as he does. But there are not many. Instead, the majority would better understand the thievish impulse motivating Brown, who sees an opportunity to make a fortune by placing a false object in front of people too greedy to notice the difference. It is not a victimless crime. In fact, in the end, all are victimized by the masquerading of false things as true. Still, in the short term, it seems almost like a victimless crime, for the people hoodwinked are, first and foremost, those who are themselves most rapacious.

We might anticipate a certain scorn toward the producers and buyers of false objects, yet in *The Recognitions* the greatest blame attaches to the art historians and critics. They are condemned by their ambition, whereas the producers and buyers are condemned by their greed. Neither situation is pretty, but it is the sin of pride that appears the most castigated. Thus Brown and Valentine, no innocents themselves, find merriment in watching the "experts" get trapped by their own theories, taking the false as genuine largely for reasons related to professional ambition. That is, until their adjudications are shown to be as flimsy as the false object they labeled genuine. Referring to the frenzy stirred up by Wyatt's fakes, Valentine says to Brown: "It's heartbreaking to watch, isn't it. They are all so fearfully serious. But of course that's just what makes it all possible. The authorities are so deadly serious that it never occurs to them to doubt, they cannot wait to get ahead of one another to point out verifications" (229). Once fooled, the expert stays fooled. Or as Brown later tells Wyatt, who has begun to wonder whether the whole project is any more than a "sanction[ing] of Gresham's law":

> —Don't talk to me now about law, just listen to me. Who would gain anything if you ran around telling people you painted these things? They'd all be mad as hell at you, most of all the people who bought them. Do you think they'd even admit they paid forty or fifty thousand for a fraud? Do you think anyone would thank you? [. . .]

—Do you think they'd even believe you? They'd lock you up, my boy. You could get up there and paint these things all over again, and they wouldn't believe you. They'd think you're crazy. That's what they'd want to think. My boy, you've fooled the experts. But once you've fooled an expert, he stays fooled. (364)

Brown has a point, certified by the van Meegeren story, and capped by van Meegeren's well-publicized 1947 trial. During the 1930s and 1940s, van Meegeren, disgruntled with an art establishment that refused to recognize his genius, had painted, in addition to canvases masquerading as original Terborchs, Pieter de Hooghs, Baburens, and Hals, several Vermeers. The most famous of these was *The Supper at Emmaus* (1937), a painting that the Vermeer scholar Abraham Bredius declared in the *Burlington Magazine* as Vermeer's own masterpiece:

It is a wonderful moment in the life of a lover of art when he finds himself suddenly confronted with a hitherto unknown painting by a great master, untouched, on the original canvas, and without any restoration, just as it left the painter's studio! And what a picture! Neither the beautiful signature 'I. V. Meer' . . . nor the *pointillé* on the bread which Christ is blessing, is necessary to convince us that we have here a—I am inclined to say—*the* masterpiece of Johannes Vermeer of Delft, and moreover, one of his largest works . . . , quite different from all his other paintings and yet every inch a Vermeer. (Werness, 31)

That van Meegeren could paint a Vermeer unlike any other, but still have it putatively recognized as a Vermeer, was in itself a remarkable achievement. The achievement, however, has its explanation. Like Wyatt, with his proposed Hubert van Eyck, van Meegeren took advantage of the fact that art historians not only study surviving masterworks but also speculate about what has not survived, or what may, in time, surface. This was the case with the scholarship surrounding Vermeer, a painter "discovered" only in the late nineteenth century, yet whose reputation was very much on the rise. Meanwhile, as scholars began to pay closer attention to Vermeer, they noticed a gap between the early works and the more characteristic paintings. The Italianate character of the early pictures led to the speculation that, apart from the influence of the Utrecht Caravaggisti, there must have been a trip to Italy, likely to have produced hitherto unrecognized Vermeers.[29] It was into this gap that van Meegeren ventured, producing work designed to confirm the Italian interlude hypothesis.[30] What was notable, then, about *The Supper at Emmaus* was how much it seemed to look back to Caravaggio's own *Supper at Emmaus*, lending support to the thesis that Vermeer had either traveled to Italy or become acquainted with the Caravaggio canvas in some other way. To Bredius, who had authenticated an earlier Vermeer canvas and who had not only assumed the Italy trip but even predicted that more Vermeers with religious themes would be discovered, the van Meegeren canvas appeared a genuine find. A big canvas, it seemed to fit in perfectly with Vermeer's early work, before his canvases became smaller and his subjects secular: "As to the period in which Vermeer painted this masterpiece, I believe it belongs to his earlier phase—about the same time . . . as the well-known *Christ in the House of Martha and Mary* at Edinburgh. . . . He had given up painting large compositions because they were difficult to sell, and painters like Dou and Mieris were already getting big prices for their smaller works" (Werness, 31).

With Bredius's authentication, the painting, despite its mysterious antecedents,[31] was successfully sold for the then astonishing price of 520,000 guilders to a consortium of buyers, including the Rembrandt Society. It was then moved to the walls of the new Boymans Museum in Rotterdam, where it would have stayed except for an unusual series of events. During the war, van Meegeren passed along *The Adulteress* (another fake Vermeer) to a fellow Dutchman, who passed it along to a Bavarian banker with an office in Amsterdam, who, in turn, passed it along to Dr. Walter Hofer, an art agent for Hermann Göring, the Nazi party leader. These events led to van Meegeren's arrest in May 1945 on the charge of collaborating with the enemy. At the time, no one suspected that *The Adulteress* was a fake, yet to evade the charge of collaboration, van Meegeren confessed to having painted it and other Vermeers. This let him off the hook as far as the charge of collaboration went, for he was no longer trading in Dutch national treasures. However, he now faced a new (albeit lesser) charge: forgery. Meantime, despite his confession, not everyone wanted to believe that this second-rate artist was the author of Vermeer masterpieces. In fact, to prove his authorship, he was required while in jail to paint yet another Vermeer canvas, *The Young Christ Teaching in the Temple*. The demonstration convinced most "experts," though there remained one, the Frenchman Jean Decoen, who "took the position that two of van Meegeren's paintings, 'The Supper at Emmaus' and the second painting of 'The Last Supper,' were actually genuine Vermeers" (Werness, 45). Decoen also sought to convince the latter canvas's owner that a wrong had been done him and that he should sue. The owner, one van Beuningen, followed Decoen's counsel and in 1955 took the matter to court, where the ruling went against him. It was, as Werness writes, a "fascinating if irrational side" to the whole Meegeren/Vermeer affair (45), though as Brown knows, not so entirely unpredictable. Or as he tells Wyatt: "These pictures of yours, do you think you could get two hundred dollars for one? No. But these poor bastards crawl all over each other trying to get them away from me for prices in the thousands. They don't know, they don't want to know" (363).[32]

Meanwhile, it is precisely the attempt to take advantage of critical speculation that fuels the project, proposed by Valentine and undertaken by Wyatt, to paint a Hubert van Eyck:

> —Yes, yes, Basil Valentine interrupted impatiently, —there are probably more badly faked Jan van Eycks then any of the others. Hubert, on the other hand . . .
> —Hubert van Eyck?
> —It might be the art discovery of the century, if it were absolutely perfect, signed and documented . . .
> —Yes, yes it might, it probably would be. (249)

Valentine explains to Brown that a Hubert van Eyck would command a quarter of a million dollars for the reason "he never existed" (254). Valentine is half serious, half teasing. He is, he admits, among those historians convinced that Hubert van Eyck never existed, yet he concedes to the now frazzled Wyatt that perhaps he did: "All right, my dear fellow . . ." (254). This, after Wyatt has protested, "But he did, he did," and before he offers the evidence of the "Ghent Altarpiece" and the "Steenken Madonna" (254), the first of which was begun, most historians agree, by Hubert and finished by Jan, and the second of which is no longer ascribed to Hubert, though Conway did so in *The Van Eycks and Their Followers*, a key source for Gaddis. Hubert's life is not so much in doubt as untestified to by any certifiable picture. There is, of course, the Ghent altarpiece, with its famous though partly damaged inscription: "The painter Hubert van Eyck, greater than whom no one was found, began [this work]; and Jan, his brother, second in art, having carried through the task at the expense of Judocus Vyd, invites you by this verse, on the sixth of May, to look at [or possibly, 'to protect'] what has been done" (Panofsky, 206). But it is not clear how much, if any, of the altarpiece was actually done by Hubert (for the inscription's authenticity has itself been questioned).[33] Panofsky, while not disputing Hubert's existence, assigns the greater credit to Jan: "The very existence of these 'subjacent rays' suffices, I believe, to prove, on the one hand, that we cannot eliminate the participation of Hubert altogether; and, on the other, that, whatever we may decide to assign him cannot include the magnificent panorama which constitutes the upper ranges of the scenery" (225).

Clearly, then, a signed Hubert van Eyck would represent an extraordinary discovery. And a forged canvas, supported by forged documentation, might, if well executed, accomplish the trick of convincing a community of experts already on the lookout for a Hubert van Eyck. In any event, this is the plan, for Valentine mentions two pieces of documentation (one authentic, one imagined) that should prove instrumental in convincing the community's more skeptical members. The first is the will of Jean de Visch, the "grand bailli" of Flanders, who in 1413 bequeathed a painting by Hubert (Conway, *Van Eycks*, 59). This, says Valentine, "goes to prove, supposedly, that such a picture was painted. Another Virgin of some sort. Proves it well enough for your purpose, at any rate" (256). The second document is "a scrap of paper" found "when they tore down that house in Ghent [wherein] they hoped to find some of Hubert's work, hidden somewhere" (256). Valentine is referring to a house on Ghent's rue de Gouvernement, the demolition of which exposed "the old walls of a building believed to have belonged to Jodoc Vyt" (Conway, *Van Eycks*, 57). Jodoc Vyt (or Vyd) was a wealthy citizen of Ghent and eventually its mayor. As noted, it was he who commissioned the "Ghent Altarpiece." Valentine mentions this and goes on to say that the scrap of paper found in the house was, in fact, "a letter signed by Jodoc Vyt [. . .] commissioning a work by Hubert van Eyck" (256). There is, of course, no such document, yet Valentine offers it to Brown for two thousand dollars. Brown thinks it can be gotten for less, and wonders whether or not it is genuine. Valentine responds that "[i]f it is not genuine, why should it exist at all?" (256). The answer is to authenticate another fake, but Brown lets this go, and wonders why if it exists, he needs to buy it. Valentine, after offering the history of blackmail among the Greeks and Romans, ends by saying that this is a case of "blackmail in reverse. You see, if you don't buy this slip of paper it will be destroyed" (256). He means that unless Brown buys it, it shall never be forged to begin with. What should be the point? But Brown has been baited, and when he asks whether Wyatt "can't paint this picture without this scrap of paper?" Valentine says, "Of course he can. But with this attached to it, it will be irreproachable" (256). Thus Brown buys in: "All right" (256).

The plan to forge a Hubert van Eyck is ingenious, but it will not get far unless the execution is brilliant. It must be this, for faking a Flemish masterwork requires extraordinary knowledge and skill. Valentine even questions, despite Wyatt's previous successes, whether he can pull off a Hubert van Eyck. Wyatt responds with indignation: "If I could do it! Of course I can do it" (249). Yet everything stands in his way. Or as Frank Arnau notes, "The working methods characteristic of paintings of this epoch [i.e., van Eyck's] present the forger with almost insuperable difficulties. To imitate them, he must employ substitute techniques which are fairly easy to detect. The ochrous oily or resinous *imprimitura* with its thin overall coat of glaze is almost impossible to simulate. The presence of contemporary varnishes and Venetian turpentine can always be established in original works to a certain degree. In section, a fake never exhibits the same authentic stratified effect, and technical shortcomings make it easy for the art historian to form definite conclusions" (62).

True, van Meegeren fooled the experts, and as late as 1955 his work was still mustering debate. However, he himself admitted at the conclusion of his 1947 trial that "the possibility of forgery of this kind, and on this scale, no longer existed" (Savage, 232). In the future, forgers would need to work closer to the present if they hoped to avoid scientific detection.[34] Still, in the late 1940s, Wyatt thinks that though "[t]here isn't one test they [the experts] don't know," there is not "one that can't be beaten" (248). In a way, Wyatt becomes too absorbed with the difficulties of fooling the experts. He needs to fool them, of course, if the paintings are to be received as genuine. But his successes leave him feeling boastful, a surprising emotion given that the paintings are imagined to foster humility as well as piety. Still, Wyatt advances further in his experiments, seeking to find a satisfactory solution to two of the more difficult problems of this field of deceit: getting the oil painting to harden and to crack. In the first instance, oils are notoriously slow to dry and will retain their moisture over a long period of years. The problem, then, for the forger is how to dry or harden the paint so that it appears much older. In the second instance, there are many ways for a forger to produce what is known as craquelure, the fine crackles on a painting's surface that are the consequence of a shrinking, over time, of either the paint film or varnish. Some of these are more convincing than others, and a good forger needs to master the technique.[35] Wyatt himself speaks of various experiments to produce the desired results:

> —Yes, that . . . getting the hard surface, it was one of the worst problems. [. . .] —I've tried everything, every different . . . I tried mixing my colors on blotting paper, to absorb the oil, and then mixing them with varnish but it dried too quickly, you see? It dried too quickly and it was unalterable. I tried a mixture of stand oil and formaldehyde, but it wasn't right, it wasn't what I wanted. I tried oil of lavender and formaldehyde and I like that better, the oil with an egg tempera, and a varnish glaze. In those two Bouts pictures, in those when I prepared the canvas I laid linen threads on the gesso when it was still wet, you see? in the pattern I wanted for the crackle. Then I baked it, and when it came out of the oven the threads came off and left the pattern. (248)[36]

If this process leaves Wyatt happy with the surface's hardness, it is still inadequate as to the craquelure. Hence, he experiments until he finds a surprisingly simple solution, the use of glair, the product of egg whites, which when ground into the pigment and left to dry will, of its own volition, produce a quite convincing cracking:

> —But I haven't told you, after all this work, this . . . fooling around. Do you know what the best medium is? It's so simple I never dared try it, it's that simple. Glair, the liquid that settles to the bottom when the whites of egg are beaten, with dry powdered pigments, and a layer of clean white egg over it and the varnish, it's so simple it doesn't need anything, it doesn't need to be baked, it crackles by itself beautifully, as though years, hundreds of years had passed over it. (248–49)[37]

At this point, Wyatt appears satisfied that he has mastered the considerable technical obstacles standing in the way of his Flemish fakes. Valentine offers no objections, nor do we hear of objections from the art community, including its conservators. Even his student work, the painting done in the style of Memling and then passed off as an original, has been certified as real by the experts at "the old Pinakothek in Munich" (74), though there is mention only of a cleaning and not of a full-fledged examination. Later, at Brown's party, a member of the Royal Academy will question the authenticity of the face in *The Death of the Virgin*—"Oh dear no, won't do at all. Zinc white, don't you [Valentine] know. Zinc white. I think you'll come upon that when you make an analysis of the pigments" (671). What he detects (i.e., the use of an eighteenth-century color) is, however, the consequence of Brown's painting over the damaged face, the damage deliberately inflicted by Wyatt, so as to make the picture appear more authentic. Here, if Brown finds it difficult to reconcile himself to the damage, Wyatt finds it more so, for he must deliberately destroy part of that which has taken him so long to create. Yet the damage must be inflicted, if the painting's authenticity is not to be questioned. The skillful forger, write Mansfield and Mills, is

> well aware that a painting, say from the early Flemish period, fifteenth century or thereabouts, is very unlikely to have escaped completely unscathed. Apart from cracking on the surface, it is possible there will be areas that have been damaged by abrasion and by unwise cleaning; therefore the forger, having completed his fake, will deliberately abrade certain areas, using possibly an agate burnisher dipped into a little fine abrasive powder such as tripoli or crocus, something that won't give an obvious scratch as would a glass paper. This trick can often be picked up if the picture in question is closely examined to see just where these abrasive or paint losses occur. If such defacements are genuine, the damage obviously may be anywhere. If the picture in question is a fake, the damage will be very carefully placed and certainly would not be over a vital feature such as a face, a hand, or some piece of elaborate jewelry. (128–29)

Wyatt is more than a skillful forger, he is an excellent forger. If the ordinary forger is too cautious vis-à-vis the damage, Wyatt himself knows that "the damage is indifferent to the composition" (333). It respects neither this nor its most beautiful elements, which in the van der Goes picture include the Virgin's face. And so the damage Wyatt inflicts proves, as Valentine notes, extensive: "Brown won't like this, you know. The face there, how badly you've damaged it" (333).

There are other things that make Wyatt an excellent forger. For instance, like van Meegeren, he knows that the best forgeries are not mechanical imitations or pastiches. The difficulty with the latter is that the forger, so attentive to getting the details right (i.e., the brush strokes, iconography, and mannerisms), can easily produce a picture wherein the whole appears too much the incoherent addition of its parts. The painting ends up looking like ten different paintings, or their parts. As Wyatt tells Brown and Valentine, after Valentine has accused him of being nothing but a forger: "Do you think I do these things the way all other forging has been done? Pulling the fragments of ten paintings together and making one, or taking, a . . . a Dürer and reversing the composition so that the man looks to the right instead of the left, putting a beard on him from another portrait, and a hat, a different hat from another, so that they look at it and recognize Dürer there?" (250). Wyatt works otherwise. He thinks of himself as a painter, a genuine painter, and while we, like Valentine, must refuse to concur so long as the work greets the public under someone else's name, it is important to understand that a principal reason why Wyatt (again like van Meegeren) proves so successful as a forger is that before he is a forger he is an artist. Thus Valentine can later say to Wyatt, "I called your work calumny once, so it was. But the face of Christ in your van der Goes, no one could call that a lie" (386). Like the paintings in general, the face speaks of a truth transcending mechanical reproduction, speaks, that is, of a freedom and a consciousness identified less with the forger than with the artist. It is thus with the likes of Wyatt in mind that Rudolf Arnheim says that the most successful forgers,

> [i]nstead of duplicating by mechanical imitation, . . . rely on fairly free invention in the spirit of the original's style. They produce analogies or equivalents, which make for better aesthetic quality. This accounts in part for the appreciation received by the sculpture of a Bastianini or Dossena or some of van Meegeren's paintings. The forger, somewhat gifted himself, can take chances, and thereby obtains an additional resemblance to the work of the great. Being an artist oneself helps when one tries to match the work of others. (237)

Are we to infer from this that Wyatt's forgeries, while spawned in deceit, possess aesthetic worth? Some critics have been prepared to discount the fact of something's being forged when attending to its artistry. For instance, Alfred Lessing argues that "[c]onsidering a work of art aesthetically superior because it is genuine, or inferior because it is forged, has little or nothing to do with aesthetic judgment or criticism" (58). And Clive Bell, well known for his advocacy of significant form, asserts that since "[g]reat art remains . . . independent of time and place," if a work were "an absolutely exact copy, clearly it would be as moving as the original" (Meyer, 78, 79). But the issue is more complicated than either is prepared to grant. With forgeries there come many gradations, and we should hesitate to pronounce a forged object a necessarily bad or good thing. Certainly, the knowledge that an object is forged cannot be dismissed from an assessment of its value. Still, it remains one factor among others, and not always the most considerable. Who, for instance, would not prefer Michelangelo's student forgeries to their originals? And who would look askance at Andrea del Sarto's copy of Raphael's Pope Leo X portrait simply for the reason that it, too, was conceived as a forgery? Da Vinci might scorn all imitations—"Stultum imitatorum pecus" (Arnau, 36)—but forgies do not all serve the same purpose or find themselves framed by the same circumstances.

Still, forgery, by definition, constitutes an intentional desire to deceive, and while circumstances may meliorate matters, in most instances forgery is a hateful thing. It is particularly odious on those occasions when it distorts the history of achievement, be it in painting, sculpture, or music. Disciplinary knowledge always entails a chronology, and requires that one understand, for example, the way Melville learns from and responds to Hawthorne or the way van Gogh does much the same vis-à-vis Millet. What the forger does, though, is to insert his or her own work, carrying with it the values of a later time, into this chronology and thereby distort the nature of what has and has not been achieved. Since no artist "has his [or her] complete meaning alone," it is very possible, through the insertion of a single art object, to change the reputation of a whole host of other such objects. This, for instance, happens with what seems an almost innocuous forgery, Wyatt's Memling. Now, rather than being simply a student's work, inspired by David's *Flaying of the Unjust Judge*, it starts to find itself positioned as that painting's inspiration: "Possibly, the experts allowed, it might be the work of Gheerardt David, but more likely that of Memling, from which David had probably drawn his 'Flaying of the Unjust Judge'" (74–75). The Wyatt picture proves to be a small gesture with outrageous consequences, though these themselves are small compared with what shall be the consequence of not only his Bouts and van der Goes forgeries, but the Hubert van Eyck. Fortunately, the Hubert van Eyck picture never gets beyond the study stage (274). Otherwise, it would have constituted not only "the art discovery of the century" (249) but also one of this century's more significant crimes, of which there have been already too many.

There is another matter that warrants discussion here, and this is the way forgery undermines our epistemological confidence. Michael Wren has written that, contrary to general opinion, "it is possible for all paintings to be forgeries, and that, again contrary to widespread belief, 'forged' is not a relational term. For although every forgery is a forgery *of* some 'thing,' that 'thing' need not exist; in this respect 'forgery of' is more like 'thought of' than 'son of.' Better, I think, to keep in mind that the logically proper locution is 'forged X,' that 'forged' is attributive, and that 'forged' is logically parasitic on 'genuine'" (199). Wren's observation would seem most applicable to Wyatt's forging of the Bosch table with the Seven Deadly Sins. The table, described by the narrator as "the original" (25), is acquired by

Reverend Gwyon, while in Italy, from the Conte di Brescia, owner of one of the world's finest art collections, who, owing to bad finances, is forced to sell off his works in secret, replacing the originals with copies. Meanwhile, Wyatt, like the young Michelangelo in Ghirlandaio's studio, creates a copy that he substitutes for the original. In order to pay for his European study, he sells the original, which ends up in Brown's hands. The table's travels do not stop here, for Valentine has other plans for it, basically to return it, along with other objects in Brown's collection, to Europe. This, as he later confesses, explains why he, before Brown and Wyatt, questions the table's authenticity, speaking of it as an intricate, cunning forgery (245):

> Of course it was the original here for so long, the one you [Wyatt] sold him. And this [an unconvincing forgery, which Valentine has substituted for the original], I picked this one up in Rome myself scarcely a year ago. Do you recall when we first met? right here, across the table? Of course that was the original. I said it was a copy simply to hear you defend it. I knew Brown would trust your judgment. And I knew Brown would be troubled enough to have it gone over again, by "experts." I brought the idea into his mind simply to let him kill it himself, so that once I'd exchanged the two, no matter who called this a copy, he'd simply laugh at them. He'd just made absolutely certain, hadn't he? (688)

Only children and naïfs expect absolute certainty from the world. Still, most people's relation to the world can be described as trusting. Over time, they learn, with some predictability, which actions pay back with ill fortune and which with good, and from this they make further speculation about the world's larger orderliness and, perhaps, immanent design. The forger, meanwhile, works against the stream of people's more general desire, for forgeries cultivate mistrust, playing people for fools and undermining the integrity even of otherwise true things. It is with great relief then that Wyatt greets Valentine's confession concerning the Bosch table, for in taking from him, if only momentarily, what he was certain about, Valentine had done more than increase the younger man's doubts about a single table, he had undermined Wyatt's fundamental relation to the world itself. A dose of skepticism is generally a healthy thing, but few are the exponents of complete skepticism, and fewer are those who practice such skepticism without enduring dire consequences. Hence, when Valentine confesses that what Wyatt, with great confidence, first held to be genuine was so in fact, Wyatt exclaims, "—Yes, thank God! [. . .] —Thank God there was the gold to forge!" (689). This is itself perhaps the most important confession (not Valentine's but Wyatt's) in the novel, as much a key to the reading of *The Recognitions* as, say, Stephen Dedalus's famous line, "The word [love] known to all men," is to Joyce's *Ulysses*.[38]

As in *Ulysses*, love is a central theme in *The Recognitions*, and I wish to conclude by speaking of love in relation to forgery. I particularly wish to remark on the deep hurt felt by Esme when she watches Wyatt damage the face in *The Death of the Virgin*, which is, of course, her face. She accuses him, before she walks out, of dishonoring death, an accusation that comes to haunt Wyatt, and whose justice he eventually comes to accept. Meanwhile, Esme reacts to the damaging of the picture as a personal hurt. If Wyatt cared about her, as she cares about him, he would be more protective of her image, again figured in the Virgin's face. We know that he does care, and it is precisely his affection for Esme that, though it comes too late, helps him to see just how immoral are his forgeries. They represent a betrayal of trust, the trust placed in one, be it either by family and friends or simply by the common citizen. The damaging of the Virgin's face, however, represents a very specific betrayal, and makes clear how interconnected are the acts of the forger and the false lover. So long as Wyatt commits himself to the calumny that is forgery, so long shall he remain outside the circle of a loving relation, at least to the degree that this relation demands honesty and openness. Actions have a tendency to come full circle, and the dishonesty that is practiced in one realm, art, is bound to manifest itself in another, one's friendships. This, at any rate, seems to be the case in the relation between Wyatt and Esme, for it appears to be precisely the forged canvases that come between them. Forgery and love are, almost by definition, incompatible, an observation that I find beautifully developed in an essay, "The Disappointed Art Lover," by Francis Sparshott, who writes like a flesh-and-blood Esme:

> What makes sexual betrayal possible is akin to what makes art forgery possible. The separability of sexual activity from the social and personal relationship that should sustain it is like the separation of aesthetic experience as such from the sharing and appreciation of artistic performance. In both cases, the simultaneous violence and shallowness of one component contrasts with the subtlety, diffuseness, and depth of the other. The quality of aesthetic experience, like that of sexual experience ("As who, in love's embrace, / Forgetfully may frame / Above the poor slut's face / Another woman's name," or vice versa), depends on imaginative construction and association, for only an imaginatively funded vision detects and responds to the meaningful structure of a picture or a musical piece. And, because all social and personal bonds are reciprocal but directly known from one end only, all the relationships we know or think we know ourselves to be living in are as fragile and subject to illusion as the art lover's confidence in the authenticity of a work and the integrity of its artist. (259-60)

Relations are "fragile" but not, as Wyatt says elsewhere, "tenuous" (113). They do not lack a reason for being, but can be sustained only if we are respectful of this reason. Wyatt, in his forgeries, forgets the equation's logic, forgets, in Stanley's phrase, that "[t]he devil is the father of false art" (464). In forgetting this, Wyatt ends up hurting those people (e.g., Esther, Esme) who care most about him. The tragedy for Wyatt is that forgetting does not preclude remembering, and there comes a point when, seeing what he has done, he finds it difficult to forgive himself, or to offer himself to Esme, after having misused her. As he tells Valentine: "You can see that I can't just go to her, like this, after what I've done and, done to her. That I couldn't just go to her and offer her this . . . what's left" (549). Yet if, in relation to Esme, Wyatt has acted unlike a "lover, not [as one] looking to find what was there," but as one who felt it his right to impose a face upon her and then "selfishly take it away" (840), it is better to know this, after having forgotten it, than never to know it at all. So while there is something terribly sad in Wyatt's remembrance of his obligation, there is also something hopeful. That is, if there can be no real tragedy without consciousness, where there is consciousness there can be no real tragedy, for consciousness is the starting point for setting things right. By this, I mean not returning things to what they were, but setting them right, introducing honesty into one's relations (e.g., to one's art, to other people) with the hope and the faith that, in time, things will come full circle.

2

J R and the Question of That Which Is Worth Doing

For instance, Milton, who wrote *Paradise Lost*, was an unproductive worker. On the other hand, a writer who turns out work for his publisher in factory style is a productive worker. Milton produced *Paradise Lost* as a silkworm produces silk, as the activation of *his own* nature. He later sold his product for £5 and thus became a merchant.

—Karl Marx, *Capital*

Children may not obey,
But children will listen.
Children will look to you
For which way to turn,
To learn what to be.
—Stephen Sondheim, *Into the Woods*

Exchange Value as the Societal Ethic

In the prior chapter, I argued that mid-century artists, lacking a genuine raison d'être, sought to make art an end in itself. The response, while not without interest, was ultimately inadequate. Here, I will also address the theme of the artist living in a largely posttheological age, but as *J R* has not yet received the fullness of attention that *The Recognitions* has, I should like to expand the parameters of the discussion more, and to attend to some additional themes—e.g., capitalism, social disorder, children's education, the ethos of the sublime, and so on. I especially wish to address these matters in the context of, or in opposition to, an even larger, more insidious conflation of means with ends, the way that in the United States reality is so often identified with an equation of commodity exchange. The business of America is business, and Gaddis's *J R* suggests that this has never been more true than in the second half of this century when other competing ethics—e.g., religion and art—have seen their constituencies flag. There are no true vacuums, and into the space vacated by the more traditional orders, business has marched like an ur-reality. Of course, Gaddis himself will always resist this scenario, and even as *J R* documents a world in thrall to Wall Street, there remain pockets of resistance. These constitute the hope of the novel, but to see what they are up against, I would like to begin this chapter by attending to American capitalism's rather successful bid to identify reality with itself.

In the world depicted in *J R,* it often seems as if the equation extant between reality and commodity exchange is the only one that can be counted on to hold good over time, for all other identities find themselves destabilized by the corroding pressure of market forces. Human identities are not exempted, and if we tend to think of them as bridgelike apparatuses connecting people to jobs, places, and even names, our disappointment will be even greater. In *J R*, names are found to be particularly lubricous. There does not appear to be a single character whose name goes unmolested, a situation confirming Julia Bast's own growing sense about "how cheap names are" (65). Edward Bast ("what was his name, bastard" [225]) is referred to as Edwerd Bast, E Gerst, B Best, and R Gast; Amy Joubert (pronounced by colleagues and relatives as "Jewbert") as Emily, Amie, Miss Moneybags, Mrs. Hyman Grynszpan, and Mrs. Richard Cutler; Jack Gibbs as Mr. Grynszpan and Greenspan; Whiteback as Whitefoot and Whitelaw; Charlotte Bast as Carlotta; Dan diCephalis as deSyph and Mister Ten-forty; Governor John Cates as Black Jack Cates and Katz; Pecci as Peachy; Coen as Cohen; and the baritone Dietrich Fischer-Dieskau as Fisher Dishcloth. Adding to the instability is the fact that some characters choose to change their names, the way, for instance, Reuben, the protégé of James Bast, decides to assume the Bast surname or the way in which the family name Engels gives way to that of Angel. Jack Gibbs appears to capture the general irreverence toward names when, asked if he is Mr. Slomin, he responds, "If I was I'd change my name" (114).

In one sense, then, names here are simply that—names, signifiers lacking any essential relation to beings, the way in which Gibbs and Eigen's Mr. Grynszpan remains an unembodied creation, even as he possesses a summa cum laude degree from Harvard, earns the attention of the *Encyclopaedia Britannica,* and acquires a Wall Street reputation as the "éminence grise behind the company's [the J R Family] meteoric expansion" (711). But in another sense, locatable outside the said equation, names can foster linkages, can be quite real. I am referring, in this instance, to Gaddis's own adeptness at making fictive names mean more, the way J R Vansant's cognomen (he has no Christian name) accents his junior status, Edward Bast's surname accents the son's sense of abandonment by the father; Jack Gibbs's name alludes to the physicist Willard Gibbs;[1] Tom Eigen's name alludes to the prominent concern here with sight;[2] and so on. The commodity equation notwithstanding, names are important in Gaddis's fiction and not unrelated to our sense of existence. This seems evident when Eigen, angered by his wife's accusation that he resents their child, draws a connection between his son's name and his existence: "Told me before he was born I said I didn't want David God damn it wasn't David there wasn't any David, got any sense what in hell do you want to bring one more helpless, one more whole capacity for suffering doesn't exist yet doesn't even have a name" (404).

A name relates to the fact of a person's existence—and by extension, worth—but it does not guarantee this existence. Nothing really does, not one's books, music, property, or family relations. All these are capable of suggesting identity, but there always remains a gap between a name and its subject.[3] This is true in any culture. However, the situation is exacerbated in the world of *J R*, where one's existence seems harder and harder to prove. We see numerous expressions of skepticism regarding the existence of one individual or another. Mr. Coen, for instance, certainly has a right to be suspicious about the existence of the Bast family's attorney Mr. Lemp ("I almost feel his existence may be open for question" [358]) for he has been dead for sixteen years, a situation that makes his subsequent suspicion ("and very frankly the figure of James Bast himself seems so ephemeral that when they tell me he is abroad somewhere accepting an award there is the sense that they may be referring to the Paris Exposition of nineteen eleven" [358]) plausible, if not finally convincing. Meanwhile, Zona Selk's skepticism regarding John Cates's existence, following from the fact that his body is a patchwork of both mechanical and organic replacements, may provoke little more than philosophical musing, but it also seems of a piece:

> —Beaton you tell him that if he tries that [to place money in escrow] I'll sue him for, dried up Raggedy Andy with his tin heart I'll sue him for impersonating himself for impersonating Mister Katz he's nobody, he's a lot of old parts stuck together he doesn't even exist he started losing things eighty years ago he lost a thumbnail on the Albany nightboat and that idiot classmate of his Handler's been dismantling him ever since, started an appendectomy punctured the spleen took it out then came the gall bladder that made it look like appendicitis in the first place now look at him, he's listening through somebody's else inner ears those corneal transplants God knows whose eyes he's

looking through, windup toy with a tin heart he'll end up with a dog's brain and some nigger's kidneys why can't I take him to court and have him declared nonexistent, null void nonexistence [. . .]. (708)

In a society that virtually grants exchange value the force of an absolute, no one's identity remains secure, not even John Cates's. This was not the intention, of course. No one starts off thinking that capitalism's ethic of use value belongs in the hospital, school, theater, town hall, and houses of worship, but when an ethic is permitted to rule in the community's main thoroughfares, its influence ends up permeating society's other segments. In fact, it is the belief that society's components can be bracketed, so that its ethical and religious beliefs are assigned one space, its culture and arts another space, and its laws of business a third, that makes it possible, in the absence of a larger, more encompassing telos, for the more aggressive of these components to infiltrate the others. Certainly this is the situation in *J R*. The society has willfully chosen to compartmentalize its workings, believing that it can avoid falling under the dominion of any single telos. It is a pragmatic decision, reflective of the community's plural antecedents. While the decision itself is well intended, the consequence is that one order—exchange value—begins to hold sway over the others. Exchange value begins to function like the telos that the bracketing was itself designed to forfend. And soon, rather than acting as separate entities, society's main institutions—its schools, universities, museums, churches and synagogues, as well as, of course, its manufacturing and retail firms—all find themselves reconceiving what they do in the light of this more encompassing order: cash nexus.

Governing this order, or ethic, is the mostly unspoken conviction that everything is either an object or its sign, and that the two are forever changing places, with the object functioning as a sign, or the sign functioning as an object or, in the parlance of cash nexus, a commodity. Whether it is one (commodity) or the other (sign) makes little difference, for the commodity by definition has little practical use value for its transitive owner. For instance, the nine thousand gross wooden picnic forks purchased by J R have for him absolutely no use value, and little more use value for their prior owner, the Navy, given their "progression" to plastic forks, though they are valuable to their prospective owner, the Army. What J R does is to buy cheap and to sell dear, thereby replicating Marx's classic formula of exchange value—M-C-M—wherein money's value is enhanced via the means of a commodity first bought, then sold. "In the . . . form M-C-M," Marx writes, "the buyer lays out money in order that, as a seller, he may recover money. By the purchase of his commodity he throws money into circulation, in order to withdraw it again by the sale of the same commodity. He releases the money, but only with the cunning intention of getting it back again. The money therefore is not spent, it is merely advanced" (249).

J R's initial deal, financed by the leveraging of the sixth graders' "class" action windfall, is a relatively simple one, peculiar, says Marx, to "merchants' capital" (256). He has used money—other people's money—to make money, a formula learnt from the master of the deal, Governor Cates:

> —You in this class of Mrs Joubert's are you? Mean she's never told you the only damn time you spend money's to make money?
> —She did too hey I mean that's what we're having where she said your money should work for you or it's like this here lazy partner which you . . .
> —Think she's pretty smart do you?
> —Sure she's real smart, like . . .
> —Real smart is she? She ever teach you what money is?
> —Like anybody knows that I mean, wait, here like this here quarter is . . .
> —What most damn fools think, next time you just tell her money is credit, get that?
> —It's what?
> —Tells you your money should work for you you tell her the trick's to get other people's money to work for you, get that? (109)

J R certainly does get it. So well, in fact, that he is able to use Cates's money, extracted by means of the "class" action suit, to finance his first major deal. Still, this merchant's exchange requires as much luck as cunning. It is possible to buy a commodity and then find it difficult to sell at more than the original price because it proves to be more available than first thought, or the demand has dried up, or some third, fourth, or fifth reason. In short, the commodity may have to be sold at a loss, in which case it would have been better never to have entered the game in the first place. There is an improvement upon the M-C-M formula of exchange, however, and that is that of M-C-M', or the formula of surplus value. Here a third factor—e.g., the rate of interest, the surplus value of production vis-à-vis labor's wages, etc.—introduces a more bankable edge than that found in simple exchange value, and makes "M-C-M' . . . the general formula for capital" (Marx, 257). What is noticeably different now is that money is used coercively, to dominate those with fewer resources, though capitalism makes a pretense of respecting the individual's freedom to sell his or her labor in the marketplace. Still, as Adam Smith observed, "Many workmen could not subsist a week, few could subsist a month, and scarce any a year without employment. In the long-run the workman may be as necessary to his master as his master is to him, but the necessity is not so immediate" (Heilbroner, 41).[4]

With his takeover of Eagle Mills in upstate New York, J R moves into a very different economic world, the sort that has repercussions not merely for a few Wall Street players but for an entire factory of workers and their families and for the town itself, so dependent is the community on the health of

this one plant. J R's interest in the textile mill is, however, purely exploitative. He cares nothing for the workers, their families, or the town. He simply
wants to take advantage of the mill's weakness by (1) selling almost everything off on a ninety-nine-year leaseback arrangement, making it possible
both to stay in business and bring in a significant amount of cash; (2) taking
tax credits for selling matériel below book value; (3) replacing aged workers
with machines which, unlike people, offer tax credits in the form of deprecia-
tion; (4) using the workers' pension fund to buy a brewery; and (5) writing
off the mill's losses against the brewery's profits, so as to keep the latter.
That J R manages to proceed with his acquisition follows from the fact that
not only do the mill workers have too few resources to combat the plan but
also the larger culture condones such activity. In J R's refrain, the action is
justified "[b]ecause that's what you do" (295).

Capitalism has built into it a rapacious, aggressive ethic, which if
unmasked would quickly make itself unwelcome. But it assumes the cloak of
anonymity, infiltrating the body politic, so that it appears, in Adam Smith's
famous phrase, to act almost as an "invisible hand," a set of laws as natural
as those of gravity and motion. Capitalism thereby encourages business people to think of themselves, almost, as the determined agents of some netherworld. Or as Robert L. Heilbroner writes, "That netherworld may be called
the Invisible Hand, or the laws of motion of the system, or the market mechanism; and its influence on the business world may be seen as propelling it in
the direction of growth, involving it in internal contradictions, or guiding it
toward a position of overall balance and stability. In every case, however, the
business world itself is seen as a mere vehicle by which the larger and more
encompassing principles of order and movement are carried out" (16). An
explanation much like this is what J R, in his own defense, offers Bast when
the latter protests the morality of the Eagle Mills takeover:

> But what am I supposed to do! [. . .] —I mean who asked them for their lousy
> mills? All I did was buy these bonds for this here investment and mind my
> own business and then they turn around and dump all these wrecked up build-
> ings and people and stuff on me and what do they expect me to do, build them
> a park? I mean holy shit . . . he ripped a paper towel down and worked it at his
> nose , —I have this here investment which I have to protect it don't I? (300)

If, as J R says, "You can't just play to play because the rules are only for
if you're playing to win which that's the only rules there are" (301), then it
seems imperative to protect one's investment whatever the human cost.
People may be important, but profits are more important. Not that this is
said; that would be unprofitable. In fact, what is attractive about the system,
from the capitalist's viewpoint, is that the pretense that people are the ultimate value can be kept up, even when the far reaches of a corporation's

activity offer persuasive argument otherwise. This is possible, says Heilbroner, because the system works to reduce "human contact in order to minimize the emotional entanglements that might interfere with the necessary stance of impersonal acquisitiveness" (59). The public marketplace, wherein seller and buyer would meet and exchange town news, finds itself replaced by a different, more impersonal marketplace, wherein exchanges are transacted as much over the telephone, one anonymous voice speaking to another, as person to person. As J R tells the Hyde boy,

> like I mean this here bond and stock stuff you don't see anybody you don't know anybody only in the mail and the telephone because that's how they do it nobody has to see anybody, you can be this here funny lookingest person that lives in a toilet someplace how do they know, I mean like all those guys at the Stock Exchange where they're selling all this stock to each other? They don't give a shit whose it is they're just selling it back and forth for some voice that told them on the phone why should they give a shit if you're a hundred and fifty all they . . . (172)[5]

Now, of course, even the telephone transaction is an anachronism, for most current trades are made electronically.[6] Nevertheless, it is a significant part of Gaddis's brilliance in this 1975 novel not only to be attuned to the newer, more anonymous manner in which economic activity takes place but also to find a way to render it fictively. George Steiner describes the novel as "a cancerous mingling of telephone calls, of crossed lines, of dial tones and static that fudges the logorrhea of the American voice" ("Crossed Lines," 106); Patrick O'Donnell speaks of J R "as a kind of talking switchboard" and the way in which "[t]his radical destabilizing of human agency via the telephone is perfectly complicit with 'doing business' in *J R*" (*Echo Chambers*, 165); and Susan Strehle observes that the narrator "leaps through television lines, or jumps telephone wires," pursuing "motion and energy inside the text" wherever it should lead him (121). The human voice, so long fettered to a physical presence, has become disembodied; originating miles away, it is the voice of someone whom the trader has probably never met, and most likely has no expectation of meeting.[7] It is a voice, like so many others, and thus almost anonymous. And because big business cultivates anonymity, its sense of right and wrong appears less responsive to human needs than to profits.

In *J R*, business leaders do not necessarily set out to contravene conventional ethics, yet they repeatedly offer "definitions of right and wrong that exonerate the activities and results of market activity" (Heilbroner, 117). This is probably the most repellent aspect of the system, the way in which all practices are prisoner to the bottom line. For instance, Bast can rightly object that J R's plan for Eagle Mills is unconscionable, that it countermands the trust that the employees, thinking it reciprocal, have placed in the company:

—Because these are real people up there that's how come! A lot of them who owned the stock still can't believe it's not worth anything and even the ones who owned bonds, a lot of them are old and when they first bought the bonds it was almost like they were lending money to, to someone in the family. And the ones who work there, even if you could see their ballfield and put their offices in the mills how long do you think they'd . . . (296)

Yet as responsible as Bast's objection may be, its suasiveness will always find itself undermined by the system's own requirements. The system sets up the making of wealth as its end, and while it would prefer to do this without trespassing against familiar moral codes, these codes will find themselves repeatedly subordinated to, or forced into a reconciliation with, this end. As Max Weber put the matter, capitalism is its own ethos:

"They make tallow out of cattle and money out of men." The peculiarity of this philosophy of avarice appears to be the ideal of the honest man of recognized credit, and above all the idea of his capital, which is assumed as an end in itself. Truly what is here preached is not simply a means of making one's way in the world, but a peculiar ethic. The infraction of rules is treated not as foolishness but as forgetfulness of duty. That is the essence of the matter. It is not mere business astuteness, that sort of thing is common enough, it is an ethos. (51)

The system makes its own demands, and people delude themselves if they think that they can participate in it, hoping to maximize their own profits, without deleterious consequences elsewhere if not locally. William James once remarked that to get through life we all need to wear blinders, for otherwise we would find ourselves too overwhelmed by the individual hardships and miseries of people we are in no position to help.[8] I suspect that he is right, but James was speaking of the hurts of which one was not the cause, whereas in capitalism, the capitalist puts on blinders to remain unaware of the consequences, made abstract by distance, of one's own actions. Pursuing wealth less as a means to a larger good than as an end, the capitalist becomes less the system's master than its vehicle, much in the manner of Thoreau's nineteenth-century traveler who thinks he rides the rails when they ride him. Or as Marx puts the matter, value, or capital, starts to be its own "automatic subject," the impetus behind an ever-expanding process: "In truth, . . . value is here the subject (i.e., the independently acting agent) of a process in which, while constantly assuming the form in turn of money and commodities, it changes its own magnitude, throws off surplus-value from itself considered as original value, and thus valorizes itself independently" (255). When this happens, it starts to seem both natural and desirable to see things, as *J R*'s Major Hyde likes to say, "at the corporate level" (23). That this means forging a system "set up to promote the meanest possibilities in human nature and make them look good" (463) occurs to some—in this instance the District Superintendent, Vern—yet not to those who define "good will" as "the excess of the purchase price over the value of [their] net tangible assets" (655).

Meantime, if "worth" becomes widely understood as "whatever some damn fool will pay for it" (201), then the entrepreneur's status is itself enhanced. He or she becomes something like a leading citizen. But who exactly are these entrepreneurs and what do they want? The obvious answer would appear to be that the entrepreneur—e.g., Moncrieff, Cates, J R—is someone motivated by a strong desire for wealth, by greed. Looking over the class six J photograph, Vern notices J R and then asks aloud, "ever see so much greed confined in one small face?" (461). Yet, if greed motivates J R, one wonders where are the tangible signs? He may now be the operating genius of a multimillion dollar empire, but he acquires only a single new possession for his own use, a pair of shoelaces (475). Like Moncrieff, whose personal material desires extend no further than the Roosevelt dimes he hoards, so as to take them out of circulation (505), J R lives a fairly spartan existence. He is in the game, playing to win, but his freneticism, at bottom, constitutes a "noisy desperation." That is, as Amy tells Beaton, Cates's corporate secretary, it all seems to be about avoidance, in the most profound sense:

> —Preferred stock doesn't vote, yes. We had it in class, preferred stock doesn't . . .
> —Yes in this case however it appeared advisable for tax purp . . .
> —Doesn't sing doesn't dance doesn't smoke or drink or run around with women, doesn't even . . .
> —Pardon?
> —Oh nothing Mister Beaton it's all so, just so absurd so, lifeless, I can't . . .
> —Please I, Mrs. Joubert I didn't mean to make an emotional issue of it, the . . .
> —Well it is! It is an emotional issue it simply is! because, because there aren't any, there aren't any emotions it's all just reinvested dividends and tax avoidance that's what all of it is, avoidance the way it's always been it always will be there's no earthly reason it should change is there? that it ever could change? (212)[9]

As for J R, there is, as Amy observes, a sad hunger driving the boy, one which his parents, school, and community have done little to satisfy. Not that they are capable of doing so, so blind do they appear to their own failures to work out a reason for being. But this makes J R's yearnings all the more poignant, for he is still a boy, and though chances are he will evolve into a Moncrieff or Cates, there remains the hope that things might be different. The odds are against this, Gaddis knows, for he is a realist as well as an optimist. Still, we are invited to read this novel in the spirit of Ernst Bloch, the Bloch who believed "[s]omething's missing" to be "one of the most profound sentences that Brecht ever wrote." And the Bloch who believed that

the ideal of "utopia cannot be removed from the world in spite of everything," convinced that "every criticism of imperfection, incompleteness,
intolerance, and impatience already without a doubt presupposes the conception of, and longing for, a possible perfection" (15, 16). Unlike Bloch,
Gaddis speaks almost sotto voce, but the attentive listener hears an analogous
hope, grounded in the fact that we could not recognize the ideal if we did not
have, at least, an intuition of the good. This does not transform evil into
good, but it does make the path from the one to the other clearer to map out.

J R appears, again in Amy's words, "eager about all the wrong things"
(497), and when she tries to introduce him to a realm of value apart from the
vulgar, it is as if she speaks another language, almost beyond translation:
"He looks like he's trying to fit what you're saying into some utterly different, some world you don't know anything about he's such an eager little boy
but, there's something quite desolate, like a hunger . . ." (246–47). This
hunger gets satisfied only in a disheartening way, through absorption in the
market or game. He becomes an entrepreneur, characterized in Gaddis's fiction as that person who, in pursuit of riches, shirks the core question of life's
meaning. This person, as in Schumpeter's classic formulation, has an almost
childlike "will to conquer," marked by an "impulse to fight, to prove oneself
superior to others, to succeed for the sake, not of the fruits of success, but of
success itself" (93–94). The entrepreneur lacks any bearing other than the
fluid game, and thus gets easily sucked into its whirlpool. Marx wrote, "His
aim is . . . the unceasing movement of profit-making. This boundless drive
for enrichment, this passionate chase after value, is common to the capitalist
and the miser; but while the miser is merely a capitalist gone mad, the capitalist is a rational miser" (254). Here, Marx suggests that the capitalist seeks
more and more profits not with the intent of converting them into things of
practical value, but for themselves alone. The game becomes an addiction.
At one point in the novel, Bast tries to draw a picture for J R of what is happening to him: "The more you get the hungrier you get" (647). To which J R
responds:

—No but that's what you do! I mean where they said if you're playing anyway
so you might as well play to win but I mean even when you win you have to
keep playing! Like these brokers these underwriters these banks everything
you do somebody's getting this percent for theirself this commission this here
interest where they all know each other so they're fixing up these deals giving
you all this here advice which they're these big experts how am I supposed to
stop everything! (647)

J R cannot stop either himself or anyone else, and so he plays to win. He
has plenty of company. For example, there's Crawley's associate Stamper:
"this man Stamper's not one who plays to play, he plays to win" (444).

There's Amy's husband Joubert, who, like J R with Bast, coerces her into a game she wishes to have no part of: "It was always a game he had to win, playing against him and helping him win" (488). And, finally, there's Amy's father, Moncrieff, "a man who likes to win" (505), who "only watched [football] because he liked to see someone lose" (499). With all this attention to winning, sports begin to function, not surprisingly, as a major metaphor for the way these people understand their lives. Here, where business activity seems divorced from any purpose more worthy than the increase of private capital, the comparison to something so gamelike seems appropriate. Weber observed this long ago, particularly as witnessed in the United States: "In the field of its [capitalism's] highest development, in the United States, the pursuit of wealth, stripped of its religious and ethical meaning, tends to become associated with purely mundane passions, which often actually give it the character of sport" (182). Thus in *J R*, Major Hyde, resorting to a plethora of sports metaphors, addresses the issue of Edward Bast's dismissal (for his Mozart lecture) plus a threatened teachers' strike without any reference to the ethical questions at hand:

> Fire him [Bast] and you'll have the whole outfield behind you running interference, there's too much milksop management sitting back in the defense zone while the opposition marches up to the basket and drops one in. Let us carry the ball for a change. I know Vern's with me on this one. Put the ball over in their court for a change. (177)[10]

Even as the language of sport obscures real issues, it constitutes the form in which the community constructs its most important narratives about itself. It is, of course, the nature of narratives that they give a form and telos to our lives; they speak of whole systems of value, and they are often the more powerful as they are unstated, speaking of those values that are taken as given, the working assumptions of a culture upon which so much of its subsequent activity is predicated. All narratives are histories, but we usually reserve the term "history" for that narrative with the greatest lineage and widest circumference, that speaks less of the society's disparate particulars than of its larger compass. So while, in one sense, all societies have histories, in another sense they do not unless they acknowledge, record, and make it. If they fail to do this, they deprive themselves of an understanding not only of the past, but also of the future. The future can barely be comprehended without a sense of destination, or telos; yet this can only be imagined as the end point of a narrative. The grander the narrative—philosophically, ethically, and even aesthetically—the greater the members' sense of purpose. Those societies lacking such a narrative or history lead, it would seem, poorer existences. Meanwhile, in *J R*, society has made cash nexus its deity and tells its story in the language of sport. The most mundane and most important events are together analogized to baseball, basketball, and football games, as if all of life came down to winning one for the Gipper. It is while locked into such a mindset that Hyde, for instance, is described as waiting for his car in the Wall Street parking garage, from where he plans to head out to Long Island:

> He watched the dollar stuffed among greased folds in a turn toward a group lunching on the hood of a distant Cadillac where, as he began to pace under the roar of an exhaust fan, he glanced with each about face to look at his watch in a heavyweight's gesture, and back, paused to study racing cars on end, in mid-air, in flames, taped to the wall, the distant picnickers again, his watch in an awkward left cross, and back; pitted navel, graveled nipple, calendar for July simmering under the exhaust fan, his watch, that lunch, dimpled cheeks bared on a diving board for August, racing cars in flame, one in mid-air, on end, he sat, stood, paced, returned to gauge the cleft in August's cheeks yawned at him from the diving board, and back, muttered, called out, sat, stood, at last himself descended, ramps, caverned ranks of cars and his, free-standing, as the third inning began, feet dislodged from the dashboard, loud words dulled to mutterings as he drove up the ramp, two men on, one out, and a called strike nearing the bridge stopped for a light [. . .]. (218–19)

Hyde will end up wishing that he had never embarked on this trip, for not only is his watch ripped off his arm by joyriding youths, but his car breaks down, forcing him to pull off the urban expressway onto its "ribbon of filth, battered hubcaps, rusted twists of tailpipe, [and] curls of tire tread," where, finally, "the whole car shook to a wrench of twisting metal" (219). The image is one not only of filth but also of breakdown, of chaos. And this latter image is, in many ways, the novel writ large.

Disorder as Symbolic of a Cultural Vacancy

As critics have noted, scenes of entropy—of things falling apart—are everywhere in the novel, beginning most notably with Gibbs's classroom lecture. Here, following a film presenting a traditional Newtonian conception of physical laws (i.e., "Energy may be changed but not destroyed . . ." [20]), Gibbs tries to introduce his students to the second law of thermodynamics (i.e., "no cyclic process is possible in which heat is absorbed from a reservoir at a single temperature and converted completely into mechanical work"), commencing with,

> —All right let's have order here, order . . . ! he'd reached the set himself and snapped it into darkness. —Put on the lights there, now. Before we go any further here, has it ever occurred to any of you that all this is simply one grand

misunderstanding? Since you're not here to learn anything, but to be taught so
you can pass these tests, knowledge has to be organized so it can be taught,
and it has to be reduced to information so it can be organized do you follow
that? In other words this leads you to assume that organization is an inherent
property of the knowledge itself, and that disorder and chaos are simply irrelevant forces that threaten it from outside. In fact it's exactly the opposite. Order
is simply a thin, perilous condition we try to impose on the basic reality of
chaos . . . (20)

Gibbs's lecture hardly ends any better than Hyde's car ride. The class bell
rings, and the students erupt into noisy disassembly, leaving Gibbs just
enough time to chalk on the blackboard the word "entropy": "t,r,o,p,y, he finished the word and broke the chalk in emphatic underline, turning past the
toss of blonde hair repeated in the thighs as she stood up and joined the surge
of disorder" (21). Evidence of disorder can be found everywhere. There is
the "[p]redictable, deliberate, you might even say prescheduled breakage"
that the school faces (26); there is the Penn Station platform that appears
"like the dawn of the world," [with] "countless hands and unattached eyes,
faces looking in different directions, rolled newspapers clutched and their
wives' umbrellas, frankfurters redolent, a muffled explosion and falling
glass" (161); there is the endless spillage, be it from badly poured drinks
("Look out Jack damn it you're spilling that" [278]) or from the "torrent"
gushing out from the sink in the Ninety-Sixth Street apartment; there is
Gibbs's concern with the "decay process of this eta particle," bringing "up
the whole question of a basic lack of symmetry in our part of the univ[erse]"
(485); and there is the pervasive sense of leakage. As Gibbs puts the matter
to Bast: "Problem Bast there's too God damned much leakage around here,
can't compose anything with all this energy spilling you've got entropy
going everywhere. Radio leaking under there hot water pouring out so God
damned much entropy going on think you can hold all these notes together
know what it sounds like? Bast?" (287).

Adding to the disorder is the way that sound has given way to noise, with
everyone speaking at cross-purposes and no one being heard. Thomas Bast
dies and the newspaper prints James Bast's obituary, having heard only the
surname; Pecci proposes that since his wife is a former Miss Rheingold,[11] she
should play a part in the school's production of Wagner's *Rhinegold*; Isadore
Duncan tries to tell the J R Family people that he is in the wallpaper business, but they hear only the name Duncan, identical with that of a prominent
publisher, and proceed with their corporate takeover; and in what Whiteback
calls "just one of those little misunderstandings" (238), the contractor
Parentucelli blacktops Vern's two-acre lawn, tearing up all the trees in the
bargain. Misunderstandings are everywhere in *J R,* and their effects range
from the inconsequential and humorous—Amy's mistaking an illuminated

ice cream cone, atop a Carvel stand,[12] for the rising moon, or the diCephalis child's trading $50 in paper currency for the assumedly more valuable 85 cents in coin—to the serious and tragic, as when the narcotics agent shoots and kills the retarded boy whose only weapon is a toy pistol or when Zona Selk is not advised of the danger of mixing her medication with strong cheeses, including the Stilton that Beaton, knowingly, offers her.

The message often gets lost in the noise, and while there are characters like Dan diCephalis who prefer to "hide in noise" (52)—that is, until he himself is tragically lost in the noise of the Teletravel transmission (707)—the overriding sense is the more complicated the message, the more likely the message will be distorted or even lost. As Gibbs says in his inimical fashion to Eigen: "read [Norbert] Wiener on communication, more complicated the message more God damned chance for errors, take a few years of marriage such a God damned complex of messages going both ways can't get a God damned thing across, God damned much entropy going on say good morning she's got a God damned headache thinks you don't give a God damn how she feels, ask her how she feels she thinks you just want to get laid, try that she says it's the only God damn thing you take seriously about her" (403).[13] Meanwhile, if disorder and misunderstanding reign, it is not because things could not be otherwise; the situation also has much to do with the choices made. That is, disorder of the sort witnessed in *J R* might be understood as just as much a problem of ethics as of physics. "'Order' implies 'disorder,' and vice versa," observes Kenneth Burke (181), and while it is important to note how entropic things are in Gaddis's fiction, it is also important to note how this very observation thrusts us into an ethical relation vis-à-vis this world. Alone, the world itself might be understood outside the realm of good and evil, but once we ourselves begin to consider it in the light of order and disorder, our own relation to it ceases to exist apart from such a realm, and must be judged by whether our actions promote one formation or the other. As Burke writes, "guilt . . . comes not from the *breaking* of the law but from the mere *formulating* of the law (that is, from the Idea of Order)" (228).

This is why Norbert Wiener couches his own discussion of entropy in the context of Augustine's understanding of evil as incompletion or negativity. Discerning a relation among Gibbs, Freud, and Augustine, Wiener writes, "in their [Gibbs and Freud's] recognition of a fundamental element of chance in the texture of the universe itself, these men are close to one another and close to the tradition of St. Augustine. For this random element, this organic incompleteness, is one which without too violent a figure of speech we may consider evil; the negative evil which St. Augustine characterizes as incompleteness, rather than the positive malicious evil of the Manichaeans" (19). This sense of things is remarkably similar to Gaddis's own understanding, wherein the world is most palpably felt in terms of its incompletion and imperfection. Implicit here is the possibility of completion, of perfection. Order follows from the pursuit of this possibility, disorder from its rejection. Thus, if *J R*'s characters often wear expressions of "vacancy"; if they "can't tell one [day] from the next sometimes" (155); and if they find it necessary "to humanize" the genius of a Mozart for the reason that if they "can't rise to his level" at least they can "drag him down" to theirs (42), might we not just as well view this as a moral statement about the culture, as opposed to a statement about the way material things decline into a state of "maximum homogeneity"? Gaddis himself has observed that when "looked at another way this collapse of Absolutes going on around us may be simply another form of entropy, a spiritual entropy winding down eventually to total equilibrium, the ultimate chaos where everything equals everything else: the ultimate senseless universe. But then that, fighting that off, or succumbing to it, isn't that what Dostoevsky, what the great fictions have always been about?" (*PR*, 77).

Does everything equal everything else? Are discriminations impossible to make? Or if they are possible, on what basis can we make them? Those who answer yes to the first question (and thereby the second) are not likely to be interested in fiction, at least not as practiced by Gaddis. The point is, his fiction speaks of a world marked by countervailing pressures requiring a response. Chaos is among these pressures, and it carries with it, paradoxically, a certain seductive appeal, the way that death, a state of total equilibrium, appeals to those overwhelmed by life's exigencies. Still, there is the possibility of resistance, of refusing to see all acts and all events as the same, or as meaningless. The resistance, when it occurs, takes many forms. Some are local and short term. Others predicate themselves on the belief that our lives are invested in a larger order, the rejection of which constitutes a moral failing. To put the matter this way also suggests the connection between language and morality. Were we not endowed with language, with the ability to say "no" as well as "yes," there would be, says Burke, no possibility of "moral disobedience," for this "is grounded in language" (187). However, we are so endowed, and can see our way toward "merging the principle of the natural order with the principle of verbal contract or covenant intrinsic to legal enactment in the socio-political order" (186). Entailed then in our formulation of Order/Disorder is the conviction that we can say yes or no to either part of the equation. Or, as Burke writes: "If, by 'Order,' we have in mind the idea of a command, then obviously the corresponding word for the proper response would be 'Obey.' Or, there would be the alternative, 'Disobey.' Thus we have the proposition: Order is to Disorder as Obedience is to Disobedience" (186).

Yet, even if "moral 'evil' is a species of *negative*, a purely linguistic (or 'rational') principle" (Burke, 195), there remains the sense in *J R* that whatever moral agents there are reside in what Oscar Wilde called "the noisiest country that ever existed" (*J R*, 289). This, in turn, makes it more difficult not only to live the "examined life" but the "ethical life," the kind wherein, said Beethoven, "the better among us bear one another in mind" (*J R*, 290). Adding to the difficulty is, again, the economic system, with its propensity to conflate human beings with commodities, reducing them to their practical use value, whether this be as a "resident psycho(metrician)," a "composer in residence," a "textbook salesman," a "program specialist," a "topflight name painter" or a specialist in "curriculum management." These appellatives validate not the individual but the system, and are, in Weber's words, part of the larger "tendency toward uniformity of life" (169). This tendency is also pressed forward, as Jack Gibbs notes in his manuscript, by industrialization, with its past and present effort to robotize people, children included. Working on his manuscript, Gibbs writes and thinks aloud:

> this aesthetic experience of Wilde's was leveling men's claims to being fine [. . .], homogenizing their fid, [. . .] their differences till by the time Horatio Alger died the hand at the machine had a distinctly childish cast and Ragged Dicks were everywhere, one and, one and? Supposed to be in, one in seven children between ten and fifteen out working for wages, a body thirty times the size of the U S Army for whom refinements on Cartwright's loom and advances in the canning, in canning machinery and the glass [. . .]. (575)[14]

This process, in turn, leads to the culture's increasing mechanization, wherein the values of pragmatism, efficiency, and numeric description and codification hold more and more sway:

> In a Cambridge house where William James was busy pasting up a collage of what worked into a philosophy, E L Thorndike emerged from actual processes of manipulation in the cellar with his book Animal Intelligence to lay foundations for modern public school testing in terms got from nature at first hand in the intelligent behavior of chickens, terms irrefragable enough to be measured and compared as time and motion were currently being strait-jacketed by F W Taylor in a Bethlehem steel plant, to be sorted and evaluated as readily as the nickel and dime items on Frank Woolworth's expanding counters, ingredients of the tangible world Mary Baker Eddy was profitably demonstrating could be classified and organized in unruffled confidence that it did not exist while, as profitably confident it did [. . .]. (581)

The economic system in place has its own logic, and while it furthers the ambitions of "Specialists with spirit; sensualists without heart" (Weber, 182), it appears largely amoral. J R's own formula for success comes down to "what works" (652). But here we find no guide to moral action, to a way of understanding people more as ends than as means. In fact, it is the latter view (i.e., means over ends) that appears to win out, and this leaves too many peo-ple—those who do not play to win, either not knowing the rules or not wish-ing to acquiesce to them—feeling left out and even defeated. And these, according to a different yardstick, may be very good people. In *J R*, they include Norman Angel, Schramm, and Isadore Duncan, all of whom are destroyed, one way or another, by the system. Thus when Thomas Bast, founder of General Roll, dies intestate and the death taxes threaten to force the company to go public, it is the son-in-law Angel who makes the valiant effort "to hold things together" (144). The company itself, a manufacturer of piano rolls, is a comparatively small one, but because all its profits have been put back into it, the company has prospered, so that its net worth equals sev-eral million dollars. It has also prospered because its owners, Bast and Angel, never lost interest in what they were doing, so that profits were never the first interest, especially for Angel. Now, however, with no excess cash, the company must find a way to pay the death taxes, and Angel fears that the company will be taken over by an outside group that has no interest in what General Roll does. As he says to the company lawyer, Coen:

> —Coen God damn it can't you see what I mean? Can't you see this is what's going to happen right here, after all it took to put all this together? Can't you see you go public and all these people owning you want is dividends and run-ning their stock up, you don't give them that and they sell you out, you do and some bunch of vice presidents some place you never heard of like the ones that turned this [a "wood" cabinet made of pressed sawdust] out, this wood product they call it, they spot you and launch an offer and all of a sudden you're work-ing for them trimming and cutting and finally bringing in people to turn some-thing out they don't care what the hell it is, there's no pride in their work because what you've got them turning out nobody could be proud of in the first place . . . He broke the piece over his knee and stood up with the bottle, —if they'd just understand I'm not just trying to grab this whole show for myself but to keep it doing something that's, that's worth doing . . . (359)

Angel is not, in fact, "trying to grab this whole show for" himself; he is a good man. But his company has attracted the attention of big investors owing to its long-standing, unsettled suit, first pressed by Thomas Bast and the long deceased attorney Lemp, against JMI Industries (formerly the Jubilee Musical Instrument Company). The suit pertains to the JMI's theft of a punch-hole technique patented by Bast for the piano rolls, but now valuable for its application to data processing. If won, the suit would bring immense wealth to General Roll, something that the outside money people, including the J R Family and Governor Cates, know too well. But the suit will not ben-efit General Roll so much as put it at risk. Trying to maneuver into the profit picture, Cates tells Beaton: "Don't matter if it's as big as your thumb it's sit-

ting there on this old patent claims suit with JMI never read your damn law
journals? Why the devil you think Stamper picked up JMI in that Dallas
mortgage deal think he needed a million used jukeboxes? Get hold of this
end of it in this receivership there's the whole punched tape industry by the
short[. . .]" (694).

In the end, Angel's company is forced to go public. Although he has done
everything to protect the company's integrity, the game's rules make Angel's
a losing hand. He eventually attempts suicide, reminding us of that other
"type of hero," recalled by Gaddis in his essay "The Rush for Second Place."
This type, mentioned in an essay indicting American business practices, is
borrowed from Japanese culture, and refers to that person whose failure is
the consequence of his own ethical probity. Or, as Gaddis quotes Ivan
Morris,

> [he] represents the very antithesis of an ethos of accomplishment. He is the
> man whose single-minded sincerity will not allow him to make the manoeu-
> vers and compromises that are so often needed for mundane success. . . . He is
> wedded to the losing side and will ineluctably be cast down. Flinging himself
> after his painful destiny, he defies the dictates of convention and common
> sense, until eventually he is worsted by his enemy, the "successful survivor."
> . . . Faced with defeat, the hero will typically take his own life in order to avoid
> the indignity of capture, vindicate his honour, and make a final assertion of his
> sincerity. (38)

Angel may, or may not, be imagined as "wedded to the losing side." He
certainly refuses to acquiesce to a predatory system; and his suicide attempt
puts him at odds with the capitalist ethos which, writes Gaddis, believes "suicide is a sin, a crime, a confession of failure, or at least a desperate avoidance
of failure" ("Rush," 38). With Angel out of the picture, it does seem, as
Gaddis argues in "The Rush for Second Place," as if "we have only 'successful survivors'" (38). Still, this last point is more despairing than true and
needs to be understood in the context not only of Gaddis's own history as a
first-class writer seeking a modicum of recognition, but also of the pressures
that push hardworking people like Angel or Schramm toward suicide. Gaddis
does not dismiss these two or those like them, and he expects the reader not
to dismiss them either. In their "failure," they still have something to say,
even if the survivors prefer not to listen, fearing that if they did, they might
undermine their own hopes for success. In the culture of *J R*, success sur-
rounds itself with success, and does its best to keep failure at bay.

Like Angel, the writer Schramm is something of a special case. He is, as
Gibbs says, "one of those men who wanted to write and had a father who
thought writing was for sissies" (246), someone who, accordingly, experienced tremendous difficulty in that the things he thought important, or worth

doing, had little value for the larger community. Certainly not for people
such as Hyde, who hearing of Schramm's accident (a thrown pencil capped
with an eraser bounces off a wall and back into his eye), insensitively
remarks, "Sounds like that painter that cut off his ear, what did he do Gibbs?
sent it to somebody in a . . ." (184). It may be true, as Gibbs angrily retorts,
that someone like Hyde would prove "a real tonic" for Schramm, for "he
feeds on outrage that's what keeps Schramm alive" (184), yet, finally, even
this would not stave off his suicide. There needs to be something more than
that which inspires the reactive gesture, be it Hyde and his corporate mentality or be it General Box's desertion of Schramm in the Forest of Ardennes.
This is apparent in Schramm's confession that there was "something terribly
lacking between what I felt and what I could do" (248). For Schramm, this
something's elusiveness remains the one true fact. Meanwhile, even his own
life story is stolen from him by his friend Eigen. Or as Gibbs tells Beamish
(an attorney for the J R Family), "Ought to know what did Schramm in
though Beamish, problem was somebody ran off with it, read all about it in
Mister Eigen's very important" novel (389). After his death, Schramm is still
being stolen from by Eigen, who walks away with his friend's unfinished
manuscript, hoping to develop it as his own. Not without reason does Rhoda,
Schramm's lover, call Eigen a "graverobber" (616).

In the end, Schramm kills himself because, as Gibbs tells Amy, it all
became too hard, and nothing truly seemed real:

> —Well god damn it Amy doing things badly because they're not worth doing,
> or trying to believe something's worth doing long enough to get it done [. . .]
> —it's just, sometimes it's too God damned long to be able to keep believing
> something's real [. . .] —Schramm standing in that tenement window he'd
> watch a truckload of smashed car fenders go by and think the poor bastard
> driving it was doing something real [. . .]. (492)

Gibbs appears to be right about Schramm. Like Angel, the writer suc-
cumbs to the pressures of living in a place where the things not worth doing
or being are given precedence over those that are. Also like Angel, Schramm
chooses suicide, a tragic act that need not require us to view the life as a failure, unless we measure it by the standards of a Cates or Moncrieff. The suicide does, however, make clear who does, and does not, fare well in this
"cash-nexus" world.

Finally, there is Duncan, whose trip to New York, where he is mugged,
hospitalized, and dies, is made necessary by the J R Family's takeover of his
Zanesville, Ohio, wallpaper business. Less like Schramm than like Angel (i.e.,
a decent man going about his business in as hardworking and honest a manner
as possible), Duncan also feels betrayed by what Gaddis has, elsewhere, called
"The System" (Grove, B 10). Hearing Coen tell Edward Bast, his hospital

roommate, about Norman and the takeover threat to General Roll, Duncan blurts out, "Sound like the same son of a bitches that got me out of the wallpaper business" (677). It is, in fact, the J R Family that is responsible for the demise of both Angel and Duncan, though neither ever knows his nemesis as anything more than a corporate abstraction. What they do know is that these corporate "families" are not to be trusted, that they prey on small businesses and unorganized labor, even as they offer pieties about "free enterprise." But, says Duncan, threaten their "expanding capital formation and they're at the head of the line whining for loan guarantees" (684). Corporations cannot, or are not allowed to, fail. They bankroll politicians and politicians return the favor, as when Senator Broos, Cates's man in Washington, makes an impassioned plea on the Senate floor for a "two hundred million dollar government loan guarantee favored by banking and investment interests" (684), interests badly hurt by J R's too friendly stance toward pork bellies (purchased at margin) which, when he cannot unload them to China, via Malwi (now at war), results in their market free fall (642). Left with the bill is the everyday worker, the waitress who must pay "the taxes on those tips she's sitting out there counting at night on her four dollar davenport" (684). It is she who truly knows the meaning of failure: "to bail them out because she's the only one who knows failure's what it's really all" about (685).

    In *J R*, we repeatedly see illustration of Heilbroner's argument that the world of capital needs the state more than the state needs it: "Remove the regime of capital and the state would remain, although it might change dramatically; remove the state and the regime of capital would not last a day" (105). The reason is that capital, while it ranges beyond borders, is still dependent upon the state to protect its investments and to guarantee its rights and claims. For instance, when Typhon's Moncrieff, prior to taking a high-level government position in Washington, negotiates the building of "a smaltite processing plant for the extraction of contained cobalt" in the African nation of Gandia, he makes sure that (1) the United States government contracts to buy so many tons of cobalt annually at a guaranteed price; (2) it will advance the company $39.7 million for the construction of the plant; (3) it will sell to the plant, at cost, a sufficient amount of smaltite ore "to yield at a minimum the amount of contained cobalt" required; (4) it will, at deal's end, sell back the plant, as surplus, to Typhon; and (5) safeguards are put in place "exempting private investment in a hazardous business climate" (96, 97). Moncrieff can negotiate such a no-risk deal not only because the Department of Defense needs cobalt for its weapons production but also because of his influence in Washington, noticeably manifested here by Senator Broos's work, in the Armed Services Committee, to get the cobalt stockpile requirements raised (97). Meanwhile, what the deal, from the government's point of view, does not taken into account is that (1) there are, in fact, sufficient cobalt deposits in the United States (in fact, the head on the beer made by J R's brewery is produced by cobalt contaminants in the water supply); (2) it will end up purchasing the ore from the Pythian Overseas corporation, which is clandestinely connected to Typhon; and (3) as a skutterudite, smaltite contains significant amounts of precious nickel, which Typhon can sell on the open market, significantly enhancing its already attractive profit picture. All of this is virtually insured by the United States taxpayer. At Typhon, the policy is to "let the damn government's money work for" the company (108).

All of these American guarantees, meantime, pertain to an operation that is carried on in a foreign country not known for its political stability. So in addition to upfront economic guarantees there also must be hidden guarantees tied to the possibility that American troops might be called on to safeguard property that is both public and private, both American and not American. Not that Typhon foresees a scenario in which American troops will be deployed. Quite the opposite, for Typhon foresees a situation wherein civil unrest in Gandia—which the company already has secret plans to abet—will actually work to its advantage. That is, Typhon executives think it to their advantage that Uaso province, the locale of their operations, should secede from Gandia, so that it may more effectively be turned into something like a company town. To this end, they have made secret overtures to Doctor Dé, Gandia's defense minister, and, with Typhon's backing, the prospective leader of the newly independent nation of Uaso. Meanwhile, when Doctor Dé's rebel forces start to get ahead of themselves, blowing up a few bridges and creating general havoc, all before the smelter contract has been signed, Governor Cates needs to engage in some serious damage control, making it clear to his Washington operatives, especially Senator Broos and Frank Black, Typhon's key (though undesignated) government lobbyist, that there is to be no intervention on the part of American troops in what is, after all, a civil war, and therefore nobody's business:

> —Broos . . . ? the phone came up clenched to a deaf ear, —no damn time to start nitpicking, if this contract's not signed sealed and delivered while Monty's still running things here his signature on it's no more damn good than Jefferson Davis', already got enough damn problems left-wing press adding two and two getting five sounds like a few blacks jumped the gun over there blew up a damn bridge or something, Blaufinger on the phone here first damn thing he'll want to know's if there's any talk about sending in troops to stabilize the situation. The answer'd better be we're damn well not and I want Frank Black to make that good and damn clear to the press corps down there and anybody else that noses in hear me? Civil war breaks out seceding this Uaso province it's nobody's business but these damn Africans', we can't get in there and support secession don't mean we want some damn fool introducing a resolution on the floor supporting the established government either hear me . . . ? (96)

Typhon's interest in Gandia is dictated by its own bottom line. The company managers give little heed to considerations of morality. They are as prepared to employ an ex-Nazi general, Blaufinger (who led the German Panzer army against the Allies at St. Fiacre in the Ardennes [706]), as to align themselves with the side of civil unrest if it means greater profits. They can even take both sides, as when they have Eigen write a speech, to be delivered in Germany by General Box (who led Allied troops against Blaufinger's at St. Fiacre), that plays both sides of the Usao/Gandia dispute. Davidoff, the company's public relations person, directs Eigen: "This Box speech for Gandia you've got a delicate situation, you've got the defense minister Doctor Dé and President Nowunda both up there on the platform, work them both in but so one of them can come out at the last minute" (216). Thus, while the company's interest equates itself with the situation that will permit it the greater legislative leeway and economic control, it is more than ready to paint the whole matter as one of freedom versus communism (428), and to have Senator "Broos speaking up in the Senate for self-determination for the people of this gallant little emerging nation," pleading "for nonintervention and sponsor[ing] a bill prohibiting imports with Gandia as country of origin" (523). So well do the company executives play their cards that they are even able to garner left-wing support, as Governor Cates tells Moncrieff: "Yes worked so damn well even got peace groups wearing signs keep out of Gandia and Africa for Africans" (428).

Typhon's operations are, of course, part of a larger process of globalization on the part of capital, or big business. Taking note of this process, the sociologist Anthony Giddens writes:

> If nation-states are the principal "actors" within the global political order, corporations are the dominant agents within the world economy. In their trading relations with one another, and with states and consumers, companies (manufacturing corporations, financial firms, and banks) depend upon production for profit. Hence the spread of their influence brings in its train a global extension of commodity markets, including money markets. However, in its beginnings, the capitalist world economy was never just a market for the trading of goods and services. It involved, and involves today, the commodifying of labour power in class relations which separate workers from control of their means of production. This process, of course, is fraught with implications for global inequalities. (72)

In J R, we see these "global inequalities" at work, particularly as capital pursues cheap labor. As I have noted, there are no compelling reasons for setting up the smelter in Gandia rather than in the United States, other than the fact that labor there stands ready to be colonized and exploited. This also explains Typhon's support for the secessionists: Uaso labor promises to be cheaper. Nor is this the line's end, for in neighboring Malwi, one finds an even more indigent people prepared to take on the most dangerous mine work. As Governor Cates puts the matter: "Little country right there east of Gandia [. . .], get all the labor for the mines there so damn poor'll work for peanuts" (429). So defenseless is Malwi that Cates gives General Blaufinger the order to annex it: "Place next door there Malwi yes I told Blaufinger to annex it" (698). Adding to the economic interest here is the desire, on Cates's part, to placate his friend Zona, perturbed by the Malwi diplomat's parking in front of her Sutton Place apartment. Or as she complains to Cates's right-hand man, Beaton: "Don't tell me it's a DPL parking space Beaton I paid good money to have it made a DPL parking space so Nick [her chauffeur] could pull in to the curb and I wouldn't have to wade through an acre of dogshit to get to my own front door, and if you think I believe stories about something called Malwi you . . ." (428).

It is hard for the Typhon people, as well, to believe in a place called Malwi, or in any of the African nations. Rather, they are places on the map, places where raw materials are mined and money made, not places where people with needs akin to their own actually live. Thus, Cates simply orders that Malwi be annexed. The plan backfires, however, and while this represents a loss of cheap labor for Cates, the consequences are tragic for the Malwi people, who stand up to the Typhon-backed invaders with nothing but toy weapons. Or as Cates, hearing the story from Senator Broos, says: "labor force whole damn Malwi labor force decimated yes how the devil'd that happen, Dé's people supposed to annex it just heard they walked in these buggers meet them armed to the damn teeth Dé's bunch panic cut them down like flies go in to clean up find all they had's toys, pistols carbeens submachineguns rocket launchers every damn weapon you can think of plastic toys poor buggers must have . . ." (709).

Corporations, unlike states, assume little responsibility regarding society's more general welfare. Nevertheless, people can and do suffer as the consequence of decisions made in their boardrooms. Gaddis knows this, and in *J R* he moves to make us more aware of just how interconnected all of our actions are; and how, in the modern world, if we disregard the fact, the consequences can be dire. "The System," then, does not appear to work. One cannot trust it to be mindful of the common person's needs. The real interests that the more powerful players—corporations, government bodies, wealthy citizens, and so on—take care of are their own. Thus, despite his ineptness as both school principal and bank president, Whiteback, in Typhon's thank you gesture for his clearing the path toward its takeover of his bank, is rewarded with a job—fitting the talent to the position—with the Federal Communications Commission (710); and though Assemblyman Pecci, a state banking committee member responsible for promoting Typhon-friendly legislation, pushes a girl out of a window, Governor Cates still plans to reward him with a judgeship, assuming he avoids prison (710).

The Schoolroom, Children, and Lost Sheep

If the system works for some, it does not work for many others, including not only the Angels, Schramms, and Duncans, but also all those who do not really participate in the game, not because they believe that what is at stake is more than a game, but because indifference has set in. They do not trust the system, and it, in turn, does not trust them, relegating their children to second-class schools, offering the adults mind-numbing jobs, and denying them any sense of purpose or hope beyond that of a more or less immediate use value. If "life is draining out of the sky out of the world it's" not simply for the reason that the season is autumn (119). Something appears to be either missing or wrong.

Take the school system. Something is wrong when insiders such as Gibbs and Vern, the superintendent, opine that teaching is "a second class profession [. . .] fill[ed . . .] with second class people" (497) or that "[t]he function of this school is custodial. It's here to keep these kids off the streets until the girls are big enough to get pregnant and the boys are old enough to go out and hold up a gas station, it's strictly custodial and the rest is plumbing" (226). And if the teachers and administrators are cynical, the students are no less so. As J R tells Bast, "school's always this bunch of crap which it never has anything to do with anything real" (649). Teachers distrust students, and students distrust teachers. The equation is not as symmetrical as it appears, however, for the teachers have a responsibility toward the children greater than that which the children owe to them—a responsibility that is being disregarded. Why? One reason relates to the culture's countinghouse ethos that encourages the fragmentation and compartmentalization of knowledge, as if it could be reduced, tallied, and Newtonized. Standardized, closed systems are the rule, so long as they are testable. Gibbs, somewhat heatedly, tells his students: "Since you're not here to learn anything, but to be taught so you can pass these tests, knowledge has to be organized so it can be taught, and it has to be reduced to information so it can be organized" (20). He appears right, and the consequence is that the students, responding to what is asked of them, begin to model their behavior accordingly. They begin to think of their education more and more as a matter of jumping certain hurdles, passing particular examinations, and garnering attractive grades. If they protest, as one does when Gibbs departs from the standardized curriculum, that "[t]his wasn't in the reading assignment" (21), it is difficult to blame them, for the system offers few rewards for pursuing questions that do not have immediate answers, for curiosity. Instead, it rewards those who can correctly fill in the blank, returning a packaged answer to a packaged question. That the students do this so willingly—as in the instance of the student who quickly offers Gibbs a Newtonian formulation of matter ("The tendency of a body which when it is at rest to . . ." [21]) when the discussion is going elsewhere—reflects an urgent need for approval, following from the fact that the culture offers them so few genuine signs of approval. In "The Rush for Second Place," Gaddis, referring to John Holt's book *How Children Fail,* notes that

> This hunger for approval appears in all its desperate trappings in John Holt's excellent, profoundly saddening book *How Children Fail.* The overriding desire of the children in his elementary classroom to please, irrespective of the lesson's content or even the question itself; the anguished search for an answer, any answer, even the wrong one, to end the anxiety; and the hapless attempts to manipulate his authority, later drove him to recommend the disbanding of schools altogether. But finally he came round: these schools were, after all, preparing these children for exactly the contentless, need-for-approval, manipulative society he saw out there waiting for them. (36)

The Holt book, first published in 1964, appears to have been an important resource for Gaddis in composing *J R.* Its thesis, perhaps more familiar today, is that educators need to instruct students as much in the principles structuring knowledge as in the discrete facts marking off one discipline from another. If there is no effort toward making clear how bodies of knowledge are bridgeable, the students will be left with the sense that something crucial is missing. Holt chastises educators for their propensity to break knowledge down into "arbitrary and disconnected hunks of subject matter, which are" then "'integrate[d]' by such artificial and irrelevant devices as having children sing Swiss folk songs while they are studying the geography of Switzerland, or do arithmetic problems about rail-splitting while they are studying the boyhood of Lincoln" (275).

Holt's examples have even more satirical and sinister parallels in *J R,* wherein the teachers, unmindful of their colleagues' efforts, offer self-contained courses that relate to nothing, except to the culture's substitution of cash nexus for a genuine raison d'être. Thus Clancy, a mathematics teacher, instructs the students in percentages by reference to a businessman's (i.e., Clancy's) desire for profits: "gross profit on a business was sixty-five hundred dollars a year. He finds his expenses were twenty-two and one half percent of this profit. First, can you find the net profit?" (29). Coach Vogel, teaching driver's education, likens the combustion engine to the human body in need of its occasional fillup: "When you pull up at the gas pump and ask for ten gallons the fuel is poured through an opening, or mouth, and goes into the gas tank, the engine's stomach" (30). Even Amy Joubert, whose motives are the best, takes her sixth grade social studies class into Manhattan so that they can, with their pooled twenty-four dollars (the same sum the Dutch settlers "paid" the Manhattan tribe for the island in 1626),[15] "vote for our share in Am[erica]" (49), by which she means buy, on the New York

Exchange, a corporate stock share (Diamond Cable), which once purchased promptly drops in price.

The school's program lacks coherence and purpose, yet the students are constantly being tested. The school even has its own psychometrician, Dan diCephalis, formerly the driver's education teacher, whose responsibility is to track the students according to their inborn talents and intelligence. He does so not by meeting with the students or their teachers, but through expensive computerized testing. The equipment is new, however, and not without problems. As Dan tries to explain, "It isn't the equipment it's the holes, in this computerized scoring the holes that have been punched in some of the cards don't, aren't consistent with forecasts in the personality testing, the norm in each case should . . ." (23). What cannot be explained at this point is how, as Hyde puts it, "[a] boy who scores out at the idiot genius level, this music-math correlation," can also be "running around town sticking people up with a toy pistol" (23), the same boy later shot dead by the narcotics agent. How, then, does one take such contradictory behavior and make it correlate with an arithmetic description? The answer, Gaddis suggests, is that one should not even try. But for diCephalis, Hyde, and Whiteback, the answer is first to establish a norm, and then to describe other behavior vis-à-vis this norm. As Whiteback, the principal, puts the matter: "Right Dan, the norm in each case supporting, or we might say being supported, substantiated that is to say, by an overall norm, so that in other words in terms of the testing the norm comes out as the norm, or we have no norm to test against, right?" (23).

Whiteback's explanation is obviously a mishmash, despite Hyde's comment to Dan that "if you can present it [the testing] at the budget meeting the way Whiteback's just presented it here no one will dare to argue with you" (23). The explanation does, however, illustrate the staff's affection for "normative behavior." Here, testing is designed to codify all behavior into the unhelpful binary of normal and abnormal behavior. Differences are erased or conflated, the way the categories "idiot" and "genius," or "music" and "math," not only merge, but even become one larger correlation (i.e., "idiot-genius-music-math"). The child who does not subscribe to the norm is, in Hyde's words, "going to get left out in the cold" (22). There is no place for this student, except in the halls of wing east seven where, Hyde tells Vern, "Whiteback had to set the little retreads up in business" (453), so as to make more room for the "new home ec center" (454). Here, in east seven, adorned with its "three dimensional paintings" covering a base of molded gum (454), the children are left to their own devices. They have been abandoned, suggesting, in Holt's words. that "retarded children are made, not born" (100).

The child whose difference makes his or her normality (i.e., humanness) suspect is an important theme in *J R*. Again one finds some parallels in Holt, especially as he attends to the embarrassment that attaches to those children who fail to measure up to our definitions of normal. Much of this embarrassment originates in expectations that are too circumscribed, confusing the commonplace with the desirable: "We take the word 'normal,' meaning *usual,* what happens most of the time, and turn it into *proper, correct, desirable,* what ought to happen all of the time" (Holt, 103). In *J R,* this occurs in the treatment of Amy's brother, Freddie. Amy herself admits to feeling uncomfortable in her brother's presence. Though she eventually goes out of her way to offer him a home, she initially found it all but impossible to summon the courage to visit him at the institution where, for ten years, he resided: "Once I, I went once and they had a concert he was learning to play the, played the cymbals I just couldn't ever go again" (210). She knows this was wrong, and even blames her father for his equally distancing response, justifying the rebuke with the words "Freddie's his son!" (211). In any event, for a long period neither sister nor father visits Freddie, a response, or lack of one, that has a detrimental effect on the boy, now a man. There was a time when his condition was less severe, when he seemed almost like the other boys, and in some respects more precocious. Gibbs, a friend of Freddie's at boarding school, speaks of him to Amy, unaware that she and Freddie are siblings:

> But if you thought that I think it's [i.e., retardation] funny because I, because a boy I knew in boarding school family so God damned wealthy all they exchanged at Christmas were three percent municipals I used to try to help him with his stamp collection, they probably could have bought him the British Guiana two cents rose if they'd ever thought of him as anything but retarded luggage but the Minuet in G you'd look at him and know he was hearing things you didn't, knew things nobody else did my throat still closes when I hear that, sweetest lonely God damned person I ever . . . (498)

Later, running into Freddie at Grand Central Station, Gibbs brings him back to the Ninety-Sixth Street apartment. As he tells Eigen: "knew me the minute he saw me he hasn't changed since he was ten look at him, what the hell could I do leave him there?" (618). At bottom, Gibbs is a good soul, prepared to keep others in mind and to shelter orphans. He himself has memories of what it is like to be a child alone in the world, to feel, as he tells Amy, that one has "been in the way since the day I could walk" (247). And this makes him more feeling for those who are, physically or emotionally, homeless. In *J R,* there are many such people, especially among the children, who are noticeably abandoned by the adults. "[K]ids are in the way that's how they're all brought up now" (247), Gibbs says, moments after Amy has commented on J R's orphanlike demeanor: "he always looks as though he lives in a home without, I don't know. Without grownups I suppose" (246).[16] She is right, of course, and so is Gibbs. In the world of *J R,* children are left to fend for themselves, as in the case of J R, or Buzzie, or the child with the toy pistol. The latter two are killed, one by a narcotics agent, the other in a car crash while driving under the influence of drugs. Other children, the victims of their parents' divorces, are simply lonely, including the children of those characters one likes most: Gibbs's Rose, Eigen's David, and Joubert's Francis. Home from boarding school, Francis, in a poignant passage, tells Amy in the taxi ride home, "I haven't got any friends" (192); and this is said before the boy's life worsens, when he is kidnapped by his father.

Like the baby Jesus in David Eigen's crèche[17]—"Look [. . .] help me find the other piece, the little Baby Jesus" (411)—children are frequently lost. A radio message solicits those interested in "adopting a foster child" (372), yet others are just as quickly being lost. Gibbs, Eigen, and Joubert all lose their children through the process of separation and divorce, though Joubert, after a trip to Geneva, is able to reclaim her son. Then there is the class trip to Wall Street, where it is not clear whether a child has been lost. Asked by Amy, who wishes to remain in the city, to chaperon the children back to Long Island, Bast finds that he has one more train ticket than he has children (twelve), leading him to the sensible conclusion, spoken to J R, "Look we must have lost somebody!" (136). It is not clear that a child has been lost. In the Wall Street cafeteria, Amy counted only twelve kids, but she was not sure if she had everyone or not: "Wait, yes six, seven there were twelve I think" (121). And while later Whiteback murmurs "something about a lost child" (179), the feeling is that since no child has been reported lost (237), the administration will simply go about its business, which includes calling an ambulance to take away the baby born in the girls' room to the school's ado-lescent Flosshilde, who will, in turn, not be able to perform in the much-looked-forward-to Spring Arts Festival "unless some adoption agency comes through" and assumes responsibility for the infant (457).

This theme of the lost child is also conveyed in the several allusions to Jesus's parable of the lost sheep. For instance, in his effort to take J R's mind off "these nickel deductions and these net tangible assets for a minute" (655), Bast asks him to listen to Bach's Cantata no. 21, which invokes both Peter's First Epistle ("Cast your cares upon God" [5.6–11]) and the parable of the lost sheep, found in both Luke 15.1–10 and Matthew 18.10–14. It is in Matthew that the sheep are most likened to children, for the parable follows the admonition that to gain heaven one needs to become like the child: "Truly, I say to you, unless you turn and become like children, you will never enter the kingdom of heaven" (18.3); and is bracketed by the warning against abusing children:

See that you do not despise one of these little ones; for I tell you that in heaven their angels always behold the face of my Father who is in heaven. What do you think? If a man has a hundred sheep, and one of them has gone astray, does he not leave the ninety-nine on the hills and go in search of the one that went astray? And if he finds it, truly, I say to you, he rejoices over it more than over the ninety-nine that never went astray. So it is not the will of my Father who is in heaven that one of these little ones should perish. (18.10–14)

The cantata is divided into two parts. The first focuses on the misery of the lost sheep, and the second on their joy when discovered by the good shepherd, Jesus. In the opening sinfonia, to make clear the depth of sorrow and hopelessness, Bach twice halts the music on discords. A tone of lament, with textual bases in Psalms 94 ("When the cares of heart are many thy consolations cheer my soul") and 42 ("Why troublest thou myself, my soul, and art so unquiet in me?"), dominates the first half, whereas the second half, which Bast calls J R's attention to, entails, as he says, "a dialogue between the soul and Jes[us] . . ." (655). Here the soul speaks of feeling lost: "ja ach ja ich bin verlor"; but Jesus replies that no, you are chosen, "nein du bist erkoren . . ." (654). Or, as Jesus, in the recitative, says to the sheep, "I am your true friend who even in darkness watches." Bast himself refers to this darkness, with the suggestion that it too can be miraculous, when he says to J R, "damn it J R can't you understand what I'm trying to, to show you there's such a thing as as, as intangible assets? what I was trying to tell you that night the sky do you remember it? walking back from that rehearsal that whole sense of, of sheer wonder in the Rhinegold, you remember it? [. . .] How it can lift you right out of yourself make you feel things that, do you know what I'm talking about at all?" (655). J R has no idea about what Bast is speaking of, even as the latter's attempt to educate the boy in the possibilities and reach of wonder represents a noble effort—represents, in short, the good shepherd's concern for the lost sheep. Nevertheless, J R's own education has been so bereft of the terms that might help him make sense of either Bach's cantata or Bast's urgings that he can respond only in the crassest manner: "I mean what I heard first there's all this high music right? So then this here lady starts singing up yours up yours so then this man starts singing up mine, then there's some words so she starts singing up mine up mine so he starts singing up yours so then they go back and forth like that" (658).[18]

It is not the first time that Bast's efforts this way fall on deaf ears. When, following Miss Flesch's accident, he was called on to take over her Mozart lecture, he tried to hold to the scripted lesson, reading the teacher's saccharine portrait of genius as well as he might: "fairy tale life of the composer Wolfgang Amadeus Mozart. Even his name, Amadeus, or in German, Gottlieb, means beloved by the gods . . ." (40). Yet, before being handed to Bast, the script had been dropped and jumbled, and after he has read Miss Flesch's narrative as far as it holds together, he finds that he must improvise. He does so brilliantly, even as the story he tells markedly departs from the fairy tale opening. Bast's reading accentuates not the effortlessness of Mozart's achievement but rather the multitude of obstacles that constantly threatened to end his work: "three more piano concertos, two string quintets, and the three finest operas ever written, and he's desperate, undernourished, exhausted, frantic about money while his wife runs up doctor bills and he's pawning everything in sight just in order to work, to keep working" (41). Finally these obstacles put a stop to both Mozart's work and his life. Bast meantime chooses not to gloss the dismal finale, with "his few friends following the cheap coffin in the rain and turning back before it ever reached the pauper's grave nobody could ever find again" (42). Bast is neither interested in, nor does he believe, stories of unblemished success, be they Mozart's or anyone else's. To know success almost requires that one know failure, for each is measured in the light of the other. Thus, genuine success requires an ability to imagine the trials of failure, the way that belief—profound belief—requires an almost scatological understanding of unbelief.[19] Or as Bast, quoting Mozart in a letter to his cousin, says, "For believing and shitting are two very different things" (42). They are two very different things, and the difference bears scrutiny. However, Bast never gets the opportunity to pursue the matter, for he is dismissed for simply reading from the letter. The school is happy to tolerate all kinds of inanity, but not profanity. This is too bad, for the letter has its value, albeit not the kind likely to impress either Whiteback or Hyde. I would like to discuss the letter (addressed to Mozart's cousin, Maria Anna Thekla Mozart) further because it, too, foregrounds the lost sheep motif, and it brings us back to what is missing in the pedagogy.

As I say, the parable of the lost sheep is a dominant motif in *J R*. For one, the more thoughtful characters all experience the strongest sense of estrangement, of feeling lost. "I see," says Gibbs, "crowds of people walking round in a ring" (479), alluding not only to Eliot's *The Waste Land*, but also to a cultural condition marked by a myopic listlessness that threatens to overwhelm adults and children alike. Children cannot prosper if there are no wise adults to guide them; and here, in *J R*, the repetition of images of "maimed [. . .] sheep" (618) and parents' disavowing their obligation to their children, and of a language that deliberately echoes the parable's diction (i.e., "little ones"), as in Gibbs's question in reference to the baby Jesus that belongs to the crèche, "Where's the little one that got away" (412), makes it clear that the choice of this Mozart letter (28 February 1778), with its long allusion to the parable of the lost sheep, is not simply coincidental. Before offering further comment, however, let me first quote the relevant passage:

> Now one day the shepherd was walking along with his sheep, of which he had eleven thousand, and was carrying in his hand a stick with a beautiful rose-coloured ribbon. For he always carried a stick. It was his habit to do this. Well, let's go on. After he had walked for a good hour or so, he got tired and sat down near a river and fell asleep, and dreamt that he had lost his sheep. He

awoke in terror, but to his great joy found all his sheep beside him. So he got up and walked on, but not for very long; for he had hardly walked for half an hour before he came to a bridge, which was very long but well protected on both sides in order to prevent people from falling into the river. Well, he looked at his flock and, as he was obliged to cross the river, he began to drive his eleven thousand sheep over the bridge. Now please be so kind as to wait until the eleven thousand sheep have reached the other side and then I shall finish my story. I have already told you that no one knows how the affair is going to turn out. But I hope that before I send you my next letter the sheep will have crossed the river. (501)

The event takes place, says Mozart, in either the village of Tribsterill or Burmesquik. His memory, he says, is uncertain, though they are both ficti-tious names born in a mad, almost Blakean dream, mixing reverence with irreverence, analogous to Bast's hospitalized state when he tells the solici-tous Coen that he has been away at a "[p]lace called Trib, Trib, place where the muck runs down to the sea . . . ," and then, when the latter appears non-plussed, that he has been at an "[i]mport export place called Burmesquik where they make the crooked [arseholes]" (667). Here, one might wish to discount the allusion's importance because so much of the letter appears manic. Yet its composition follows immediately that of a letter to Mozart's father where, in a calm voice, he echoes themes (i.e., the longed for reconcil-iation of the child to the parent mediated through a larger trust) expressed in both Cantata no. 21 and *J R*.[20] We need, then, to take this lost sheep motif seriously, not only as we find it in the Mozart letter, or as we read the letter back into the novel, but as we find its moral on practically every page of *J R*. This is a novel wherein children are too regularly shunted aside, so that if the kids come across, in Bast's words, as "a generation in heat" (142), it has everything to do with the fact that the parents either are absent or are, like the mother of the pregnant Flosshilde, "ugually asleep" (228).

This might bring us back, briefly, to a discussion of the classroom, for the teachers are also usually asleep. They do too many things—lessons, exams, administration—by rote, and thereby fail in their obligation to the children. There is, as mentioned, a countinghouse ethic in place, one most esteemed in the ludicrous reform that, in the wake of the J R Family's takeover of the school, substitutes for the traditional letter grade, itself a "petty and con-temptible reward" (Holt, 274), a monetary bribe: "a dollar is A, fifty cents is B C is a quarter D is like nothing see then instead of E you have to pay a nick[el]" (649). School and business merge, so that the school is run for prof-it, an idea whose ludicrousness would be self-apparent were the community members less smitten with proposing monetary answers to all their problems.

In a sense, the J R Family takeover only makes emphatic an ethos that is already in place. Certainly, under Hyde and Whiteback, the school is no enemy of business. Hyde, who professes to see everything "at the corporate level" (23)—until his own corporation lets him go (461)—puts loyalty to his company, Endo, before all else: "the only place left for loyalty if you've got any's the company that's paying your way, when my company says jump I jump!" (455). Unfortunately, his corporate loyalty here includes, in a public relations gesture (426), pressing a lot of unneeded equipment onto the school, including equipment (for the home ec center) that displaces the kindergartens and the children with learning disabilities. Like Dan diCephalis, an alleged recipient of manufacturer's kickbacks (455), Hyde cannot dissociate the children's interest from self-interest. And though one might expect that his bosses would appreciate this blurring of responsibilities, Hyde has, in fact, been acting against the clear interests of Moncrieff and Cates, whose Diamond Cable tender is tied to a Justice Department mandate that the smaller company (Endo) be divested from the larger one (Diamond Cable); until then, the smaller company's activity must be curtailed. As Cates complains to Beaton, "nothing left to that Endo outfit but its damn inventory he's giving away with one hand while we're complying with this Justice Department ruling to sell the company with the other, already jeopardized the Diamond tender with this damn fool news story tell me what in hell he thinks he's been doing?" (426). Sadly, Hyde does neither the schoolchildren nor himself a favor.

Whiteback's mistakes are less dramatic, yet he also does no one a favor by trying to wear two hats, as school principal and bank head. And he also gets sucked into a corrupt financial maelstrom, composed of "an overabundance of bad home improvement loans" and ill-advised mortgages (327), a large unsecured loan to Parentucelli, owner of Cantania Paving, and a conflict-of-interest gift of bank shares to Assemblyman Pecci's wife, "possibly in connection with a corporation [Flo-Jan] formed in both their wives' names to collect fees under contract with the same contractor [Parentucelli] under a leasing arrangement involving the local town dock" (434–35). He would do well, of course, to choose between the school and bank positions, but he first needs, says he, to determine which stands the better chance of surviving. As long as he leads, neither's prognosis can be thought attractive. Certainly, as school principal, his time goes almost entirely toward obliging those—Hyde, Parentucelli, diCephalis, Pecci, Haight, Skinner, Stye, et al.—who think they have some god-given right to tap into the budget for their own profit. Two thousand dollars goes toward funding diCephalis's "reading accelerators" (330), thirty-five thousand for his "Edsel Responsive Environment" (329), and a million dollars for Pecci's pet, in-school television (331). Meantime, the Great Books program gives way to all the "stoves, washers, [and] dryers" (223) that Hyde has given the school to spur on its "[h]ome catering and slipcover making" program (176). This makes sense if one believes, as Hyde does, that with "[b]ooks you don't know what you're getting into" (25). If not, it would seem as if education gets lost in the technology, the gimmickry. DiCephalis may wish to "key the technology to the individ[ual]," and Hyde, "the individual to the technology" (224), but in both instances, the children's true needs are not being addressed. As Vern, noting the rot pouring out of the in-house television, says, "don't try to describe what flows through these tubes as educational content, [. . .] when I said plumbing I meant plumbing, doesn't matter who pulls the chain" (221).

The school's greatest problem has less to do with budgets and equipment than with its inability to instill in students a larger sense, vis-à-vis the world, of trust and curiosity. This brings us back to Bast's lecture on Mozart. What is wonderful about this lecture is that it starts by raising questions, including unpleasant questions requiring the students to think about poverty and its consequences, even if "we don't like to think about poor people" (42). Of course, one cannot predict exactly where these questions will lead, but this is part of their value. Unlike Miss Flesch's lesson, so encouraging of complacency, Bast's takes the students a distance from where they began. His questions do not disclose their solutions beforehand; rather, they lead the curious student on by a promise of discoveries to be made, though what these will be may, at first, take the form only of a guess responding to a hint. Still, they are posed with the trust that questions entail answers, just as answers entail further questions. Together, in time, questions and answers begin to suggest a pattern and a way to proceed, so that even if we begin with an open question, we start to find that the world tends more to satisfy than to obstruct our need for answers. That is, so long as we ask the questions. Paradoxically, then, though Miss Flesch's bracketed questions are meant to instill in the students confidence and trust, Bast's more open-ended questions actually accomplish this better. This is because Flesch's questions leave the student underprepared to deal with contingencies, whereas Bast's inscribe these into the program. The purpose is not to promote contingency over truth value, but to decrease the student's fear of the former, thereby making it easier to pursue the latter.[21]

The Long Island schoolchildren do not learn to trust their world, to see it as suggesting larger reassurances. For them, as for their mentors, knowledge assumes a material and pragmatic form. Things are what they are; there is no wish to see them symbolically. J R's way of dealing with the green aspirin—"Why should it have to mean anything! It's green, explanation ˙ ɔint" (471)—functions as the paradigm by which the school and communi-
live. Why should a color, or anything else, mean something? And yet it might, there is that possibility. Bloch has cautioned, "The meaning is not yet clear and not yet decided" (139). Gaddis I think would agree, for the tenor of not only *J R* but all the novels seems to point this way. Thus while I readily grant that J R is an exceptional child—and, to my mind, the most interesting fictional child since Huck Finn—there is still the sense that he is as much

victim as hero. There may seem nothing extraordinary about his victimhood; he does not live in a time of war or experience persecution. Yet had he wiser parents and mentors, he would make a much more impressive figure, especially as an adult, after his ingenuous earnestness and eagerness—charming in a boy, but not likely to be so in the adult[22]—give way to other emotions. His press clippings may speak of him as a "man of vision" (656), but we err if we are taken in by his rationalizations, the essence of which is that the system always wins, and that those who comply with it and use it shall be the real winners. Questions of morality—of yes and no, of obedience and disobedience, of innocence and guilt—give way, in J R's understanding, to ones of simple expediency. Made uncomfortable by Bast's ire, J R offers the familiar apology that he does only what everyone does or would like to do: "No but holy shit Bast I mean that's what you do! Like I mean these here Indians is it my fault they think corn is this here god they don't even have electricity? is it my fault if I didn't get these here leases off them and leave them stay there somebody else is going to screw them out of the whole thing? Is it my fault if I do something first which if I don't do it somebody else is going to do it anyway? I mean how come everybody's always getting mad at me!" (659).

The answer to J R's question—"Is it my fault?"—is both no and yes. No, in the sense that true, there is *a* system in place, and it makes its own demands. The system is coercive, and to play by its rules raises a question less of guilt—though it raises this too—than of complicity. All of us, whether we approve of it or not, are in one way or another (large or small) complicitous with the system, fulfilling its demands, whether it be taking advantage of the extant laws to steal another group's land—J R: "I mean why should somebody go steal and break the law to get all they can when there's always some law where you can be legal and get it all anyway!" (660)—or simply paying taxes, enabling the government to pay for bad, even unethical, projects, as well as good ones. Complicity seems unavoidable, but guilt would seem to attach more to the spirit, or will, with which a person does things; it calls forth more the question of what a person knows and then does with this knowledge.

Amy Joubert, Edward Bast, and the Need for a Larger Trust

Readers may not wish to attach too much moral responsibility to J R. He is an eleven-year-old boy, and his actions reflect his upbringing as much as his character, or lack of.[23] I myself take this stance, though I do not mean to suggest that I find J R, as he would have Bast find him, faultless. For a boy his age, he does have a rather developed sense of what is, and is not, right in the larger scheme of things. He knows, for instance, that his handling of the

Indian land matter, while legal, is wrong; and he knows, though not palpably, that the system which he inhabits is but one system—that there are other ways to measure value, to determine what is right and wrong. That he knows this follows particularly from his dealings with such adults as Amy Joubert and Edward Bast.

Two of the novel's most poignant scenes are those in which Amy and Edward try to introduce J R to another order, different from and opposed to the prevailing logic of cash nexus. I have briefly referred to both, but I would like to examine them more closely. In one, J R, seeking Amy's attention, follows her out of the school and into the autumn evening. He wants her to share in his excitement, in the thought that behind every common object (e.g., water fountain, lightbulb, etc.) there must stand a millionaire: "like did you ever think Mrs Joubert everything you see someplace there's this millionaire for it?" (473). When Amy, somewhat taken aback, asks him if that is what he really thinks about, J R goes further, saying, "Sure, I mean look back there [. . .] —like right now someplace there's this water fountain millionaire and this locker millionaire and this here lightbulb one I mean like even the lightbulb there's this glass millionaire and this one off where you screw the [. . .]" (473–74). The child's ingenuousness is cute, yet it is a serious matter. He may be full of wonder—a good thing—but its object is too circumscribed, and may end up being a bad thing. Amy knows this. It is what, among other things, makes her different from a Hyde, Whiteback, or diCephalis. Accordingly, she takes J R by the shoulder, folds him in her embrace and makes him look at the evening sky and what she takes to be the rising moon:

> —Just stop for a minute! she caught an arm round his shoulders, —just stop and look . . . !
> —What? at what . . .
> —At the evening, the sky, the wind, don't you ever just stop sometimes and look? and listen?
> —Well, I mean sure, I . . . He stood stiff in her embrace, his armload holding her off between them, —like it's, I mean it's like getting dark real early now . . .
> —Yes look up at the sky look at it! Is there a millionaire for that? But her own eyes dropped to her hand on his shoulder as though to confirm a shock at the slightness of what she held there. —Does there have to be a millionaire for everything?
> —Sure well, well no I mean like . . .
> —And over there look, look. The moon coming up, don't you see it? Doesn't it make . . .
> —What over there? He ducked away as though for a better view, —No but that's, Mrs Joubert? that's just, wait . . .
> —No never mind, it doesn't matter . . . (474)

I quote this passage at length for its extraordinary tenderness. At this point, Amy is feeling the absence of her son, stolen away by Lucien, the boy's father. Naturally, some of her maternal affection for Francis is displaced onto J R. But the situation is more complicated than this. Amy is intelligent, thoughtful, curious, trusting, and generous. She is almost everything that one would want a person to be. And here she is simply trying to say to J R, look, there is another way in which to live in the world; it is not exploitative or proprietary, but instead is the way a child might meet a teacher, open, trusting, prepared to learn, and hoping to gain a wisdom hitherto denied. Her words ("look," "listen," "see"), of course, like Bast's own, intentionally (though the intention is Gaddis's) recall Conrad's memorable explanation of what he sought to offer his reader: "to make you hear, to make you feel—it is, before all, to make you *see!* That—and no more; and it is everything!" (preface to *The Nigger of the "Narcissus"*).[24]

"It" is everything, even as the pronoun's antecedent escapes definition. What Amy wishes to show J R is that wonder reaches much further than the realm of the countable, that its circumference is always expanding. The world offers satisfaction to one's curiosity; and yet it no sooner does than it alerts one to all that one does not yet know, and thereby sets curiosity once again in motion. This, too, was what Bast meant when he, like Amy, directed J R's attention to the night sky, and then later to the Bach cantata. It was not as if Bast expected either experience to reduce itself to a truth statement; but he hoped that one or the other might awaken some larger sense of wonder in J R. That, after all, was the reason that Bast allowed himself to be "used" by J R, that he might introduce the boy to all the things that Bast himself found so real, so extraordinary. But J R sees another reality, and the teacher-student relation flounders:

> —What tell me what! I mean you're telling me how neat the sky looks you're telling me listen to this here music you even get pissed off when I . . .
> —I asked you what you heard! that's all, I . . .
> —What like it lifted me out of mysel . . .
> —Not what I said no you! what you heard!
> —What was I suppose to hear!
> —You weren't! you weren't supposed to hear anything that's what I'm . . .
> —Then how come you made me lis . . .
> —To make you hear! to make you, to make you feel to try to . . . (657–58)

Amy and Edward's efforts to invoke the night sky as a means to introduce J R to a larger, more sublime sense of the world's possibility recalls not only Wyatt's attempt, in *The Recognitions*, to show Ludy the sublimity of an El Greco sky, but also Kant's invocation in *The Critique of Judgment:* "if we call the sight of the starry heaven *sublime*, we must not found our estimate of it upon any concepts of worlds inhabited by rational beings, with the bright spots, which we see filling the space above us, as their suns moving in orbits prescribed for them with the wisest regard to ends. But we must take it, just as it strikes the eye, as a broad and all-embracing canopy: and it is merely under such a representation that we may posit the sublimity" of such things (I.121–22). Kant's point is that the starlit sky constitutes an introduction to that which escapes our capacity to formulate it, or to make it companionable with instrumental reason. Its sublimity functions, in a sense, as a negative, offering instruction, but delivering little by way of information. Responses to this situation differ, but for Kant—and I believe for Gaddis—the feeling is that the mature person experiences an awe, inflected by trepidation, and a respect, not unlike that which moves the devout:

> delight in the sublime in nature is only *negative* . . . : that is to say it is a feel-
> ing of imagination by its own act depriving itself of its freedom by receiving a
> final determination in accordance with a law other than that of its empirical
> employment. In this way it gains an extension and a might greater than that
> which it sacrifices. But the ground of this is concealed from it, and in its place
> it *feels* the sacrifice or deprivation, as well as its cause, to which it is subjected.
> The *astonishment* amounting almost to terror, the awe and thrill of devout feel-
> ing. . . . (I.120–21)

Of course, in addition to expressing a stance toward the unknown, Kant's remarks also constitute an aesthetic statement. He speaks of the imagination engaged in an act—the act of its own self-deprivation. By this act, something is lost—the separate discriminations that mark the empirical—and something gained: a wholeness in which the self and the aesthetic are united.[25] I bring this point up not to take up the question of the aesthetic—this I wish to hold off a little longer—but because it ties in with a remark made by Gaddis elsewhere, yet relevant to the present discussion. The remark, tying the polar night to an aesthetic theory, is offered in the closing paragraph of his review of Saul Bellow's *More Die of Heartbreak*: "The long polar night offers a sharp image for this or indeed any well-wrought novel in its claim as art, iso-lating people in small groups hemmed in on every side by their inadequacies where they are bound to find one another out, which is fundamentally what the task of the novel is" (16). Here again, Gaddis refers to the night sky (in this instance, to the aurora borealis) as that which, like the author's own sense of art, offers a unity to what is otherwise characterized by separation and division. It is a Kantian formulation, which should not surprise, for there are numerous resemblances in Gaddis's work to Kantian thought.

This said, I wish to return to the question of trust, for what distinguishes Joubert and Bast is their willingness to place themselves—vis-à-vis the world—in a relation of trust. For them, the night sky does, in fact, suggest a transcendental, even a spiritual, realm which, if acknowledged, might offer itself as a means to the overcoming of the terrible atomism afflicting the general culture.[26] The consequence of this atomism is reflected in the fear that grabs at even well-intentioned characters like Gibbs, who speaks of being "afraid of failing at something worth doing" (491), not yet convinced that, as Amy rightly puts the matter, if one commits oneself to something worth doing, there is no failure, not in any event akin to that attaching to the thing that never was worth doing from the start: "the only bad failure's at something you knew wasn't worth doing in the first place" (491).

Here, I can imagine more skeptical readers complaining that in directing J R's attention to the rising moon, Amy, this scion of wealth, only makes clear how hollow and romantic her beliefs are, for she actually points not to the moon but to an illuminated ice cream cone atop a roadside stand. As J R later tells the story, "What tell her it's this top of this here Carvel icecream cone stand? tell her does she want to bet her ass if there's this millionaire for that?" (661). Similar criticism might be leveled at not only Edward's attempt to impress upon J R the magnificence of the night sky and of the Bach cantata, but also his attempt to write an opera based on Tennyson's "Locksley Hall," an ambition that his cousin Stella ridicules as a sign that he is simply "a boy with a lot of romantic ideas about himself and everything else" (148). In truth, Amy and Edward are romantics. Early in the novel, Edward asks Amy if she would be interested in going with him to a concert and whether she likes Chopin. To the latter question, she responds, "Oh of course I do yes, that ballade the Ballade in G? it's simply the most roman[tic]" music (113). However, in the context of the novel, I am not sure this altogether makes for a bad thing. At worst, it is innocuous. But here, I think it suggests something more positive. For one, *J R* is not a novel bursting with romantics, certainly not of a thoughtful sort. Amy and Edward are perhaps the only two. It is, in a sense, what makes them different and attractive: both are caring, sincere, and vulnerable. And though many others also appear vulnerable, most protect themselves by something like a "do unto others before they do unto you" ethic.[27]

It would be a mistake, then, to dismiss either Amy or Edward as lacking substance. Yes, there is an innocence about them, connected to their youth and stances vis-à-vis the world. The first, however, will give way to something else as they grow older; and the second will not give way, for it speaks of a desire to hold if not to an innocent, then to a youthful or, in Emerson's words, "an original" relation to the universe. This is what makes them most attractive. At least for this reader, for it strikes me that in Gaddis criticism there is a readiness to discount character—by which I mean thinking and feeling individuals who, while acted upon, also act. John Johnston, for instance, argues (in a reference to *The Recognitions* but also, it seems, more generally) that "Gaddis's depiction of character is postindividual and post-

Freudian in the sense that his characters are not fully autonomous and intelligible in the terms of bourgeois psychology, and do not develop in self-awareness and moral perception" (3). And Patrick O'Donnell, specifically referring to *J R*, argues that "there is no 'one' who attains the status of integral or singular identity in the novel" (*Echo Chambers*, 175). I grant the justice of Johnston's and O'Donnell's comments to a full range of characters in Gaddis, yet not to all; and it is the difference to which we are, I believe, asked to attend. There are, in fact, quite a number of Gaddis characters rich "in self-awareness and moral perception," and while in the larger context of the novels they may appear a minority, we make a mistake if, propelled by our postmodern ambitions, we choose to conflate, or reduce, all of Gaddis's characters into this single posthumanist type. In fact, if reductions are permitted, we might do better to call out E. M. Forster's chestnut regarding flat and round characters, for it does seem that Gaddis's own ambition as a satirist leads him to represent character either as unusually cartoonish or as complex, leaving the broad middle swatch to novelists like John Cheever, Richard Ford, Joyce Carol Oates, Peter Taylor, John Updike, et al. Or, to go further, we might borrow the terms employed by Glancy in his speculation about life on other worlds and then picked up by Gibbs: one-, two-, and three-dimensional characters. As Gibbs tells Amy, "Run into a two dimensional people sideways you couldn't even see him . . ." (346).

Thus, among the two-dimensional characters, there are figures like the cafeteria manager Mister Urquhart, whom Gibbs speaks of as "creeping around picking up napkin wads like something out of Dickens" (118); Ann diCephalis, about whom Gibbs tells Amy, "Ann, she's sort of you in a cheap edition, twentieth printing of the paperback when things begin to smear" (245); Dan diCephalis, who, in practicing his corporate role playing, takes to making faces in mirrors (162); and Nurse Waddams (Duncan's "Waddles"), whose conversation is ticlike, as she repeatedly replies to Coen's calls with the genial yet vacuous phrase, "I sure will Mister Coen so how's your other patients you really got your hands full haven't you you must be . . . you bet Mister Coen goodbye" (670). What joins most of these characters, apart from appearing caricatural, is a persistent fear that (as with their counterparts in *The Recognitions*) rules their lives. Or as Gibbs says of Urquhart:

—What who Urquhart? I'm God damn it I didn't invent him look at him, think he hasn't got a skinful to get through the day in a place like this? That almost distinguished profile that authority in his face but it won't stay still afraid people will notice his teeth don't fit, afraid he'll lose them and we'll all laugh so he's telling that sloppy busboy to clean up a table he's almost finished anyhow keep his authority intact just those God damned teeth can't relax for an instant he's . . . (118)

These characters properly belong to the novel's chorus. They are the "bystanders" referred to by Gibbs, assisting Bast with his opera: "All those God damned bystanders there's your chorus" (398). As with the "young man carbuncular" or the "typist" in Eliot's *The Waste Land*, the sense is that the system provides these people with only the most routine and boring jobs, forcing them to pursue distractions, even to the point of turning sexual relations into just another distraction, something to blot out the more encompassing ennui. Here, Norman Angel's secretaries, Terry and Myrna, appear updated versions of their *Waste Land* counterpart. Terry, for instance, finds that the days all begin to seem the same and that "Sometimes I get real bored" (155). Her affair with the salesman Kenny, who treats her badly, is one consequence of this boredom. Meanwhile, Leo, Angel's assistant, finds that the boys in shipping have been circulating lewd photographs purportedly of Terry taken with soldiers stationed nearby. As for Myrna, Gibbs later picks her up in the subway and takes her to the Ninety-Sixth Street apartment where they engage in freewheeling sex. Not surprisingly, then, when Terry and Myrna get together during breaks, their conversation weaves the most intimate details of their lives with the most banal, as if sexual relations and shopping were simply variations on a theme:

—You still using his apartment?

—No his kid's still home sick we been using this friend of his, Kenny said he's a musician someplace I think he's a fag the way the place is decorated, you know? It's real nice.

—I can't make it like that, like that time with Ronnie I'm always scared somebody's going to walk right in when you're wait is that all the pink polish?

—We made it four times up there Monday before he went, I'll get more at lunch you want to go shopping? I saw this like silky yellow blouse over on Steinway it would go real nice with your coloring turn it [the radio] up a little ... (154)

It is not Gaddis's point to make fun of these people, these bystanders. Granted, he paints them with a comic brush, but like Gibbs's anger at the Larchmont millionaire who employs the poor black girl at three dollars a day to steam shirts in a Grand Central Station storefront, where she must stand and watch all the dashing Westchester and Connecticut commuters (496), Gaddis's anger is directed more to those who control, and have a vested interest in, the system. The bystanders are, like the Eagle Mill workers, "real" people (296),[28] and Gaddis's sympathies go out to them even as he deplores what has become of them, reduced to cogs in Instrumental Reason's monstrous machine. Still, it is not these people alone who are victimized by a system that celebrates expediency, for in the long run all suffer. One cannot make it a point to use people, as J R is so fond of doing, without promoting a situation wherein other people wish to do the same thing back. And when this happens, when the manipulation proceeds full circle, trust breaks down.

Mistrust on a large scale is a central theme in *J R*. Naively, the community's leaders, corporate and political, seem to think, à la Dale Carnegie (685), that while it is unwise to trust anyone at first, trust can be purchased and commanded. One just needs enough money, enough power. Hence Cates's maxim, later picked up by J R, that if you "don't own them you can't trust them" (98), an assumption that turns out to have ruinous consequences for him. He trusts Beaton, Typhon's corporate secretary and general counsel, principally because he owns him; it is hard for Cates to imagine Beaton doing him any harm, for, in his own mind, Cates believes he is the corporation. Yet Beaton, entrusted to inform Cates when the fourth dividend on the nonprofit health insurance corporation is due (212–13), tells him only when it is too late (twenty minutes before the deadline and with the octogenarian about to be wheeled into the hospital's operating room). As a consequence, Cates loses control of the foundation that he was adamant about holding onto; he also, on the operating table, loses his life (718). The suggestion is that Beaton, captivated by Amy—"you're such a stunning woman a stunning young woman I, I, I . . ." (214)—decides to act in Amy's, rather than Cates's, interest, knowing that if the dividend is missed then control of the foundation will pass over to her. And this is what happens (712).

Here we see that trust cannot be coerced; it is a willful, not a reactive, gesture; it entails a placing of faith in another, not as the consequence of an obligation but as an act of good will, free and unentailed. It does not exist outside the sway of contingencies, yet it also does not function in the fashion of a quid pro quo. It is something that either does or does not permeate behavior, for it is attentive less to particulars than to histories of affection and disaffection. In *J R*, trust exists in the occasional byways of society but not in its main thoroughfares. There are, as noted, the exceptional characters like Edward and Amy, the first of whom embraces Tennyson's lines "And I said, 'My cousin Amy, speak, and speak the truth to me, / Trust me, cousin, all the current of my being sets to thee," as when he turns to his own cousin, Stella, and says to her, "Wait wait! trust me cousin! you wanted to hear this part" of my opera (142). He is serious; Stella is not. He is also serious when he gives his word on the land leases to the Indian Charley Yellow Brook. As he tells J R, "I gave him my word, I expect to live up to . . . [it]" (639). But he will not be allowed to, for as J R tells him, he has already been fired (after Bast uses the company's stock for collateral, the company's lenders demand, from J R, his dismissal) (639–40).

Amy also offers trust. She takes a genuine interest in J R, something no other teacher, with the exception of Edward, has done. She also takes an interest in Edward and his work; and while she does not exactly comprehend the pressure he is under, her questions evince a genuine curiosity—e.g., "Yes but that's what you meant isn't it, about creating an entirely different world when you write opera, about asking the audience to suspend its belief in the . . ." (111)—and her encouragement is sincere: "But I think it's marvelous, that you couldn't write their nothing music? I mean just because you can't get paid to play Chopin or even write music that's . . ." (112). Some might think this solicitude dismissable. After all, Amy knows little about contemporary music or its career pressures. Still, she cares about and has confidence in Edward, and this has a value of its own. It is the sort of support that Edward desperately needs, especially as his own family members—the absent father James, the steely cousin Stella—have withheld emotional support. So while I grant that Amy's support has its limitations, I would stress its importance in fostering a climate in which good work may be done. Trust breeds trust, to the point that Amy's confidence in Edward communicates itself to others, notably Crawley and Gibbs, who then go out of their way to assist the young composer. Crawley tells Edward that if he "hadn't come so highly recommended" (200), he would not demonstrate a companionable interest. Likewise, Gibbs offers Edward the Ninety-Sixth Street apartment keys only after Amy's urging. As the now intoxicated Gibbs, offering the keys, says to Edward, "Told me you're talented sensitive purpose Bast sense of purpose need help and encouragement lock yourself in write nothing music, take defeat from any brazen throat get to be like Bizet only not like Bizet" (131). Of course, the value of Crawley's and Gibbs's assistance is open to question. Susan Strehle, in her first-rate chapter "*J R* and the Matter of Energy," thinks the Ninety-Sixth Street apartment an important step for Edward, for it forces him out of his studio, with all its romantic associations with the solitary artist. The apartment's "clutter, entropy, chaos and openness to invasion make it," she argues, "an apt microcosm for the larger world" (114). Perhaps, yet I suspect that this gives away too much to the rule of "clutter, entropy, [and] chaos," and I myself am more inclined to see Crawley's and Gibbs's assistance as in line with that offered by J R—it is well-meaning but ultimately takes Edward away from something more important and real.

As J R's teacher and Bast's colleague, Amy takes a heartfelt interest in their needs, but she is naturally more emotionally attached to Francis, her son, and Gibbs, her lover. Again, for both of them, she creates an environment of affection and trust—that is, to the extent that other factors do not enter in, and they certainly do enter in. Meanwhile, there is a wonderfully touching scene in Penn Station, wherein Gibbs—standing in a telephone booth talking to Eigen, yet at the same time recalling the place's significance in his own history, remembering the return from boarding school, the "looking for a familiar face" but finding none, thinking that it has been "like this since I was seven" (190)—is stopped in the middle of his thoughts by the sight of Amy. He steps out of the booth and calls to her, yet she, arms reaching out, does not hear him, for she is reaching out not for him but for her son, himself just back from boarding school:

> —Amy . . . ? as though that had constricted it, knotted his voice and his face in consternation as hers filled with her smile, her arms extended open passing him where he sank back against the booth and then into it watching her come half to her knees to embrace the boy who stood away quickly in embarrassment to pick up a suitcase, straighten the school blazer, as he caught the dangling phone —like, like one of those old Shirley Temple movies, Jack Haley goes in one side of the revolving door and she comes out the other but Christ, Tom? Imagine having her, having anybody that glad to see you? (190–91)

Later, Amy will in fact show a like enthusiasm for Gibbs, but he, jealous of her past and present affections, will find it difficult to place his full trust in her. This happens despite the fact that he trusts her more than anyone. Or as he says to her, "it's not you I don't trust Amy it's life, it's the whole God damned . . . [thing]" (507), and not trusting this, there is very little chance that he can truly trust Amy, no matter how much she reaches out to him. This is made clear in the incident with the douche in the bathroom, which Gibbs immediately thinks is hers, but this is Lucien Joubert's apartment, and the douche belongs to his lover, the dancer. Gibbs makes an accusation, through innuendo, that forces Amy to confront him: "look at me, because I said that ['it happens to everybody,' said after Jack proves impotent] you think I sleep around?" (502). The suggestion is ridiculous and, apart from the whole question of a double standard, leaves aside, as Amy points out, the possibility that she may have cared enough about someone actually to wish for physical intimacy: "Or because I sleep around with older men I don't but what if I had, not if I've loved someone or why I'd love anyone or want them to love me but who I've slept with or you're afraid I might sleep with isn't that what you're saying?" (503).

Despite his great affection for Amy, Jack Gibbs is something of a misogynist. His attitudes toward women are too often inflected by contempt, most notably in his stances toward Stella, Mrs. Schramm (Schramm's young stepmother), Marian (Eigen's wife), and his own ex-wife. This contempt is, in part, a protective mask for his own self's uncertainties, the shield of a boy, now a man, who has been made to feel "in the way since the day I could walk" (247). Like Schramm, Schepermann, Freddie, and so many others in this novel, Gibbs belongs to the walking wounded, never having felt cared for, and unable now to think himself worthy of care. Meanwhile, he seems aware of how unjust his attitudes toward women are. For instance, when Amy, first hearing about Gibbs's manuscript, says she wishes it were a novel, he responds, "Only problem is a novelist has to understand women":

—You don't?

—Apparently not, from all the . . . turned full to share her smile he found it gone, only her eyes wide through the lenses. —What's the matter.

—I wish you hadn't said that, she said looking away as quickly.

—What?

—I hope it's not true. (248)

Here, Gibbs is still putting the onus on others, notably women, and not fully acknowledging his own fault. Between the Scylla and Charybdis of mid-century American male attitudes and his own personal history, he will always find it difficult, try as he may, to think of women outside the angel/whore paradigm. Meanwhile, Amy tries to disabuse him of the notion that love should be reduced to sex:

—Jack is that why you'd want me to love you? for the one thing any other man can replace? The one thing a woman's afraid of a man loving her for when she thinks that's the only reason he please, Jack no please . . . (503)

As messy as his life is, Jack is not a bad soul. He is not only the sort who will offer his apartment to one such as Bast, but also the sort who can be found pressing a dollar bill in the hand of a homeless man. If he does the latter, as Stella says, "because what he saw coming toward him was himself" (359), it does not really matter. In fact, it is what we all need to do, to make the connection between our life and that of others. And if his attitude toward women often seems harsh, there are times when it is otherwise. It is Jack who defends Rhoda, Schramm's druggy girlfriend, from Eigen's abuse, saying, "Look Tom she's just a, little outspoken but there's not a mean bone in her body really just a sweet kid" (620). It is Jack who dearly loves his daughter, Rose, even as his insecurity leads him to overreach, to assume the character of the lamed war hero (modeled on Schramm) each Thursday, his visitation day. Finally, it is Jack who seems to make everything okay when, asked why he should act so oddly in Tripler's elevator, he tells Amy: "I just do things sometimes that, I'm crazy about you and sometimes I just seem to do the wrong things I God damn it I always do I . . ." (497).

This is the Jack whom Amy sees and loves. Jack of course does not see himself this way; he is too mindful of his own inadequacies to feel that he might merit another's love. Certainly not Amy's, for he is painfully aware of the difference in class and manners: "Amy you're so, just so damned elegant wherever we went today everybody so damned deferential, in the bank they would have kissed your feet and that woman in Bergdorf's and I felt like . . ." (496). If Jack could overcome his insecurities, it would not be a bad match. This does not happen, however, and the relation, by Jack's choice, ends. But before this happens, Amy, trying to reassure him, says, "I love you

for reasons you'll never know anything about" (507). It is one of the loveliest lines spoken in the book, and it points out, again, not only the strength of
Amy's character but also the fact that trust is never a quid pro quo matter,
that trust, while responsive to the contingencies, is not mechanistically
reducible to them.

The relation between Amy and Jack falters not because of anything that
Amy does or does not do, but because Jack, lacking trust in himself and,
more generally, in life itself, finds it difficult to believe that Amy loves him.
As he tells her, just before she leaves for Geneva with the hope of recovering
her child: "But Amy with you gone the whole God damned thing will, get
out and see myself in the daylight wonder what in hell you ever saw in me
that . . ." (507). It is not that Jack is not initially buoyed by Amy's love; he is,
and the immediate sign of this is his beginning to work once again on his
book. As he tells Bast, "Getting a fresh start on a book I was working on
Bast, getting a fresh God damned start on everything really going to get
down to work again" (565). He also begins with the belief that he has a reason—i.e., the desire for Amy's approval—to finish the book. But Jack's book
is not a simple, straightforward project; it is a young man's book, with all the
attendant ambition this suggests.[29] It is encyclopedic, an attempt to bring a
multitude of discourses together into a single order. One sentence reads, "For
the first time government, invention, art, industry, and religion have served
all the people rather than the patrician classes" (576). Thus, while the hope
remains that the disparate discourses also possess a commonality (hence *The
Recognitions* and *J R*),[30] Jack has the sense that he is no Diderot—"must
have thought I could, like Diderot good God how I ever thought I could do
it" (588)—and that the book's timeliness has passed: "Ten years later stag-
gers out God damned pianist already shot God damned sunshine everybody
step right over him God damned hurry go noplace nobody give a God damn
book everything's happened book about everybody knows hate it!" (605).

Then, when Rhoda attaches a question to an observation—"like I mean
look at all the fucking books in this place who asked you to write another
one anyhow" (605)—Gibbs's resolve begins to break down, for he begins to
believe the project no longer doable. "[S]he told me," Eigen says to Gibbs,
referring to Rhoda, "you hate it you can't finish it you're afraid of losing
your rotten opinion of yourself" (620). It appears true. He just cannot muster
the faith necessary to see the book through. The reason is, as suggested, partly one of temperament. For instance, Norman Angel, reminiscing about
Gibbs's work at General Roll, recalls "[h]ow he'd work out some cracker-
jack idea right to the point you could do something with it then he'd leave it
there, like it wasn't worth just getting down and doing it" (147). But it is also
more than this, for what also defeats Gibbs is the overriding sense—culled
from everything (i.e., the hurts, the greed, the ignorance, and the chaos) that
he sees around him—that in the end nothing is really worth doing, or

redeemable. Hence, when Eigen tries to place the blame for Schramm's suicide on Rhoda, Gibbs reacts angrily, saying,

> —Christ look can't you see it wasn't any of that! it was, it was worse than
> that? It was whether what he was trying to do was worth doing even if he
> couldn't do it? whether anything was worth writing even if he couldn't write
> it? Hopping around with that God damned limp trying to turn it all into some-
> thing more than one stupid tank battle one more stupid God damned general,
> trying to redeem the whole God damned thing by . . . (621)[31]

"An individual lifestyle is . . . hard to sustain against the grain," writes
Charles Taylor (9), and Gibbs appears to bow out of the competition by
novel's end. He talks about how "it's going to be hard [. . .] to tell her
[Amy] this, about this book tell her I'll never finish it never write it Christ
one thing the one God damned thing she ever really thought I . . ." (625). At
this point, he has just been diagnosed as having leukemia (a diagnosis later
reversed), and he wants Eigen to believe that he will not be able to finish the
book owing to his illness. He has, in fact, convinced himself that this is the
case, and in the cab ride uptown, listening to Gluck's *Orfeo* and its celebrated song "Che farò senza Euridice?" (What shall I do without Eurydice?), he
begins to identify Amy with Eurydice—earlier in the novel Julia Bast, hearing Amy's voice, likens her to Louise Homer playing Eurydice in the Gluck
opera (235)—and himself with Orpheus (619). Yet when he reaches the
Ninety-Sixth Street apartment and tells Eigen of his tragedy, the latter refuses, in effect, to hear him: one, because Eigen is so absorbed in his own problems (i.e., telling David, his son, about his and Marian's decision to separate
permanently); and two, because he believes that the illness represents one
more excuse on Jack's part not to finish the book: "this excuse you've got
now for not writing this book" (626). Then, when Jack protests, Eigen goes
further: "I just meant look I mean being objective Jack facing it honestly
instead of this turning it into this Tolstoy play this, to make the whole world
know what it lost that's all I'm saying, this I shall write nothing the world
will have to understand all by itself . . ." (626).

Eigen's response is both cruel and knowing. The diagnosis of his illness
has, in fact, let Jack momentarily off the hook; for as Tom has noted, the
decision not to proceed with the book was made prior to the diagnosis, the
testimonies to which are the torn and stamped-on pages of Jack's notes that
litter the apartment: "footmarks pages torn look at them Jack it was all over
before you found this out wasn't it, before you even went down to the hosp
. . ." (626). Tom places Jack back on the hook; and this, coupled with the
news from the IRS that he owes $28,000 on the stock given to his ex-wife,
leads to his more final withdrawal: he bows out of Amy's life, answering her
calls in the voice of "an old black retainer" (725) who tells her that Gibbs has

"clear[ed] out to a place yonder cal[led] Burmesquik" (725), the village of lost children. Unfortunately, this too has its consequences, and they seem not to match the happy ending of Gluck's opera, wherein the two-times dead Eurydice is restored to Orpheus.

Amy, as I have said, is a strong woman. She tells Jack at one point that "I've never done anything I thought wasn't right" (503), and one believes her. But she is not without her points of vulnerability. Like Jack (and so many other Gaddis characters), she is the child of an emotionally withholding father and has learnt firsthand the truth of the quotation, found among Jack's belongings, about "[g]rowing up as a difficult thing which few survive" (486). Amy has survived, yet when she returns from Geneva and finds that Jack not only refuses to see her but that he purportedly has been only toying with her—"dat ole Mistah Gibbs he a genuine rascal to play de ladies so" (725)—something in her breaks. In a reactive gesture, she marries Dick Cutler, the man urged upon her by her father, and the same man she once thought a union with would be "like marrying your issue of six percent preferreds" (214). It is, in short, a mistake, one that finds its antecedents in the failure to trust, on the part of not only this or that individual but the whole community. There are, at novel's end, events that ameliorate the sadness of this scenario, including Amy's decision to take responsibility for her retarded brother's well-being, and Stella's decision to seek Jack's forgiveness for past hurts.[32] Still, the failure of Amy and Jack's relationship to get off the ground is, I think, one of the more regrettable consequences of, as I say, a larger failure.

That Which Is Worth Doing, or Responding to Ought

Both Jack and Amy act in a way they ought not. This seems clear, but where does this sense of an ethical imperative originate? Geoffrey Harpham, discussing ethics and the novel, comments that the "is" of instrumental reason puts all sorts of pressure upon the "ought" of ethics: "At the dead center of ethics lies the *ought*" (18). In *J R*, meantime, instrumental reason certainly puts the ought to a tough test. For instance, J R's "that's what you do!" (659) appears almost the operating rule, with scarcely an acknowledgment of an obligation outside that of the expedient. Or as Davidoff, working under J R, puts the matter, success requires "see[ing] how things are not how they ought to be whole approach is what works" (530). Nevertheless, there remains a sense that the realm of *ought* will not go away. "America" may have, as Jack writes in his manuscript, "sprang full in the face of that dead philosopher's [Aristotle's] reproach to be always seeking after the useful does not become free and exalted souls" (571), but some individuals still hold to the belief that some things are worth doing more than others, and not

necessarily because they are useful. Music, Bast tells J R, is not a business—"Look I'm not trying to write tunes for money" (134)—and while its
exchange value is negligible, it remains worth creating: "It's just what I have
to do!" (134). Bast speaks more full-heartedly than Amy, who, while
wealthy, chooses to teach "just to have something to do, something alive to
do even if it's, even if I hardly know what I'm teaching them just following
the lesson guide but it's something it's, something . . ." (211). It is something, and while she expresses uncertainty, as later does Bast, one feels the
kinship between her need and Bast's. Both feel compelled to respond to an
order larger than themselves, one that makes demands upon them and is not
to be equated with immediate self-interest.

   In a historical place where, as Gibbs notes, there seem to be "so many
opportunities to do so God damned many things not worth doing," so many
opportunities to flout Thoreau's admonition "to live deliberately," what distinguishes Bast, Amy, and others like them (e.g., Schepperman, Schramm,
Gibbs, Eigen) from the majority is a readiness to listen, by which I mean
turning an ear to that which "opens the path towards a state of redeemed
utopian promise."[33] Here, listening entails a receptivity to that which is not
identified specifically with one's self or interests but which nevertheless, if
heard and attended to, immediately begins to direct one's self and interests. It
is, in this sense, quite like Lyotard's understanding of what it means to think:
"In what we call thinking the mind isn't 'directed' but suspended. You don't
give it rules. You teach it to receive. You don't clear the ground to build
unobstructed: you make a little clearing where the penumbra of an almost-
given will be able to enter and modify its contour" (19).

   It is with reference to this "almost-given" that Amy speaks when she asks
J R, as previously noted, "At the evening, the sky, the wind, don't you ever
just stop sometimes and look? and listen?" (474). This "almost-given" also
pertains to that which Bast rightly believes Stella will not understand in his
opera: "I said you wouldn't understand it anyhow that's why I, what it's
about that's what this is about if you'll listen . . ." (72). But neither J R nor
Stella is a listener. Of course the novel's last words are J R's, "So I mean listen I got this neat idea hey, you listening? Hey? You listening . . . ?" (726),
meant for Bast, but heard only by the reader as they pour out of a dangling
telephone receiver. In a sense, they *are* meant for the reader, for their meaning transcends J R's specific utterance, as if the novel or novelist were speaking through J R directly to the reader, asking whether this person has been
truly listening. This may be what characters and narrative always do—mediate the exchange between author and reader—though things here seem more
direct than usual.[34] Meanwhile, to the degree that this is simply J R speaking,
the word "listening" has a different meaning than it has when used by either
Bast or Amy. That is, for J R, it is a more self-directed matter, as in "Are you
listening to me?" This is not surprising, for the child has largely been ignored

by his elders, so for him to ask that Bast or anyone else listen to him seems the right thing to do. Still, it speaks of a quite different sense of listening than that entailed in Bast's command that he listen to the Bach cantata:

—I don't care what it [the tape] was! I didn't know I had it I forgot I'd even sit still! Now listen. Once, just once you're going to listen to something that . . .
—No but ho . . .
—And stop saying holy shit! it's all you, you want to hear holy you're going to hear it wind the tape back, just once you're going to keep quiet and listen to a piece of music by one of . . . (655)

Bast's exasperation with J R perhaps gets the better of him, but it is not difficult to understand the cause, the simple failure of J R to take an interest in anything that does not offer an immediate payback. He appears deaf to the music and all efforts to imagine the world as a sacred place. Obviously, the choice of the word *holy* here is not an accident. Gaddis is not a writer who relies upon accidents; he is probably our most deliberate writer, an author who, as he says, "even outline[s] paragraphs" (Grove, B 10). In addressing the question, then, of what is heard, we need to widen the discussion's parameters somewhat. I have already noted how Gaddis, in the motif of sight and hearing, looks back to Conrad, especially the Conrad of the preface to *The Nigger of the "Narcissus."* The motif has even more resonant biblical antecedents, notably the passage in Matthew 13.13–17 where Christ, quoting from Isaiah, explains why he speaks in parables:

This is why I speak to them in parables, because seeing they do not see, and hearing they do not hear, nor do they understand. With them indeed is fulfilled the prophecy of Isaiah which says:

"You shall indeed hear but never understand,
and you shall indeed see but never perceive.
For this people's heart has grown dull,
and their ears are heavy of hearing,
and their eyes they have closed,
lest they should perceive with their eyes,
and hear with their ears,
and understand with their heart,
and turn for me to heal them."

But blessed are your eyes, for they see, and your ears, for they hear.
Truly, I say to you, many prophets and righteous men longed to see what you see, and did not see it, and to hear what you hear, and did not hear it.

Hearing and seeing go together here, as they do in the Gaddis novel. So far, my textual references have focused more on the problem of hearing, but the novel offers just as many references to that of seeing. Repeatedly, we find characters whose sight is in some way impaired. These include Whiteback, who finds himself blinded by the sun, catching "him flat across the lenses, [and] erasing any life behind them in a flash of inner vacancy" (18); Coen, who is arrested for reckless driving after he breaks his glasses (150); Schramm, who puts out his eye in a freak accident with a pencil (182); Eigen, who experiences a "detached retina," something "practically unknown in medical [history]" (622); Angel, who shoots himself with a bullet "beside the eye" (669); and all the "one-eyed men" (576) spoken of by Gibbs in his manuscript, the pioneers of the Gilded Age whom Mark Twain saw "through a glass eye, darkly" (576).

In the art world, says Adorno, "[t]here is always the expectation of hearing the unheard-of and seeing the unseen" (196), but in the corporate world, as witnessed in *J R*, people like to see things straight on, as they are, the way in which Hyde—"I'm the only one around here with my eyes open" (462)—sees the threat posed to the white, middle-class community from African Americans: "Look Vern [. . .] talk about history you haven't seen history you haven't seen anything, Watts Newark you haven't seen anything yet wreck my car, clean out my house, rip off my watch rip it right off me right off my wrist" (462). Hyde's racism is seldom abated, though on one occasion, when he thinks the African American insurance representative, Stye, might, through the offering of a school board seat, be made to take a more sympathetic stance toward the school's claims, he does what he can, producing Vern's apt query: "All sounds a little like Saul on the road to Damascus Major, something blind you on the drive out here today?" (222). No such conversion has taken place, of course. Hyde simply sees things, as he has always seen them, "at the corporate level" (23). One other person who sees things this way is J R, our "man of vision" (661). For him, as with listening, sight always attaches to the realm of the cash nexus. If Bast tries to make him listen to a sound he cannot hear, it is only after J R has tried to make him "see" things he sees only too well:

> —No well *see* we'll keep that separate because I have to like discount these
> here tickets, you know?
> —No I don't know! look . . .
> —No but *see* that's what you do hey, *see* [. . .]. (135; italics added)

J R is trying to explain the concept of discounting, wherein the borrower pays interest in advance of a loan, the consequence of which is "he never ever *sees* it [the $1,000], *see* I mean like he loaned it off them only all they do they just take it out of this one pocket and like put it right back in this here other one I mean that's what discounting is, *see*?" (136; italics added). What one does *see* is how incompatible this sort of vision or value system is with one extolling the world's mystery and sacredness. Heilbroner writes, "Capitalism would be impossible in a sacralized world to which men would relate with awe and veneration, just as such attitudes cannot arise in a society in which exchange value has reduced to a common denominator all use-values" (135). Empathy for nature gives way to indifference, reverence to appropriation, so that the value of nature, or anything else, gets reduced to what it will fetch in the marketplace. Not surprisingly, then, morality—a system of principles necessarily abstract—is undermined. Heilbroner writes: "It is part of the nature of capitalism that the circuit of capital has no intrinsic moral dimension, no vision of art or idea aside from the commodity form in which it is embodied. In this setting, ideas thrive but morality languishes, and the regime of capital becomes the breeding ground for an explosion of ideational and esthetic creations that conceal beneath their brilliance the absence of an organizing moral force" (140).

Capitalism seeks to change everything into coin. Agapē, the love that God expresses for humankind, and that humankind is asked to emulate, is, in *J R*, capitalism's opposite. It expresses not the law's letter but its spirit; and if capitalism sides with distrust and discreteness, agapē sides with trust and the seeing of people and things sub specie aeternitatis. Agapē is also, as in *J R*, a "love feast" (605), which the dictionary defines as "(among the early Christians) a meal eaten in token of brotherly love and charity" or any similar "gathering of persons to promote good feelings." It is defined by Gibbs—"I'm the one who told him [Eigen] about agapē" (290)—simply by quoting Beethoven's belief that "the better among us bear one another in mind" (290). Finally, it appears to refer to the spirit—the "positive" matter/antimatter—located at the very center of one of history's most touching testimonies of a parent's love for a child, the Pietà. This we *see* if we conflate Gibbs's remarks about the "eta" particle with his remarks about his manuscript's title, *Agapē Agape*. The first are drawn from a discussion with Amy and relate to the particle's decay:

> you see it's both a particle and an antiparticle, it has no electric charge nothing to distinguish it as matter or antimatter, for every class of particle there should be its kind of mirror image antiparticle same mass and spin and an equal but opposite charge and this reaction they're talking about should produce fragments of equal energy but the positive ones are coming out more energetic than the negative ones, brings up the whole question of a basic lack of symmetry in our part of the univ . . .
> —And could you get your foot off the table Jack it hardly . . .
> —Only find one shoe yes but you see there might even be galaxies made of antimatter to balance ones like ours that are made of matter [. . .]. (485)

The second are drawn from Gibbs's attempt to suggest the importance of his manuscript's title to Rhoda:

—Man I [Rhoda] mean that's what I mean, like I mean if it says it why doesn't it say it? And I mean this is the name of the book agape agape? that's the name of it?

—Can't, look pē mark right over the God damned e pi eta pē agapē can't see God damn it? pi eta pē?

—Man like who's supposed to know piéta I mean . . .

—Didn't Christ! didn't say pietà whole God damn different Christ any God damned use look, book don't bring a God damned thing to it can't take a God damned thing from it [. . .]. (604-5)

In this later passage, Gibbs will go on to speak of why agapē's agape and of the Gordian Knot, making it clear that something also needs to be cut or solved here, whereby Gaddis, in Nabokovian fashion, says something without saying it. As suggested above, I think we particularly want to attend to the way in which this "positive" matter/antimatter particle—which sounds like a physicist's definition of God—resides smack in the middle of the Pietà. If this is a novel that both posits and resists the idea of the world as an orphan's place, this scene—wherein Divinity appears present in the mother mourning her child—functions as a sort of key, making clear how much the author wishes us to understand the responsibility of parents (or adults in general) to children in the light of a larger responsibility or ethos. This thought is also enhanced here by the presence of "pi," which, as Gibbs uses it, is, first, simply a sound offered to clarify the pronunciation of agapē's last syllable, but also, second, the symbol for the ratio of the circumference of the circle to its diameter (Derrida: "the symbol of the symbolic itself" [*Given Time*, 7]), a number (3.141592+) that stretches out to infinity, and that again functions as an apt metaphor for the intersection of the quotidian with the timeless.

Art as a Form of Perfectionist Thinking

Agapē makes its demands, capitalism its counterdemands. And if in *J R* their conflict remains unresolved, the pressure marshaled against all efforts to resist the law of capital also remains extraordinary. Those in the arts are not excluded from this pressure, even as they make all sorts of efforts to escape. "More than anything," Apollinaire wrote in 1913, "artists are men who want to become inhuman," even as circumstances stand in their way, as they do for all the would-be artists in *J R*. Eigen, for one, the author of "a very important novel" (389), finds it easier not "to compete with himself" (269) than to finish his play-in-progress, and what he has written seems too packaged and safe. Recounting Schramm's counsel to Eigen, Gibbs tells Bast the play lacks agapē: "[Schramm] told him to drop the first act it wouldn't change a God damned thing, told him it was undigested Plato, told him he

didn't leave the actors or director an inch to move in because he didn't trust
them told him the ending was too neat [. . .], writer who's run out of agapē
same God damned thing tell him Tom, squeeze the universe into a ball and
. . . " (282).[35] As Gibbs suggests, Eigen's Prufrockian side leaves him too
weak and self-pitying to do what is required, and that is to practice his art.
Eigen ill fits his part. Still, the countervailing forces do not make things any
easier. For instance, despite the critical acclaim his novel garners, his publisher does nothing to promote the book, even as he refuses to yield the
book's rights. As a consequence, this prize-winning novel remains, for the
longest time, available only in "a rare book dealer's for twenty dollars a copy
after" the publisher "remaindered practically the whole first edition" (269).
A paperback copy eventually does appear, though Eigen learns about it only
by coming across the book in a shop window. Meantime, the publisher grabs
what profits he can and moves on, offering only the most transparent excuses
to explain away his irresponsibility.

There are reasons for believing, with Bast, that "music's not a business"
(134), but in doing so, we ought to be prepared to acknowledge all the ways
in which it and all the arts in the United States are treated exactly as if they
were.[36] In fact, the arts here are quite frequently converted into coin. Note,
for instance, the way Thomas Bast kidnaps the musicians visiting his brother
and presses them into "cutting piano rolls" (63); the way Whiteback seeks to
make the "cultural drive pay off like never before in mass consumers, mass
distribution, mass publicity, just like automobiles and bathing suits" (19); the
way Davidoff, wishing to soften Typhon's big-business image through a calculated public relations gambol ("that big color spread we got on business
and the arts"[257]), pays $12,000 for a Schepperman canvas after Eigen
vouches that the artist is, in fact, a "name painter" (257); the way Typhon is
able to "subsidize name art and get a tax break at the same [time]" (195); the
way Zona, a practiced speculator, attempts both to create and then to corner
the market in Schepperman paintings, signing the struggling artist to a seven-
year contract that does not require that she exhibit the work (421); the way
Eigen's play, stolen by Gall, gets sold to Angel West for $1,500, then sold to
Angel East (which, like Angel West, is owned by Walldecker) for $100,000,
then produced with the hope of creating a tax loss, so that when, to the back-
er's chagrin, *The Blood in the Red White and Blue* proves a hit, they immediately pull it out of production (723). All in all, things seem little better than
in the days when Mozart could not command even $300 for his Concerto in
D Minor (112); and so if Eigen, whose royalty check for the novel proves to
be a paltry $57 (417), comes to believe, as Gibbs says, that things are "so
God damned real" that he cannot "see straight long enough to write a sentence . . ." (492), no one should be surprised.[37]

In this culture, the arts seem most "useful" not so much for what they
might say or express as for their exchange value. As Lyotard, observing the

contemporary scene, notes, "In the current state of techno-science and capital, the identification of the community with itself has no need of the support of minds, it does not require any shared great ideologies, but takes place through mediation of the whole set of goods and services exchanged at prodigious speed" (124). So if in former epochs a Socratic dialogue, a van Eyck nativity scene, a Shakespeare history play, a Mozart mass might all be thought of as expressive of something more exalting than free trade, here artists are required to do very little by the larger community. The artist need not, of course, acquiesce to the society's lower expectations. Both Gaddis and Lyotard enjoin the artist to do exactly otherwise: to resist the leveling and commodifying of the arts. Speaking of the pressure under which any contemporary painter works, Lyotard writes: "To the extent that this postmodernism, via critics, museum and gallery directors and collectors, puts strong pressure on the artists, it consists in aligning research in painting with a *de facto* state of 'culture' and in deresponsibilizing the artists with respect to the question of the unpresentable. Now in my view this question is the only one worthy of what is at stake in life and thought in the coming century" (127). It is a rare artist, not to say individual, who can resist the "demands of States (make it cultural!) and the market (make money!)" (128). One of the ironies this situation breeds is that this sort of success can sometimes be easier to achieve than what the same standard deems a failure. By this, I refer to public success and public failure, measurable in money and fame. Here, Jeff Koons and Madonna are successes, and William Gaddis a failure. The first two, despite their bad boy and girl pretensions, are too much the prisoners of society's demand that its more tawdry emotions and desires be reified; whereas the latter serves a different master, for which he perhaps pays dearly in coin—much in the manner of James Bast, whose "work is always money going out not coming in" (65)—but not in self-respect. In *J R* meanwhile, we find an equivalent of the Koons phenomenon "in the soaring steel sculpture Cyclone Seven," which, according to the newspapers, "promises to set precedents in art and insurance circles alike." The only thing that really distinguishes this "most outstanding contemporary sculptural comment [. . .] on mass space" (672), however, is its hype. So many—i.e., exhibitioners, critics, corporate money people, and fellow artists—seem to have a stake in its success, and then when a child gets caught in its clutches, these same interested parties come together to urge that the sculpture's well-being be given precedence over the child's. This gesture matches the culture's more general stance toward children. In any case, the prevailing argument, as made by the attorneys for MAMA (Modern Allies of Mandible Art), is that no harm should come to this "unique metaphor of man's relation to the universe," so movingly evident in "the arbitrary arrangement of force and line that pushes Cyclone Seven beyond conventional limits of beauty to celebrate in the virile and aggressive terms of raw freedom the triumphant dignity of man" (672).

"Society today," Adorno wrote in the 1960s, "has no use for art and its responses are pathological" (22), a judgment reiterated in *J R*. "Cyclone Seven," for instance, qualifies as a success only for the reason that the community at large has ceased to care about what does and does not function as art. In effect, the community says to its artists, "You decide what is and is not good, and let us know. We will accept your adjudications, for our chief concern is not with art per se, but only that some works be esteemed more valuable than others, in order that they might be more swiftly transmuted into coin." To their credit, some artists refuse the offer's terms, but others do not. Among the latter is the creator of "Cyclone Seven" who, with his sculptural Rorschach test, only furthers the diminishment of art's role in the community. The community's estimation of art (never high to begin with) declines because its own interests lie elsewhere, and too many artists acquiesce to its ethos (which the community itself recognizes as materialistic and self-interested).

Not surprisingly then, in *J R*, the larger community seems uninterested in, if not disdainful of, its artists. Examples abound: there is Hyde who, when told that Schepperman has been selling his blood in order to afford paint, says, "Fine let him! Who asked him to paint it [his work] anyhow!" (48); there is Rhoda who, as we have seen, offers a similar rebuke, asking Gibbs, "who asked you to write another one [book] anyhow" (605); there is Governor Cates who, responding to Schepperman's painting, says, "Don't match the carpet don't match the walls don't match a damn thing" (110); there is Zona who, while thinking of herself as Schepperman's patron, believes that she has "seen monkeys do better" paintings (421); there is Crawley who, wishing to "help along a struggling artist," commissions Bast (for $200) to write "Zebra music" (206, 202); there is Coen who thinks that artists are "notoriously impractical" (357); there is Schramm's father who thinks all writers "sissies" (246); and there is Davidoff who tells Bast, "wrote a novel once myself you know, maybe a little jealous of you boys with a knack for the arts luxury I can't afford never finished it, couldn't just sit on my butt and indulge myself like that" (540).

This final comment raises, again, the question of whether the artist does not withdraw too much from society. Bast is sensitive to the charge, especially as it comes from his cousin Stella, who forces him to rethink the significance of his studio as a retreat wherein he can "shut it all out so" (70). Not too much later, Bast tells Amy of what he now takes to be his own youthful romanticism: "I was laughing at myself when I was young, at what I thought all composers were like I'd read something about Wagner somewhere, about how he couldn't stand books in a room where he was working and how he stroked soft folds of cloth and scent, he liked attar of roses and someone sent it to him from Paris, that's what I thought it was like all silk, silk and attar of roses" (111). This is immediately followed by talk of Wagner's fear of the

garden path, which Amy, retelling the story for the benefit of Gibbs, a new
arrival, begins:

> —Oh and the garden path yes I forgot, that he couldn't concentrate if he
> looked out and let his eyes follow the gardens paths because they led to an out-
> side world, to the real . . .
> —Led in.
> —Pardon?
> —They led the God damned outside world in. (116)

It is not quite clear what we are to make of the distinction here between
the garden path's leading the artist out into the world and its leading the
world into the studio. It first seems that Gibbs offers his correction based on
a greater intimacy with the Wagner story. But, in fact, Amy's telling of the
story, picked up from Bast, is a more faithful rendering of the story as told by
Ernest Newman in *Wagner: As Man and Artist*. Newman writes that Wagner
"could not endure even books in the room he was working in, or bear to let
his eyes follow the garden paths: 'they suggested the outer world too defi-
nitely and prevented concentration.'"[38] Newman's telling is in line with his
criticism of Wagner for "expound[ing] the doctrine of renunciation from the
centre of a bower of satin" (134). Gaddis, too, wishes to criticize Bast's
desire to shut the world out, and we are reminded several times of just how
young and romantic he is. But if Bast is at first too anxious to place a wall
between his studio and the world, we do not, as I stated earlier, wish therefore to extol the Ninety-Sixth Street apartment and its entropy as a solution
to the problem of the artist vis-à-vis the world. Rather, we might liken Bast's
situation to that of *The Recognitions*' Wyatt who also wished to "lock it ['the
whole world'] out," yet who was wisely answered by Fuller, "Seem like such
a measure serve no good purpose, sar. Then the mahn lose everything he suppose to keep, and keep everything he suppose to lose" (347). One does not
lock out the world, but one does not let it flood in either. At this point, Bast
has learnt the first lesson but not the second. This, I think, explains Gaddis's
reorienting, via Gibbs, of the Wagner story, for he wants us to attend to the
way in which the world's multitudes, having no other place to go, can, if the
artist is not careful, come "pounding down the garden path" into his or her
life (117). Later, Hyde will seek to ask Whiteback a question "before Vern
leads you down the garden path" (454), a scenario suggestive of what sort of
guests Bast can expect to—and does—entertain.

Here, the need of the modern artist for privacy appears crucial. Granted,
the world cannot, and must not, be shut out. Still, if modern art sets itself in
opposition to the larger culture's self-involvement, it also seems imperative
that a space be set aside in which the artist can work. The artist does need a
place, in Bast's words, "just to be alone so I [can] work" (364), so that if

money has any value for a Bast, Schepperman, and Schramm, it connects to the value of privacy and the freedom to work more or less uninterrupted. James Bast is, for instance, said to believe that "money buys privacy and that's all it's good for" (231). Or as his son, Edward, says to J R: "Look I just told you I did this to earn some money so I can do my own work" (305).[39] Were the culture set up along more utopian lines, there would be no need to separate means from ends. There might not even be a need for art. (Adorno: "If the utopia of art were actualized, art would come to an end" [47].) But it is not set up along these lines, and if the artist is often ensnared by the world of means—the way, for instance, in Marian's words, "[t]he great Thomas Eigen's talent" finds itself "thrown away in a stupid job because he has to make a decent living for his wife and son" (270)—this is not to be entirely regretted. While art does not seek to be one with the world as found, it does not seek to turn its back on it either. At the same time, this ensnarement is not to be taken as proof that the world as found is all, and that all attempts to hear an unheard music are vain and misguided.

In *J R*, as in all of Gaddis's work, the artist must live with the knowledge that "in the arts [. . .] one's best is never good enough" and identify, like Tolstoy's Fedya, with "the self who could do more" (604, 389). This is the perfectionist self, which, sensing that something is missing, seeks to find it, knowing, in the words of Stanley Cavell, that "perfectionist thinking" is itself "a response to the way's being lost" (*Conditions*, 55). It is what makes thinking something like "a stopping," a "finding a *way back*, as if thinking is remembering something" (*Conditions*, 55).[40] It is also what makes the artist's own self intrinsically so uninteresting. The artist is in quest of something beyond the self, and if this is not found in the work, no amount of personality will offset the failure. Just as Eliot reasons that "[i]t is not in his personal emotions, the emotions provoked by particular events in his life, that the poet [or artist] is in any way remarkable or interesting" (*Selected Prose*, 43), the belief here is that the artist is most true when he or she, in Lyotard's words, "bear[s] witness that *there is*," and "respond[s] to the order to be" (88). Accordingly, Bast speaks for more than himself when, addressing Rhoda's charge that he is "not very interesting," he protests, "Well why should I be interesting! I mean I want my work to be interesting but why do I have to be interesting! I mean everybody's trying to be interesting let them I'm just, I'm just doing something I have to do so I can try to do what I hope I . . ." (561).

Bast's "hope" is connected to a belief in something larger than himself, a belief—again to quote Lyotard—"that something will happen, despite everything, within this threatening void, that something will take 'place' and will announce that everything is not over" (85). And it is also connected to a belief that "[t]he music of the world is free to all" (*J R*, 283), there being "things only music can say, things that can't be written down or hung on a clothesline things that" speak, apophatically, of the ineffable (655). Still, this music requires someone to hear it, someone capable, in this "noisiest country that ever existed" (289), of, as Gibbs says of Freddie, "hearing things you didn't" (498). Bast tries very hard to be that person, that genius, even as he feels threatened by his own inadequacy, a feeling abetted by Stella who, in her allusions to James Bast's virtual adoption of Reuben, insinuates that the orphan son had the real talent. The insinuation, with its implicit betrayal, leaves Edward grasping for words:

> —That's what she said! Just the boy not the talent, that's what you meant isn't it Stella? Because there wasn't any talent that's what you meant isn't it? [. . .]
> —isn't it? The talent yes that he [Reuben] had it and I didn't that's what you meant when I, when you came out here and wouldn't even listen to what I'd . . . (141)

Stella has ulterior motives for her unkindness, having more to do with Edward's father than with him (716-17), but her rejection still seriously undermines the young man's confidence.[41] Edward has wanted to believe that he has, if not genius, at least talent, an understandable enough desire given his father's brilliance. It is Gibbs, at the Wall Street cafeteria, who speaks most fully of the elder's achievement: "that whining tenor part he gives Ulysses [in his opera *Philoctetes*] real stroke of genius, comes off as a real sneak the only man who's ever seen Ulysses clear whole opera's the God damnest thing I ever . . ." (117).[42] It is also Gibbs who in his preface to these remarks—"genius does what it must talent does what it can" (117)—most notably alludes to the Kantian conception of genius, which is so important to Gaddis's own work, and which Kant, in *The Critique of Judgment*, defined as "the innate mental aptitude (*ingenium*) *through which* nature gives the rule to art" (I.168). Here, genius is conceived to be both original, "a *talent* for producing that for which no definite rule can be given," and exemplary, not itself "derived from imitation," though it "serve[s] that purpose for others" (I. 168–69). What distinguishes genius is an ability to hear nature's music, an ability whose workings remain mysterious even to the auditor, for the reason that while intellectual and aesthetic achievement can embody genius, genius itself resists being reduced to precepts. Kant writes: "where an author owes a product to his genius, he does not himself know how the *ideas* for it have entered into his head, nor has he it in his power to invent the like at pleasure, or methodically, and communicate the same to others in such precepts as would put them in a position to produce similar products" (I.169).

Kant's statement recalls a brief allusion to Beethoven made by Gibbs: "Never compose in a room where there's a God damned piano Beethoven told Cipriani Potter because you may be tempted to consult it" (287). The suggestion is that the music somehow exists prior to its performance, even as its existence, in a more familiar sense, depends upon its performance. This

passage also has it own amusing analogue in a scene where a genuinely curious J R peppers Bast with questions about what conditions are required to
compose music and where does it actually come from, this right after Bast
has told him, "It's just what I have to do!":

> —I know, that's what I mean. [. . .] —hey? I mean when you're writing
> this here music do you need to be someplace with a piano or a horn or some-
> thing? or like can you make it up anyplace. Hey? Mister Bast . . . ?
> —What.
> —I mean when you make it up right inside your head do you hear it playing
> like? I mean if I think of some song I can like hear it playing only if you're
> making up this here music which nobody ever heard it before do you hear
> these here instruments playing like tee, boy I'm getting out of breath, like tee-
> dle leedle leedle right inside your head then you go write down these little
> notes? Or, or first do you think of all these little notes which you write them
> down then when you read them you get to hear . . . (134–35)

These are good questions, not easily answered. Still, I think the answer
for Bast, as for Gaddis, is that the music paradoxically exists, in one sense,
prior to its being heard, and, in another sense, only after its composition and
performance. In the first instance, it may be, as Geoffrey Harpham main-
tains, that "the belief that the work already exists is a useful, even essential
belief for the creator, who otherwise might be overwhelmed by the spectacle
of an infinite number of possible paths leading to a destination that itself
might be reconceived at any moment" (189). To go further with this suggestion, it may be that "[o]ne becomes a creator by persuading oneself that one
is not a creator in the pure sense, but only a superior listener, observer, servant[,]" that "[t]he narrative of the imperative is the necessary fiction" of art
(189). Or it may be that the music, in fact, does exist before its composition—the way, for instance, the rules of geometry speak of relations that
were extant even before Euclid. Gaddis approves of the idea and has confessed that "I'd like to think of it all, what's eventually completed and what
isn't, in terms of Samuel Butler's books 'coming to him wanting to be written'" (Kuehl and Moore, "An Interview," 6).

The notion that the music exists prior to the composition also ties in with
that of virtuality. In his interview with Thomas LeClair, Gaddis speaks of the
realized art object as exemplifying a "consistent entity of its own," alive in
the space of "unfragmented time" (52). It is a view reminiscent of Suzanne
Langer's contention that "[a]ll music creates an order of virtual time, in
which its sonorous forms move in relation to each other—always and only to
each other, for nothing else exists there" (109); and it is in this same vein that
Gaddis also contends, à la Pater, that all art aspires to the condition of music,
the "highest of the arts, totally abstract and ungraspable" (LeClair, "Missing

Writers," 52). Meanwhile, for Bast there is also the conviction that a composition hints at a more perfect completion, though ever deferred. And because this is so, there is something almost preferable about an unfinished work, for it remains open to the possibility of perfection in a way that a completed work—with all the determinations made—does not. This is what Bast, alluding to his father and the studio where they both work, tries to explain to Stella: "Well he, of course he did [i.e., worked in this same studio] yes I, because it's one place it's the one place an idea can be left here you can walk out and close the door and leave it here unfinished the most, the wildest secret fantasy and it stays on here by itself in that balance between, the balance between destruction and realization until . . ." (69).[43] Stella rejects Bast's notion of the studio "where a vision can exist unfinished with a life of its own till the moment" the composer puts down the last note (116), and the possibility of perfection vanishes. For her, it is too naive and romantic; and in a way, it is. Still, in another way, it is not. While music, like any art, exists within a realm of contingencies, there remains the hope that it bespeaks formal properties that are not only incommensurable with this realm but also more virtual. In any event, Bast makes a distinction between music's "real form" and the "message," as when he explains to Amy what is being asked of him by the producers of the "nothing music": "they [the producers] said they had three minutes of talk on a track or tape they needed music behind it but it couldn't have any real form, anything distinctive about it any sound anything that would distract from this voice this, this message they called it" (112). Bast, like Gaddis, puts much stock in form or design, believing with Kant that "the *design* is what is essential" (I.67). The argument, while currently not in great favor, remains strongly suggestive, as in Bast's attempt to explain his work to Rhoda:

> —Oh a cantata yes that's, it's a choral work voices and a large chorus with an orchestra, it's a sort of dramatic arrangement of a musical idea that . . .
> —I mean it's all this messy?
> —Yes well this is just the, it's like a sketch a painter does before he starts painting, to work out the form and structure so every note and measure will . . .
> —So like you never heard this, right? I mean how do you know what it even sounds like.
> —You don't yes that's one of the, you don't really know till you hear it performed that's one of the . . . (370–71)

To believe, as Bast does, that "every note and measure will" find their proper place is to believe that in art, as in morals, "is" needs to show itself respectful of "ought."[44] It is to define art not only in terms of its cultural and historical boundedness, but also as it seeks to "rise above" these limits (658), as it seeks, in Eliot's words, to "penetrat[e] to the core of the matter, . . . to arrive at the truth and to set it forth" (*To Criticize the Critic*, 144). Art, understood this way, has a strained relation with democratic institutions. It shows itself, in Gibbs's words, reluctant "to open the arts to Americans for democratic action" (289), believing that left to its own offices there is nothing that democratic capitalism "can't destroy" (658). Or as Bast in his Mozart lecture puts it, "democracy in the arts is all about" humanizing the genius of a Mozart, for "if we can't rise to his level no at least we can, we can drag him down to ours" (43, 42).[45] Nevertheless, the hope remains for Bast, Gibbs, and most of all Gaddis himself that the possibilities of art reach beyond the reproduction of the community's values. Obviously, art does not altogether escape such values. As Adorno notes, "While art opposes society, it is incapable of taking up a vantage point beyond it. Art's opposition is thus in part identification with what art opposes" (194). Still, the feeling is that art, at its best, is about opening possibilities rather than closing them down. "By their presence art works signal the possibility of the non-existent," says Adorno; "their reality testifies to the feasibility of the unreal, the possible" (192). So also believes Eliot: "What poetry proves about any philosophy is merely its possibility for being lived. . . . For poetry . . . is not the assertion that something is true, but the making of that truth more real to us" (Eldridge, 20). And, most significantly, so believes Gaddis, who speaks of a desire to escape the welter that transforms "the creative artist into a performing artist" (LeClair, "Missing Writers," 52).

The creative artist responds to an imperative, an "ought"; and though the nature of this imperative remains mysterious, it enjoins a formal response. As Harpham, speaking of the "creator" or artist's artist, observes:

> The only intention appropriate to the creator . . . is obedience to the strictly formal and self-justifying imperative imposed by the task of creation itself. The power of "form," conceived as a principled indifference to intentions or even to meaning as such, is absolute over the creator. An "artist's artist" is distinguished by her reverence for technical facility or formal competence, her respect for and curiosity about materials. The primary task of such an artist is likely to be the full exploitation of the medium—especially the solution of "problems" or the overcoming of "difficulties"—rather than the urgent communication of a meaning. (196–97)

J R's artists (Bast, Gibbs, Schramm, Schepperman, and Eigen) seem, much like *The Recognitions*' Stanley and Wyatt, to think of themselves as creators, drawn to the still point of a turning world. This is what moves Bast to speak of his studio as "the one place [. . .] where nothing happens," the antithesis "of all that out there . . ." (69). This is also what moves Gibbs (who thinks of his writing as the working out of a problem, the solution of which—even in its absence—is understood to exist) to say, "that's what any book worth reading's about, problem solving" (499). For them, Schepperman's canvas, a large abstract mural, appears, in Eigen's words, as "the one thing that's real in that whole God damn place [the Typhon office]" (408). What these artists, in effect, ask of art is that it disarm the viewer, that it leave him or her in some perpetual now, wherein the chaos of events is placed in relief by something more permanent. They do not anticipate that everyone will understand, especially those who live otherwise. Eigen himself, mistakingly, accuses Bast of not understanding that which motivates Gibbs, Schepperman, and Schramm:

> —Look Bast you don't have to understand nobody expects you to! What you just threw in that box on the sink nobody expects you to know what it [Gibbs's manuscript] cost him, nobody expects you to see what he saw there all these papers, these boxes what we saw here that painting back there [Schepperman's] it's magnificent, the way it looks right now it's still magnificent [after the old man upstairs has brought the ceiling down upon it] he's down on his knees picking plaster out of it nobody expects you to see what he saw there! what Jack saw, what Schramm . . . (725)

Bast does understand, however. He also understands, more than the others, that the creative artist needs, in some sense, to be a performative artist, particularly if by this we accent the need to get things done, to do the work. Granted, the work might somehow demand its writing, but until it is written, until, in the instance of music, it is performed, there is the strong sense that it does not exist. Or as Bast tells Gibbs, "there are some things you can't really write down especially simple things, they just have to be left for the performer and till the music's actually performed it doesn't really exist at all" (287–88). Gibbs will later admonish Bast about not "finish[ing] things" (383), and while it is at this point true, it is Bast, more than the others, who by novel's end evinces the greatest determination to get on with his work. Here, the catalyst is Duncan, who gave his life to his wallpaper business, only to see it taken over by the J R Family, but who also has enough acquired wisdom to tell Bast that he can, in fact, call himself a failure if he has "never done anything," never made the attempt (683). All the self-pity in the world does not make one an artist, nor is the artist's work the only thing worth doing. As Bast, recalling Duncan's counsel, tells Coen:

> I told him this morning I don't have to anymore I don't have to try to write music [. . .] —I never had to, it was just something I'd never questioned before I thought it was all I was here for and he, everybody thought that they thought I was doing something worth doing he did too but he, nothing's worth doing he told me nothing's worth doing till you've done it and then it was worth doing even if it wasn't because that's all you . . . (714–15)

No life is worth living unless someone lives it. Otherwise, a person lives in a world of perpetual deferral, a world wherein one refuses to acknowledge the authorship of one's own actions, in the false belief that life has yet to commence. Then this person awakens and realizes, in Gibbs's words, that "life is what happens to us while we're busy making other plans" (394). At the junior high school, Typhon and the J R Family, Gibbs, Eigen, and Bast, respectively, are found making other plans, and yet unbeknownst to them, their lives have already moved on.[46] The need is not necessarily to live one life rather than another, assuming each is honest, but to live and to commit to *a* life. If a person does this, the suggestion is that it will, in a kind of metaleptic reversal, begin to assume the aspect of necessity. It will turn out to be the life worth living, or the thing worth doing. Bast, in first realizing this, thinks that perhaps he has made a mistake in setting out to be a composer: "I always thought I had to write music all of a sudden I thought what if I don't, maybe I don't have to I'd never thought of that maybe I don't! I mean maybe that's what's been wrong with everything maybe that's why I've made such a" mistake (687). The mistake, however, was not in the dedication to that which he loved, the music, but in the dedication to that which he did not love, the J R Family. This is not to say that he was forever destined to write music. It is to say that it will seem that way if he goes ahead and lives the composer's life. Hence, if Bast's first impulse, after the Duncan conversation, is to throw away his composition—"Just, just throw it away it's, throw it away" (714)—his later, more considered act is to recover his papers from the wastebasket, determined to succeed or fail on his own terms: "No, no I've failed enough at other people's things I've done enough other people's damage from now on I'm just going to do my own, from now on I'm going to fail at my own here those papers wait, give me those papers . . ." (718). So, at novel's end, it appears much more likely that it will be Bast, rather than the others, who will see his work through to completion. Thus when Eigen makes his accusation respecting Bast's failure to understand, the latter can, Thoreau-like, testify to his determination to live life deliberately:

> —I mean until a performer hears what I hear and c⌐⌐ make other people hear what he hears it's just trash isn't it Mister Eigen, it's just trash like everything in this place everything you and Mister Gibbs and Mister Schramm all of you saw here it's just trash!
> —Listen will you, God damn it will you just go do what you have to and . . .
> —That's what I'm doing yes! (725)

3

Carpenter's Gothic's
Bare Ruined Choirs

> Things fall apart; the centre cannot hold;
> Mere anarchy is loosed upon the world,
> The blood-dimmed tide is loosed, and everywhere
> The ceremony of innocence is drowned;
> The best lack all conviction, while the worst
> Are full of passionate intensity.
> —William Butler Yeats, "The Second Coming"

Things Fall Apart

Like *The Recognitions* and *J R*, *Carpenter's Gothic* speaks of a culture where "the centre cannot hold," or hardly. It speaks in a tone noticeably more grim than before. The opening scene is particularly foreboding, a mood reflected as much in events' symbolic value as in the events themselves. Gaddis once said, in reference to his first novel, that "[e]verything I have observed has been only for its symbolic (simile) value" (Koenig, 80), a statement as applicable here as elsewhere. For starters, there is the dove, the traditional symbol of both peace and the Paraclete, which is, like a shuttlecock, battered about by boys who seem bereft of all innocence. Further along, there is the evening with its dying light, and then the season itself, the autumnal d   leading up to Halloween and the Day of the Dead. All of this enhances the mood of eclipse, of events moving toward completion or some bleaker end. Even the boys appear helplessly drawn to complete their capers at "the yellow dead end sign on the corner opposite the house where they'd end up that time of day" (1).

146

There is an incipient violence, a sense that things are unraveling. Evidence is everywhere, including the clock that has stopped (2); Billy's boots which are "falling apart" (3); the "hole" in his pants knee (3); the broken-down truck with its nonworking heater (3); Paul's "broken" car with its disintegrating flywheel (3); the stopped-up toilet (4); the house with the ceiling "ready to fall down" (6); and the city which, in Liz's judgment, is on its deathbed: "it's filthy, everything, the air the streets everything, and the noise" (7). Things are entropic, deteriorating, running down. Even the brilliant colored leaves are, finally, "reduced again to indistinction in this stained monotony of lifelessness" blanketing the back lawn (227). While the leaves' change might, elsewhere, signify the promise of renewal as well as death, the suggestion, as furthered by McCandless, is that this change symbolizes a larger change and disintegration, promising no later spring: "all those glorious colours the leaves turn when the chlorophyll breaks down in the fall, when the proteins that are tied to the chlorophyll molecules break down into their amino acids that go down into the stems and the roots. That may be what happens to people when they get old too, these proteins breaking down faster than they can be replaced and then, yes well and then of course, since proteins are the essential elements in all living cells the whole system begins to disinteg . . ." (228–29).

McCandless is but one character—albeit an important one—in the novel, and it is best to hold back from any identification of him with the author. The warning might seem unnecessary, except that, like those of Gibbs in *J R*, McCandless's pronouncements occasionally parallel views publicly expressed—few though they may be—by Gaddis himself. Still, like any good novelist, Gaddis is more than capable of holding together opposing ideas, and this is perhaps why the reader can feel the force, even threat, of McCandless's outlook without wishing to give in to it. McCandless is a man worn down by experience, who, like the hero in V. S. Naipaul's *The Mimic Men* (which McCandless is found reading), cannot quite offset his despair with his hope. The latter emotion, attached to a desire for order, appears too romantic, too untrue, and McCandless, at this point, seems almost more willing to acquiesce to a state of disorder than to fight it. Or as the relevant novel-within-the-novel passage reads: "*A man, I suppose, fights only when he hopes, when he has a vision of order, when he feels strongly there is some connexion between the earth on which he walks and himself. But there was my vision of a disorder which it was beyond any one man to put right*" (150). In the end, neither the Naipaul hero nor McCandless can justify despair as a response. Even if the world appears headed toward dissolution, meeting the situation without hope only insures that the future will be more like the present, and more likely worse.

In *Carpenter's Gothic*, hope and despair—and by extension, order and entropy—are in conflict. It is difficult to say that one wins out, though I see hope and order managing to eke out a small victory.[1] Still, we cannot speak of hope and order here without, again, conceding that they are inhabited by their opposites. As already noted, there is plenty of evidence to suggest that things are falling apart. Yet there are also efforts the other way. For instance, McCandless, despite his despair, spends his life cleaning up things. He spends a good portion of the novel doing just this in the room housing his books and papers. When asked by Lester, who has broken into the house, what he is doing, McCandless replies, "Cleaning things up. I came up here to get things cleaned up what about you" (125). Lester ignores the question, and wonders what things. McCandless tells him, "All of it. Everything" (125). Later, Mrs. McCandless remarks, to Elizabeth, on his inclination to be always cleaning up: "That's really all he ever does, isn't it [. . .] —and it's always once for all isn't it, to get things cleaned up once for all" (249). It might be, as McCandless says, that you "spend the first damned half of your life complicating things in that eagerness to take on everything and straighten all of it out and the second half cleaning up the mess you've made of the first" (230). Yet with McCandless, the need to impose order upon disorder has always been there and is not likely to go away. It is telling that in his last day with Elizabeth, after the morning break-in, it is McCandless who, without prompting, telephones the cleaning woman, Madame Socrate, to come and help clean things up: "en désordre, la maison oui . . . demain? tôt le matin, oui? certainement" (226).[2] Almost the last thing he says to Elizabeth is to mention this: "I, incidentally I called Madame Socrate she'll be here first thing tomorrow to, to clean up . . ." (245). Chaos may threaten and even strike, but the need to put things right, or in order, remains.

Others also try to impose an order on a recalcitrant reality. Paul Booth, for instance, is absolutely determined to make his business dealings cohere. For him, it always seems as if there is just one piece missing, that if he could locate and properly place it, he should master the situation. To do this, he thinks, requires an ability to see "the big picture" (18), to be capable of "some good clear hard headed thinking [. . .] to put them [the pieces] together" (39). The centrifugal forces, however, threaten to pull everything apart. Seeking to explain to Elizabeth the part the expensive flower crucifix sent to her hospitalized friend Cettie, Senator Teakell's daughter, plays in the puzzle, Paul says:

> Trying to get things together here look, getting things lined up everything's just about ready to fall in place so God damn many pressures why I don't try to tell you everything I don't want to upset you. Try to give you the big picture you take one corner of it and run, jump like I said you jump to some conclusion the whole God damn thing falls to pieces like these flowers, I send these flowers you jump to some conclusion we end up arguing about the flowers, see what I mean? (76–77)

Paul never gets the pieces to fit, though they do seem, less through planning than through brutish fortune, to fall into place for him at novel's end, when he achieves control of the Vorakers empire. For anyone else, the price of this ascendancy would be considered too costly, for it includes the deaths of his father-in-law, brother-in-law, and wife. And while there is no evidence that Paul seeks their deaths, he is, first and foremost, a confidence man who has married Elizabeth in the expectation of advancing his own interests and whose grief over his loss appears mitigated by his winnings. Meanwhile, if he has not engineered their deaths, he has known for some time what their deaths would mean to him. This is why Billy, sensitive to the possible reaches of Paul's machinations, seeks out the trust instrument, to learn what would be the consequences for Paul should Billy die before the forthcoming trust distribution:

> —It's the exact wording Bibb, I have to see the exact wording. I mean when I was talking to Adolph and I'm thinking like suppose something happened to me before this distribution and like where does that leave Paul, you and Paul. I mean your share by the time it comes through it won't be there and like if something happens to me he steps in and blows everything, could you look for it? now? I mean it's important. (175)

Unfortunately, Paul is one step ahead of Billy and has already squirreled away the trust instrument. So when Billy dies in the shot-down plane, and Elizabeth dies in her kitchen, Paul finds his position significantly reversed. No longer is he forced to supplicate Adolph, the trust's manager: "Look God damn it Adolph get one thing straight, you're working for me now I don't give one God damn what you think" (258). He becomes what he has longed to be, rich and powerful. At novel's close, he is seen seducing the very rich Edie Grimes, friend of Elizabeth and daughter of Grimes, the powerful successor to Elizabeth's father as head of Vorakers Consolidated Reserve (VCR). His seduction line—"you know? [. . .] I've always been crazy about the back of your neck" (262)—is the same line he first used on Elizabeth, also on the occasion of a funeral, that of her father (22).

Another character who would not like to see things fall apart, though for different reasons, is Elizabeth. More than once, she is spoken of as "the only thing that holds things together" (177). She is the center through which the axes of Mr. Vorakers, Billy, Paul, McCandless, Cettie, and Edie all intersect. Without her, they would be, more or less, strangers to one another, and there would be no story. However, this is very much a narrative wherein characters imagine their lives as either the locomotive or the caboose to a whole train of events, itself identified with one character or another, and exemplifying the Guarian notion that there are no more than six degrees of separation between oneself and the most distant stranger. Characters act and are acted upon, the way "Paul thinks he's been using Ude but Ude's been using him and Lester's been using them both" (236). Here, determinations never move in but one direction, and each character is as much determined as determining.

Meantime, Elizabeth, while vexed, holds onto the belief that things may be brought back to a more accommodating order. If the world refuses to cooperate, there is always her fiction which, fleshed out by her hopes and dreams, helps remedy the "sense of something missing" (247). "[H]ere in her hands at least," there remains "some hope of order restored, even that of a past itself in tatters, revised, amended, fabricated in fact from its very outset to reorder its unlikelihoods" (247). Beyond her fiction, there are all the hopes wrapped up in a domestic order. She herself has not been able to do much in the way of creating such an order: all her furniture, including the prized mar-quetry chests, is in storage, and is later auctioned off when Paul neglects the payments. Her situation is made worse by the fact that she and Paul are renters. She cherishes the house and would like to make improvements, including tearing out the wall separating the living room from the back porch, substituting an arch for the missing wall, and enclosing the porch in the fashion of a winter garden (14). But as things stand, she feels like an out-sider in what should be her own home. Thus when McCandless, insensitive to such needs, intrusively returns, Elizabeth feels even more dislocated, "looking round her as though for something to do, to explain her presence here in the kitchen, her own kitchen, her own house" (60). It is an almost useless gesture, for she can hardly think of the house as hers if no one else will grant the fact. Certainly, neither Paul nor McCandless does, though she yearns for at least one of them to see the connection between her longings and the house. Frustrated, for instance, by McCandless's continual disparage-ment of ordinary people and their dreams, she tries to suggest to him what the house means to her, if only potentially:

> Because when I woke up again that morning after I'd loved you and I knew you were in the house, I heard you cough downstairs and I knew you were here and it was the first time I, when I came up the hill that night in the dark and the lights were on and you were in there in front of the fire, sitting reading in front of the fire because it had never been mine, it had never been like coming home. Because we've never had one. Because Paul it was just a place to eat and, to eat and sleep and fuck and answer the telephone because he'll never have one, he'll never have a home and when I came down that morning and I knew you were here and I thought, and I felt safe. (244)

Elizabeth's hopes are intertwined with the house and the possibilities of domesticity. For her, the house is a good place to begin setting up a home, a place where she could feel safe, surrounded by family and cared-for objects. On the surface, it appears a simple thing to desire, and yet its true possibilities, Elizabeth fears, will always escape her. This helps to explain her fascination with the house as found, that is, Irene's house. Irene is the woman with whom McCandless shared the Hudson Valley house until she, frustrated by his stoniness, left both him and the house. Or so I conjecture. The details of McCandless and Irene's relation are in fact obscure, though the few that are offered seem telling. There are, for example, the surviving fragments —"anyone's fault, the last thing I, for you to believe me, what else to do" (31)—from what appear to be Irene's final letter to McCandless, since torn to pieces by him.[3] There are also the house and its furnishings, which have been left as they were for Paul and Elizabeth, and which bespeak a loving attention to detail and, in a larger sense, an enormously hopeful feeling for how a house might be a home. As Elizabeth more than once observes, it feels like a "petit musée," with the owner temporarily absent but sure to return. She tells Edie over the telephone: "No not yet we've just rented it, not from anybody I mean nobody we know but you'd love how it's furnished it's all, rosewood chairs and sideboards and the draperies in the alcoves all heavy silk lined and gold and the loveliest lamps and silk flowers I can't wait for you to see it it's just, c'est comme un petit musée, tout . . ." (33).

This "petit musée" exists as an alternative logic to that offered by McCandless, Paul, Grimes, Adolph, Teakell, Lester, Cruikshank, et al. The latter logic declaims its importance, bullying when it cannot persuade, and inveighing against its opponents in apocalyptic terms. The former speaks in a softer voice, but should not be dismissed. Clearly the difference has something to do with gender. Those identified with the former order—Irene, Elizabeth, Edie, Mrs. McCandless—are all female, whereas those identified with the latter are all male. It need not always be this way, but it is true that historically domesticity, a created value, has always been closely identified with women. For this reason, no doubt, domesticity has been long undervalued. This is unfortunate, for domesticity is one of our most valuable possessions, and we would greatly feel its loss. In any event, in *Carpenter's Gothic*, it is the appreciation of the house as home that links Elizabeth to Irene, and the two of them to Mrs. McCandless. In the first instance, there is the sense that the approximate agemates Elizabeth and Irene have an almost sisterlike relation. Certainly, they both seem to value the same things. For example, not only does Elizabeth take delight in the way Irene has furnished the house, but her own imagined addition—the winter garden—turns out to be Irene's own prior plan, as McCandless, unaware of the matter's importance, tells her: "She wanted to take this whole wall out, put in an arch here and glass the whole porch in with all the plants out there, kind of a wintergarden" (67). Irene and Elizabeth both love the house and invest it with their hopes. It is apt, then, that Mrs. McCandless, making a short visit at novel's end, should think that Elizabeth is Irene (Elizabeth herself thinks Mrs. McCandless is Irene). It is also apt that all three women should take note of the house's possibility as a home and pay it the compliment of either working to make it so or simply acknowledging what has been done. Just before Mrs. McCandless exits, she wistfully tells Elizabeth, "you have lovely taste" (252).[4] Finally, because Elizabeth is in some way very much like Irene, she can in a sense speak for her, as when she castigates McCandless for being blind to the other woman's hopes, so evident in the furnishings and overall domestic order:

> it was all your despair locked away in that room there with the smoke and the cobwebs, pouring a drink with that old man and his dustpan pretending there was some reason to get up in the morning? locked away from her hopes all out here in the open? The silk flowers and the lamps and the gold draperies all her own hopes spread out like she'd be back in the morning until they were mine, spread up there in her bed? (244-45)

Domesticity may be a delicate order, lacking the firepower of the more self-brandishing orders elsewhere in evidence. Yet it remains a crucially important order, and to ignore it would be a serious mistake. In *Carpenter's Gothic*, domesticity (a friend of the aesthetic) may be the most viable order about. McCandless himself is not as insensitive here as I have perhaps suggested. It is he who has left the house untouched, added the china dog (65), expressed the wish to see his books unboxed, and made plans for repainting the porch (67) and for cooking a veal scallopini dinner, something that Elizabeth says "I've only had [. . .] in restaurants" (171-72). Still, his most obsessive concerns take him far away from domesticity, to Zaire, to Smackover, to Rio de Janeiro, and to Papua New Guinea. Thus while his final promise to Elizabeth is that he will do what he can to stop the impending conflict over what are, as only he knows, spurious mineral fields in Africa, his overriding sense is that "[t]hings fall apart" and "the centre cannot hold."[5] His "vision of a disorder"—substantiated by the multiplying outbreaks of greed, rapacity, vengeance, and madness—pushes him to the point that he wishes to disengage himself from the larger world. As he earlier tells Lester: "I don't read the papers and I don't give one damn what's going on out there [. . .] I'm through with it, I've been around the ring twice and I'm not going round again" (138). McCandless, albeit more angrily, has come to believe with Thoreau that "[i]t is not a man's duty, as a matter of course, to devote himself to the eradication of any, even the most enormous wrong; he may still properly have other concerns to engage him; but it is his duty, at least, to wash his hands of it, and, if he gives it no thought longer, not to give it practically his support."

Yet as twentieth-century experience has repeatedly shown, as a like experience earlier did for Thoreau (if we identify slavery with "the most enormous wrong"), it is not ethically possible to wash our hands of a situation that has already been acknowledged as grievous. It is too late; the wrong has been recognized; and from this point we are judged—at least in a just society—by the actions we take to put things right. It is a mistake, then, to think it possible to stand on the sidelines, for there are no sidelines; we are implicated in a situation once it is acknowledged, if not before. In this sense, Lester is right when he tells McCandless, "You came up here to clean it up and you can't clean it up, you know why McCandless? You can't clean it up because you're part of it" (144). McCandless would step back from it all (i.e., the world's troubles), or clean it up, put it in order, and then remain apart from it. But while it is possible to clean things up and put them right, it is best not to think it done for the last time. Things do not work this way; the job is never finished. This does not mean that the urge toward order is self-defeating. It simply means that as long as there is something (i.e., a world) rather than nothing, the forces aligned with order will perforce need to do battle with those aligned otherwise. McCandless appears to acknowledge this at the end, with his promise to Elizabeth. It may not be a promise backed by great conviction, but it does accord with the way that McCandless has always conducted his life: toward putting things right.

Conspiracies, or Forcing Things Together

In his classic essay "The Paranoid Style in American Politics," Richard Hofstadter distinguishes between the "clinical paranoid" and the "spokesman of the paranoid style." The first tends to believe the world a hostile and conspiratorial place that directs all its animus "specifically *against him*" (4). The second, however, tends to be worried less about himself than about a way of life or culture. Millions will suffer if the conspiracy is not rooted out, and because this second type resists the imagined tyranny, he or she may feel a "righteousness" and "moral indignation" befitting the "unselfish and patriotic." As Hofstadter points out, the paranoid style has always had its proponents in the United States, as anywhere else. In earlier times, the object of fear might be the Masons, Catholics, or Mormons, but holding together these antipathies was the conviction that the threat came from outside the community. The proponents "felt that they stood for causes and personal types that were still in possession of their country—that they were fending off threats to a still well-established way of life in which they played an important part" (23).

   Something started to change halfway into this century, however. The threat is now seen as coming as much from the enemy within the community as from that without. There is a sense of dispossession, that one's country is being pulled out from under one. Hofstadter writes that for the contemporary representatives of the paranoid style,

America has been largely taken away from them and their kind, though they are determined to try to repossess it and to prevent the final destructive act of subversion. The old American virtues have already been eaten away by cosmopolitans and intellectuals; the old competitive capitalism has been gradually undermined by socialists and communist schemers; the old national security and independence have been destroyed by treasonous plots, having as their most powerful agents not merely outsiders and foreigners but major statesmen seated at the very centers of American power. Their predecessors discovered foreign conspiracies; the modern radical right finds that conspiracy also embraces betrayal at home. (23–24)

This brings us back to *Carpenter's Gothic*, particularly to Paul, who is convinced that conspiratorial parties are seeking "to destroy all our churches, our free press and our rights of assembling peacefully before God" (203). Of course, Paul is not above exploiting people's fear of conspiracies, and there are times when he puts an extra spin on his own deep-seated suspicions about the world so as to separate people—poor and uneducated—from their money or, more sinisterly, to use them to effect his own megalomaniacal designs. The campaign—Christian Recovery for America's People—that he promotes on behalf of Reverend Ude's church (if one can call it a church) is purposely launched "in these rural weeklies out in the boondocks all these hicks read anyway" (203). The less savvy the people, Paul reasons, the easier it is to take away their money, especially if one can persuade them that they "are witnessing the most satanic and unconstitutional attack on the very fundamentals of American freedom, the dark beginnings of a Marxist dictator state casting the shadow of the powers of darkness over the entire world" (204). Still, if Paul exploits the fears of those less knowing, his own knowingness is only slightly less paranoid. Among the things he believes are that Victor Sweet, the African American senatorial candidate, is in collusion with the KGB (97); that big business and the federal government are controlled by the same people (206, 44); that the country is manipulated by a Jewish-controlled, liberal media (105); that the nuclear freeze movement is a euphemism for appeasement (215); that the FBI and the federal marshals are, by design, determined to destroy Reverend Ude (215); that the federal government is in collusion with marxists (215); that all Vietnamese are "gooks" (24); that McCandless is "a God damn traitor" (75); that secular humanism is a threat to both the Constitution and religious freedom (103); and that the Vatican, under the guise of a "big God damn third world peace offensive" run by the Jesuits, has designs on Africa (212). For Paul, the enemy is everywhere. The evening he returns to the house after having been mugged ("A spade of course it was a spade!" [200]), he launches into a tirade about how "they," or the "same God damn bunch," are after Reverend Ude:

—can't get him on that *they* want to kill his tax exempt status, bottling plant sending out this Pee Dee water join his Pray for America club he suggests a ten dollar donation *they* say he's running a profit making business that's where *they* bring in the FDA, *they* all know each other that's how it works down there. That's what Washington is *they* all know each other, get one of them he's penetrated the IRS calls his buddy at FDA and *they* dig up a couple of cases of typhus out in the boondocks, seize their mailing list send out agents in Georgia Arkansas Mississippi Texas digging up typhus nobody told them to drink the Pee Dee water, a lot of God damn ignorant people out there see a bottle *they* open it and drink it that brings in the Post Office Department and the FCC, *they* all know each other. (206; italics added)

For Paul, the aim is to get a handle on how the ubiquitous "they" operate, how they pool their resources together to make one formidable enemy. Repeatedly, he attempts to get the "pieces [to] fit together" even as there are "just too God damn many pieces" (212). Paul feels his own limitations here, but believes that the conspiring "they" move about unimpeded, that their reach has "penetrated right down to the county level" (212). The enemy is like that for Hofstadter's paranoid, "a perfect model of malice, a kind of amoral superman: sinister, ubiquitous, powerful, cruel, sensual, luxury-loving. Unlike the rest of us, the enemy is not caught in the toils of the vast mechanism of history, himself a victim of his past, his desires, his limitations. He is a free, demonic agent" (31). Such are the powers, for instance, that Paul attributes to the Belgian syndicate whose members, Paul tells Elizabeth, have "Grimes in their pocket," who in turn has Teakell in his pocket, who in turn is nicely fixing things up—for instance, the investigation into unfair business practices—in Washington.

Not all the relations that make Paul anxious, and to which he attributes conspiratorial motives, are necessarily imagined. The Belgians probably do have Grimes in their pocket, as he has Teakell; the federal government's branches do intersect not only with one another but also with the offices of big business and law, where many a pensioned government employee finds a lucrative second career; and the Catholic Church, under Pope John Paul II, has demonstrated an interest in the harvesting of African souls. In fact, a notable feature of the conspiracist temper is its rationalistic tinge, its belief that everything holds together, that everything makes sense of a sort, albeit demonic, and that it can be understood and explained. While to an outsider all of Paul's ascriptions might appear a madman's ravings, the real difficulty is not that they lack coherence but that they are too coherent. As Hofstadter explains the temper: "the paranoid mentality is far more coherent than the real world, since it leaves no room for mistakes, failures, or ambiguities. It is, if not wholly rational, at least intensely rationalistic; it believes that it is up against an enemy who is as infallibly rational as he is totally evil, and it seeks to match his imputed total competence with its own, leaving nothing unexplained and comprehending all of reality in one overreaching, consistent theory" (36–37).

These judgments are themselves not disinterested. Hofstadter, Gaddis, and *Carpenter's Gothic*'s readers are likely to identify themselves in one way or another (e.g., through social class, education, careers) with mainstream American culture, even with the establishment. Yet the logic of this culture is very much at odds with that of Paul, and certainly with that of the Reverend Ude and his flock. The latter's logic, if not thought a mania, is confidently dismissed by the mainstream as "rationalistic," i.e., as having only the semblance of rationality. I pretend not to take a different stance. Still, it is useful to acknowledge one's own position and to grant that what appears rational to one community can appear complete madness to another.[6] Also, it seems especially important in the present instance to urge caution for the reason that many of the readers who discount Paul's fears are, simultaneously, likely to embrace McCandless's. Yet while I wish to differentiate McCandless from Paul, and even to admit a preference, we should note their similarities. Like Paul, McCandless also appears unusually gripped by a demonic other that he would like to exorcise from the American mosaic. The object of his fears is not godless marxists or secular humanists, but those working either in or at the edges of the military-state-industrial complex, most notably the large operators and smaller field agents typified by Grimes, Adolph, Teakell, Cruikshank, and Lester. (Cf. Gibbs's emotions, in *J R*, about the Larchmont millionaire [496].) In addition to these, McCandless also fears the radical right, especially the Christian fundamentalists.

McCandless's fears will strike many, this reader included, as not out of bounds. His suspicions of Western mining interests in Africa, and his conviction that they work hand in hand with United States military and intelligence operatives, do not appear ludicrous. In the postwar period, United States industrial and political strategies vis-à-vis Africa have been interventionist in nature. The reason is that, following the war, Africa's mineral wealth came to be seen as a prize that could not be allowed to fall under the influence of the Soviets. David N. Gibbs, in his excellent book *The Political Economy of Third World Intervention: Mines, Money, and U.S. Policy in the Congo Crisis*, notes how during the Truman administration what had been a strong anticolonial policy began to be something different:

> The Cold War came to dominate Africa policy during the Truman presidency, while anticolonialism, which had previously characterized U.S. policy, diminished or disappeared entirely. Declassified documents confirm that the United States pursued procolonial policies during the late 1940s and 1950s. The Belgian Congo in particular was now regarded favorably, as an anticommunist bastion and as a supplier of strategic raw materials. American officials opposed independence, fearing that it would threaten the security of the minerals. Indeed, the United States offered financial support for colonialism. The USA provided aid through the Economic Cooperation Administration, which administered the Marshall Plan, while the Export-Import Bank and the (U.S.-domi-

nated) World Bank issued loans. These pro-Belgian policies continued during
the Eisenhower administration. Documents from the Eisenhower presidential
library indicate a continued, and even intensified, procolonial policy. (65)

What the postwar period particularly offered, in Brian Urquhart's words,
were "postcolonial power vacuums" (46). The French, English, Belgians,
and Portuguese no longer had the resolve that they once had to maintain
colonial regimes in Asia, Africa, and the Middle East. As they retreated, the
now powerful United States and Soviet Union saw opportunities and, as they
understood matters, obligations to step in. The Suez Crisis in 1956 was, says
Urquhart, a significant watershed, "dramatically marking the demise of the
traditional British and French influence in the Mediterranean and the Middle
East. That historic role vanished overnight, and as a result both the United
States and the Soviet Union became increasingly concerned with the effects
of decolonialization in the Middle East itself, in Africa, and later on in
Indochina" (46). The upshot, as we know, was that for several decades the
United States and the Soviet Union engaged in a series of proxy wars, many
of which, unlike the Vietnam War, were fought with great secrecy. They were
hidden wars, wherein the real combatants appeared, to borrow Adam Smith's
metaphor, very much like invisible hands.

The United States and the Soviet Union, from their perspectives, had
every reason to take a new interest in sub-Saharan Africa. The mineral
deposits were extraordinary, and neither side wished to see this wealth pass
into its enemy's coffers. In 1960, United Nations Secretary General Dag
Hammarskjöld, sensing the gravity of the situation, made something of a
plea, saying, "Africa is part of the world which at present is outside the conflict, the competition, the Cold War . . . under which we are all suffering at
present, and I would like to see that part of the world remain outside"
(Urquhart, 56). The plea went unheeded, however. U.S. and Soviet interests
were considered too strategic, and when the Belgians acceded, in 1960, to
the Congolese demands for independence, the competing interests of the
Americans and the Soviets succeeded only in complicating the whole process
of independence. Urquhart writes: "From the start, a major problem for the
UN in the Congo was the anxiety of both the United States and the Soviet
Union about the strategic control of this important and rich country. The
Soviet Union did not want to see the Congo fall completely under American
domination, and the United States had no intention of allowing it to fall
under Soviet domination. Thus, in addition to all the other problems of the
Congo, something like a proxy war—a war of secret agencies, the KGB and
the CIA—was soon going on for what was left of the hearts and minds of the
Congolese" (51).

One event that led to so many others, including the American and Soviet
interventions, was Katanga province's attempt to secede from the Congo.

Katanga represented the heart of the Congo's mineral wealth, and it was where the infamous Société Générale de Belgique most powerfully operated. As Gibbs notes, in 1960 the "government of Katanga . . . was really a joint stock company, partly owned by the Compagnie du Katanga, an SG affiliate" (60). The secessionist move was, then, an attempt by Western interests to extract the heart of the matter. It was about this time that the London *Metal Bulletin* wrote, "it would be asking too much to expect—human nature being what it is—that anybody is going to overlook the fact that the immense mineral riches of Haut-Katanga represent a really 'glittering prize'" (Gibbs, 103). It was sadly true. Thus when the United States, in the last days of the Eisenhower administration, supported the secession attempt, instability in the Congo increased and the Soviets found it necessary to intervene (Gibbs, 144). The immediate consequence was that "[t]he original government split up after two months, the West backing Kasavubu [president of the Democratic Republic of the Congo] and Joseph Mobutu, and the East backing Lumumba; Lumumba was murdered in early 1961; and after many vicissitudes Mobutu came to power, apparently for life" (Urquhart, 51).

The sinister dealings of American corporate and state interests vis-à-vis Central Africa have been on Gaddis's mind for a while. In *J R*, Governor Cates brags about how he has the situation under control in Gandia (a fictitious country resembling the Congo, facing a Katanga-like secession that is being promoted by a lot of behind-the-scenes work on the part of Western mining and financial interests):

> Pythian's interest in Typhon is nobody's damn business, got [General] Blaufinger coming in here this morning and that whole situation in Gandia should be cleared up in a week or two, had Nowunda up there on the platform when [General] Box gave the groundbreaking speech and Doctor Dé declared the secession of Uaso province same night, Nowunda sending in troops but there's not a damn thing he . . . No, talked to him on the phone, won't see us intervening to support that red regime of Nowunda with all the . . . what . . . ? Yes worked so damn well even got peace groups wearing signs keep out of Gandia and Africa for Africans [. . .]. (427–28)

Governor Cates does not give a damn about the politics of the Patrice Lumumba-like Nowunda, though he knows that, given his Soviet backing, the Gandian leader will refuse to be a puppet of Western interests. Accordingly, he marshals all his weapons. These include encouraging the Moise Tshombe-like Doctor Dé to act as the leader of the secession; sending his topflight lobbyist Frank Black to the White House (428); and commanding Senator Broos to make an impassioned plea "in the Senate for self-determination for the people of this gallant little emerging nation" (Uaso province) as well as to sponsor "a bill prohibiting imports with Gandia as country of origin" (523). All these weapons are deployed despite "the UN resolution supporting Nowunda's government" (523). The weapons do, in fact, prove effective, so that after a period of strife and warfare, the Nowunda regime collapses and the leader flees (709). Nowunda meets a less dire fate than does Lumumba, whose murder was abetted by the CIA. Still, the final upshot is more or less the same: the country's wealth will be open to Western appropriation.[7]

In both *J R* and *Carpenter's Gothic*, Gaddis is also attentive to how Cold War tensions constitute a cover for a second conflict between European and American corporations over Central Africa's mineral wealth. In the latter novel, for instance, McCandless is quite savvy to the fact that Western intervention in Central Africa has, historically, had less to do with our fears of communism than with the protection of corporate interests. Look, says McCandless to Billy, brandishing the statistical evidence that makes clear how dependent both the United States military and industry are on Central African mineral deposits: "Over there sitting on half the world's diamonds and chrome, ninety percent of its cobalt, half the gold, almost half the platinum, the whole length of the copper belt and that huge bauxite deposit at Boké in Guinea" (189). In addition, there are "[v]anadium, platinum, manganese, chromium[, . . .] four key minerals to our industry and defense" (190). McCandless's statistics are not imagined. At approximately the time of the narrative, according to *U.S. News & World Report*, Africa accounted for a startling proportion of the U.S. mineral and other imports: "100% of industrial diamonds; 58% of uranium; 48% of cocoa; 44% of manganese, used in producing steel; 40% of antimony to harden metals; 39% of platinum; 36% of cobalt, for jet engines and high-strength alloys; 33% of petroleum; 30% of beryll, used in weapons and nuclear reactors; 23% of chromite, used in gun barrels; 21% of columbium-tantalium, for heat-resisting alloys in missiles and rockets; and 21% of coffee" (Offiong, 181–83). No wonder, then, that Cruikshank, first as a CIA station chief and then as a Vorakers Consolidated Reserve operative, should, in McCandless's words, seek "to recolonize the whole continent[, . . . to] take it back a hundred years when Europe cut it up like a pie and they all took a piece" (142). No wonder that those who have spent time in Central Africa should think of "Vorakers Consolidated Reserve like the name of a country," for "it's bigger than most of them, [and can] buy and sell half of them out of its back pocket" (229).

In *Heart of Darkness*, Joseph Conrad wrote, "The conquest of the earth, which mostly means the taking it away from those who have a different complexion or slightly flatter noses than ourselves, is not a pretty thing."[8] The ugliness, while it has changed its face, has not subsided. McCandless can therefore make the argument that the United States's staunch support, in the 1970s and 1980s, of South Africa was part of this continuum, for he conceives of the U.S. policy of "constructive engagement" as little more than a fig leaf disguising patent economic interests. The South African and United States governments may speak loudly of their fear of the Soviets, but this fear, while not unreal, functions more as a smoke screen for policies that are rapacious and often murderous. Or as McCandless says to Billy:

> the cause of unrest anyplace in the world you find it [in the Soviets] no, take a look at every country bordering South Africa you'll see who's doing the destablizing. They've got no damned rights at all in Namibia but who's making them leave, diamond fields running up the west coast but that's not why they're there oh no, no no no they're holding back the powers of darkness up in Angola going right in there and shooting to kill. This great global Marxist conspiracy behind every insurgent movement, who recruited these wretched Ndebele for this secret Matabele brigade to destabilize Zimbabwe handing them over to rape, torture, murder by the Shonas. Who set up the Mozambique National Resistance Movement in the Transvaal when Rhodesia went down, want to write to them they're at Clive Street, Robindale, Randburg, want to see a reign of terror see them raiding into Mozambique beating, raping, disfiguring the locals, teachers, health workers all the forces of darkness and the whole rickety thing collapses, Mozambique's brought to its knees like Lesotho, there's a country as big as your hat and they've ground it right into the dirt but a hundred and fifty thousand of them cross the border to work in the mines and it's that or starve. (189–90)

All the while, says McCandless, "we're right in there cheering them on" (190).[9]

McCandless's fears, unlike Paul's, seem bound up with fact. He is not mad, as Cynthia Ozick (18) and John Johnston (211) suggest, or suffering from paranoia. Rather, he is, as Billy observes, simply "pretty wound up" (192), exercised by his country's engagement in economic colonialism and the fact that those in the know represent the endeavor as an honorable defense of freedom, and those not in the know, including most Americans, should be so incurious as to what practices underprop their material well-being. It is not that he believes that Americans are by and large bad people. Rather, like Gaddis, who sees in the United States "a country of decent people who do terrible things" (Grove, B 1), McCandless believes that Americans help perpetuate what must be understood as genuine evils—e.g., economic subjection in third world countries—less out of guile than out of innocence and thoughtlessness. He tells Elizabeth, in what becomes something of a refrain, "There's much more stupidity than there is malice in the world" (118).[10]

Earlier, I linked McCandless with Paul, stating that they are preoccupied with their fears. It should, however, be clear not only that I think the former generally an honest and good man and the latter the opposite, but that I give greater credence to McCandless's fears than I do to Paul's. I can see how some might, as I do not, see McCandless as a promoter of baseless conspiracies. But I would counter the charge by arguing that McCandless, the beneficiary of a fine intellect and atypical life experiences, sees things that the majority does not. For the latter, the connections between, say, Cold War politics and colonial economics remain obscure, if not invisible. To them, McCandless (who vigorously argues the existence of these connections) must appear almost crazed. He is not, for his fears have an evidentiary object. This does not make his harangues any more attractive. Still, it does mean that we can distinguish between his claims and Paul's. If the former is not a conspiracy monger, the latter is, for his claims lack evidence. The determination is, as said above, reflective of the interests of those judging, though it does not necessarily reduce itself to these interests.

McCandless is something like the classic American Adam, taciturn and somewhat alone in the world but also possessing unusual hands-on knowledge and a reservoir of kindness that waits to be tapped. To state this is also to suggest his weakness, the kindness that has retreated, fearing that the world requires a tougher front. This behavior speaks of a certain skepticism, maybe even cynicism. It also connects to McCandless's own blind spot, one that Elizabeth calls to his attention. She rightly tells him, vis-à-vis his contempt for religious fundamentalists, that among the things he despises is their hope: "you despise their, not their stupidity no, their hopes because you haven't any, because you haven't any left" (244). McCandless is smart enough to recognize the charge's truth, and thus matters are not altogether hopeless. Still, there are realms of feeling and experience that remain largely invisible to him. Included among these are people's need to believe that their lives make sense, not only in a day-to-day way, but also in a metaphysical or religious sense. McCandless's indictment of the religious right, while often pointed, fails in a way that his indictment of the corporate state's exploitation of the world's poor does not. Yet because the theme of religion, as it encourages hope, both false and otherwise, is an important one, I would like to hold off its discussion to a later section. Meanwhile, I would like to turn briefly to a discussion of the motif of "inside/outside" that figures so prominently in the novel.

The Complement of Inside and Outside, of Truth and Fiction

In *Carpenter's Gothic*, Gaddis repeatedly employs, as well as deconstructs, the opposition between inside and outside. For starters, it is a novel, unlike the first two, that seems almost classical in its respect for the unity of time and place. "When I started I thought," says Gaddis, "'I want 240 pages'— that was what I set out for. It preserved the unity: one place, one very small amount of time very small group of characters" (Grove, B 10). All the immediate action takes place in, or immediately outside, one Hudson Valley Victorian house, owned by McCandless and rented to the Booths. In the opening paragraphs, Gaddis speaks of, yet also questions, the division between outside and inside, something he does throughout the novel, particularly as he uses the motif of the open and closed door. In the opening scene, note the frequency of words such as "out," "in," "door," "open," "inside," "closed":

> Somebody hunched down, peering *in* where she'd stood staring *out* there a minute before, a line straight through from the kitchen past the newel to the front *door* fitted with glass, shuddering *open*. —Wait! she was up, —wait stop, who . . .
> —Bibb?
> —Oh. You frightened me.
> —He was *inside* now, urging the *door closed* behind him with his weight against it, bearing up her embrace there without returning it. —Sorry, I didn't . . .
> —I didn't know who you were *out* there. Pushing *open* the *door* you looked so big I didn't, how did you get here? (2; italics added)

Here, as elsewhere, Elizabeth's sense of threat is attached to something that comes from "out there." It may then appear somewhat ironic that despite the suggestion that danger comes from without—e.g., from the mean-spirited neighborhood boys, the intruders, the fire next door but meant for her house—Elizabeth's later death is consequent less on an intrusion from outside than on her own body's internal failing. Or is it? If I am right about the cause of Elizabeth's death, I would say that the situation might, in fact, be spoken of as one wherein outside and inside lose their qualities of discreteness. In a sense, her death does indeed come from something out there. Still, I will have to make my case for this later. At the moment, I think what can be said about Elizabeth's death—whether the reader suspects that it follows from a long-term ailment, a heart attack, injuries sustained in the plane crash, or even, as more than one critic has argued, from murder—is that a certain mystery will always attach to it, and that whatever the reader's ambition to separate the truth of the matter from its fiction, the latter will always render the former suspect.

There is a "very fine line between the truth and what really happens" (130). So McCandless told Lester when they were together in Africa. Lester reminds him of this, and McCandless picks it up again, to the point that it becomes a major motif. The suggestion is that truth easily gets lost, that no sooner do we take notice of an event then we start to place it in a new narrative or fiction. The fiction becomes the truth, and the truth the fiction. Then, as happened in both *The Recognitions* and *J R*, the question becomes whether all is not a fiction from which truth has fled, assuming it had ever been present. McCandless himself is conscious of how much a life begins to

resemble a fiction. This need not be a bad thing. In fact, it is an unavoidable
thing. As McCandless says, "this fiction's all your own, because you've
spent your entire life at it" (169). All lives have a fictive dimension, but not
all lives have a truth dimension—that orientation toward something beyond
the self and its interests which imparts to the life its feeling of necessity. This
necessity speaks of "who you are, and who you were when everything was
possible, when you said that everything was still the way it was going to be
no matter how badly we twist it around first chance we get and then make up
a past to account for it" (169). Fiction, thus understood, requires a consenting
reality, and reality depends on a marshaling fiction. This appears the gist of
the story McCandless tells about the gold:

> I told you [Elizabeth] they all thought I was crazy when they brought me in,
> when I said there was gold there, well I was. Two or three days out there roast-
> ing alive, drinking rusty water from the truck's radiator and I was delirious but
> I'd sworn to myself if I ever got through it that I'd remember what really hap-
> pened. That all that kept me from losing my mind was knowing I was losing
> my mind but that it was there, the gold was there. And when they found it
> twenty years later it didn't matter anymore [. . .]. All that mattered was that
> I'd come through because I'd sworn to remember what really happened, that
> I'd never look back and let it become something romantic simply because I
> was young and a fool but I'd done it. (168–69)

It would be tempting to read this as an allegory for Gaddis's own experience with *The Recognitions*, and the novel's initial failure to find an audience
or critical response comparable to the occasion. But the passage also functions as a crucial testimony (analogous to Wyatt's "Thank God there was the
gold to forge!" [*R*, 689]) to the fact that however much truth is obscured as it
gets figured and disfigured in its retelling, something real did happen. The
figuration of the real event may not be one with it, but it implies a third thing
(i.e., an equation of correspondence) by which this figuration is judged. This
third thing is elusive, but that does not stop the search. "[T]o recover what
had been lost and found and lost again and again (155)," says the narrator,
borrowing from Eliot's "East Coker," is an unending search, or narrative,
wherein presence and absence take turns canceling one another, and yet also,
paradoxically, confirming one another's existence. What the experience
means for McCandless and for Gaddis, whom I quote, is a truth that goes
"deeply enough to unfold, not the pattern, but the materials of the pattern,
and the necessity of a pattern" (Koenig, 81).[11]

McCandless is prepared to think of his life as a fiction but not as something romantic. Fiction and reality are interdependent. They exist in a chias-
muslike relation, wherein fiction speaks of—and, in effect, is—reality, and
reality, in turn, makes fiction possible. But for McCandless, the romantic
refuses this interdependence. It is autotelic, too satisfied with its own origi-

nality, which it assumes without antecedents. It is thus judged by McCandless as wayward and untrustworthy. This judgment is borrowed from Gaddis's prior fiction and, before that, from Eliot. One recalls, for instance, Herr Koppel's conflation in *The Recognitions* of romanticism with the disease of originality—"That romantic disease, originality, all around we see originality of incompetent idiots, they could draw nothing, paint nothing, just so the mess is original" (89)—and Eliot's belief that "as genius tends toward unity, so mediocrity tends toward uniformity" (*Varieties*, 52), as well as his belief that poetry is less about personality and emotions than an escape from them, for "only those who have personality and emotions know what it means to want to escape from these things" (*Selected Prose*, 43). McCandless shares this view and, when questioned by Elizabeth as to why he does not write about "the things only you know," says: "Maybe those are the things that you want to get away from" (168).

For those who "think if something happened to them that it's interesting because it happened to them" (158-59), McCandless professes contempt. Contempt is not an attractive emotion, and McCandless does not make it seem otherwise. Elizabeth therefore does well to correct him, reminding him that most of those whom McCandless condemns are, in fact, "doing the best they can" (159). He acknowledges the fact, and admits his error. Yet despite his harshness, the conviction remains that a poetics of personality is ill-advised, and that unless one is responsive to something more profound than personality, the life will seem shallow. Here, what is inside depends on what is outside, making it clear that one without the other would disappoint, something that Elizabeth realizes as soon as she tries to imagine what it might be like to look back in time through the lens of a telescope: "But you'd just see the outside though, wouldn't you. You'd just see the mountain you'd see it go down and you'd see all the flames but you wouldn't see inside you wouldn't see those faces again and the, and you wouldn't hear it, a million miles away you wouldn't hear the screams" (153–54). The screams too are important; they are part of the reality, which the person who attends only to the visible, outer dimension misses. The outside determines the inside, and the inside the outside.

In *Carpenter's Gothic*, perhaps the most potent symbol of the distinction between outside and inside—and its permeability—is the house. The house is remarked upon early on, but it is Lester who first speaks specifically to its class ("it's a classic piece of Hudson river carpenter gothic" [123]) and its uniqueness: "All designed from the outside, that tower there, the roof peaks, they drew a picture of it and squeezed the rooms in later" (124). He also makes us aware of how porous are the boundaries between outside and inside when he draws McCandless's attention to the "roof leak" (124). Leaks (not all in houses) constitute a motif in the novel, one to which I plan to return later. For the moment, however, I would like to remain with the theme of the house, and to insist on the importance of Lester's ostensibly off-the-cuff recall of his architectural history. We know it is important, for Gaddis has McCandless restate, at greater length, the history, while talking to Elizabeth:

> —Oh the house yes, the house. It was built that way yes, it was built to be seen from outside it was, that was the style, he came on, abruptly rescued from uncertainty, raised to the surface —yes, they had style books, these country architects and the carpenters it was all derivative wasn't it, those grand Victorian mansions with their rooms and rooms and towering heights and cupolas and the marvelous intricate ironwork. That whole inspiration of medieval Gothic but these poor fellows didn't have it, the stonework and the wrought iron. All they had were the simple dependable old materials, the wood and their hammers and saws and their own clumsy ingenuity bringing those grandiose visions the master had left behind down to a human scale with their own little inventions, those vertical darts coming down from the eaves? and that row of bull's eyes underneath? He was up kicking leaves aside, gesturing, both arms raised embracing —a patchwork of conceits, borrowings, deceptions, the inside's a hodgepodge of good intentions like one last ridiculous effort at something worth doing even on this small a scale, because it's stood here, hasn't it, foolish inventions and all it's stood here for ninety years . . .
> (227–28)

The McCandless discussion is interesting for numerous reasons. For starters, there is the matter of architecture, which here has its own suggestiveness. Like Lester, McCandless observes that the American Gothic was designed from the outside in. First, there was the idea of how it should look vis-à-vis the landscape, and then the builder set out to make the rooms concur with that design. It does not surprise that John Maass, an expert in such houses, says exactly the opposite: "It [the American Gothic] is planned from the inside out, the free layout of rooms determines the outward look" (64). In a sense, "inside-out" and "outside-in" result in the same thing, "a happy, hide-and-seek quality of surprise" (Maass, 64). The point is, one of the purposes of this design is to merge the inside with the outside, and the outside with the inside. As James Early writes, the architectural design's asymmetry was thought "desirable . . . because it seemed to follow the scheme of nature and hence enable an irregular building to fuse more easily with its natural surroundings" (61), surroundings that were themselves, in the words of the nineteenth-century architect Calvert Vaux, attractive for their quality of "well-balanced irregularity" (Early, 61). Vaux, like his contemporary Frederick Law Olmsted and his mentor Andrew Jackson Downing, felt that the picturesque American landscape was hospitable to the Gothic style. It was not, at least in the Northeast, a land noted for its gentle plains or cultivated terrain, and accordingly the classical style, with its emphasis upon geometrical regularity, would prove unfitting. But the Gothic style, wrote

Downing, with its "rich variety of gables, turrets, buttresses, towers, and ornamental chimney-shafts, . . . harmonize[s] agreeably with the hills and tree tops, and all the intricacy of outline in natural objects" (Early, 62). Downing was a Hudson Valley native, and the style he championed in the 1830s proved popular there, and then throughout the country, thereby marking a revolution in architectural design.[12]

Here, the Gothic style refers first and foremost to structures built of stone—e.g., granite, freestone, brownstone, and slate. Structures built of wood, like the McCandless house, became known as "Carpenter Gothic."[13] Whether Gothic or Carpenter Gothic, the structures were designed to break down the distinction between house and landscape. They did this not only via the mentioned spatial language of gables, towers, and chimney shafts, but also via the addition of "porches, windows mouldings, blinds, [and] brackets," all designed "to eliminate the unnatural monotony of plain broad surfaces" (Early, 67). These, said Downing, "confer the same kind of expression on a house that the eyes, eyebrows, lips, etc., do upon the human countenance" (Early, 67). They likewise heighten the play of light and shadow on the structure's surface, a play that minimizes "the blockly forms of the house" (Early, 66) and makes it, again, more semblable with the landscape. And it is this last feature (i.e., the transformation of outside and inside) that frames McCandless's own discussion of the style, first prompted by Elizabeth's remark that she had never "really looked" at the house from the outside (227), and then followed by her reply: "All I meant was, it's a hard house to hide in [. . .] —seeing it from outside, looking up there and seeing myself looking out when everything was green, it all looked so much bigger" (228).

The landscape with which the house almost merges is autumnal and dying, and the emptiness of the two upstairs rooms—one with "an empty bookcase and sagging daybed" and the other with "a gutted chaise longue voluted in French pretension trailing gold velvet in the dust undisturbed" (226–27)—looks out upon the fallen "leaves of scarlet oak here and there in the blackened red of blood long clotted and dried" (227). The mood is one of loss, and this is carried forward in McCandless's (already quoted) remarks about the house's history. Here the house becomes something like a symbol for Western civilization in decline. Decline, particularly, from a moment when there appeared to be a purpose to everything one did, signified here in "[t]hat whole inspiration of medieval Gothic" with its "grandiose visions" (227), visions that, thinks McCandless, the modern cannot truly share, only parody. For him, the present seems too much about images, shows, outsides, all bereft of substance at the core. Contemporary culture verges on being a simulacrum, a hodgepodge of tricks and feints that makes a pathetic attempt to mask the fact that its reason for being has been lost. What we are left with is one grand confidence game, "a patchwork of conceits, borrowings, [and] deceptions" (227). Or so it almost seems, for there remains something that saves the matter from being only a ruse; and this is the residue "of good intentions," even if they be no more than "one last ridiculous effort at something worth doing even on this small a scale" (228).

Good intentions—signifying a refusal to despair—do not, by themselves, guarantee that there will be an answer to people's longings. Still, they keep alive the sense of possibility, the desire for a meaningfulness that is not itself mean. And here, though we see evidence that the scale of vision has shrunk, brought down "to a human scale" (227), this diminishment need not be regretted altogether. There is, in truth, something comforting about "a human scale," for it is, after all, our scale. So, if it is best not to make the human both the center and the circumference of our circle, there remains something brave, in an existential sense, about these carpenters working within the limitations of their "simple dependable old materials" (227). Their "ingenuity" does count for something. The carpenters, by working in the face of what *seems* to be a blankness, transform that blankness and make it a more amenable reality.

The matter is not without allegorical import, for McCandless also thinks of himself as working against the grain, as trying to live an ordered existence in a world that is anything but ordered. I spoke earlier of his preoccupation with cleaning things up, of setting them right, and to this we might add his conviction that the world has a facticity to it that makes some interpretations more true that others. Certainly, his objection to the creationists has everything to do with what he takes as their refusal to make their beliefs accord with "known facts": "they jump on the Piltdown fraud, the Nebraska man that turned out to be a pig's tooth so the missing link is a fraud, evolution's all a fraud and geology astronomy physics all of it's a fraud, nothing in there about the fossil fragments in the Samburu hills where the strata's fifteen million years old, nothing about those fossil bones in three million years of volcanic ash up in the Afar Triangle, nothing about all those hominid fossils at that site in the Gregory Rift" (181).

The allegory of the carpenters also extends to Gaddis, for he clearly imagines himself as working at the end of a great tradition—that of the novel. After Austen, Dickens, Eliot, Hawthorne, Melville, Dostoevsky, James, Tolstoy, Conrad, Joyce, Woolf, Nabokov, it is understandable that a novelist should despair of making any new contribution. Still, there is a dignity attached to the mastery of an inheritance, to demonstrating a competence to marshal what Gaddis refers to as the discipline's "[s]taples." Of course, in novels such as *The Recognitions* and *J R*, there is the clear desire to extend the novel's boundaries. The achievement certainly appears equal to the desire. But in *Carpenter's Gothic*, the ambition is more reined in. Like the carpenters, working with "the wood and their hammers and saws and their own clumsy ingenuity," creating nice little effects like the "vertical darts coming down from the eaves" or the "row of bull's eyes underneath" (227),

Gaddis, too, thinks of himself here as working with common materials or staples, and somehow making them work. Referring to his ambition in *Carpenter's Gothic*, Gaddis has said: "Staples. That is, the staples of the marriage, which is on the rocks, the obligatory adultery, the locked room, the mysterious stranger, the older man and the younger woman, to try to take these and make them work" (Grove, B 10). He does make them work. In the end, *Carpenter's Gothic* is, in fact, "something worth doing" (228).

Before moving on, we need finally to note that while Carpenter Gothic is a name for an actual architectural style, it also recalls, in the present instance, Christ as carpenter. The allusion is made plain in Doris Chin's newspaper story on the Reverend Ude, read aloud by Paul:

> And as his [the Lord's] will came down upon me, trembling, I suddenly heard the voice of the profit Isaiah, wherein The carpenter stretcheth out his rule; he marketh it out with a line; he fitteth it with planes, and he marketh it out with the compass, and maketh it after the figure of a man, according to the beauty of a man; that it may remain in the house. And as I pondered the meaning of these words from on high, what had been a day of mourning burst before me as a day of glory! For did not they ask, when Jesus came unto Nazareth, Is not this the carpenter's son? He who built this great edifice of refuge for the weak, for the weary, for the seekers after his absolute truth in their days of adversity and persecution, as we are gathered here today before the onslaught of secular humanism, builded with his simple carpenter's tools from the humble materials closest to his hand his father's house, wherein are many mansions? (80)[14]

Like Paul, Reverend Ude is a confidence man who has no right to appropriate the religious narrative for his own profit. This, however, is what a confidence man does: he cloaks himself in the dress of the worthy so as to mask his own far from worthy ambition. Here, outside once again becomes inside, and inside outside, as that which is sinister assumes the form of that which is good, and that which is good is forced outside of itself by that which is sinister. The "Gothic" here is not that which conforms with the picturesque, with, in Downing's words, the "poetic, aspiring [and] imaginative idea" (Early, 61). Rather, it is that which speaks of the horror of things turned against themselves. Carpenter's Gothic is Christianity—McCandless: "the greatest work ever produced by western man" (134)—turned into a grotesque business venture, selling salvation to the poor and credulous, all the while appealing less to their sympathies and hopes than to their fears, prejudices, and superstitions. As McCandless, savvy to the tactics of an Ude and his brethren, puts it: "You can't put the fear of God in them put in the fear of something right here and now, it's all fear, Satan wears a little thin so you tie him in with godless Marxism and you've got a crusade to scare the hell out of everybody, a crusade against the powers of darkness over there washing these Africans in the blood of Jesus and you'll have enough bloodshed to float the Titanic" (187).

Faith is not at issue, as Elizabeth astutely enough realizes when Paul presses her to admit her apostasy:

> Ude gets his message of faith and prayer in papers all over the God damn country, says divine providence brought them [Ude and Senator Teakell] together in the shadow of the valley of look, just because you don't believe in faith and . . .
> —Oh stop it Paul stop it! Honestly.
> —What. Honestly what.
> —Don't believe in faith and . . .
> —What I just said isn't it? (100)

The question is faith in what or in whom? Faith—religious faith—does not require charlatans and confidence men as intermediaries, or an allegiance to biblical literalism. In fact, unless the literal can in some way be understood as allegorical, there cannot be religious belief, which speaks of a trust in what cannot be handled or seen, in what must be known symbolically or not at all ("Now faith is the assurance of things hoped for, the conviction of things not seen" [Hebrews 11.1]). But for Ude and his followers, the spirit gives way to the word, and the consequence is monstrous, for it inverts that which is most attractive in the biblical narrative: its offering of consolation and hope.

It seems, then, as McCandless notes, that by "defending the Bible against the powers of darkness," the fundamentalists do "more to degrade it taking every damn word in it literally than any militant atheist could ever hope to" (134).[15] They build another kind of church, another kind of Carpenter's Gothic. But even as they do, it is still possible to discover, as Elizabeth does gazing down on the fallen, lifeless foliage, "a dove carp[ing] among last testimonies blown down from somewhere out of reach, out of sight" (227). What the dove signifies is difficult to say, though a too literal reading would prove unsatisfactory. Again, there is "a very fine line between the truth and what really happens" (130), and while some might wish to repress the world's ambiguities so as to promote a truth capable of cleaving saints and sinners, the Gaddis novel suggests that the wish is both dangerous and impossible. Relations are too complicated and multivalenced to encourage the notion that inside can confidently be distinguished from outside and vice versa. Thus when, as often happens, someone does attempt to "draw [. . .] the line" (235), to separate friend from foe, madness often follows. As McCandless, hearing Elizabeth tell of how Paul was fragged, says, "It's madness then isn't it, it's just madness [. . .] —madness coming one way and . . . [going back the other]" (240). The madness follows despite (and, as I say, somewhat because of) all the participants' efforts to control events, to "put the pieces together" (19) and to see that they stay together, that there be no weak links, no sieves or leaks.

Leaks, however, are everywhere, and no one knows where they come from. Cruikshank and Company speculate that McCandless is the source. As Lester tells him, "Maybe they think you're where these leaks are coming from" (130). Billy, meanwhile, believes that Paul is responsible, and, more important, Grimes believes this too and tries to bait Paul in a trap. Or as Paul tells Elizabeth, "he still thinks I'm the one that blew the whistle on those payoffs you know what he tried on me? Some press leaks on VCR and some hushup deal he's sitting in on in Brussels tried to string me along and see what I knew, tried to pin me down on the . . ." (47). In fact, though our first inclination when confronted with Lester's break-in is to imagine it connected with McCandless's findings, there is good reason to think that it has just as much to do with Paul. Lester, as he tells McCandless, works for Cruikshank (130); but Cruikshank, remember, now works for Grimes: "Cruikshank earning his fee [as a consultant] and Grimes' syndicate damned glad to pay it" (237). Lester's break-in, then, is as likely to have been prompted by the suspicions that surround Paul as by the desire to get hold of McCandless's findings, which Lester procures easily enough by paying McCandless $16,000. But at first, Lester believes McCandless and Paul are linked, a warrantable surmise given that the latter is living in the former's house. One of the first questions Lester puts to McCandless is "Who are you working for[?]" (126). Thus when his suspicions that McCandless is in league with Paul prove valueless, Lester tries to elicit information about the latter:

—What do you know about the redhead's husband.
—He's behind two months' rent, that's what I know about him.
—You ran a credit check on him didn't you? when they rented your house here?
—I didn't run anything. They gave the agent a bad check for a month's rent they made good a week later and that was it.
—You don't look out for yourself very well do you. You never did . . . (133)

The suggestion is that Paul is dangerous, and that Grimes and Cruikshank will do what they think necessary to see to it that he does not interfere with VCR's plans. What others then speak of as a mugging, with Paul the unfortunate victim in a crowd, appears to have been an attempt to kill him. As Paul tells Elizabeth: "I think he was waiting for me [. . .] —tried to get his hands on this [the envelope with the $10,000 bribe, originally intended for Senator Teakell, but stolen by Paul] I think he was waiting for me" (200). This suspicion is enhanced by the subsequent attempt to set their house on fire, with the intention of either destroying McCandless's papers or murdering Paul, if not both. Fortunately for them, the arsonist sets ablaze the wrong house (217).

Whose side is Paul really on? Is he, as Billy believes, "on the inside" (175), or is he only an outsider who wishes to be on the inside? The answer is that there is no real answer. For one, every inside is also an outside some-where else; and then, so much disinformation has been sowed and so many players have been doubled and tripled that it would seem impossible to dis-entangle all of them so as to discern their real motives and positions vis-à-vis one another. For instance, we are told by Paul that Victor Sweet, the black senatorial candidate, gets his backing "from the outside" and one should "know what that means" (77). But he also gets his backing from Edie Grimes and when that runs out from her father. The father, of course, has his motives: he wishes to set Sweet up so that Senator Teakell will gain an easy November victory. Yet Senator Teakell's prospective victory starts to look much more uncertain after the bribery scandal. Then there is a question of whether Sweet's people have had anything to do with the bribe story and, if so, where did they get the incriminating photograph linking Senator Teakell with the Reverend Ude (221)? From Paul? From Grimes? If so, does this change Sweet's status from outsider to insider? I do not think we can say for sure, and it seems as if the players themselves do not even know who is and who is not on their side. There is so much confusion, and all rush forward to garner the kernels of any rumor and to squelch any leak. The anxiety respect-ing leaks is truly Nixonian, and when a leak is detected, all the plumbers are sent out in full force. Or as Lester tells McCandless, who cannot fathom the depth of concern, thinking it a waste of time:

—I'll tell you who'll waste the time. I'll tell you who'll waste more time than you've left alive McCandless. That's somebody who thinks there's a leak and brings the pressure down from the top, and won't stop till they find it. Maybe three or four agencies running down sources and none of them knows what the other ones are after. They don't know who else is after what they're after. They're so jealous they won't share the time of day. They don't know if the other side's in there too, they don't even know who's on the other side and every one of them thinks the other ones have been penetrated so they penetrate each other. They're afraid they're being fed disinformation so they put out a little disinformation of their own, the only thing they know is if somebody says he's got what they're after and they haven't got it, if the other side says they've got it and pulls out the rug there's no way to prove they haven't. (140–41)

Who use whom? Well, it seems that everyone seeks to use everyone else. VCR needs Senator Teakell to protect its mineral rights abroad; Senator Teakell needs Ude for his mailing list; Reverend Ude needs Senator Teakell's help with the FCC; and it goes on and on this way. At one point, Paul tries to diagram the confluence of relations, and ends up with something looking like a hail of arrows: "Grimes to Teakell, Teakell to Ude, Ude to the point every-thing goes both ways . . . more arrows, —everything to everything else . . . and a hail of arrows darkened the page like the skies that day over Crécy" (107). Outside becomes inside, inside becomes outside; and while there remains the sense that the newel of events is locatable if you "know what you're looking for" (140), few here do. Confusion thus reigns, not because order does not exist, but because the will to discern and, in turn, trust this order has largely given way to more immediate and even rapacious ambitions.

Elizabeth and the Desire for Something More

Elizabeth "turned on the radio, to be told there was a forcible rape in this country every six minutes" (197). As in *The Recognitions* and *J R*, startling, yet sadly apropos, information has a way of filtering into *Carpenter's Gothic*, as if through the narrative's cracks. News about the frequency of rape is pertinent because, among other things, *Carpenter's Gothic* is a story about male domestic violence. Like rape, domestic violence entails an attitude toward women that is indefensible, but all too common. Elizabeth is a battered woman and has the wounds to prove it. In the opening chapter, she provokes Paul's anger by wearing a sleeveless outfit exposing her bruises:

—No please . . . she pulled away, cringed lower, his hand on her bared shoulder —you're hurting my . . .
—Well what the hell are you wearing this thing for! He was back out of reach, a hand out for his glass, —you haven't worn it since summer.
—But what, I just . . .
—Show off your bruise? Sleeveless thing to show off your God damn combat badge to the neighbors and anybody who . . .
—I don't know any neighbors!
—And your brother what about your brother, your . . .
—I said I'd bumped into a bookcase. When do you want supper.
—A bookcase . . . He held the bottle over the glass, held it the way he poured drinks, two handed, one holding the bottle up and away against the other forcing it down, forcing the neck down over the glass, and —a bookcase, he muttered again at the sink for a splash of water, turning past her through the doorway. —Where. What bookcase. Will you show me one God damn bookcase? Everything else here but a bookcase it's like a museum, like living in a museum. (22)[16]

It is a classic instance of "battered-woman syndrome," a phrase/condition introduced into the vernacular by the psychologist Lenore Walker in 1984. The syndrome is characterized by a pattern of domestic violence, wherein the wife is emotionally coerced into assuming part of the responsibility for the husband's brutality, even to engaging in its cover-up. Elizabeth does everything that she can to protect Paul from the condemnation of insiders (e.g., her brother) and outsiders (e.g., Edie). She deflects her brother's question about her bruises—"I said I don't want to talk about it!" (9)—though it is Billy, not Elizabeth, who concocts, albeit cynically, the story about the bookcase: "Bumped into a bookcase, great . . ." (9). And when Edie raises the topic on the telephone, Elizabeth passes the matter off as an occasional thing that Paul cannot truly be blamed for: "no, it's, it's all fine Edie honestly Edie it's fine, it's not really Paul's fault he's just, he gets short-tempered sometimes and things haven't gone that well for him since Daddy but he's really trying hard to . . ." (33–34).

Paul's mistreatment of Elizabeth is part and parcel of a more omnipresent violence. This includes the violence of the neighborhood boys with their "bold obscenities" (35); the hidden violence inscribed in the economic system, so dependent on colonial-like relations with poorer nations; and the violence of warfare and its aftermath. Paul is a veteran of the Vietnam War, a war for which the nation's leaders were tragically unable to articulate a rationale, allowing the warfare's violence to become more and more about itself. So it was that the 1968 massacre at My Lai came to symbolize, for many, the too frightening truth about that war: that the American soldiers could not distinguish friends from foes, and that having no real understanding as to why they were there, and frightened to boot, they began to make fewer discriminations about whose hamlet they destroyed or whose father, mother, wife or child they killed—or murdered. Certainly, Paul has participated in, and been victimized by, that violence. Memories of both a martial wilding and being fragged by his own men are activated by the assassin's attempt on his life:

> you see me take him out? Cameras set up out there for some candyass politicians at that prayer breakfast two chops blew him away, that mother was waiting for me Chick. You see him? looked just like Chigger didn't he? you see his face? Same yellow shit in his eyes that last day out pouring that M60 into those hootches kids chickens pigs wasting that whole fucking ville same shit, see it in his eyes before I saw the blade, he . . . mother creased my arm that's all, told him that Chick when I turned him in, looking for somebody to tear you out a new asshole just step right up told him that, every mother out there got five minutes to be crazy, two weeks short Kowalski couldn't wait? walks right up route seven trying to draw fire? (213)

Paul is a violent man, and while we are witnesses more to the emotional than to the physical violence, everything about him suggests an extraordinary potential to do harm. This helps to explain why Elizabeth does not leave him. Certainly, there are attempts to convince her to leave. Billy asks her to accompany him to California: "why don't you pack up. Pack a bag and get out of here Bibbs, listen. I'm going to California I'll wait for you. Tonight pack a bag and I'll wait for you" (89). And McCandless asks her to go with him to the South Seas: "I've got some cash, got my hands on about sixteen thousand dollars and a ticket to anywhere, we can . . ." (246).

Her reasons for refusing are complicated. For one, there is the fear of what Paul's reaction would be to her disappearance, a common reaction among battered women. Del Martin writes, "Battered wives give many reasons or rationalizations for staying, but fear is the common denominator. Fear immobilizes them, ruling their actions, their decisions, their very lives" (76). Others note the same thing: "women don't flee because, ironically, they are afraid for their life. Law enforcement experts agree that running away greatly increases the danger a woman faces. Angered at the loss of power and control, violent men often try to track down their wives" ("Til Death Do Us Part," 42). Elizabeth has real reasons to be afraid. Her inheritance is about to come due, and Paul has banked all his ambitions on this prospect, just as he has taken every advantage of her family's connections. As Billy says to her, "I mean you know why he married you, we all . . ." (9). Elizabeth does know, though she prefers to repress the knowledge. She also knows that if she does flee, there is no telling what Paul might do, except that it will be out of proportion and violent.

Paul does his best to keep Elizabeth cloistered in the house. "Keep the door locked" (88) is almost his refrain. But it is fair to wonder, as Billy does, what Paul fears most: someone coming in from outside or Elizabeth herself escaping outward. "That's why he's got you locked up here," says her brother, "he's scared shitless some old friend will find you he's scared something will happen" (89), and that she might leave. Explaining why she stays, Elizabeth shows herself to be a genuine Gaddis hero: "I don't know what it is, as long as something's unfinished you feel alive it's as though, I mean maybe it's just being afraid nothing will happen . . ." (89). Like the anxiety felt by Wyatt in *The Recognitions* and Bast in *J R*, Elizabeth's fear is that finished things are really dead things, that the world exists within the frames of possibility and chance, and that it is best to accept this. It is not that she, like the others, does not wish to see smaller, individual projects completed; she simply wishes to keep a horizon present, holding to the conviction that what is is but a shadow of what might be. This way, hope is kept alive. This, however, puts Elizabeth at odds with both Paul and McCandless, who ceaselessly try to nail things down, to complete them. It is not surprising then that Elizabeth, borrowing McCandless's own metaphor, should "feel like a nail [when] everything looks like a hammer" (223).

Elizabeth is taken for granted and treated badly by all the men in her life. Her father, like Amy's father in *J R*, was an emotionally limited and withholding man, too wrapped up in his business empire to take notice of his wife and children. Billy says that their father "bullied anybody that got near him like he bullied us, like he bullied mother like he bullied you till you'd do anything to get out" (90). The irony, Billy tells Elizabeth, is that she has married a man much like her father, at least emotionally: "You find this inferior person, you know he's fucking inferior and you've married the same thing you tried to get away from" (90–91). Unfortunately, Billy's contempt for Paul influences his feelings for Elizabeth: he thinks less of her because of the marriage. There is a way, then, in which his statements are, as Elizabeth realizes, meant to hurt, to get back at her for marrying Paul and, paradoxically, for making him think less of her. As solicitous as Billy can be, his remarks about Paul and the likeness to their father—"why do you think the old man took Paul on in the first place, because he'd found somebody just as fucking inferior as he was" (91)—are thoughtless and cruel. Elizabeth rightly reproaches him, making clear that she understands the purpose of the attacks: "Because it's not to hurt Paul, it's me isn't it. It's to hurt me" (193). And while it would be a mistake simply to conflate Billy with the father and Paul, this bullying does foreground the resemblance. Hence Elizabeth's angry retort:

> —Well maybe I did! [married her father's clone]. Because I, because some-
> times I almost can't tell you apart you and Paul, you sound the same you sound
> exactly the same the only difference is he says your God damn brother and you
> say fucking Paul but it's the same, if I closed my eyes it could be either one of
> you maybe that's why I married him! If you think the only men I appeal to are
> fools, if all I ever look for is inferior men then maybe that's why! (194)

It is no coincidence, then, that McCandless is spoken of, by Lester, as "an inferior character" (140). He is not this, but the statement seems to speak to another matter: his uneven treatment of Elizabeth. McCandless can be as much like the father as can either Billy or Paul. Like them, his respect for her appears to be almost in inverse proportion to his dependence on her. He does not take her concerns seriously, even as he is asking her to leave her husband and go away with him. Repeatedly, Elizabeth must ask him not to make fun of her, as when she tells him about the "babies trying to get born": "Now you are! [. . .] —making fun of me, aren't you . . ." (156). The dilemma is clear: Elizabeth's thoughts about reincarnation and babies wishing to be born are, to a rationalist like McCandless, worse than far-fetched. The fantasy aside, they also express something else about Elizabeth, the extent of her longing. There is something attractive about her need to see her dreams realized or, barring this, to return somehow to that time "when things were still like you thought they were going to be" (154). She longs for the world to make sense, for it not to let her down. This is not something McCandless can easily identify with, for he has lost whatever hopes he might have had this way. It is too bad, for his knowledge would serve him better were he wiser.

Elizabeth appears wiser. She does not believe, as he does, that most things can be explained by referring to people's fears, nor does she fear, as he does, becoming "the prisoner of someone else's hopes" (155). Better to be attached to someone else's hopes, she reasons, than someone else's fears: "It's being the prisoner of someone else's hopes but that was, but that's not being the prisoner of someone else's despair!" (244). In fact, Elizabeth has cause to resent the tenor of McCandless's address, not only as it questions her longings, but also as it shifts from intimacy to formality—"I'm not a writer Mrs. Booth!" (165), this after they have spent the night together—depending on what it is that he wants from her. Even his apologies can be patronizing:

> —No I'm sorry, Elizabeth lis . . .
> —And stop calling me that! That's, what's sorry no, that's what my father always did, saying I'm sorry and he'd pat me and try to give me a kiss no, it's always something else, saying I'm sorry it's always for the wrong thing that's why people say it. I'm sorry I disturbed you Mrs Booth, loading all those books on him [Billy] and driving away filling his head with, with I don't know what; that whole show you put on for him in there from the minute he, the minute you found out his name, that his name was Vorakers. (223)

McCandless, as suggested by the novel's multiple allusions to *Jane Eyre*, plays Rochester to Madame Socrate's housekeeper and Elizabeth's Jane Eyre. He is the stern, taciturn owner of the house, who has a hidden past, known to the servant but otherwise unspoken of. We do not need to search far for the evidence of this past. It is present—in the form of Irene's furnishings—right there in the house. And if there is no madwoman in the third-story attic, McCandless does have a history of alienating women's affections. Yet Elizabeth, only vaguely aware of this history, yearns for the older man's tutelage and protection. In the end, as in *Jane Eyre*, she becomes more valuable to her imagined protector than he is to her. And in the midst of this evolving relation, Gaddis offers a specific allusion to *Jane Eyre*, or at least to the 1944 movie version, watched on the bedroom television by Elizabeth:

> from the screen where a demoniac laugh, low, suppressed, and deep, came uttered it seemed at the very keyhole of the chamber door. As she gazed, the unnatural sound was reiterated, and she knew it came from behind the panels. As though her first impulse was to rise, and her next to cry out, something gurgled and moaned, and steps retreated up the gallery toward the third story staircase. The door came open under her trembling hand and there was a candle burning just outside, left on the matting in the gallery where the air was quite dim, as if filled with smoke. Something creaked: it was a door ajar and the smoke rushed from it in a cloud. Within the chamber tongues of flame darted round the bed: the curtains were on fire: the very sheets were kindling. In the midst of blaze and vapour Orson Welles lay stretched motionless, in a deep sleep. (55)

The scene draws from chapter 15 in the Brontë novel, and employs a fair amount of quotation. Gaddis also quotes freely from Brontë in his own chapter's final scene, wherein, as in the first instance, two realities seem to merge, that of Elizabeth in the bedroom and that of the laurel walk where Rochester asks Jane to marry him just prior to the storm that splits the chestnut tree (Chapter 23). Later, Gaddis, returning to this image seen on the television, raises a question as to what has, and has not, been real. This is when Elizabeth notices that the television is missing, that it has been stolen:

> when she looked up sharp, straight before her: the television set was gone. It was simply not there; but her stare where it had been was as simply one of a blank insistence that the furnishings of memory prevail as though, if it were so abruptly nonexistent as to never have been there, then neither had the man flung from the train on the trestle, nor everything in shadow while wind roared in the laurel walk, near and deep as the thunder crashed, fierce and frequent as the lightning gleamed striking the great horse chestnut at the bottom of the garden and splitting half of it away. (248)

The passage recalls a prior passage where Lester tells McCandless that it was he who persuaded him to join the Agency. Initially, Lester recalls, McCandless would talk and he would listen: "Helen Keller in the woods when the tree falls and all the rest of your, the truth and what really happens" (146). In both instances, the suspicion of the real seems not so much to deny the real as to find in it an essential ambiguity. The fictive and the real are discovered to be inseparable. In fact, if we examine the closure of the earlier Gaddis chapter with the allusion to *Jane Eyre*, we can see just how intertwined the two realms are. In the chapter's last paragraph Elizabeth lies with Paul in bed. She has asked him for money for Madame Socrate (whom she has asked not to return), and he is complaining about Haitians, at the time of the Vietnam War, selling their blood. Though the television is on, playing *Jane Eyre*, both Elizabeth and Paul fall asleep: "Lids closed against the streetlight's gleams scattered on the wall, the empty mirror, it scarcely mattered: the chase continued on what passed for sleep taking with it what passed for time" (56). Sleep and time are both spoken of with some suspicion, as if their realities were something less than or different from what they purport to be. Soon, however, Elizabeth wakes up and finds herself, in a sense, in *Jane Eyre*'s laurel walk: "till finally, eyes fallen wide again crowded with movement still as the breathing beside her, she came off the edge of the bed and brought the room and her own face back to ashen life down a winding walk, bordered with laurels and terminating in a giant horse chestnut, circled at the base by a seat, leading down to the fence" (56). At this point the storm, which will soon engulf the laurel walk, is already real outside Elizabeth's window: "She drew the blanket close against a sudden burst of rain at the window spattering the streetlight out there over its panes" (56). But then, once again, her eyes dim, only "to come wide again with the lashing rain" (56). Here, it is difficult to distinguish the real from the fictive. Which "lashing rain" does she awaken to, that outside her window or that on the television screen? It is hard to say:

> what had befallen the night? Everything was in shadow; and what ailed the chestnut tree? it writhed and groaned, while wind roared in the laurel walk, near and deep as the thunder crashed, fierce and frequent as the lightning gleamed striking the great horse chestnut at the bottom of the garden and splitting half of it away. (56–57)

Gaddis's prose here is mostly a borrowing from Brontë's, particularly from the chapter 23 paragraphs:

> But what had befallen the night? The moon was not yet set, and we were all in shadow: I could scarcely see my master's face, near as I was. And what ailed the chestnut tree? it writhed and groaned; while wind roared in the laurel walk, and came sweeping over us.

> Before I left my bed in the morning, little Adèle came running in to tell me that the great horse-chestnut at the bottom of the orchard had been struck by lightning in the night, and half of it split away.

With this borrowing, other questions about what is and what is not real are raised, for most readers will assume the prose Gaddis's. But what is assumed to be true is not true, or not entirely true, truth "lying" somewhere between the two possibilities. So it seems with the events of the narrative itself. For instance, there are other moments when the two narratives appear to intersect, as with the fire and Elizabeth's attempt to wake Paul—"Paul please! both hands on him pulling him over, eyes sealed and his mouth fallen open" (217)—which recalls Jane's similar attempt to waken Rochester, as the flames begin to engulf his bedroom: "'Wake, wake!' I cried—I shook him, but he only murmured and turned: the smoke had stupefied him. Not a moment could be lost: the very sheets were kindling" (chapter 15).[17] There are also parallels between Elizabeth's presentiments and Jane's own. Jane, at one point, tells the reader:

> Presentiments are strange things! and so are sympathies; and so are signs: and the three combined make one mystery to which humanity has not yet found the key. I never laughed at presentiments in my life; because I have had strange ones of my own. Sympathies, I believe, exist: (for instance, between far-distant, long-absent, wholly estranged relatives; asserting, notwithstanding their alienation, the unity of the source to which each traces his origin) whose workings baffle mortal comprehension. And signs, for aught we know, may be but the sympathies of Nature with man. (chapter 21)

In the case of Elizabeth, the presentiment is, it seems, of her own death:

—wasn't that a strange dream? She held his [McCandless's] face pressed against her, —but they always are aren't they, when they're about death, I mean when they're about somebody dying and you don't even know who it is? (152)

Not surprisingly, she reads the dream as being connected not with herself but with her father: "it must have been about him, that dream. Don't you think so?" (152). Even what strikes the reader as a clear-cut presentiment is, in a Gaddis novel, made ambiguous, "baffl[ing] mortal comprehension."

In this same section, McCandless recalls Elizabeth's having said that her father had died when pushed off a train, and he (testing her, for he has seen the film that inspires Elizabeth's fiction) wonders whether maybe that was not also a dream (152). She says no, but then deflects the question, knowing that the story's source was neither in real life nor in dream. It is an emblematic instance wherein her fantasies insert themselves in the place of the real, so that her life must be thought of as inseparable from her fictive imaginings. There are many instances when she simply slips into fictions—even deceits—designed to make her own life less bare or oppressive. Thus, in a telephone conversation with Edie, Elizabeth, feeling the pain of her suburban isolation, speaks of her Spanish lessons and charity work. She also transforms Madame Socrate into a new and lovely French-speaking friend: "I mean the woman who came in to, today, who came in to lunch today yes a lady I've just met here, she lived a lot in Haiti and came over for lunch and all we spoke was French" (33). And later, when Billy telephones, she feels the need to create, for the benefit of McCandless, who is nearby, an exotic life completely unlike her own. Billy, not knowing what is going on, finds himself addressed as an important senator:

When finally she heard it again she started at the loudness of her own voice, —Hello . . . ? rising with conviction at each word, —no I'm terribly sorry Senator, Paul's not here . . . talking at the phone, past it to the open doorway —I think he plans to be in Washington very soon, he's had to make a trip south something suddenly came up with in connection with, pardon . . . ? gathering aplomb and even cordial condescension, —that's terribly kind but I honestly can't say, we do want to get down to Montego Bay for a few days with friends if Paul can possibly take the time but you know how busy he's been with the . . . (61)

It is in her fiction, however, that her fantasies take their most elaborate shape. Like *J R*'s Tom Eigen, who attempts to "hypothesize backwards," Elizabeth's thoughts often alight on what might have been: "what it might all have been like if her father and mother had never met, if her father had married a schoolteacher, or a chorus girl, instead of the daughter of a stayed Grosse Pointe family, or if her mother, lying silent even now in the cold embrace of a distant nursing home, had met a young writer who . . ." (63–64). For Elizabeth, a shadow reality never lurks far away from what

passes as reality. The experience might be likened to our own general aware-
ness of the difference between the events that are, and those that should have
been, had we, sometime in the past, simply made one less, one different, or
one more decision than we did. That we did not does not mean that the other
realities altogether cease to exist. Rather, there is a sense in which they live
on: they constitute the what might have been, and this too is an aspect of
reality, if only, as in Eliot's "Burnt Norton," as a mode of "speculation."

At one point Elizabeth tells McCandless that she thinks that "people write
because things didn't come out the way they're supposed to be" (158). The
suggestion, which has its parallel in Gaddis's work, is that the facticity and
the potentiality of events constitute two different modes but remain sem-
blant. "What might have been and what has been" figure in one another, and
there is a constant movement back and forth between them, a movement that
measures the realm of what is by what is not but might have been. If this
involves an element of regret and loss, it also speaks of hope and the possibilities of a future fulfillment, as we steer our lives toward a horizon that
may force us to reimagine all past events, both lived and not lived, as the
fragments of a larger perfection. As Ernst Bloch so expressively contended,
hope matters, and when we live in the light of its anticipation, it becomes the
equivalent of a utopian function: "Only when reason starts to speak, then
hope, which has nothing false to it, will begin to blossom again. The not-yet-
conscious itself has to become *conscious* of its own doings; it must come to
know its contents as restraint and revelation. And thus the point is reached
where hope, in particular, the true effect of expectation in the dream forward,
not only occurs as an emotion that merely exists by itself, but is *conscious
and known* as the *utopian function*" (105).

Elizabeth's fantasies are, I think, best understood in light of her hope for
something better and as evidence that she has not stopped caring about either
herself or others. If this means occasionally masking the reality with something more interesting, she will not shrink from doing so, particularly if this
helps her to move toward her sense of how things should be. McCandless, of
course, cannot see the point of whitening things, grim though they be, and
forces the matter by asking Elizabeth why she lied about the death of her
father, an ignominious suicide:

—Tell me . . . he'd lit the cigarette, and he coughed. —Why did you tell me
your father had been pushed off a train.
    —What's the difference . . . She hadn't moved, her back to him rigid as the
table between them —he was dead, wasn't he?
    —Going over a trestle? off the roof of the train? Because I remember it, I
remember that scene, I saw the same movie.
    —That wasn't kind, was it . . . and her shoulders fell a little, —because
when people tell a lie . . .
    —No I didn't mean, I didn't say that you'd . . .

—I'll tell you why yes, because why people lie is, because when people
stop lying you know they've stopped caring. (226)

With her father a suicide, her mother in a nursing home, her brother at
loose ends, and her husband an abusive alcoholic, Elizabeth needs something
that she can place her hope in. Paul, Billy, the house, her novel, all are
entwined in her hopes. In her novel, Elizabeth works hard to make things
come out as they should. For her, the novel is more than a fiction, for it is set
in a dialectical relation with outside events, including the appearance, or
reappearance, of McCandless. When McCandless first returns, Elizabeth
inserts him into the alternative past that she has imagined for her mother. At
this point, she thinks him a writer, "a man with another life already behind
him, another woman, even a wife somewhere" (64). But as she learns more
about him, she revises the description, changing "another life" to "other
lives"; "another woman" to "other women"; and "somewhere" to "a wife
hidden now in Marrakech" (93). It is doubtful that her fiction will ever be
one with the truth that is McCandless's life, but this does not mean the fictive
approximations are not worth pursuing. And the suggestion that Elizabeth's
fiction approximates a truth is enhanced by the fact that it also merges with
Gaddis's own fiction. For instance, her last additions—"livid erection where
her hand closed tight on its prey swelling the colour of rage" (248)—recalls
the author's own prior description of sexual relations between Elizabeth and
McCandless: "her hand closed tight, its prey swollen the colour of rage"
(162). In a sense, then, Elizabeth's and Gaddis's efforts are collaborative,
both of them reaching for a truth that lies somewhat beyond their reach.

In addition to her fiction, Elizabeth also places her hope in the house,
McCandless, and Paul. They are not necessarily bad places to locate her
hope, though the results are mixed. The house, as mentioned, is a focal point
of Elizabeth's hopes, especially as her longing for a settled domestic arrangement finds its symbols in Irene's furnishings and McCandless's reassuring
presence. But when summer changes to fall, the house and its grounds start
to lose some of their luster, at least as seen from the outside. For Elizabeth
remembers, she tells McCandless, "seeing it from outside, looking up there
and seeing myself looking out when everything was green, it all looked so
much bigger" (228). But now, in autumn, she sees that "it's, look at it, it's
just a horrid little back yard" (228). The same seems true with respect to
McCandless, who disappoints her. This happens when, learning that Billy is
Vorakers's son, McCandless appears to drop everything, and runs down to
the city with her brother. At the end, she tells him, "I think I loved you when
I knew I'd never see you again" (245), making it clear that something has
changed and that her love for him has shifted to the past tense. Nor is this
simply a matter of her becoming sensitive to his detachment with regard to
her. She is even more troubled by his larger detachment, particularly as it

connects to matters that he might, in a positive way, alter. For instance, his willingness to dissociate himself from the African mining matter truly upsets her, for she believes he might help avert a tragedy. If the possibility is there, how can he refuse it when lives are at stake? In the end, then, she turns down his invitation to run away with him, and chooses to remain with Paul. Why she should remain is difficult to say, for he treats her so badly. But perhaps it is because, unlike McCandless, he orients his life toward the future, even if this future is imagined in terms that are self-aggrandizing. For a long time, Elizabeth tries to believe that Paul's dreams are worthy, though even she appears to give up the night that she tries to tell him about her furniture being sold: "they sold the, they sold all of it Paul they sold all of it!" (202). Not hearing a word, Paul tries to tell her the problem is that she does not listen. She responds, "Paul honestly, don't tell me what the problem is" (203). Finally, she is left staring out a blackened kitchen window, reflecting back her own image and pain:

> She'd turned back to the sink holding an empty pan, looking through darkness carved her own shape from the reflection on the glass of the walls behind her and the cupboard and the doorway, and the lamp on the table and the reach of the torn arm [Paul's] for the bottle beside her, through to the darkness outside. (205)

Given Paul's mistreatment of Elizabeth, there is an inclination to agree with Billy when he tells his sister that her medical problems have more to do with Paul than with the air crash: "I mean he's the one that's wiping you out Bibb not some old plane crash" (92). Still, like so many other things here, there are several possible explanations regarding her failing health and premature death. Respecting the last matter, no one explanation can be put forward with certitude. Steven Moore argues that Elizabeth dies of a heart attack (*William Gaddis*, 114), and John Johnston argues that she is murdered (211).[18] Both explanations, while possibilities, seem inadequate. Murder is unlikely, for the evidence here (e.g., Paul's interest in and appropriation of the trust instrument, and his hiring of an assassin to kill Reverend Ude) still does not explain how Elizabeth, alone in the house, comes to her death. Nor does a heart attack appear the cause of death. At the age of thirty-three, women seldom die of heart attacks. More likely is the possibility that she has suffered an aneurysm (hinted at by her high blood pressure) or that, experiencing arrhythmia, she faints and hits her head against the counter, a blow that can easily result in death. She has felt faint several times in the narrative, a symptom (along with headaches) that Paul connects with the airplane crash (16), but which, again, is more logically connected with arrhythmia. In any event, we see her, feeling faint, grab the newel for support just before she retrieves the two books dropped in the autumn leaves by McCandless (197). Later, she almost faints in the kitchen: "But she was up coming toward him

[Paul] reaching out, suddenly holding to the handle on the refrigerator door and he caught her elbow —what is it, what's . . ." (240–41).[19] Then, finally, she faints for the last time:

> For a moment longer she held tight to the newel as though secured against the faint dappled movement of the light coming right into the room here and then suddenly she turned back for the kitchen where she rushed into the darkness as though she'd forgotten something, a hand out for the corner of the table caught in a glance at her temple as she went down. (253)

While there is a good chance that Elizabeth's death is connected to arrhythmia, the fainting that is associated with it, and, crucially, the blow to the head that she suffers in her final fall, we need to note still another possible cause of death: Elizabeth's severe asthmatic condition. Asthma can kill, but when it does the warnings are usually more dramatic than as found here.[20] Still, Elizabeth's asthma is a concern, and partly explains the move from New York City up to the Hudson Valley. When Billy first visits, he questions Elizabeth about the change: "You any better up here? your asthma?" (9). She thinks so, but she is not sure. It would seem that she is better by being outside the city, yet the house has its own pitfalls. For one, the residue of McCandless's chain-smoking is everywhere; and cigarette smoke is a particular irritant to Elizabeth. She repeatedly must ask Paul to put out his cigarette. McCandless's smoking, however, goes unchecked; and this certainly could be a factor in her death, if it caused a severe asthmatic attack.[21] Also, in the house, there is the matter of the dust, one of the things Madame Socrate has been brought in to take care of. There is a difficulty, however, with the vacuum cleaner. It is old and in need of replacement. As Madame Socrate tells Elizabeth, she needs "un nouvel aspirateur" (26), which on the surface simply means that, again, she needs a new vacuum cleaner, but also calls up, in both French and English, the thought of an aspirator. In the exchange between Madame Socrate and Elizabeth, Gaddis clearly wishes to bring forward all these things (e.g., dust, vacuum cleaner, aspirator) in connection with the asthma:

> —On a besoin d'un nouvel aspirateur.
> —Yes a, a what, quoi?
> —On a besoin d'un nouvel aspirateur, Madame.
> —Oh yes. Oui.
> —Celui-ci est foutu.
> —Of course yes the, the vacuum cleaner oui yes it is quite an old one isn't it mais, mais c'est très important de, qu'on nettoyer tout les, le dust vous savez le, le dust? Parce que mon asthma . . . (26)

Also to be noted is that after Madame Socrate's first visit, Elizabeth tells her that she need not come again until called. The reason is not that Elizabeth does not like her work, but she feels that if she does the work herself, she can, by not telling Paul, pocket the money meant for Madame Socrate. The one time Elizabeth does try to clean the house, however, she becomes ill and throws up (116), making it clear that Madame Socrate's assistance is needed. Meantime, the dust begins to build up, contributing to her asthmatic condition. In the course of the narrative, Elizabeth experiences several attacks. The first and the third attack, during her respective visits to Doctors Shak and Kissinger (14, 50), seem connected with the city. The second attack ("her chin sunk in an effort for breath" [31]), coming shortly after McCandless's first visit, might be related to the residue from his smoking. And then the most violent attack, aside from the final attack, if attack it was, comes when she is in bed with McCandless, the owner of the "smoking gun" (160), which is to say his cigarettes. At this point, he has not smoked since the night before and his cigarettes remain downstairs (157), but if the evening is anything like the later morning when the "[p]lanes of smoke" are said to settle "through the room" (164), then the house is filled with his chain-smoking residue. And this plus his breath (163) seems to set off Elizabeth's asthmatic attack:

> for his breath at her shoulder, on the glints of perspiration beading the white of her neck and his hand down her back spreading the rift wide, his weight coming over when that suddenly she turned seizing him with her arms to bring him in, head thrown back and the full swell of her throat rising in the hollowed arch of her jaw surging to meet him with choked bleats of sound for as long as it lasted until he came down, fighting desperate for breath himself [. . .]. She lay with her head on her right shoulder, eyes drawn and her mouth hung open with no betrayal of life but the uneven trembling of her lower lip sucked in with each effort at breathing and then falling away spilling the stilled tip of her tongue and [. . .] legs flung wide and her arms loose beside her, her thumbs still crushed into the palms of her hands and as he leaned down to pull the sheet over her [. . .]. (163)

The description is strikingly similar to that attending Elizabeth's death (253), and strengthens the view that her death follows from an asthmatic attack, set off by McCandless's smoking. Before his final departure, McCandless has spent the time, mostly in Elizabeth's presence, chain-smoking—"He started making another cigarette" (245)—and the house remains thick with his smoke even later, when his first (and only?) wife appears. Twice, Mrs. McCandless comments on the smoke—"it's the smoke isn't it, it clings to everything for ages" (251)—and her own entrance is introduced by mention of two boys sharing a cigarette: "The shrill of a car's horn brought her over to snap up the shade. In what light remained out there two waist high boys sat sharing a cigarette under the bare tree [. . .]" (248). Then, before she leaves, Mrs. McCandless takes note of Elizabeth's paleness, again most likely a reaction to the leftover smoke.[22] It is after Mrs. McCandless's exit that Elizabeth, hearing the two telephone rings (the signal adopted by both Paul and McCandless), rushes into the kitchen, only to be overcome by a fainting spell, caused, it would seem, either by an arrhythmia or an asthmatic attack set off by the smoke. Granted, the front door remains open, but it admits only a "wind scarce as the gentle rise and fall of breathing in exhausted sleep" (253). I suspect that Elizabeth, indeed, dies from an asthmatic attack, if only because of the almost identical description linking this scene with Elizabeth's most violent attack. Still, in Gaddis's fiction, clues are everywhere, and the attempt to move toward conclusion often gets derailed by yet more clues.[23]

Geology versus Scientific Creationism

In his fine book *The Creationists*, Ronald L. Numbers offers a cogent history of how it was that an essentially religious objection to a scientific theory, evolution, should turn into a rival scientific theory, albeit persuasive only to those of a particular mindset. The matter is central to understanding McCandless's "outrage," and thus merits discussion. As in *Carpenter's Gothic*, Numbers's narrative often revolves around events in Arkansas, where it continued to be illegal to teach evolution until 1968 when the Supreme Court struck down the relevant statute. This, however, was not the end of the matter. A turning point actually took place in California, where creationists, unhappy with what they felt was a too dogmatic insistence on evolution in the state curriculum, pressed the board of education for a revision. In the ensuing compromise, the board's statement was revised to read: "While the Bible and other philosophical treatises also mention creation, science has independently postulated the various theories of creation. . . . Therefore, creation in scientific terms is not a religious or philosophical belief" (Numbers, 244).

For the creationists, a window had been opened. Creationism could be taught in the public school if its proponents could leave aside biblical references. As Henry M. Morris, Creation Research Society president, said at the time, "Creationism is on the way back, . . . this time not primarily as a religious belief, but as an alternative scientific explanation of the world in which we live" (Numbers, 244). It thus became important among proponents to speak of creationism as either "scientific creationism" or, better yet, "creation science." They also began to promote the contention that science, especially paleogeophysics, was by its nature theoretical and that scientific creation was but one theory among others. Yet if creationism was a science, it needed a more precise material description. The 1981 Arkansas "balanced treatment" law sought to offer this, defining creation science as follows:

(1) Sudden creation of the universe, energy, and life from nothing; (2) The insufficiency of mutation and natural selection in bringing about development of all living kinds from a single organism; (3) Changes only within fixed limits of originally created kinds of plants and animals; (4) Separate ancestry for man and apes; (5) Explanation of the earth's geology by catastrophism, including the occurrence of a worldwide flood; and (6) A relatively recent inception of the earth and living kinds. (Numbers, 245)

As Numbers writes, the description "looks suspiciously like old-fashioned biblical creationism" (245). Still, there are notable differences. "Few biblical creationists before the 1960s," he writes, "would have included an appeal to geological catastrophism. Scientific creationists, in contrast, identified the Genesis flood as 'the real crux of the conflict between the evolutionist and creationist cosmologies'" (245). One also notes the deliberate repression of the biblical narrative, making the whole project seem like an end run.

What McCandless most objects to is the end run itself, the refusal to study the geological record and the refusal to grant the difference between biblical narrative and scientific fact:

show them a zircon from Mount Narryer in Australia that's four billion years old, show them these fossilized skeletons of Pronconsul africanus from eighteen million years ago that have just turned up in Lake Victoria, that may really be the missing link and they'll say fine, just fine, if this creator could produce the heavens and earth and the whole shebang in just six days he'd certainly be able to produce a real interesting history to go along with it now wouldn't he? They'll point to billion year old Precambrian rocks on top of Cretaceous shale to disprove geological sequence and lump the whole thing into the flood here [. . .]. And God destroyed the earth's inhabitants with water because of man's wickedness. And Noah only remained alive, and they that were with him in the ark and the whole geologic record goes down under forty days of rain [. . .]. (180–81)

The creationist movement, as Numbers points out, has always lacked for geologists among its supporters. For instance, the most influential statement on flood geology, John C. Whitcomb, Jr., and Henry M. Morris's *The Genesis Flood* (1961), is authored, respectively, by a fundamentalist theologian and a civil engineer (Numbers, 207). Here, they argue that the earth, prior to the Flood, was canopied by a body of water that, when it fell, covered the entire earth. Before this, God instructed Noah to build his ark (the size of eight freight trains each numbering sixty-five cars). The animals saved were both domestic and nondomestic, and, eventually, all the animals were released on Mount Ararat and guided by God to their respective homes. Geological layering meanwhile is explained by "the early death of marine creatures, buried by sediments deposited during the first stages of the flood; the hydrodynamic selectivity of moving water, which sorted out particles of similar sizes and shapes; and the superior mobility of vertebrates, which allowed them to escape early destruction" (Numbers, 202). Thrust faulting, as McCandless complains, is dismissed by reference to a single mountain in Glacier National Park, where "old" Precambrian limestone is found to sit on "young" Cretaceous strata. According to Morris, "all of the rock strata which contains fossils of once-living creatures" can be dated "as subsequent to Adam's fall" (Numbers, 203), or between five and seven thousands years ago.

Flood geology might have been an amusing geological footnote except for the fact that in the effort to transform a biblical narrative into a scientific one that could be taught in the schools, creationists sustained its prominence.[24] The consequence of all this—that is, of the effort to transform creationism into a respectable science, so that it could be argued that "teaching it did not violate the constitutional restrictions against religious instruction, while not teaching it violated the free-exercise rights of creationist students"[25]—was that in the early 1980s, two state legislatures, those of Arkansas and Louisiana, after a decade of increasing sympathy for creationism, passed legislation mandating that it be taught in the public schools. The Arkansas law was the more demanding, and it was the one that, when it was contested by the ACLU and went to trial, attracted both national and international attention. Surprisingly, the bill moved through the state senate, by a vote of 22 to 2, with hardly a word of debate. The Arkansas House of Representatives mustered up a few more nays but also passed the bill along, without debate, to Governor Frank White. Known as "Balanced Treatment of Creation Science and Evolution Science Act," the bill's stated purpose was to "protect academic freedom by providing student choice; to ensure freedom of religious exercise, to guarantee freedom of belief and speech; to prevent establishment of religion; to prohibit religious instruction concerning origins; to bar discrimination on the basis of creationist's or evolutionist's belief; to provide definitions and clarifications" (Nelkin, 138). The bill was, as one legislator complained, "worded so cleverly that none of us can vote against it if we want to come back here" (Larson, 152). This was less of a problem for Governor White, who admitted to not having read the bill, though he signed it. The matter was a simple one, he thought, saying, "If we're going to teach evolution in the public school system, why not teach scientific creationism? Both of them are theories" (Larson, 152).[26]

Still, there are theories and there are theories, some predicated on a significant body of evidence and others entirely speculative and even, as with scientific creationism, promoted in the face of compelling counterevidence. Thus, convinced that Arkansas had passed legislation that sought to promote not a science but a religion, the ACLU felt it imperative to challenge the new law. The two-week trial took place in December 1982. It was billed as "Scopes II," but it was nothing of the sort. As Edward Larson writes, "Too many differences separated the two cases. Two world views clashed at Dayton as leading protagonists for each side debated the reasonableness of evolutionary teaching, which was then the central constitutional issue. New constitutional principles against religion in public education now refocused the debate" (156). Meanwhile, confident that it had a strong case, the ACLU lawyers brought to Little Rock an array of religious leaders, scientists, and educators to testify on its behalf. The trial was a battle less of science versus religion then of the left versus the radical right.[27] In the end, the judge, William R. Overton, expressing skepticism with regard to the state's case, found for the plaintiffs. In his opinion, he wrote that there could be "no doubt that a major effect of the Act is the advancement of particular religious beliefs," and that if science is "what scientists do," then "creation science is not science" (Larson, 161). The case's aftermath left many creationist supporters quite upset. The preachers Pat Robertson and Jerry Falwell even accused Attorney General Steve Clark of "collusion with the ACLU" (Nelkin, 144). But it was a serious blow to the movement, at least as it sought to live beneath the umbrella of science. Later, the ACLU also protested the Louisiana legislation, but the case never went to trial, for a judge ruled, beforehand, that the legislature, in mandating what the public schools' curriculum must include, had usurped the board of education's rights (Larson, 164–67). A major consequence, then, of the Arkansas trial is that whereas close to twenty states had creationism legislation pending, no further legislation to this effect was enacted. This does not mean that the controversy has died. Convictions here are unamenable to compromise, and any judicial decision holds sway only so long as the community's opinion does not demand another.

In fact, as McCandless points out, popular opinion is somewhat evenly divided on the matter: "Almost half the damned people in this country, more than forty percent of them believe man was created eight or ten thousand years ago pretty much as he is today" (136). McCandless's accuracy is confirmed by a 1991 Gallup poll that found "47 percent, including a fourth of the college graduates, continued to believe that 'God created man pretty much in his present form at one time within the last 10,000 years'" (Numbers, ix). It appears, then, as the ACLU's lead counsel observed, that "[n]otwithstanding the Arkansas victory, . . . the problem of creationism will persist because it is a legal problem only in part. The law can only provide temporary relief" (Larson, 171). The truest relief depends on "meaningful scientific education" (Larson, 171). This too is what McCandless thinks and what makes him fearful, for in his brief career as a textbook writer, his work has been repeatedly bowdlerized by state education commissions afraid of offending their constituencies. His article on Darwin, for a high school encyclopedia, is a case in point:

> see all this blue penciling? They cut it from sixteen hundred words to thirty six, evolution theory went from three thousand to a hundred and ten the next

edition it won't be there at all. Origins of life get twenty eight, twenty eight mealy mouthed words listen . . . he had a book, or what was left of one, pages torn from it —here's what they want now, listen. Some people believe that evolution explains the diversity of organisms on earth. Some people do not believe in evolution. These people believe that the various types of organisms were created as they appear. No one knows for sure how the many different kinds of living things came to be. No one knows for sure how many smug illiterate idiots are out there peddling this kind of drivel [. . .]. (167)

Actually, the companies "peddling" these textbooks are in the hands not of "illiterate idiots," but of business people who can read the bottom line, which says that to ignore a market such as Texas, with its statewide purchasing policy, is to give the game away. In 1982 Texas spent $64 million on school textbooks, making it the largest and most influential of consumers. Each year, "the Texas State Textbook Committee, as an arm of the Texas Education Agency, approves not more than five and no less than two textbooks in specific categories" (Jenkinson, 61). A company that finds even one of its textbooks selected stands to make handsome profits, so it is not surprising that textbook publishers slant their books in the direction of this state's requirements. As *Education Week* observed, "Because the Texas market is so important and because it is impractical for publishers to print separate editions for use in Texas schools, some industry officials have noted that changes that are made in textbooks to be eligible for the Texas market are also included in books offered to schools throughout the country" (Jenkinson, 62). Texas has a history as the most prominent bulk purchaser, but it is not the only state to order its textbooks this way. At the time of the Gaddis narrative (mid-1980s), the practice was mimicked by twenty-one other states. It was, and continues to be, a practice with inbuilt dangers, and it fuels McCandless's anger:

> there must be twenty of these states where local school boards can't buy textbooks that haven't been selected by the state committee. You think Texas wants one that talks about land redistribution in Central America or anyplace else? You think Mississippi wants a history book that tells the kids Nat Turner was anything but a coon show? You talk about censorship and they howl like stuck pigs no, they let the publishers do that for them. Sixty five million a year, that's what Texas spends on schoolbooks, that kind of money the edition's so big it wipes out everything else, you think any publisher that wants to stay in business is going to try to peddle a fourteen dollar biology textbook to these primates with a chapter on their cousins back there banging around Lake Rudolf with their stone hammers? (184)

McCandless most objects to the vulgarizing of truth, forced to prostitute itself to popular prejudice. Respect for evidence is subordinated to political pressures, as shown in the way the Texas Education Agency, pressured by grassroot fundamentalists, wrote to the nation's publishers to demand that "[t]extbooks presented for adoption [in the state's schools] which treat the subject of evolution substantively as explaining the historical origin of humankind shall be edited . . . to clarify that the treatment is theoretical rather than factually verifiable" (Jenkinson, 63). Assumedly, the agency administrators knew the difference between science and religion, but they also knew the political strength of the movement, led by the Longview couple Mel and Norma Gabler, challenging its purchase of "secular humanist" textbooks. McCandless refers to this same "charming Texas couple who keep an eye out for schoolbooks that undermine patriotism, free enterprise, religion, [and] parental authority" (184).[28] In fact, the Gablers wielded, largely via their textbook reviews, extraordinary influence over education officials, both in Texas and throughout the country. In the early 1980s, the Gabler reviews were being used in all fifty states and twenty-five foreign countries (Jenkinson, 56). As the *New York Times* observed, "The Gablers are at the center of a growing network of parent groups, emboldened by what they see as the new conservative mood in the nation, who are demanding the alteration or removal of teaching methods, curriculums and individual textbooks that they contend are in large part to blame for the high teenage pregnancy rate, venereal disease, declining test scores and other problems of today's youth" (14 July 1981, C 4). It was from this same *Times* article that Gaddis appropriated quotations for use in *Carpenter's Gothic*.

Perhaps more crucial to McCandless's objection to the Gablers and their followers than their "vigilante spirit" is their conviction that education should entail the inculcation of absolute values. He speaks of them as exemplifying "just your good American vigilante spirit hunting down, where is it, books that erode absolute values by asking questions to which they offer no firm answers" (184). There is a certain irony here, for creation science has advanced itself precisely by accenting the theoretical side of science. Contrariwise, McCandless's professed promotion of questions over answers[29] roots itself in a real attachment to answers (e.g., those provided by paleontology), paralleled by a singular disbelief and anger when others refuse to acknowledge them:

> I'm not talking about ignorance. I'm talking about stupidity. If you want ignorance you can find it right there, that site on Lake Rudolf up in the Gregory Rift, hominid fossils, stone tools, hippo bones all of it caught in a volcanic burst two or three million years ago that was ignorance, that was the dawn of intelligence what we've got here's its eclipse. Stupidity's the deliberate cultivation of ignorance, that's what we've got here. These smug idiots with their pious smiles they can't stand the idea they're descended from that gang at Lake Rudolf banging around with their stone hammers trying to learn something no, they think God put them here in their cheap suits and bad neckties in his own image [. . .]. (182)[30]

McCandless' distinction between ignorance and stupidity does not show him at his best. There is too much anger and too little empathy; and the tone points to something else. That is, what is at issue is not simply a matter of evolution. For starters, it is not, to use Stephen R. L. Clark's phrase, only "ill-educated noodles" who think the distinction between science and pseudoscience less than clear and who distrust evolutionary science. Nor do the political abuses run all one way. Those suspicious of evolution, Clark states, were right to suspect that it "was more than a hypothesis. It had become a creed, and not one easily assimilable to ancient ideas of truth or justice" (24). Clark himself is not an opponent of evolution. Still, he can see, from the point of view of those who are, the imagined dangers:

> Evolutionism has been seen by them not simply as a scientific theory but as a worldview, with its own morals and metaphysics. Social Darwinism, with its "survival of the fittest," lay at the core of an oppressive capitalism, and was seen to be the ethos of the German war machine in *both* world wars. And evolutionists were supposed to think that there were "backward" peoples who might justly be erased from history, to think that traditional moralities were biological accidents that might properly be surpassed, to think that evolutionary success is all that matters. The scientific establishment denied that there was any radical difference between human beings and brutes, and simultaneously insisted that animal experimentation was certainly allowable. (24)[31]

Clark does well to point out just how enmeshed in politics the whole discussion is—and not only the politics of Southern fundamentalism. McCandless speaks of the smugness of those who object to evolution, but there is also the smugness of those who think evolution's narrative an indisputable fact. Again, this is less to dispute the "facts" of evolutionary theory than to suggest that scientists themselves need to demonstrate sensitivity regarding larger axiological concerns, and would do well to refrain from riding roughshod over those beliefs—e.g., ethical, humanistic, religious—that communities hold. Nor is it best to view an event too completely in the frame of a prior event, the way McCandless views Smackover as Scopes II:

> —In Smackover no, no you don't kid about Smackover. People get up in the morning and go to bed at night in Smackover till the day they die and go someplace else, someplace that must look just like Smackover at two in the morning believe me, that's as serious as things can get, Reverend Ude in there washing them all in the blood of where are those little books, those damned little books [. . .] —here, here's one, Genesis to Revelation the whole thing boiled down to ten pitiful little pages of illiteracy and hideous cartoons [. . .]. (179-80)

Of course, one may wonder whether there is not a good bit of Gaddis in McCandless's denouncements of the Southern fundamentalists. The critic

Michael Wood has observed that, on this subject, Gaddis has something like "a bee in his bonnet" (20), and I think he is right. In any event, it is interesting to note Gaddis's change of the court case's venue from Little Rock, its historical site, to Smackover, a small town, or backwater, about an hour southeast of Hope, Arkansas.[32] The change accentuates the parallel with the Scopes trial (held in rural Dayton, Tennessee [1925]), even when the differences between Scopes and Little Rock are perhaps more noteworthy. For instance, an unpredicted element of more recent anti-evolution legislation—in Arkansas, Louisiana, and Tennessee—was just how much support it garnered in urban districts. In fact, as Larson notes, especially notable about the Louisiana legislation was its representing "the first preponderantly urban state assembly to approve an anti-evolution measure. Over 60 percent of the state lawmakers represented counties having more than 100,000 people, and those urban legislators voted for the bill in substantially the same ratio as their rural colleagues. At least in Louisiana, and to a lesser extent in Arkansas and Tennessee, the stereotype of creationism emanating from the rural backwaters of American civilization simply did not hold up" (155). And yet the picture that *Carpenter's Gothic* offers of the anti-evolutionist movement and of the fundamentalists in general—with their comic books, snake handlers, day of rapture, Survival Handbook, and illiterate preachers—is broadscale caricature, suggesting that Gaddis does not think the distinction between Snopes and Little Rock worth making, so benighted do they both seem. This conclusion is, undoubtedly, too strong. Still, Gaddis does at times offer evidence of being rather wearied by the intellectual torpidity of Southern fundamentalists and their political allies, almost as if he would prefer to remove himself from the debate, important as it may be. In the Grove interview, he comes close to saying as much: "As one grows older one realizes that the people who listen to you are the people who agree with you, and you agree with them. And the others just get harder in their positions. So there is a sense of futility, finally, in the effort. But the effort is worth continuing to make" (B 10).

Still, however weary Gaddis must be from the failure of his novels to garner an attention commensurate with their achievement,[33] he is as much different from McCandless as the latter is from the protagonist of his own novel, Kinkead. As McCandless tells Lester, who has speculated about the resemblance, "Not supposed to be anybody, what do you think a novel" is? (136). Here, a novel is understood as something that borrows from, and comments upon, real people and events, even as it retains its element of difference and detachment. Thus, not only is Little Rock not Scopes II, but Smackover is not Little Rock, and Gaddis is not McCandless. Or at least not exactly, for though I wish to be mindful and considerate of the difference, I do not want to let go of resemblances entirely, and of the tension that novels (Gaddis's included) have historically maintained between the real and the fictive. In any event, there is enough about Gaddis's description of McCandless to suggest the distance between the novelist and his protagonist. For starters, we can hardly overlook McCandless's intellectual aggressivity. That is, Gaddis's portrait shows us a man inclined toward teaching, yet handicapped by an inability to acknowledge the intelligence of others. Expecting people to concede their comparative ignorance, McCandless angers when they do not, and begins to harangue them, as he harangues Lester. Lester, however, is familiar with McCandless's tactics and refuses to be bullied: "You think you're back in one of these broken down schools where you can rave and rant like this? bully and browbeat everybody in sight because that's what you do. Because you've smarter than anybody else aren't you, like this hero you've got in this rotten novel, this Frank Kinkead" (136). And it is not only Lester who helps us to put McCandless's character in perspective. There are also the women, notably Elizabeth and Mrs. McCandless, the latter of whom, as Cynthia Ozick observes, "appears out of nowhere like a clarifying messenger" (18), offering a history of McCandless that cuts through some of his more self-protecting accounts. Seen from this perspective, McCandless is well-intentioned but adrift, not really knowing which way to proceed or what stance—censor or savior—to take toward the world. And when Mrs. McCandless hears Elizabeth say that she does not know what he is up to, she illuminatingly says: "I don't think anyone does [. . .] —anything he could get his hands on, even Greek drama and you can imagine that, but he didn't even really teach history no, no he wanted to change it, or to end it, you couldn't tell" (252). Here, the woman's calm self-possession, combined with her preparedness to meet difficulties in their time, makes McCandless's stance appear almost manic.

Elizabeth also forces us to reconsider the thrust of McCandless's pronouncements. Unlike both the creationists and McCandless, she does not feel the need to read things—e.g., the Bible or science—imperiously. Her openness is especially attractive when juxtaposed with Paul's or McCandless's stridency. Neither man demonstrates much empathy for others. For them, the world divides into those who are with or against one. Elizabeth is different, however. She may not agree with the way the fundamentalists read the Bible, but this does not prevent her from seeing that for these people, the Bible, taken literally, helps to front the world and to answer the question that dogs us all: to what purpose does the world exist? To an educated Northeasterner like McCandless, the beliefs of a Southern fundamentalist may, indeed, register as wrongheaded. Yet Elizabeth, more sensitive to the need to reconcile realities to desires, particularly after her brother's death, thinks there is something equally wrongheaded about despising people for their longings and hopes, no matter how sentimental. "[A]ll these sad stupid, these poor sad stupid people," she tells McCandless, mimicking his language, "if that's the best they can do? their dumb sentimental hopes you despise like their books and their music what they think is the rapture if that's the best they can do? hanging that gold star in the window if, to prove that he didn't die for nothing? Because I, because I'll never be called Bibbs again . . ." (245). Fortunately, McCandless's insensitivity is not so intractable that he does not feel the error, and at narrative's end, he promises Elizabeth that he will do what he can (i.e., make his geological findings public) to stop the madness over the African mineral fields.

In *Carpenter's Gothic*, McCandless stands as an almost classic representative of a class, a region, and a temperament, the last of which is rational, scientific, and masculine. It is tempting to see events through his eyes. But his is a perspective on the world perhaps definable as much by what it does not see as by what it sees. What it does see, when the gaze is directed toward the Southern fundamentalists, is illiteracy, stupidity, militarism, greed, and self-righteousness: "convicts locked up in some shabby fiction doing life without parole" (186). What it does not see, as Elizabeth's response makes clear, is the longing on the part of ordinary people for their lives to make sense, to assume a pattern, and to speak of a future equal to, if not greater than, their hopes. It might be that "the resurrection and the life" amount to no more than "the life starting to bulge in" the pants of a fourteen-year-old (186) and that these people are just stupid hicks, taking up precious space. So McCandless believes. However, we make a mistake if we embrace McCandless's point of view too readily, for it is too severe, too short on compassion and sympathy. On the other hand, we do need to pay more attention to Elizabeth. In many ways, she is a very ordinary woman: alcoholic, superstitious, ill educated, lonely, and abused. And while there are superficial resemblances between Elizabeth and *J R*'s Amy Joubert, the latter woman makes a much more impressive figure as the world judges these things. Instead, Elizabeth is an isolated middle-aged woman, trapped in a Hudson Valley Victorian house, less surrounded than visited by men—Paul, Billy, and McCandless—whom she loves in one way or another but whose real lives are lived elsewhere. And while, like Elizabeth herself, none of these men is noticeably religious, they each have some connection—if only that of antipathy—to the realm of the spiritual or religious. Thus, Paul is Reverend Ude's public relations man; Billy practices an Eastern mysticism and believes in karma; and McCandless, who (as noted) believes the Bible "the greatest work ever produced by western man" (134), is exercised by the way so many appropriate and do "business with" it (190). Elizabeth's connection is, perhaps, less obvious, and Paul, we know, even accuses her (in his cynical manner) of having no faith at all. Still, the connection is there, and it is among the things I would like to comment upon in the next and final section.

Elizabeth's (and the Novel's) Mediating Hope

Among *Carpenter's Gothic*'s characters, Elizabeth is the most hopeful and even the most religious, if by this one means a readiness to think of the world as a purposeful place. She is not outwardly religious. She even tells Paul, when he asks her to impersonate a television evangelist's mother, that she cannot "[b]ecause I'm not a good faithful illiterate Christian mother because I'm not Sally Joe!" (112). She may not be Sally Joe (who, aside from Paul, would want her to be?), but in her belief that "[i]t's an amazing thing to be alive" (151), there is a hope quite counter to McCandless's own more macabre understanding: "Sikhs killing Hindus, Hindus killing Moslems, Druse killing Maronites, Jews killing Arabs, Arabs killing Christians and Christians killing each other maybe that's the one hope we've got" (185–86). And it seems as if we are asked—not by Elizabeth but by Gaddis—to understand this hope in the light of a religious understanding, vestigial or otherwise. This sense, while never emphatic, is suggested by the symbols that attach to Elizabeth. These include most notably the doves, but also smaller things such as her age, thirty-three, the three falls that precede her death, her belief in transmigration, and her experience of exaltation or rapture. The dove is introduced in the novel's very first sentence: "The bird, a pigeon was it? or a dove (she'd found there were doves here) flew through the air, its colour lost in what light remained" (1). Its placement suggests its importance, which can also be said of Gaddis's return to it in the chapter's very last line: "It was a dove" (24). Later, when McCandless and Elizabeth stand in the backyard, enshrouded in dead leaves, the doves reappear: "But she'd turned away looking out on the fading turmoil of the terrace, the overturned chairs and the leaves and doves, three or four of them, picking indiscriminate, specked like the leaves in the sun still casting a warmth, or the look of it out there, like her voice when she'd spoken just beginning to fail" (226). The doves counter the mood, otherwise autumnal and elegiac. They mingle amidst mention of a "rapture" and "fall" and (in what almost seems an echo of Stevens's "Sunday Morning," e.g., "Palestine / Dominion of the blood and sepulchre") the suggestion of ancient sacrifice:

> and the leaves before they'd cried out their colours, before they'd seized separate identities here in vermilion haste gone withering red as old sores, there bittersweet paling yellow toward stunted heights glowing orange in that last spectral rapture and to fall, reduced again to indistinction in this stained monotony of lifelessness at her feet where a dove carped among last testimonies blown down from somewhere out of reach, out of sight up the hill in its claim as a mountain, leaves of scarlet oak here and there in the blackened red of blood long clotted and dried. (227)

What specifically ties the dove(s) to Elizabeth is that they both emit an identical sound: a bleat. There are her "choked bleats" (163, 253), including, as she lies dying, the "choked bleat of sound [that] came lost from her throat in a great sigh" (253), which recalls both her own prior sound and that of the dove that has previously awakened her from sleep: "The sound that waked her was already gone when she listened, the movement no more than the dapple of sun on the wall, on the bed empty beside her, and then again, the bleat of a dove in the branches outside and she was up" (164). In addition to the dove, we should note here the use of the word *dapple*. As it is difficult to hear the word *incarnadine* without thinking of Shakespeare (*Macbeth* II. ii. 59), it is also difficult to hear the word *dapple* and not think of Hopkins ("Pied Beauty": "Glory to God for dappled things—"), yet Gaddis uses the word at least three times here (32, 164, 253). Likewise, Hopkins's spirit seems present in that same backyard scene when McCandless asks Elizabeth whether she has ever seen the sun rise over the river, but then quickly moves to an image that more matches his mood, sunset: "get toward the end of the day like the sun going down in Key West if you've ever seen that? They're all down there for the sunset, watching it drop like a bucket of blood and clapping and cheering the instant it disappears, cheer you out the door and damned glad to see the last of you" (230). By itself, it is a frightening and despairing image, and, as far as McCandless is concerned, I believe an authentic emotion. But the description also echoes the second stanza of Hopkins's "God's Grandeur":

> nature is never spent;
> There lives the dearest freshness deep down things;
> And though the last lights off the black West went
> Oh, morning, at the brown brink eastward, springs—
> Because the Holy Ghost over the bent
> World broods with warm breast and with ah! bright wings.

What are my reasons for making the comparison, when the Hopkins passage so reverses the apparent significance of the McCandless story? Well, there are several. For one, we want to remember the other time in the narrative when McCandless's pessimism seems to win out, at the conclusion of the fourth (unnumbered) chapter, as he reads from Naipaul's *The Mimic Men*, and seems to identify with the narrator's statement that his "vision of disorder" had so much gotten the better of his "hopes" that he had lost his will to fight. There are two things to note here: (1) the Naipaul character's "vision of disorder" is, we know, a path of transition to "a vision of order" (150); and (2), even as McCandless reads the passage, "the chords of Bach's D major concerto heaved into the room around him and settled like furniture" (150). Both facts make us rethink the finality of the pessimistic mood.

Meanwhile, with respect to letting McCandless's despair dictate the novel's closing, we want to take note of something else in the penultimate chapter, and this is Elizabeth's account of her own feeling of exaltation or rapture. It came, she says, when in bed with McCandless:

> All your gentle, your hands on my breasts on my throat everywhere, all of you filling me till there was nothing else till I was, till I wasn't I didn't exist but I was all that existed just, raised up exalted yes, exalted yes that was the rapture and that sweet gentle, and your hands, your wise hands, meeting the Lord in the clouds [. . .]. (245)

It may be objected that Elizabeth's experience is strictly sexual, and not to be confused with spiritual rapture. However, we need think only of Bernini's *Ecstasy of Saint Theresa* to see how the two might be one. I believe the two—the sexual and the spiritual—here are one. If Elizabeth's experience were strictly sexual, it might more likely, as with the woman in the pornographic photograph, be felt as "without a gleam of hope or even expectation" (117). But built into Elizabeth's experience are all the hopes and expectations that McCandless, in a very short time, comes to embody for her. True, he cannot satisfy these. The reason, however, has to do less with his philosophy than with his temperament. His temper is too despairing, and this makes love—which predicates itself on a hope respecting the future—an impossibility. Elizabeth does not realize this at first, but then comes to understand the nature of McCandless's self-imprisonment. There can be no rapture when there is no hope, and McCandless, with his bets placed on Apocalypse (Elizabeth: "you're the one who wants Apocalypse, Armageddon all the sun going out and the sea turned to blood you can't wait no, you're the one who can't wait!" [244]), cannot truly help her, so afraid is he of "being the prisoner of someone else's hopes" (244).

In the end, McCandless, with his "smoking gun," kills Elizabeth. Yet unlike McCandless's narrative, which ends with its blood-red sunset, the Gaddis narrative, which began at sunset, ends with a sunrise. Why should this be, emotionally? symbolically? Certainly, the novel seems to end grimly enough, with Teakell, Billy, and Elizabeth dead, the Reverend Ude shot, war in Africa imminent, and Paul victorious. Can there really be any consolation in the identification of Elizabeth with the doves, the first of which, in its death, is knocked about like a "battered shuttlecock" (1)? Steven Moore thinks not. That is, while acknowledging the symbolism's religious tenor, he argues that it only makes the novel's conclusion more bleak:

> when this "sweet bird" emits "a choked bleat" as she dies, even a reader hardened by the savage ironies of modern literature must feel that peace and innocence have indeed fled from this world for good. The dove of the Holy Ghost is treated no better by the novel's militant Christians, and at the symbolic age of thirty-three Liz even has aspects of Him the fundamentalists profess to worship. (*William Gaddis*, 125)

I agree with the substance of Moore's statement, but not its tone, for it makes the novel darker than I find it. Nor would I, with Moore, be so quick to offer a "No comment" (134) to the argument, made by Richard Toney, that in *Carpenter's Gothic* Gaddis "makes his optimism plain enough on the surface. The book ends with no period, indicating continuation. It hints at reincarnation, if only as a fly" (Moore, *William Gaddis*, 134). I have not had the chance to read the Toney review,[34] so I am not sure what he does with the suggestion of reincarnation. But the suggestion—or more accurately, the suggestion that death's finality is open to question—is very much part of the book, and we should make a mistake to ignore it. That is, much like the reader who misses the fact that Nabokov's narratives are often ghost stories—think, for instance, of the way that in *Pnin* Mira Belochkin, Pnin's youthful but murdered "sweetheart," lives on as the protagonist's guardian angel in the form of (what else?) her namesake, a squirrel—misses the whole spirit of the plot, the reader who rejects the less commonsensical elements of Gaddis's narrative also misses a great deal. Gaddis, I would argue, is much like Nabokov in this respect, and I would direct the reader's attention to a statement by Nabokov that nicely articulates what is at issue here:

> That human life is but a first installment of the serial soul and that one's individual secret is not lost in the process of earthly dissolution, becomes something more than an optimistic conjecture, and even more than a matter of religious faith, when we remember that only commonsense rules immortality out. A creative writer, creative in the particular sense I am attempting to convey, cannot help feeling that in his rejecting the world of the matter-of-fact, in his taking sides with the irrational, the illogical, the inexplicable, and the fundamentally good, [the true artist] is performing something similar in a rudimentary way to what the spirit may be expected to perform, when the time comes, on a vaster and more satisfactory scale. (Alexandrov, 56–57)

Of course, Gaddis is not Nabokov, and his interests in an other world appear mild by comparison. Also, Toney's "hints at reincarnation" are simply this: hints. Nevertheless, they are strong enough to warrant attention. In the case of Elizabeth, I would argue that her death does lack finality. That is, in the identification of Elizabeth with the dove, which of course is, in turn, identified with the Paraclete (often referred to in the novel), there is the sense, as in the Hopkins poem, that "morning . . . springs— / Because the Holy Ghost over the bent / World broods with warm breast and with ah! bright wings." The dove does appear in the last chapter, after Elizabeth's death. Or it seems to appear, and whether it does or not depends on what importance we attach to it, for its appearance is flitting and skeptics might deny its presence. However, it makes its presence known, I think significantly, right after Paul has picked up and read Elizabeth's diary description of her own, quite sexual but also spiritual, rapture: "she brought him in, surging to meet him for as long as it lasted" (257). It is just after Paul flees to the bathroom, from which he exits "shaved, scarred and shirtless," that "a movement no more than the flutter of a wing caught his eye through the glass at the foot of the stairs, someone on tiptoe, peering in" (257).[35] What does it mean? Well, it may mean nothing. I believe, though, it works in concurrence with the theme of resurrection, itself noticeably introduced in an early conversation between Elizabeth and McCandless, wherein the former mentions the things she learned or borrowed from her friend Edie: "she'd talk about living in this previous existence and I believed that too. I mean she was really the one that thought of that telescope, if she got far enough away where she could see herself in this previous existence? As what, he wanted to know, or pretended to" (156).

McCandless will have nothing to do with the subject, and suggests that "all the nonsense [. . .] about resurrection, transmigration, paradise, karma the whole damned lot" is a consequence of people's "fear" (157):

> —you think of three quarters of the people in this country actually believing Jesus is alive in heaven? and two thirds of them that he's their ticket to eternal life? [. . .] just this panic at the idea of not existing so that joining that same Mormon wife and family in another life and you all come back together on judgment day, coming back with the Great Imam, coming back as the Dalai Lama choosing his parents in some Tibetan dung heap, coming back as anything —a dog, a mosquito, better than not coming back at all, the same panic wherever you look, any lunatic fiction to get through the night and the more farfetched the better, any evasion of the one thing in life that's absolutely inevitable . . . (157)

McCandless has a point, and it would be unwise to ride roughshod over it. The universe is large, men and women and their planet are small; and it is more than likely an act of extraordinary hubris to think that in the larger scheme of things, our affairs are of any central importance, with the universe playing the role of wallpaper to our domestic dramas. Yet it would also be unwise to think that all is not open to question, that any knowledge that we might profess should ever be absolute, including that about "the one thing in life's that absolutely inevitable." Thus, in the final chapter, when the dog's owner, the little girl who is "all timidity" (257), and the fly both appear for the first time, it is hard, when we recall McCandless's own cynical imaginings of reincarnation's possibilities, not to identify, for whatever it is worth, these two with Elizabeth and Billy. Certainly, there is something about the little girl—her vulnerability and shyness—that make the connection with Elizabeth seem natural. There is also something about Billy—his readiness to make Paul's life difficult—that makes the connection with this fly, which will not leave Paul be, somehow logical. Paul, in a telephone conversation with Shelia (Billy's girlfriend), even introduces the idea, though he does not wish to believe it: "God damn it Shelia listen nobody gives one good God damn about his karma getting him off the wheel whether his next incarnation is a look, look there's a God damn fly just landed on the table here you think that's him? just went up to the ceiling doesn't know where the hell he's going you think that's him?" (256). Despite Paul's initial dismissiveness, the fly continues to hold his attention, yet escapes the multiple efforts to end its existence: "he banged it [the newspaper] down, pulling a deep breath and then taking the newspaper, rolling it stealthily, raising it over the fly's new foray across PREACHER SHOT IN BRIBE CASE and bringing it down hard, up slamming it at the refrigerator, the counter top, the table, finally standing there wiping his hand down his face and slumping back in the chair" (260). Something akin to a personal dislike has entered into the relation between Paul and the fly, making the link between the latter and Billy at least emotionally plausible.[36]

The point about the last chapter—and it is with this that I should like to conclude—is not that Elizabeth and Billy are reincarnated as a little girl and a fly. I cannot believe they are. Still, the suggestion is important. It reminds us that despite the coerciveness of McCandless's materialism, of his common sense (Nabokov: "Common sense at its worse is sense made common, and so everything is comfortably cheapened by its touch" [Alexandrov, 23]), it has not been the only point of view offered. Both Elizabeth and Billy have spoken of beliefs that are quite irruptive of McCandless's own. And there is, of course, the novel itself, constructed not only on the principle of the dialogic, but also (and without contradiction) on the notion, says Gaddis, of a timeless "unity" (Grove B 10). In the end, however, we ourselves assume some interpretative responsibility. We may prefer one character's reading of reality more than another's, or we may prefer a second or third possibility, including elements not mentioned. But while our beliefs differ, I suspect that most readers will agree that Gaddis, in *Carpenter's Gothic*, leaves the question of final determinations open, and that only those who think otherwise will experience the novel as "savagely pessimistic."[37] Finally, I would argue that *Carpenter's Gothic* reflects a modality of belief, exemplified by Montaigne's (or is it Pascal's?) lesson: "Our inability to prove quite forbids dogmatism. Our instinct for truth quite forbids skepticism."

4

A Frolic of His Own:
Whose Law? Whose Justice?

Now then, Glaucon, is the time for us like huntsmen to surround the covert and keep close watch that justice may not slip through and get away from us and vanish from our sight. It plainly must be somewhere hereabout.

—Plato's Socrates, *The Republic*, IV

If I . . . speak at length about ghosts, inheritance, and generations, generations of ghosts, which is to say about certain *others* who are not present, nor presently living, either to us, or outside us, it is in the name of *justice*. Of justice where it is not yet, not yet *there*, where it is no longer, let us understand where it is no longer *present*, and where it will never be, no more than the law, reducible to laws or rights.

—Jacques Derrida, *Specters of Marx*

"There may be something in the notion," Gaddis once mused, "that every writer writes only one book and writes it over and over and over and over again" (Grove, B 10). Gaddis's fiction certainly seems cut from the same cloth, as he returns again and again to themes (e.g., that which is worth doing; the struggles of the artist in a noisy world indifferent to the effort; and the hurts inflicted by a cash-nexus ethos) that fixate him. Justice is one of these themes, and if I have not addressed it directly as yet, it is because other matters got in the way. With *A Frolic of His Own*, however, the subject can no longer be put off, for the novel is, first and foremost, a meditation on justice.

Like Plato's Socrates, who believed that "it is no ordinary matter that we are discussing, but the right conduct of life" (603), Gaddis conceives the question of justice as crucial to our lives, even if it promises no easy answer. Yet, if Socrates thought it possible to postulate a theory of justice that should hold sway regardless of time and place, Gaddis, living in the twentieth century, must, whatever his longings, take history more into account. Certainly, the tragic dimension of history (with all its manifest injustices) has been on display in this century's two world wars, the Holocaust, the Gulag, the Cold War, the Vietnam War, the Cambodian genocide, the African famines, Rwanda, and Bosnia. Seldom, if ever, has the world been witness to such wide-scale brutality, misery, and murder, so much so that the *New York Times* has claimed that "At its worst, this has been Satan's century."[1] Thus while it may be true, as Socrates felt, that people in the main are well-meaning and predisposed to the good, this century's atrocities have forced us to take a more skeptical stance toward this truism and, more seriously, to rethink the question of justice itself. It is one reason why the meditation on justice has become one of the epoch's major intellectual forms. Think, for instance, of the impressive work (artistic, legal, political, philosophical, sociological, and theological) that has assumed this form, from such intellectuals as Hannah Arendt, Ronald Dworkin, Michel Foucault, Jürgen Habermas, Vaclav Havel, Agnes Heller, Martin Luther King, Jr., Emmanuel Levinas, Adam Michnik, John Rawls, Alexander Solzhenitsyn, and Charles Taylor, among others. Witness to this century's tragedies, these men and women have not pretended that they could undo or even offset all that has already transpired. Still, they have thought it imperative to reject the politics of fear and hatred, and to move in another direction, commencing with the conviction that justice is misnamed if it does not extend beyond the realm of the privileged few.

A *Frolic of His Own*, like its author, belongs to this tradition. It is a masterpiece that offers us less a blueprint for justice than a powerful meditation on where it might and might not be found. Its opening line—"Justice? —You get justice in the next world, in this world you have the law" (11)—makes clear just how difficult this search will be, even as the narrative's main East End Long Island locale appears almost walled off from the world's more devastating woes. And yet not only does news of the world's miseries seep—via newspapers, radio, and television—into this semiprotected bower, but it is also the case that this well-to-do exurban community cannot truly isolate itself from the larger national landscape. And here, in the United States, everything is clearly not okay, especially as the country has resorted more and more to resolving its genuine societal tensions through the means of an adversarial winner-takes-all practice. That is, a nation that has increasingly projected itself (notably during the Reagan, Bush, and, now, Clinton presidencies) in terms that are less cultural or political than economic (i.e., in terms of competition and free markets), has grown accustomed, Gaddis's novel would suggest, to a parallel adversarial practice in its courts and in its more encompassing sense of a judicial ethos. "This free enterprise society is an adversarial society," Gaddis told a *Washington Post* reporter, "so the law emerges from that adversarial attitude. So here we are, all adversaries" (Schwartz, C 2). Justice, if it exists, is more available to those with "deep pockets" than to the citizen of ordinary or less than ordinary means. In *A Frolic of His Own*, justice carries a very expensive price tag, and ends up looking much more like injustice.

To say this, however, implies another standard of justice. To make this standard clearer, we need to examine the novel, for it presents a range of possible understandings, sometimes allied and sometimes in conflict. Specifically, I wish to examine five such understandings: Oscar's sense of justice as something akin to natural law, albeit personally applied; Judge Crease's justice as common law; Harry's justice as legal right; Christina's justice of the heart; and, last, justice as an aspect of the otherworldly, something that makes its presence known in the space of the novel even as it resists specific formulation.

Oscar's Version of Natural Law

More than most, Oscar thinks of justice—eternal, transcendent justice—as something owed him. Others might think of it as an ideal, as something about which we might hope to gain an approximate cognition. That is, most people share Socrates' sense that "perhaps there is a pattern of it laid up in heaven" (Plato, 819), but that it is not likely to be discovered unblemished here on earth. Oscar, however, is something of an innocent, a man-child, unmindful of how even such a sincere wish as his "I only want justice after all" (28), said to the insurance adjuster, must find itself frustrated. His desire for justice is at the heart of his play, *Once at Antietam*, and of his two lawsuits, the first seeking damages for the injuries suffered when run over by his own car, and the second for a film company's alleged theft of his play. As for the play, not only is justice its theme (Oscar: "that's what it's about, my play that's exactly what it's about justice" [54]), but its composition is also thought of as an exercise in justice. That is, Oscar writes the play out of a sense of obligation, first to his grandfather and then to his father. *Once at Antietam*'s protagonist, Thomas (a Southerner and diplomat's son, who, after fighting in the Civil War, takes over his deceased uncle's Pennsylvania mine), is modeled after Oscar's grandfather, Thomas Crease, whose similar history ended with an illustrious career as a Supreme Court justice. As with Learned Hand, who once, parting from Oliver Wendell Holmes, exhorted him to "'Do justice, sir, do justice!,'" only to have Holmes reply, "'That is not my job [. . .]. It is my job to apply the law'" (285),[2] Justice Crease's reputation was of one obedient to a transcendent justice, an obedience that often put him at odds with the more pragmatic Holmes. Oscar's play, then, is a homage to his grandfather, even as it represents an earnest attempt, in the present, to win recognition from his father, a cold, judgmental, and selfish man, brilliant though he may be. Oscar, whose mother died when he was a child, has been clearly scarred by his father's ill treatment of him. He has never truly grown up, and while he thinks of himself as "the last civilized man" (386), the truth is quite different. Virtually friendless, he lacks social skills and sees the world largely through the lens of his own interest and self-pity. Even when tragedy strikes those near, as it does when Lily's breast implants rupture or, more seriously, when Christina's husband suddenly dies, he cannot imagine that the two women might have more on their minds than the status of his lawsuits. He is a sad, pathetic figure, and had his growing up not been so hard or had his stepsister not shown us another way to view him, he would be rather difficult to like. Still, as his lawyer Basie says, "Always have to like a man that's at the end of his rope" (125), and most readers will take this view. Oscar is the quintessential dangling man, and if he is largely responsible for his adversity, it is also true that an additional share of adversity, in the form of modern civilization, simply comes knocking at his door.

One of the most surprising things connected to Oscar is the quality of his play. It is quite an interesting play, and if, as Jonathan Raban has observed, its "more immediate debts are to the thoughtful, talkative middlebrow theater of the 1950s, to plays like Anouilh's *Antigone* and Bolt's *A Man for All Seasons* in which large moral questions were acted out by people in period costume," it still "has a lot of their dusty charm" (4).[3] The success of the play has much to do with its borrowings: whole dialogues are borrowed, if not lifted, from *The Republic* and *The Crito*; and there are further debts to Rousseau and Camus. Given such antecedents, it is not surprising that the play should seem wiser than its author. Nor is it so surprising that Oscar should be such a poor interpreter of his own play, for his identification with the character Thomas, whose obsession with justice is more innocent than thoughtful, leads him to miss the more encompassing suggestion of the play: that justice is best imagined as an ideal to guide and judge action. But Thomas seeks out justice as if it were reducible to a piece of property; and like Oscar, with his identification of his teacher's salary with injustice ("That salary! that miserable salary month after month just to remind me what injustice really was" [418]), he conflates justice with material success:

> It was an insult, that pension, coming year after year to remind us what injustice was, in case we'd forgotten. In case I'd been able to forget all the plans that he had for me, for a great career in public life, bringing me up to read Rousseau, believing the "natural goodness of man . . ." (71)

Thomas is speaking here of his father, the diplomat, but the lines originate in Oscar's own experience with his grandfather, who also urged the boy to read Rousseau and to imagine a life dedicated to the fostering of justice. Both Thomas and Oscar, however, have rather myopic conceptions of justice. They want justice for themselves, particularly economic justice, yet they seem oddly indifferent to the wants of others this way. Thomas, for instance, is an unrepentant slaveowner, who takes the escape of his slave, John Israel (a "black Epictetus" [101]), as a personal affront, much in the way that, later, Oscar reacts to the departure of Basie (a black ex-con now in flight from the authorities) only in terms of how it relates to himself: "What about me[?]" (307). Meanwhile, with respect to Thomas's inheritance, the Pennsylvania mine (a nineteenth-century Plato's Cave), its new owner is less interested in the workers and their conditions than in the fact that his patrimony restores him to some rightful place in the world's hierarchy. Thomas becomes a walking illustration of George Fitzhugh's 1856 polemic *Cannibals All!* which compared Northern industrial practices unfavorably with those of Southern slavery: "You, with the command over labor which your capital gives you are a slave owner—a master, without the obligations of a master!" (Fitzhugh, 17). Likewise, Oscar, when it seems that he will, as a consequence of his suit, be the recipient of tens of millions of dollars from the Hollywood producers of *The Blood in the Red White and Blue*, appears completely indifferent to the labor that went into the film, convinced that this massive transference of capital from many pockets to one represents justice. Were the behavior of Thomas and Oscar reduced to a principle, it would be: what is good for me must be thought good for everyone. Needless to say, it is not a very satisfying equation.

There are, of course, smarter heads in Oscar's play. Thomas's mother, who lives by the wisdom of Matthew 6.19—"Do not lay up for yourselves treasures on earth, where moth and rust consume and where thieves break in and steal, but lay up for treasures in heaven"—is one; and Kane, modeled on Socrates, is another. Unlike Thomas, Kane sees an injustice both in the owning of slaves and in the exploitation of so-called free labor. He speaks of the "terrible silence of slavery" (167) and speaks up for Thomas's unnamed attacker, not because he thinks what he did is right, but because he knows that when a system parcels out its wealth inequitably, justice itself suffers, and it becomes harder to tell right from wrong. Like Socrates, who felt that "when wealth is honored in a state, and the wealthy, virtue and the good are less honored" (Plato, 779), Kane proposes a system of justice that would require Thomas to shed the bulk of his possessions, something that he is not prepared to do. With his "mind stuffed with ambition and the Social Contract in" his pocket, yearning for "a great career in public life" (90), Thomas exhibits the familiar signs of the man of social conscience, but they are trappings only. His proper place is among the "'arms-bearing aristocracy'" (102), and from him, as from Oscar with all his conventional prejudices, we can expect little real contribution toward the righting of present injustices.

Rather, we would do better to look to the Kanes or perhaps the John Israels for such contributions, though their fates in the play—with the first sentenced to death on a trumped-up charge of spying, and the second free only until someone captures him or shoots him down—make this hope seem wistful.

In the meantime, Oscar pursues his lawsuits. The first of these, the liability claim consequent upon his accident with the car (the Japanese-made "Sosumi"), can be dealt with more summarily than the second suit. The reason is that this is a classic "pain and suffering" liability suit that, despite Oscar's claim otherwise, has very little to do with justice. Generally, in an accident of this sort, the victim is covered by a no-fault provision, whereby he or she is spared the trouble of proving blame, so that an adequate recompense (e.g., for hospital bills and vehicle damage) can be more quickly disbursed. In a country suffering from a litigation explosion, no-fault has been a godsend in those states, such as Oscar's own New York, where automobile insurance claims once often took months, if not years, to settle. Obviously, there is something—i.e., profits—in this for the insurance companies, but mostly the system has worked well. Regardless, Oscar cannot help seeing in all this civilization's decline: "this No Fault idea it's not even an idea, it's a jerrybuilt evasion of reality of course someone's at fault. Someone's always at fault. It's all a cheap dodge chewing away at the basic fabric of civilization to replace it with a criminal mind's utopia where no one's responsible for the consequences of his actions, isn't that what the social contract is all about?" (251).[4] Convinced that he is mounting the barricades, Oscar employs Lily's lawyer, Kevin, to press a $1.5 million liability claim to make him, once again, whole.

In this first suit, Oscar's lawyers (Kevin is, in time, replaced by Preswig) are classic ambulance chasers, though this appellation speaks of a group whose work, following the relaxation of the professional code, is no longer thought so peripheral to what lawyers do. That is, there was a time when lawyers were forbidden to "stir up litigation." It was against the law to advertise or to seek business, for it was felt that the society would be more at peace with itself if only those disputes that were heartfelt and otherwise irresolvable found their way to court. It was the specter of lawyers drumming up business, bringing neighbor against neighbor, that led even New York City, as recently as 1954, to break "up a circle of eighteen lawyers and nine accomplices operating with 'all the efficiency of a supermarket'" (Olson, 17). Still, over the decades, the prohibitions began to give way, and then, in 1977, following the Supreme Court's extension to lawyers, in the *Bates* decision, of the right to advertise, things began to accelerate in an opposing direction. In 1985, in the *Zauderer* case, the Court ruled that lawyers could solicit parties against particular sorts of defendants, giving encouragement thereby to what used to be known as "bill of peace" cases but what are now more familiarly known as class action suits. A consequence of such climatic changes was that not only did a state such as New York see, in the course of a generation, a three hundredfold rise in the "payouts in suits against doctors and hospitals" (Olson, 5), but there also grew the sense that the rules themselves had been turned upside down. Walter Olson writes:

> On the matter of promotion, the American legal profession did not just relax its old ethical strictures, which would be a common enough sort of thing, but stood them on their head. Down through the mid-1960s the A.B.A.'s ethical canon number 28, against "stirring up litigation," was still very much intact. Within a few years many had come to see stirring up litigation as an inspiring public service, in fact morally obligatory. By 1975 one of the most quoted of the newer legal ethicists, Monroe Freedman, could write provocatively but in all seriousness of a "professional responsibility to chase ambulances." (31)

Along with the turnabout in the rules of promotion, the legal profession also witnessed something like a reversal in its attitude toward contingency fee suits. Traditionally, contingency fee suits were thought an unpleasant necessity. Not everyone could afford a lawyer, yet everyone deserved his or her day in court. Lawyers were, of course, under an obligation to take *pro bono publico* cases, but the obligation was more moral than legal. This being the case, it seemed preferable to allow contingency fee suits, wherein the plaintiff's attorney worked for a percentage of the hoped-for award, rather than to let clients with good cases but weak resources go begging. Over time, all the states moved to legalize such suits, Maine being the last state to do so, sometime in the early 1960s. Still, the contingency fee suit has its downside. The real problem, says Olson, "derives not so much from the conflicts it creates between the interests of lawyer and client as from the even more dangerous identity it creates between their interests as against everyone else's" (44). That is, the contingency suit promotes claims against, and the zealous pursuit of, "deep pockets." It may make overnight millionaires of some, but it has not been a positive experience for justice in general. Rather, as Olson nicely puts it, "Suing people for a share of the proceeds has become, like one or two famous television ministries, a venture in hellfire preaching and unctuous handwringing that enables the practitioners to live in the luxury of Babylon" (46). So attractive have contingency fee suits become that a recent Federal Trade Commission report "showed that 97 percent of lawyers took injury cases only on contingency, refusing to consider hourly rates, however generous" (Olson, 47).

Oscar's own injury suit is less about justice than about money or greed. Kevin, Lily's lawyer, jumps on Oscar's claim, and though the two never meet, he is able, via Lily, to convince him that the $50,000 no-fault coverage is a travesty of justice. So while Oscar's employer continues to pay him and while he suffers no long-term injury beyond an almost undetectable facial scar, he files, on a contingency fee basis, a major suit against his insurance company. Or as he explains to Harry and Christina, "Because she [Lily] says Kevin said I'm probably already well past the threshold limit on all these medical bills so what we're talking about is all this pain and suffering and lost income because of this permanent disfigurement" (57). It is all nonsense, of course, and what makes it even more nonsensical is that, through Kevin's ineptness, Oscar's legal complaint has him, in effect, suing himself (283). There is probably some justice in that, for Oscar would do well to face his own responsibility for both the accident and the nuisance suit. But the long and short of the matter is that Oscar is exploited by a lawyer who views him as an avenue toward riches. Or as Christina rightly tells him: "It's not your constitutional rights this socalled lawyer is asserting, can't you see? He's asserting his own right to exploit your misery for every dollar he can, it's not his pain and suffering is it? his brilliant lecturing career that's in jeopardy? Is he going to pay your hospital bills when you lose? doctor bills? lab bills? this therapist? By the time you get into a courtroom that scar will look like you fell off your tricycle when you were five" (183). Eventually, Oscar sees things this way, agreeing to the insurance company's offer, but not before he, disgruntled with Kevin, seeks out the assistance of another firm, Mohlenhoff Shransky, brought to his attention through its matchbook advertisements. And with the assistance of the firm's Jack Preswig, things threaten to become truly Dickensian, for it is in the nature of product liability suits that not only do the makers of products find themselves sued but so do a whole line of subcontractors, all on the speculation, writes Olson, "that one of them will turn out to be vulnerable" (105). Or as the Ace Worldwide Fidelity agent, Frank Gribble, explains the matter to Oscar:

> —Because liability attaches to anyone who sells the product going back to its manufacturer including the makers of parts supplied by others since it is marketed under the manufacturer's name, if you follow me? Our legal department sought out the person you bought it from who had joined the Navy and so proceeded against the dealer from whom he'd purchased it new and the dealer then sued the wholesaler who has brought suit against the manufacturer who in turn is suing the assembler of the defective component parts whose makers are as you observed in your summons as a witness in the suit being brought against them by the assembler all over the globe [. . .]. (547)

When it becomes evident to Oscar that he is in tow to a "global car chase" (547), he gives up the suit, wisely if belatedly. Besides, by this point he has already learned something, via his Erebus pictures suit, about the fictiveness of pots of gold lying at the end of litigation rainbows. But I do not wish to equate the two suits too much, for they are different; and if the "pain and suffering" suit is virtually without merit, the latter suit seems otherwise.

Whatever the Erebus suit's merits, however, it too starts off as something like a nuisance suit. That is, Oscar, noting the narrative similarities between *The Blood in the Red White and Blue* and his own shelved play, *Once at Antietam*, begins an infringement suit against the Hollywood company even though his most important evidence seems like hearsay. By this, I mean that he starts the suit in motion before he has even seen the film. In fact, the suit travels through two courts and is resolved before he does so. Of course, his convalescent state prevents his attending a movie house; and he sees the film only when the studio, the injunction against its showing lifted, decides to revive the public's interest by showcasing it on television. But the whole early portion of Oscar's legal action has about it the nature of a fishing expedition.

Oscar's legal counsel, Lepidus & Shea's associate Harold Basie, tells him as much. Unlike Kevin or Preswig, Basie is a fine attorney, and ethical to boot. Or as ethical as one who has done time "for something that would curl your hair" (278), and who later lies his way into the profession, can be. Hence, when Oscar tells him that he wishes to press a suit on what looks to be solely coincidental similarities, Basie comes right to the point, telling him that given what he has heard added to the fact that the one tangible piece of incriminating evidence, the purported 1977 rejection letter from Kiester to Oscar, has yet to be located (it never is), he (unlike Szyrk, the creator of "Cyclone Seven") has no case:

> He's got a way better case than you do here. He could shit on a shingle and call
> it a protected statement under the First Amendment, you can't find that letter
> rejecting your play you don't even know who you sent it to. You go and serve
> a complaint on this Kiester they'll respond with an answer and motion to dis-
> miss and they'll probably get it. If they don't and you have to subpoena their
> records they come after yours too and that means that letter and all that doesn't
> even come till the discovery process, depositions, documents, interrogatories
> all the rest of it, motions for summary judgment if that's denied you get ready
> for pretrial conference maybe get a settlement. If you don't you go to trial, you
> lose there and you go to appeal spending your money every step, every step
> you take, disbursements, stenographers, transcripts, all that plus your legal fee
> I'd just hate to see it, case like this where it looks like you've hardly got one
> [. . .]. (114–15)

At first, it does seem as if Oscar has no case. What changes the matter, however, is that Basie, captured by Oscar's evident desperation, begins to take a personal interest in the matter. On his own time, he goes to see the film and becomes more intrigued by the narrative coincidences. Then there is also the matter of a parallel suit, lodged by a film student against Kiester and pertaining to the earlier film *Uruburu*. This suit gives further reason for thinking Kiester neither a careful nor an honest businessman. Together, these factors incline Basie to pursue the case further. It is a considered judgment, mindful of the fact that if he, in the name of his white-shoe firm, should pursue suits without merit, the firm will be the loser in the long run. Or as he tells Christina:

> —Just let's make sure we have one thing real clear Mrs Lutz, see we're not out looking for business, not ambulance chasers. Sam put me on this like kind of a favour to look into it, if I go and get us into some drawn out tangled up case just because the client's got money where I know we'll probably never win it I'm out on the street tomorrow. Maybe we've got something here, maybe worth a try, have to admit it all kind of intrigues me. And now Oscar here, see I've come to like Oscar. (125)

Basie gives an honest assessment of the situation. Still, at this point in the case, it must be thought of as something of a fishing expedition. Basie says as much: "Fish in these waters here a little today and see if we come up with enough to file this complaint he's hell bent on" (124). It is not an unethical strategy, given present legal practices, but it does give evidence, once again, of how much the standards—in this instance, of claimant's notice—have changed over time. That is, in the old law, prior to the 1938 adoption of the Federal Rules of Civil Procedure, "pleadings, among their other functions, served as an immensely important filter in keeping many kinds of litigation out of court entirely" (Olson, 94). It was expected that the claimant's lawyer had already exhaustively investigated and formulated the case, and that the pleading would deal in specific accusations. If it did not, it would be thrown out. Even when the claimant was granted trial, the subsequent proceedings would be framed only within the context of the alleged injustices. There was little room for reconceiving the case in mid-process. Thus while the old system was not without problems, most noticeably when a good case might be thrown out of court because of a failure, in pleading, to foresee the full nature of the injustice at hand, there was also good reason for maintaining a certain strictness in the pleading, or notice, requirements. Olson, summing up the objections of O. L. McCaskill, a prominent mid-century legal scholar, to the proposed changes in the rules of notice, writes:

> Justice was better served, McCaskill maintained, when lawyers did their best to investigate claims carefully before turning them into lawsuits. Once they were allowed to get away with it, however, many would follow the path of least resistance by filing the suit first and then checking out its merits at leisure. Even when they did know the facts and theory on which they planned to proceed, they would succumb to their natural incentive not to reveal more of their cases than necessary. The minimum commitment to detail needed to get their clients into court would soon become the norm. (99–100)

This is a fair description of what happens with Oscar's suit. Basie has a strong inkling that *The Blood in the Red White and Blue* is, in fact, an infringement upon Oscar's play, but he has no concrete evidence. He knows that he will not have to prove his claim until the trial, so he is willing to take certain chances at this point. Hence, he tells Oscar, with regard to Kiester's rejection letter, "Don't have to produce it right this second Oscar, state in complaint they had this access and face the problem of proof when we have to, taking a little chance on these reasons they gave for rejecting it when we try to claim breach of implied contract as a cause of action" (128). Under the old law, he would have been prevented from going further, but an important element of the 1938 Federal Rules of Civil Procedure was to allow the claimant to state the causes of action in general terms. "Pleadings," writes Olson, "would serve only to put the parties on notice that they were being sued, and briefly state the general subject matter of the dispute" (99). The problem with the new rules of notice is that they often, in the words of Fleming James and Geoffrey Hazard, allow a lawyer into the courtroom even though this person has stated "his claim in very general terms, so that it cannot clearly be discerned what he thinks the facts might be" (Olson, 99). Basie is a better lawyer than this, and though it is true that he proceeds with a case before he knows whether he has one, he does make an effort to specify the nature of the charges. He even warns Oscar, who wishes to charge Erebus with a potpourri of grievances: "Thing is Oscar this is an action for infringement. You get privacy and things like that in there you just confuse things, run a good chance they throw the whole thing out, just stay right with your play there" (164). Accordingly, Basie states four causes of action, all pertaining to Erebus's alleged infringement of Oscar's play. In addition to the allegation of infringement, the complaint alleges "fraudulent conduct" on the part of the several defendants (executives, director, screenwriters, et al.), conduct that has subjected Oscar "to extreme mental and physical distress," so that he should be entitled not only to damages but "to a constructive trust benefit on all profits and gross revenues from 'The Blood in the Red White and Blue'" (178).

Because of the nature of the suit (an infringement action)[5] and because of the fact that Erebus's general counsel has an office in New York, Oscar's complaint is filed in the United States District Court for the Southern District of New York. The choice of venue turns out to be important. Basie has the choice of filing in the defendant's home district—i.e., the Central District of California—or the district wherein the defendant's agent resides. Largely for the reason that Oscar is still convalescing, Basie files the complaint in New York, but this leads them into what is spoken of as "the trap" (299) laid by the Swyne & Dour associate Madhar Pai, counsel for Erebus, Kiester, et al. Pai prefers the New York jurisdiction because his defense strategy, assuming that the court should not grant a dismissal, is to represent Oscar's suit as one about property rather than copyright. And since compared with the laws in other states, California's laws have been unusually liberal in "giving property protection to ideas" (Goldstein, 41), Pai knows that he has a stronger case in New York. This helps to explain the logic of his questions during Oscar's deposition. Here, he knows that the 1976 Copyright Act, while granting protection to the expression of an idea, does not grant protection to the idea itself, and that, as Paul Goldstein writes, "[i]dea submitters rarely succeed on a property theory. . . . When courts invoke property doctrine in idea cases it is usually as a gentle way of telling the submitter that he will not recover his action" (41). In addition, when what is being contested, as in the present case, is an implied rather than an expressed contract, courts have tended to give more weight to the question of novelty (Goldstein, 44). Pai's defense very much relies on the decision handed down in 1972 by the New York Court of Appeals, in the *Downey v. General Foods Corp.* case (407). There, Chief Judge Fulk wrote, "The critical issue in this case turns on whether the idea suggested by the plaintiff was original or novel. An idea may be a property right. But, when one submits an idea to another, no promise to pay for its use may be implied, and no asserted agreement enforced, if the elements of novelty and originality are absent, since the property right in an idea is based upon these two elements" (Goldstein, 40).

In his deposition questioning, Pai seeks, without of course announcing his strategy, to turn Oscar's case into one that hinges on the protection of an idea:

> Q And the idea, the idea that a man of split allegiances might find himself in a situation obliging him to send up a substitute in his place in each of the opposing armies, while it was hardly an everyday occurrence, was certainly within the realm of possibility wasn't it?
> A Yes, it . . .
> Q And that the two might even meet in battle?
> A Yes, yes that's . . .
> Q In fact there was at least one such documented instance, was there not?
> A That's what my . . .
> Q Where both were, in fact, slain? In other words, a sort of quirk of history, the kind Shakespeare drew on freely when he needed a plot or a character? He could have pointed to Holinshed and advertised King Lear as based on a true story couldn't he?
> A If he, I suppose so, yes.
> Q So that in this action you're not claiming protection for an idea. What you claim has been infringed here then is not the idea which occurred to you over a period of time. (203)

Pai's performance at this stage of things is brilliant. He moves Oscar into making protective claims for an idea—"I claim protection for the idea too yes, if the . . ." (204)—and, at the same time, makes much of the fact that a good many of the ideas are borrowed from Plato, Camus, and Rousseau: "Plato attributes the idea and the words to Aeschylus whom he names, whereas you have simply lifted them from Plato without ascribing them to anyone the way you've done elsewhere I might add, Camus and Rousseau and I don't know who else" (224). It is largely on the basis of this deposition that the district court judge grants a summary judgment in favor of Erebus pictures. According to the Federal Rules of Civil Procedure (rule 56), a court can hand down such a judgment when there appear to be no triable issues of fact, and when what is at issue is simply the law's application. Here, the judge feels, in the words of Circuit Judge Bone, that the

> story idea central to the play was not sufficiently novel to create "property interest" entitled to protection under New York law in action against the motion picture makers for unfair competition and unlawful use, misappropriation and conversion; that notwithstanding the author's alleged submission of his play to defendant there was no evidence of any intent to contract with regard to the said play by defendant and thus its alleged unlawful use could form neither any basis for action for breach of implied contract, nor any basis for plaintiff's unjust enrichment action, nor for fraud action in that the defendants could not have enriched themselves at the author's expense on the ground that "plaintiff's alleged submissions lack the requisite novelty under the applicable law" and so falling into the public domain where he could not be defrauded of property he did not own. (405)

As fine as Pai's strategy appears, it is difficult to feel confident about an infringement defense that is so dependent on the issue of novelty. Granted, there have been occasional rulings that concur with the district judge's decision. In a fairly recent decision, for instance, involving the playwright Christopher Durang (*See v. Durang*, 1983), the United States Court of Appeals, Ninth Circuit, supported the lower court's summary judgment decision ("Summary judgment is proper if reasonable minds could not differ as to the presence or absence of substantial similarity of expression"), holding that "the court properly applied the doctrine ['*scènes à faire*'] to hold unprotectable forms of expression that were either stock scenes or scenes that flowed necessarily from common unprotectable ideas. 'Common' in this context means common to the works at issue, not necessarily, as plaintiff suggests, commonly found in other artistic works" (Goldstein, 728). Still, if the well-known United States Appeals Court decision involving Cole Porter (*Arnstein v. Porter*, 1946) seems to have overstated the case—"The principal question on this appeal is whether the lower court, under Rule 56, properly deprived plaintiff of a trial of his copyright infringement action. The answer depends on whether 'there is the slightest doubt as to the facts'" (Goldstein, 726)—there remains a handsome body of precedents suggesting that novelty, as it pertains to artistic properties, is a less than relevant concern. Key cases include *Sheldon v. Metro-Goldwyn Pictures Corp.* (1936) and *Alfred Bell & Co. v. Catalda Fine Arts, Inc.* (1951), both cited by Circuit Judge Bone. In the first case, Judge Learned Hand famously wrote:

> We are to remember that it makes no difference how far the play was anticipat-ed by works in the public demesne which the plaintiffs did not use. The defen-dants appear not to recognize this, for they have filled the record with earlier instances of the same dramatic incidents and devices, as though, like a patent, a copyrighted work must be not only original, but new. That is not however the law as is obvious in the case of maps or compendia, where later works will necessarily be anticipated. At times, in discussing how much of the substance of a play the copyright protects, courts have indeed used language which seems to give countenance to the notion that, if a plot were old, it could not be copyrighted. But we understand by this no more than that in its broader outline a plot is ever copyrightable, for it is plain beyond peradventure that anticipa-tion as such cannot invalidate a copyright. Borrowed the work must indeed not be, for a plagiarist is not himself pro tanto an "author"; but if by some magic a man who has never known it were to compose anew Keats's Ode on a Grecian Urn, he would be an "author," and, if he copyrighted it, others might not copy that poem, though they might of course copy Keats's. (Goldstein, 573)

Here, Hand sounds a little bit like Borges (in "Pierre Menard, Author of the Quixote"), but what he most authoritatively did in this case and else-where (see also *Nichols v. Universal Pictures Corp.* [1930]) was to make the dependence of artistic originality on novelty seem almost nonsensical.[6] Goldstein writes that "[i]t is some measure of the originality test that Learned Hand propounded in *Sheldon* that, in a long career deciding copyright cases, Judge Hand never once found that a work was insufficiently original to qual-ify for copyright protection" (578). Art is different from trademarks and patents, and Pai's attempt to conflate them, to argue that Oscar's case should be understood as one of unfair competition rather than copyright infringe-ment, is a clever yet suspect defense. And even if he can get Oscar to state that he wishes to protect the novelty of the play's idea, there are all the other instances when Oscar accents the inseparableness of idea and expression: "When the idea is used in the context of the expression, combined with the expression, then the idea becomes part of the abuse I'm referring to" (204). A judge has only to treat the case as one of copyright infringement for Pai's line of defense to crumble. The reason is, as Goldstein explains, "Copyright law possesses none of the search mechanisms for determining novelty that have developed around patent law's novelty and nonobviousness require-ments. The few recorded and largely vain efforts at introducing prior art on the issue of copyright novelty only dramatize copyright law's incapacity to measure novelty systematically" (580).

Oscar, then, wins his case on appeal. By this time, Basie has fled from the scene, the facts of his past having come to the attention of the authorities. That Oscar does win has everything to do with his father's intervention, an intervention carried forward unbeknownst to Oscar. That is, Judge Crease, reading the district court judge's opinion, and seeing that she has let herself be led by Pai's argument, perhaps for the reason that, new to the bench, she is hesitant to preempt state law, takes it upon himself to write the appeals brief; and then sends a young lawyer up to file it. The Judge acts, it seems, less as a father than as a husband of the law. Or as his law clerk later tells Oscar, "When he got his hands on that decision he was mad as hell. He acted like the closest person in his life had been raped, like he'd come on the body of the law lying there torn up and violated by a crowd of barbarians, what was the matter with you? What in hell was wrong with your lawyers not following it up, letting a wide open trap that was laid for you slip by them for this new judge to fall into" (559). Whatever his motives, his appeal goes to the heart of the matter by making clear that not only are there triable issues of fact to be sorted through but that in an infringement case such as Oscar's, federal copyright law should be thought more applicable than New York's unfair competition law. It is, in fact, a little surprising to see an unfair competition law applied to the relation between a play and a film, for it is the nature of such law that it serves to regulate the relation between commercial ideas and products. Understanding it as an ally of trademark law, Goldstein writes, "Unfair competition embraces a broad continuum of competitive conduct likely to confuse consumers as to the source of goods and services—from the appropriation of relatively nondistributive names and symbols accompanied by acts passing off, to the appropriation of distinctive symbols" (55). Judge Bone himself is receptive to the appeal argument that state law should give way to federal copyright law, summarizing the argument as follows:

> The courts have frequently debated whether laws of unfair competition are similar enough to copyright jurisdiction in its aims to be preempted by Federal copyright law, to which defendant argues that preemption is not absolute in the area of intellectual property. However under the doctrine of pendent jurisdiction a Federal court may take jurisdiction over a State law if, as established by the Supreme Court in United Mine Workers v. Gibb, that State law claim rises out of a 'common nucleus of operative fact' with the Federal claim, and here plaintiff argues for such a common nucleus residing in all his claims rising from defendant's use of his playscript. (406)

In the federal court, Oscar is the recipient of justice—not the ideal justice that he sought, but an apportioned justice, following from the fact that subsequent to the appeals court decision, no legal representative showed up to contest the award's apportioning. In any event, by the nature of the evidence, it would seem that the appeals court decision is, more or less, a sound one. That is, there is every reason to think that *The Blood in the Red White and Blue* makes use of copyrighted materials without permission. The question, however, is who stole the materials and precisely which materials did this person steal? Was it Kiester, the designated recipient of Oscar's play thirteen years before, who, as Oscar has maintained all along, stole the play? Or was it someone else, stealing perhaps something else (e.g., not the copy but the original)? Kiester himself denies, under oath, any remembrance of the play. And it does seem unlikely that besieged as he should have been (while working for network television) with unsolicited scripts, he should remember it, even if he rather than an assistant had been the script's reader and respondee. It is not impossible, but unlikely.[7]

Yet if not Kiester, who? The answer, I think, is John Knize, the Holmes Court scholar, "Civil War 'buff,'" schoolmate of Kiester, and, of course, screenwriter for *The Blood in the Red White and Blue*. Knize himself first comes to our attention not in connection with the film but through his letter to Oscar, asking whether the latter might be willing to share his reminiscences respecting his grandfather, Justice Thomas Crease. "Professor Crease," he writes,

> Perhaps my earlier letter did not reach you. I am researching material for a book on the Holmes Court, of which I understand your grandfather, Justice Thomas Crease, was a colourful member, well known for his conflicts with his associate Justice Holmes though it was said they were warm friends through their shared youthful experience in the Civil War, both having suffered wounds, I understand, at Ball's Bluff and Antietam. (23)

The point is, Knize knows the whole Thomas Crease story. He has read all the archival material, if, as I believe, he is "the outsider" the historical society's "old biddies" let "in to read them" (501). He did not need Oscar's play to write the screenplay for *The Blood in the Red White and Blue*. And according to sworn testimony, Knize and the other writers have never seen or read Oscar's play. Bone: "All these five were examined by deposition; all denied that they had ever encountered, known of, read or used the play in any way whatever; all agreed that they had based the picture on material in the public domain provided by Knize" (405). Judge Crease knows this. That is why in his Seventh Cause of Action, "which is against Kiester and his head writer Knize only" (412), he "claims misrepresentation, deceit and fraudulent conduct in the misappropriation and conversion of copyrighted material on deposit at certain public institutions" (412). It is also why he "read them [the biddies] the riot act" when he discovered that Knize had been allowed to see his father's papers. It might even partly explain his own decision to have his law clerk burn all of his private papers upon his death.

If Knize rather than Kiester is the main culprit, we still have a case of the misappropriation of copyrighted materials. Not of Oscar's own materials but of his grandfather's—the ownership of which belongs to Judge Crease and then, only after his death, to Oscar. Justice has been done, sort of, yet again we find evidence that there was too little investigation before Basie filed Oscar's claim. In fact, if the defendants are judged strictly in terms of the original claim, they should be found innocent and Pai's argument the right one. But they are not judged so, for the accusation changes its form on appeal. Hence, we have a case that the changes in the rules of notice have allowed to go through the courts before its import was properly understood even by its claimant.

Judge Crease and the Common Law

No one can accuse Judge Crease of not understanding the law. While Oscar's notion of justice would leap over legal particulars, Judge Crease's entire understanding of justice is rooted in these particulars, in those Hamletian "Words, words, words" (181) that leave Oscar so baffled, yet which, as Harry tries to explain, are for his father the law's heart and soul. Law and language, language and the law—they have the Judge's entire attention. As a craftsman, he knows that language is slippery, that laws are never perfect; but he also knows that some things—language and law included—are better than others, not better per se, but better in the world in which men and women live. After his death, his clerk speaks of "this love he had for the law and the language," but also of how he would "diddle them both sometimes because when you come down to it the law's only the language" (559). Crease's faith finally rested on the law as expressed in language, a faith that, the clerk says, served him well enough: "what better loves could a man have than those to get him through the night" (560). This is why Harry, mindful of the Judge's fidelity here, earlier speaks of him as one who is "[t]rying to rescue the language" (285).

This sense of the man is evident in the three extensive examples we have of his work: the two decisions pertaining to the Szyrk case and the instructions to the jury in the Fickert case. Like his spiritual father, Justice Holmes, Judge Crease is a strict constructionist, sharing the former's view that a judge's "first business is to see that the game is played according to the rules whether" he likes them or not (Holmes, 394). The judge may be a representative of authority, but authority itself lies elsewhere, in the laws that the legislative and executive branches, both state and federal, have hammered out. These laws all have a specific aspect about them, reflecting the needs and demands of their communities. There is no universal law, no Mount Sinai-like commandments that can be said to supersede ordinary common law. It is because Judge Crease believes this that he holds Holmes's dissenting opinion in the "Black and White Taxi Co." (1928) case in such high regard (46). There, Holmes wrote:

> Books written about any branch of the common law treat it as a unit, cite cases from this Court, from the Circuit Court of Appeals, from the State Courts, from England and the Colonies of England indiscriminately, and criticize them as right or wrong according to the writer's notions of a single theory. It is very hard to resist the impression that there is one august corpus, to understand which clearly is the only task of any court concerned. If there were such a transcendental body of law outside of any particular State but obligatory within it unless and until changed by statute, the Courts of the United States might be right in using their independent judgment as to what it was. But there is no such body of law. The fallacy and illusion that I think exist consist in supposing that there is this outside thing to be found. Law is a word used with different meanings, but law in the sense in which courts speak of it today does not exist without some definite authority behind it. The common law so far as it is enforced in a State, whether called common law or not, is not the common law generally but the law of that State existing by the authority of that State without regard to what it may have been in England or anywhere else. (199)

The Holmes dissent does, in fact, go to the heart of Crease's understanding of the law. For him, laws have a strict purview. He is quick to dismiss the appeal, by Szyrk's counsel, to early English common law "as ornamental" and demonstrating "no clear parallel in the laws of this Commonwealth" (32). He takes little notice of a similar appeal made in defendant James B's crossclaim (35). And later, in the Fickert case, he instructs the jury to disregard the Reverend Bobby Joe's testimony attributing the boy's death to Satan, reminding it of one Pennsylvania case wherein a complaint against Satan had to be "dismissed for its failure to discover Satan's residence within the judicial district" (430). For Judge Crease, people make laws so as to designate what is, and is not, acceptable behavior within a given community. These laws may conceivably embody a greater, more divine justice, but that is no reason to invoke such justice in the courtroom. As far as he is concerned, "God has no place" in his courtroom (293).

Crease himself may, or may not, believe in the Deity. It is impossible for us to say, though he clearly has no allegiance to any organized religion, and goes so far as to stipulate in his will that his grave not be "marked by a cross or any other such barbaric instrument of human torture" (444). It is true that, like Holmes, he does not entirely refrain from appeals to some sort of universal justice. His understanding of art, as reflected in the Szyrk case, certainly appears dependent on some undefined notion of transcendental truth: "there remain certain fine distinctions [respecting the argument that 'Cyclone

Seven' is art] posing some little difficulty for the average lay observer persuaded from habit and even education to regard sculptural art as beauty synonymous with truth in expressing harmony as visibly incarnate in the lineaments of Donatello's David, or as the very essence of the sublime manifest in the Milos Aphrodite, leaving him in the present instance quite unprepared to discriminate between sharp steel teeth as sharp steel teeth, and sharp steel teeth as artistic expressions of sharp steel teeth" (34). Like Holmes who once ruled that "[i]t would be a dangerous undertaking for persons trained only to the law to constitute themselves" as art critics (Goldstein, 576), Crease refrains from letting his own poor opinion of Szyrk's work interfere with the plaintiff's claim for justice or blunt him to the fact that there are many others who think the work important. Still, Judge Crease clearly has another standard of art in mind, and this cannot be thought a complete irrelevancy.

But the point remains that Crease's philosophy of justice is a version of Occam's razor, the principle reminding us that "[w]hat can be done with fewer [assumptions] is done in vain with more." Law, which has no theory, never having worked one out,[8] does best in this view when it refrains from making appeals to ancient precedents, or other forms of justification otherwise distant. This explains why Crease, in the James B decision, quotes Holmes's famous cat's clavicle remark (from *The Common Law*): "But just as the clavicle in the cat only tells us of the existence of some earlier creature to which a collarbone was useful, precedents survive in the law long after the use they once served is at an end and the reason for them has been forgotten. The result of following them must often be a failure and confusion from the merely logical point of view" (292). Precedents themselves are highly valued—they are the law's basis—but not those precedents that have lost their relevancy.

In this view, law is less about logic—though logic continues to be central—than about experience. That is, if "[t]he official theory is that each new decision follows syllogistically from existing precedents" (Holmes, 54), going back to some original law or constitution, the truth is that "[t]he felt necessities of the time, the prevalent moral or political theories, intuitions of public policy, avowed or unconscious, even the prejudices which judges share with their fellow-men, have had a good deal more to do than the syllogism in determining the rules by which men should be governed" (Holmes, 51). The courts are legislative, no matter how much its officers disavow such intentions. The fact is that each generation rewrites the laws according to its own axiology, so that, says Holmes, "[w]e could reconstruct the corpus from them [the newly written decisions] if all that went before were burned" (73). Perhaps, but the rewritten rules are not identical with their predecessors. Some rules are maintained over time, yet even when they are it is, as Holmes states, because present-day interpreters have found a way to make them cor-

respond with current values: "as the law is administered by able and experienced men, who know too much to sacrifice good sense to a syllogism, it
will be found that, when ancient rules maintain themselves . . . , new reasons
more fitted to the time have been found for them, and that they gradually
receive a new content, and at last a new form, from the grounds to which
they have been transplanted" (55). It is a situation that, as Sanford Levinson
has more recently put it, "highlight[s] one of the central mysteries of . . . constitutional faith: the process by which 'best constitutional analysis' is subtly
transformed in the passage of time so that A becomes not-A, without amendment ever being deemed necessary" (302).

  Here, while law refuses to seek mooring in a universal, it does not pretend
to be unmoored. It recognizes legal precedents as well as the opinions of the
time, though Holmes and Crease, as strict constructionists, give more weight
to the former than to the latter. All in all, the law is understood as a tacit
thing, something that exists whether we will it or not, and something that has
existed for as long as anyone can remember. This does not transform it into a
universal, but it does suggest that the law has a gravity and a continuity
about it which should be respected. Certainly, Holmes and Crease feel this
way about the law, for they revere it; and they know their way about as if
they were born to it. In a sense, they exemplify Stanley Fish's contention that
"[t]o be a judge or a basketball player is not to be able to consult the rules
(or, alternatively, to be able to disregard them) but to have become an extension of the 'know-how' that gives the rules . . . and the meaning they will
immediately and obviously have" (258). Never quite a complete body of
knowledge, the law is always reaching out to that point when it shall perfectly realize itself. Were this to happen, however, it would be a dead thing, for
transformation and growth are as crucial to the law as to any other living
body. Thus Holmes writes, "The truth is, that the law is always approaching,
and never reaching, consistency. It is forever adopting new principles from
life at one end, and it always retains old ones from history at the other, which
have not yet been absorbed or sloughed off. It will becomes entirely consistent only when it ceases to grow" (55).

  Holmes and Crease are both sensitive to the fact that law is as much the
consequence of a community's values as their molder. This does not prevent
them from wishing to free the law from the realm of individual circumstances. Crease, in the Fickert case, supports this view with a Holmes quotation: "The law . . . takes no account of the infinite varieties of temperament,
intellect, and education which make the internal character of a given act so
different in different men. It does not attempt to see men as God sees them,
for more than one sufficient reason" (429). Here, the law is best thought of as
indifferent to a person's particular fortunes: it judges the homeless person no
differently than the corporate executive. And it tries to escape not only all
forms of sentiment—as when Judge Crease instructs the Fickert jury to eval-

uate the testimony "unclouded by either prejudice or sentiment" (426)—but also all moralizing. True, a community's morality and its law often share the same field, yet they are different things, and both Holmes and Crease would almost prefer that the law were able to strip itself of morality's terminology. As Holmes wrote: "For my own part, I often doubt whether it would not be a gain if every word of moral significance could be banished from the law altogether, and other words adopted which should convey legal ideas uncolored by anything outside the law. We should lose the fossil records of a good deal of history and the majesty got from ethical associations, but by ridding ourselves of an unnecessary confusion we should gain very much in the clearness of our thought" (78). And, no doubt, lose something quite valuable in the process.

My point is that Holmes and Crease, while brilliant, seem short on compassion and empathy, making them less complete justices than, say, Learned Hand. In fact, Hand himself spoke of Holmes's limitations this way, writing that "He slipped, if slip he did, only because his imagination was too narrow. Man was more richly endowed than he supposed" (47). It is a fair judgment of a man who, in the end, let his war experience too fully color his understanding of life in general. For Holmes, life was always interpreted as a Darwinian struggle, always "red in tooth and claw." Here, human beings are likened to "a predatory animal," "the sacredness of" which "is a purely municipal idea of no validity outside the jurisdiction," it being clear "that force . . . is the *ultimate ratio*" (Aichele, 144). Was Holmes simply being honest? Perhaps, but I also find a hardness of heart, of the sort that made his description of African Americans as an "impulsive people with little intelligence or foresight" and his still hurtful words in the *Buck v. Bell* sterilization case ("it is better for all the world if instead of waiting to execute degenerate offspring for crime, or to let them starve for their imbecility, society can prevent those who are manifestly unfit from continuing their kind"; "three generations of imbeciles is enough") seem of a piece (Aichele, 148; 149).

Crease shares this same gravelish temperament. He would, says Christina, "give Jesus thirty days [in jail for contempt] if he could" (433), and one believes it. Determined to execute the law without regard for the more ordinary emotions that people attach to their affairs, Judge Crease comes across as insensitive and even cruel. His allusion, in the Fickert case, to Catholicism as one of "those widespread cults of mainly foreign origin" (428) is an example of plain bigotry, and his dealings with Southerners (the court's chief petitioners) are likewise seldom free of bigotry and condescension. No wonder Christina describes him as "one of the most selfish men who ever lived," and as one whose only interest in people was as "pawns" before the law (487). He thinks of himself, as do those near to him, as something like the Old Testament God ("for I the Lord your God am a jealous God, visiting the iniquity of the fathers upon the children to the third and fourth generation of those who hate me," Exodus 20.4), and is almost always spoken of as "Father." Christina says that he never "forgives and forgets" (326); and Oscar, while granting Christina's suggestion that his father is familiar with the Bible, comes back with "all right then maybe the Old Testament" (432). Certainly, his relation with his son has this cast to it, for he is always the stern judge and never the loving father. Here, the story that Christina tells Harry about Oscar as boy, building his canoe, is quite poignant and explains much about the older Oscar's relation—so inimically desperate—to his father:

> Harry don't tell, don't get Oscar's hopes up, I mean this whole brittle shell he's put together for who he thinks he is now but suddenly I look through that mangy beard and cigar smoke and see the face of the little boy down there by the pond that day with the little canoe he'd made, he'd spent days at it stripping the bark off a beautiful white birch that stood there and Father, Father looking at it without a word like some terrible open wound, looking at the canoe sunk in the mud and he had the poor tree cut down the next day without a word, gone without a trace he never mentioned it again but he never let Oscar forget it, just with a look, it was all too heartbreaking [. . .]. (397)

There is, then, good reason for thinking justice a more complicated and richer thing than even Judge Crease imagines.

Harry and the Justice of What Is Right

Harry is a fitting recipient for Christina's story, for he, like Oscar, had a troubled relation with his father, a Chicagoan who made a fortune in textiles. The father was especially troubled by Harry's early ambition to be a writer. Thinking it "an unprofitable vocation for 'sissies'" (526), he forced the son into permanent exile. The son, however, did not become a writer, though it was as a consequence of his reading, particularly of Dickens, that he turned to law. Initially, Harry's motives were that of the idealist; he saw "the law as an instrument of justice" (527) and wanted to help right the world. His youthful enthusiasm moved him to work for "a number of small public interest law firms" (527) before disillusionment set in. We are not specifically told why he became disillusioned. However, it is suggested that as with his prior experience in divinity school, where he found his instructors and classmates responding to difficult questions with easy answers (527), he turned away from public interest law for the reason that his object—justice—seemed too removed. In short, he was naive; and in reaction he turned to corporate law, a practice with no pretensions about justice, but extraordinarily remunerative. In a moment of pique, Harry tells Christina that he went in to corporate law because it was about money and nothing else: "Why I went into corporate law in the first place where it's greed plain and simple. It's money from the start to finish, it's I want what you've got, nobody out there with these grievances they expect you to share" (44). But the explanation is not entirely true. Harry capitulated to the values not only of his father but of the society, but he also knows that he has given in to something that he does not believe in. Thus, if he does not altogether like the person whom he has become, he is still capable of admiration for those, like Oscar, who struggle against the odds to make something worth doing work (e.g., Oscar's play), as opposed to seeking an easier success in something that was not worth doing in the first place. Or as Christina, after Harry's death, tells Oscar: "I think he admired you, that he really admired what you'd tried to do because he'd tried it himself that's what he used to say, about failing at something worth doing because there was nothing worse for a man than failing at something that wasn't worth doing in the first place simply because that's where the money was, it was always the money . . ." (529).

Harry sells out. In a society where corporate lawyers earn ten to twenty times the average citizen's wage, corporate law is a privileged demesne, whose lords appear indifferent, if not hostile, to the reformer's desire for greater economic and social justice. More than once Christina refers to Harry's firm, Swyne & Dour, as "William Peyton [the] third and his four hundred thieves" (395), and this seems an apt description. Certainly, the firm's major case, defending Pepisco against a suit by the Episcopal Church over trademark infringement (Pepsi-Cola is an Episcopal anagram), is about nothing so much as money, and to devote to it years of one's life, as Harry does, can make sense only if money is a paramount value. Money is not Harry's paramount value, but it has become something like a necessity. Driving back from the Hamptons in their Jaguar, Harry turns to Christina and asks her whether she could really "live in a place like Massapequa [a middle-class Long Island town, where Gaddis himself was raised] and drive around in a broken down Japanese" car (308). The matter comes up in response to Christina's complaint that Swyne & Dour is overwhelmingly white and male: "Out of two, three hundred lawyers you've got there every one of them white? male? and you need a black face or two in the window before some antidiscrimination law wakes up and hands out a good stiff fine in the only language they speak up there, money?" (308). Harry grants the truth of the charge, but, thinking more about survival than justice, defends the practice:

—Look Christina, a place like Swyne & Dour you're not even proposed as a lateral partner unless you're bringing along a million and a half or two in billings with you, I've told you that. You think Basie or any of them's got that kind of client base? Never been a black partner the whole time I've been there, never even more than two black associates at once and they didn't last long either, did I ever say it wasn't about money? (308)

Despite Harry's corporate values, he retains a strong vestigial sense of why he first went into law. He has turned away from thinking of the law "as an instrument of justice" and toward thinking of it as "a vehicle for imposing order on the unruly universe" (527), but he still feels an obligation toward what is "right." The word or concept occurs repeatedly in reference to him, as in Christina's "It's simply what's right that's what Harry always [said]" (531), or as in his own critique of Pai's work: "but you get a feeling that he's got the answer ready before he hears the question, takes short cuts, doesn't look back, sets up the game himself as if he's the only player. He'd rather win than be right" (388).

What does it mean to "be right" in this context? We know that Harry has become disillusioned with the concept of an ideal justice. He seems not to use "right" as a synonym for it, though the term clearly retains a strong ethical aspect. It also retains, without evincing the strictness of the law, a legal aspect, as if to say that the right can, in its best evocations, combine what is good with what is required. In fact, right might be thought of as a circumscribed justice, as that which declares itself true within the domain of historical, political, and social circumstances. Here, where true justice is thought out of reach and where the law often vindicates the crook and the fool (399), right appears like a quasi-ideal. It is the sort of compromise that gets articulated in the idea of the social contract, be it Rousseau's eighteenth-century version or, for us today, John Rawls's "justice as fairness." People are understood to have both rights and obligations, not one without the other but both together. People live in a state of interdependency, and if they wish to be the recipients of social justice, they need to do all in their power to extend such justice to others, even those about whom—for reasons of economic, ethnic, regional, religious, or gender difference—they might feel indifferent or worse. Rawls writes, "Political liberalism assumes that, for political purposes, a plurality of reasonable yet incompatible comprehensive doctrines is the normal result of the exercise of human reason within the framework of the free institutions of a constitutional democratic regime" (xvi).

Harry himself subscribes to this form of political liberalism. He wants a system that protects him from other people's systems and orders. When Christina mentions that all Oscar wants "is some kind of order," Harry quickly follows with an allusion to European fascism:

> —Make the trains run on time, that was the . . .
> —I'm not talking about trains, Harry.
> —I'm talking about fascism, that's where this compulsion for order ends up. The rest of it's opera. (11)

But even if political liberalism is what it purports to be—i.e., measured, moderate, tolerant—it still is a system in its own right, one that, when in place, displaces other systems. Rawls appears hesitant to acknowledge this—i.e., hesitant to acknowledge that as a system, political liberalism does not simply referee conflicts among society's groups but also influences the direction of resolution, and thereby assumes a more than passive role. Rawls would like to think that political liberalism is categorically different from other systems, that it is less like an epistemology and more like a place holder, facilitating people's interactions without also determining them. To this end, he proposes a theoretical model that sharply distinguishes between "background culture," which is social (e.g., "religious, philosophical, and moral"), and "justice as fairness," a political operating system that, again, impartially mediates conflicts (14). The background culture is said to be made up of numerous "comprehensive doctrines," doctrines that, individually, entail beliefs that place their members at odds with those professing different allegiances. Such doctrines are, Rawls suggests, inherently oppressive, and would, were it not for political liberalism's intervention, battle for state power so as to ensure their own hegemony: "a continuing shared understanding on one comprehensive religious, philosophical, or moral doctrine can be maintained only by the *oppressive* use of state force. If we think of political society as a community united in affirming one and the same comprehensive doctrine, then the *oppressive* use of state power is necessary for political community" (37; italics added).

Rawls's use of the word *oppressive* here, like his pairing of religious belief with gestures of intolerance, is not without significance. It is true that communal systems are, by nature, coercive. They predicate themselves on some real or imagined authority, and they expect their members to acknowledge this and to display a certain ascesis, itself part of a more general sacrificing of individual wants before societal needs. Coercion, however, is not oppression, and communities that predicate their togetherness on moral, philosophical, or religious grounds need not, ipso facto, be thought more oppressive than the community that predicates itself on the ground of political liberalism. In particular instances, much will depend on where persons stand in relation to the community's doctrinal ground, a situation that Rousseau acknowledged could prove oppressive, even in a liberal state, to the individual opposed to such ground: "In order, then, that the social pact may not be a vain formulary, it tacitly includes the engagement, which can alone give force to the others—that whoever refuses to obey the general will shall be constrained to do so by the whole body; which means nothing else than that he shall be forced to be free" (22). Here, coercion is ratcheted up a notch or two, to a point where it begins to look exactly like that which the liberal state seeks to oppose: oppression. Yet this state's own freedoms can to some, especially those lacking the resources to use them to advantage, appear oppressive. And even when the liberal state is in place, there is no guarantee that acts of intolerance will be banished.

A Frolic of His Own offers plenty of evidence to suggest that even those people—Harry, Christina, Oscar, Judge Crease, Pai, Trish, et al.—philosophically opposed to intolerance may, in their blindness, act in ways that smack of bigotry. For instance, Basie has disparaging things to say about "those Jews in Hollywood" (99); Oscar tries to honor Basie's race by telling a story of "the sheer artistry, smooth[ness], [and] unhurried[ness]" of the black men who pickpocketed his money on the Fifth Avenue bus (106); Pai believes that "blacks lack a counting gene" (364) and further believes that religion as practiced by "Sikhs, Iraqis, Afghanis," among others, testifies to the fact that "they're all raving maniacs" (375); Trish sees in her mother's long devoted servant "a thousand years of Irish Catholic ignorance" (359); Harry speaks of Pai, whom he calls "Mudpye," as the firm's "token ethnic," a "real red brick university product" (241); Christina, meanwhile, when she is not offering fine discriminations between wealth and riches ("you don't become wealthy building parking garages you simply get rich there's quite a difference" [503]) or consigning Catholics to slums ("these millions of Catholics jamming every slum you can think of" [269]), works on perfecting her Stinking Creek accent:

> Just a good thing they had a fine man like the Judge to hold this trial [the Fickert trial], had it down there at Wink County Court with some jury from Tatamount and Stinking Creek where everybody knowed how Billye Fickert shacked up with that fertilizer salesman before she married Hoddy Coops after Earl took off for Mississippi when they run him out for throwing lye down Hoddy's well a jury like that would have give the whole store away, can you tell me how Father could have put up with that for thirty years? can you? (498)

Actually, it is not so clear that the Judge's tenure on the federal bench for the Southern District of Virginia has been "a good thing." This is not to deny the incommensurableness of his legal mind. It is to wonder, however, whether a man of his opinions, so emphatically at odds with those of the local community, can actually weigh the concerns of his court's constituents fairly. I do not say "justly," for that, once again, invokes standards of a larger order. But can he rule fairly? That is, do the people of his jurisdiction believe that when they enter his courtroom their own concerns and values will be respected, or do they believe that Federal Judge Crease is, as Thomas Jefferson once wrote, part of that "corps of sappers and miners, steadily working to undermine the independent rights of the States, and to consolidate all power in the heads of that government in which they have so important a freehold estate" (Levinson, 295)? They clearly believe the latter; hence the wide-scale approval that meets Senator Bilk's call for his impeachment following the Judge's overturning of the jury verdict in the James B case. Before a large outdoor crowd, the Senator stirringly reminds them of:

where this government interference with our sacred state's rights so many died for is leading us, sending in these Federal judges that take our great American language and twist the words around to mean whatever they want, calls God no better than a cat's shinbone, calls this beautiful land of ours a botched Creation and throws God right out of the courtroom, you heard him, do whatever they please because they're appointed for life. Well we have an answer for that, call it impeachment right there in the Constitution and that's the message I'm taking back up to Washington. They pay him with your good U.S. tax dollars and I'm going to tell them to take a look at one, take a good look at a U.S. dollar bill where it says In God We Trust and that U.S. dollar's gospel enough for me. (295)

It is not necessary to like or agree with this Jesse Helms incarnation to wonder whether federalism, with its adherence to the principles of political liberalism, is not experienced as something like an encroachment by a significant minority of communities and even states. At one point, Pai, taking note of the fractiousness of American life, comments to Oscar: "It's not a country it's a continent, eight or ten million Italians, Swedes, Poles, fifteen or twenty million Irish, thirty million English descent, twenty five million Germans and the same for blacks, six million Jews, Mexicans, Hungarians, Norwegians and this horde of Hispanics pouring in it's a melting pot where nothing's melted" (373–74). It is true enough to make one pause, and to wonder whether such diversity can ever be reconciled under a single rule of law, federalism, and under a single political principle, liberalism. To wonder whether *E Pluribus Unum* is not itself a contradiction in terms. And to wonder whether we (political liberalists) should even think such a situation desirable.

To repeat my point, liberalism may not only be coercive, it may, to use Rawls's word, be "oppressive." There is plenty of evidence in *A Frolic of His Own* to suggest that what we have in the United States is something like an undeclared civil war, wherein things are held in check, to the extent that they are, by a federalism that, in its less attractive moments, appears to stifle rather than to mediate differences. Here, I would like to quote a critic of political liberalism, Bhikhu Parekh, who, in his essay "Superior People: The Narrowness of Liberalism from Mill to Rawls," points out that, despite liberalism's claim of inclusion, it has always had an oppositional, and thereby excluding, dimension:

> Since the Millian liberal developed liberalism against the background of colonialism and since he presented it as the major source of difference between the Europeans and the non-Europeans, he was led to define it in contrastive terms. Liberalism was seen as the opposite, the antithesis, of the allegedly tradition-bound non-European ways of life. Not surprisingly, it became obsessively anti-tradition, anti-prejudice, anti-custom, anti-conformity, anti-community, and both defined extremely narrowly and exaggerated the importance of such val-

ues as autonomy, choice, individuality, liberty, rationality and progress. Since the Millian liberal needed sharply to separate himself from non-European ways of life, he also redefined *himself* in the light of the way he had defined them. Liberalism thus became the other of its other and gave itself an impoverished identity. (12)

Parekh is particularly attentive to Millian liberalism and its semblance to colonial politics. But he also sees present-day liberalism (i.e., Rawlsian) as part of the same continuum, and as opposed to many of the same values (e.g., tradition, custom, community, and religion). The opposition tends, of course, to be less explicit than implicit. Liberalism does not so much oppose local traditions and customs so much as try, through the federal government's offices, to coerce recalitrant state and local communities into submitting to "enlightened" behavior. The point is, whether this behavior be enlightened or not, the long-term effect has, good consequences notwithstanding, also fostered an often banal, and sometimes deleterious, cultural homogeneity, parts of which are on display in inner-city blight, suburban tract housing, and mall culture. Here, I am not arguing one side or the other, so much as suggesting that political liberalism has tended to focus more on those things it would eradicate (e.g., local prejudice, illiteracy, and poverty) and less on the consequences of its actions, which, constructed as the anti-image of the other (e.g., local patterns and behaviors), have not always been pretty. The long and short of the matter is, as Thomas Nagel writes, that "[w]hen we try to discover reasonable moral standards for the conduct of individuals and then try to integrate them with fair standards for the assessment of social and political institutions, there seems no satisfactory way of fitting the two together. They respond to opposing pressures which cause them to break apart" (*Equality and Partiality*, 4–5).

In *A Frolic of His Own*, Nagel's insight is played out even in the federal courtroom, the space most identified with a disinterested respect for rights. That is, the court experiences pressures from all directions, and in the end it is not always clear that an impartial justice is the result. But before pursuing this point, I should point out once more that there is also a strong reformist edge to Gaddis's satire. His critiques are the consequence of outrage, the outrage of one who (in the tradition of a Swift or Twain) witnesses something good turned on its head and who would like to see things righted. Gaddis offers an indictment less of the entire legal profession than of that segment—e.g., "pain and suffering" specialists and corporate lawyers—that has made self-enrichment its true object. For other segments, and especially for the judiciary, he seems to have great respect. Or as Jonathan Raban notes in his review, "This is not *Bleak House*. In *A Frolic of His Own* the language of the law is treated with affection and respect, and the lawyers themselves are honored as the last surviving instruments (even though some of them are very imperfect ones) of order in this disorderly world" (4). I would qualify the Raban statement somewhat. For again, while it is true that Gaddis shows respect for the skills of a Pai or a Basie, and for both the skills and the integrity of a Harry, it is also clear that he sees litigators as knuckling under to greed. "It's always about money" (58), in fact, becomes a refrain here. Still, for the writings of a Learned Hand or an Oliver Wendell Holmes, Jr., Gaddis has nothing but respect. As he told one interviewer, "I would much rather read legal opinions than most fiction. . . . I'm fascinated by legal language. I think it is stunning—it's always trying to anticipate contingencies" (D. Smith, 38). A byproduct of this respect and fascination is that we get characters like Judges Crease and Bone, learned elders who chose the law, long ago, because it was a place where a love not for money but for justice and language could be entertained.

However, to return to my argument, even with the best-intentioned jurists, the law has a way of being partial. For one, the expense of litigation makes it difficult for anyone without impressive means to bring suit. The bill for Oscar's own suit against Erebus is well over a hundred thousand dollars. In cases such as Oscar's, those parties with "deep pockets" can, by drawing the process out, via discovery, petitions, and counterclaims, often force the other party to settle for less than its claim or even to drop the suit for lack of means. Oscar himself is offered a two-hundred-thousand-dollar settlement by Erebus, and only his foolhardiness makes him turn it down.

Meantime, even when the legal process aims, in Harry's words, to arrive at the right answers "within the framework of the law"—"what the whole of the law's all about, questions that do have answers, sift through all the evidence till you come up with the right ones" (454)—the process is still filtered through the interests and biases of the participants. I have already mentioned Judge Crease's bias against Southerners, but there are others to take note of as well. For instance, the various biases of all the people involved play a crucial part in Oscar's case. For one, Oscar is referred to Lepidus & Shea because he wants to be represented by a Jewish lawyer. When Basie, a black man, is assigned to his case, his hopes decline. It does not matter that Basie is a fine attorney. Oscar will judge him as prejudice, not evidence, dictates. Thus when Christina tells him that Harry thinks the man "brilliant," Oscar responds: "Brilliant! I had to do all the work myself Christina, lead him along step by step pointing things out trying to get a straight answer from him, trying to get him to take the whole thing seriously while he rambled on about his acting career in some thimble theatre sitting there blowing smoke rings as though we were having a chat about baseball" (121). None of this is true, but Oscar has a hard time seeing beyond his prejudices. So, of course, does Pai, who similarly underestimates Basie's skill owing to his skin color, and who, in the deposition meeting, treats the latter with noticeable condescension. Later, he tells Oscar, "I spotted that black they palmed off on you for a fraud the minute we got into your deposition" (363), a remark that goes unsupported by evidence. Meanwhile, Basie seems to know the lay of the land. He is aware of the fact that the appeals court for the Second Circuit has a history of reversing the district court's decisions, and he knows that this is likely to occur in their own case, overseen as it is by a woman new to the bench. In such a case, he reasons it might be better to lose the first decision and then win on appeal. Or as he tells Christina:

> See they've assigned this case to this brand new district court judge, no track record you can't tell which way she'll go [. . .]. Say she finds for the defendant and throws it out, then what. Maybe that's good Mrs Lutz. You take how many cases lose in the district court and win on appeal because that's where this Second Circuit appeals court's got a real appetite for cutting down the court below so maybe you play to that. Maybe that's how we play it. (264–65)

In fact, it is not a bad strategy, though Harry is aghast when Christina relays it: "But that's not, you go in to win you don't plan to lose so you can win on appeal" (300). Still, as the facts stand, it turns out not to be a bad plan, for the appeals court is presided over by Judge Bone, who possesses, as someone said of Holmes, a streak of "the mean Yankee" (E. Wilson, 756). Or as Harry puts it:

> sitting on the Second Circuit bench as long as anyone can remember, cut from the same cloth as old Judge Crease, he doesn't suffer fools gladly I've seen him take a young woman prosecutor right off at the knees, got himself a name over the years for being a sort of misogynist so this wild card Oscar drew on the bench better have had her act together [. . .]. Little bit of the old puritan xenophobe too, get Mudpye up there with his secondhand red brick arrogance trying to deliver his oral argument and you can't tell. (396-97)

Like Crease, Bone is a first-rate jurist, yet when justice is filtered through his misogyny and his xenophobia, it starts to seem less and less like justice. And then, as happens here, when Bone recognizes the appeals brief as the work of his own colleague, Judge Crease, whatever chance Pai had successfully to defend the appeal goes out the window. Pai cries "conspiracy," as well he might, for as stated above, strictly understood, there is good reason for thinking his the better legal argument. Here, however, "justice as fairness" turns out to be not quite so "neutral" as Rawls imagines. Thus, while the Gaddis novel honors jurists like Crease and Bone, it does so knowing that the system's dedication to right will always be skewed in the direction of this or that interest or bias.

Christina and the Justice of the Heart

Christina offers yet another take on this question of justice. She has not Oscar's Platonic sense of justice, nor does she demonstrate much interest in the more legal and political ascriptions of her stepfather and husband. Her sense of justice tends to be more intuitive, more from the heart. For her, Oscar's suit, like so many others, has nothing to do with justice. Rather, it is about his need to be taken seriously, for people to listen to him, even if he has to threaten them in the only language most people understand: money. Or as she tells Harry:

> Trains? fascism? Because this isn't about any of that, or even the "opulence of plush velvet seats, brilliant spectacle and glorious singing" unless that's just their way of trying to be taken seriously too—because the money's just a yardstick isn't it. It's the only common reference people have for making other people take them as seriously as they take themselves, I mean that's all they're asking for isn't it? (11)

I am tempted to describe Christina's sense of justice in the context of Carol Gilligan's category of "the ethic of responsibility." Gilligan, author of *In a Different Voice*, opposes this ethic, predicated "on the concept of equity, the recognition of differences in need" (164), to that of rights, which itself "is predicated on equality and centered on the understanding of fairness" (164). Beyond this, Gilligan, now famously, identified each of these ethics with one of the sexes. For her, the ethic of rights, with its attempt to balance "the claims of other and self" (164–65), is identified with men; the ethic of responsibility, with its fostering of "compassion and care" (165), is identified with women. The thesis has been both highly praised and scorned. In the first instance, many were happy to find that women had a unique contribution to make to the discussion of justice. In the second instance, many were also upset to find the differences between men and women essentialized this way. The fear was that the old head-and-heart distinction was being refashioned but not rethought. If this were the case, Gilligan's book would not be of much long-term help to those women wishing to break free of traditional stereotypes.

There has, in fact, always been something quite traditional about Gaddis's women characters. One recent reviewer has spoken of the "sexism, even misogyny" of the earlier novels (Feeley, 87). While that charge needs proving if it is to be taken seriously,[9] it is clear that the novels' ethical arguments are closely identified with female characters, e.g., Esme in *The Recognitions*, Amy in *J R*, and Elizabeth in *Carpenter's Gothic*. This is also true in *A Frolic of His Own*. Raban himself goes so far as to call Christina "the reader's representative in the novel" (5), though this overlooks how dialogic this novel, like its predecessors, is. Still, Christina is an attractive character, often endeavoring to hold everything together when most others are on frolics of their own. In the opening scene, she furnishes Harry with a present (ginger preserves) for the hospital patient, Oscar, and gently admonishes him for what he intended to give Oscar (Judge Crease's opinion in the Szyrk case): "That was very thoughtful Harry, it was just the wrong thought" (12). She has a way of responding to others' needs as if they were her own. This is something that none of the others appear capable of, though if the commandment to "love thy neighbor as thyself" is to be taken seriously—and not as, in Pai's words, "a plain oxymoron" (376)—behavior of this sort appears requisite. The fact is, it is the aptly named Christina who is there for Oscar during his convalescence; for Harry when the stresses of his job become intolerable; for Trish when she needs someone to take her situation seriously; and for Lily when she needs to have an operation. She is also the person to whom Basie is truly able to talk about Oscar's case, and perhaps the reason why he stays with it despite Oscar's obduracy.

In short, Christina practices an ethic of love. While events sometimes make her seem peremptory and shrill, to the point that she begins not to like what she sees in the mirror—"and I look at myself and see somebody I don't like because I can't stand what it's [the overworking of her husband] doing to me either" (396)—her deep attachments to both Oscar and Harry, as well as her concern about Basie, attest to her singularity and importance. In a novel in which people's declarations of affection almost always have an ulterior motive—Oscar likes Lily for her youth and beauty; Lily likes Oscar as her sugar daddy; Trish likes her boyfriend for his youth; he likes her for her money; Trish likes Bunker for his money, and Bunker likes her for her comparative youth; Trish likes Pai for his success, and Pai likes Trish for her money—Christina appears different. She affects no fake emotions. If she does not like one, one knows it:

> —Just, I just wish you liked me.
> —So do I Lily. (24)

Her attachments appear sincere, even for Oscar, who is not an easy person to like. Christina has known and lived with him since they were children and knows the causes of his disquiet, knows that his bluster hides all kinds of hurt. She feels for him, even as she is put in the unhappy role of having to mother him. Her affection for Harry, meantime, is for an equal, a person of intelligence, maturity, and kindness. What she resents here, however, is that she has a rival, Swyne & Dour, that demands from him every waking hour. Repeatedly, she must remind Harry that she is his wife, that she has reason for expecting him home, and so on. Harry's attempts to explain his situation often only make things worse. Christina tells him, "I mean you talk about language how everything's language it seems all that language does is drive us apart" (386). Still, despite the friction, the relationship is a loving one. Christina can, in fact, be quite eloquent as to why this is so:

> —I mean I love you Harry, I love your hands and your stubborn fighting your-self that drives me crazy when you won't take the shortcut like the rest of them and I love your hands on me and what they do and the stiff stubborn hairy Ainu that's like all the rest of you when I look around us at the pieces of my absurd pointless life before we met all strung out in front of us worried about Father, about the house and poor Oscar out there with his whole life in the lap of the gods and your smile, shaking your head it's such a patient, sad smile looking for what's right, what you said once, not what is just but what is right? (396)

Perhaps it is Christina's liking for Basie that best reveals her depth. The two get along together right from the start. Basie has previously met Harry, and this gives them a common handle, leading to Christina's story about the hairy Ainu. Liking Christina, Basie later clips out a newspaper story on the Ainu, which he presents to her. It is a simple but telling gesture. It also allows the making of a connection between the plights of the Japanese Ainu and the American black. The long despised Ainu turn out, it seems, to be the ancestors of the Samurai, "this fancy top elite warrior class way up there in the nobility" (265–66), and the suggestion is that a similar reversal—from being denigrated to being respected—might follow for African Americans. The possibility, of course, depends on the receptivity of the community's majority to minority members' contributions. It is a simple matter of justice, but rights, if not justice, can be blinkered. The paltry gestures of Swyne & Dour, with its two or three minority associates, testify to what sort of atten-tion the mainstream community is prepared to bestow. While sensitive to such realities, Christina does not patronize Basie. There are even times when she gets quite upset with him, believing, for instance, that his trip to Hollywood for depositions might have been carried out less expensively. Still, she attends to what he has to say in a way that Oscar, for instance, can-not. She comes, then, to see that Basie's involvement in Oscar's case gave evidence that "[h]e wasn't just a smart lawyer and a sweet natured man a real man, he was our friend!" (565). Or as she tries to explain to Oscar:

> —I mean can't you see what happened, Oscar? that it was really Basie who laid the trap? Sitting here with the clock running and he kept saying we'll take them on appeal, that the Second Circuit likes reversing district judges to keep them on their toes didn't he say that? and that Harry said Judge Bone on the appeals court was a crusty old misogynist he'd seen him take a smart young woman judge right off at the knees once like this new woman judge just to teach her a lesson, don't you think Basie knew it too? (564)

Christina goes on to argue, to a deaf Oscar, that Basie knew the district court judge was mistaken on a point of law—i.e., the question of whether federal copyright or New York State's unfair competition law was most applicable—and that "he let it pass, he let their error pass on purpose so he could base the appeal on it that was the real trap!" (564). Basie did an impressive job with Oscar's case, though there were a few things, particularly during discovery, that he might have done better. Still, much of what Christina says in defense of Basie's handling of the case strikes me as true, and what seems even more true is her conclusion—reached via the heart rather than the syllogism—that Basie was their friend. This may seem a sentimentalism, particularly when placed alongside Judge Crease's more astringent notions of justice. However, I personally prefer Christina's notions of justice to those hitherto examined. Unlike Oscar's notion, with its myopic failure to take into account others' needs, or his father's notion, with its failure to weigh the heart's concerns, Christina's notion of justice seems more empathic and intuitively sound. And this last point is not irrelevant. Thomas Nagel has argued, in *Equality and Partiality,* that in any theory of justice

> the use of moral intuition is inevitable, and should not be regretted. To trust our intuitions, particularly those that tell us something is wrong even though we don't know exactly what would be right, we need only believe that our moral understanding extends farther than our capacity to spell out the principles which underlie it. Intuition can be corrupted by custom, self-interest, or commitment to a theory, but it need not be, and often a person's intuitions will provide him with evidence that his own moral theory is missing something, or just that the arrangements he has been brought up to find natural are really unjust. Intuitive dissatisfaction is an essential resource in political theory. (7)

Among *A Frolic*'s characters, Christina is the most intuitive, the person whom one most trusts to do the right thing, even if her solutions lack Oscar's urgency, Judge Crease's dispassion and her husband's pragmatism. Of course, there is no one right path here, not even Christina's, for they all must be considered and weighed against one another, and even then justice will often be "found and lost again and again." This said, I would like to examine one more place where justice appears to lurk: the domain of nature.

The Pond as Evocative of a More Encompassing Justice

I like what Nagel has to say regarding the relation of intuition and justice, and I think it applicable not only to Christina's notion of justice but also to something larger. That is, if it would be helpful or wise to seek out one person or location wherein justice—albeit so constitutionally dialogical—is most fully present in this novel, I would point to the pond. A living thing, the pond is not, however, a thinking thing, and it offers us no theory of justice per se. Still, it appears to exemplify justice, particularly in its moments of virtual timelessness, when it is so at odds with the the ethic of billable hours. Repeatedly in *A Frolic of His Own*, there are descriptions of the pond and its visitors that make Oscar's freneticism and its variants seem almost meaningless, as if Christina were onto something when she tells her stepbrother that "if you'd had a fatal heart attack it wouldn't have mattered whether you had tenure or not would it?" (20). The point is not that life's small victories do not matter or that things are meaningless. Rather, it is that things need, in one form or another, to be understood sub specie aeternitatis. That is, much like the night in the "Time Passes" section of Woolf's *To the Lighthouse* or the snow in Joyce's "The Dead," the pond seems to wrap, or threaten to wrap, everything "in a chill mantle of silence":

> Down the bare hall the outside doors clattered again, the obstinate whine of a car's starter, the cough of the engine, the wrath of crows down there on the lower lawn where she looked out over the brown grasses stirring along the edge of the pond's surface teeming with cold which seemed to rise right up here into the room to wrap them each in a chill mantle of silence pillaged by the clatter of all that had gone before the more intense in this helpless retrospect of isolation where their words collided, rebounded, caromed off those lost boundaries of confusion echoing the honking tumult of Canada geese in skeins blown ragged against the uncharted grey of the sky out over the pond, each thread in the struggle strung to its own blind logic from some proximate cause blinded to consequence and the whole skein itself torn by the winds of negligence urging their hapless course [. . .]. (317)

It is a scene that is both enigmatic and beautiful. "[B]ut my God, it is beautiful isn't it," Christina says, making us wonder whether it might not be the artist rather than the jurist who is best able to speak to its justice, its truth. Kant writes that "[a]n *aesthetic idea* cannot become a cognition, because it is an *intuition* (of the imagination) for which an adequate concept can never be found" (I.210). The definition accords with Christina's own conception of the artist as one who, unlike the jurist, seeks to escape the containment of laws: "where it's all laws, and laws, and everything's laws and he's done something nobody's told him to, nobody hired him to and gone off on a frolic of his own I mean think about it Harry. Isn't that really what the artist is finally all about?" (399). The answer seems to be yes, but to the extent that the artist is, like the Conrad quoted by Pai ("You remember Conrad describing his task, to make you feel, above all to make you see? and then he adds perhaps also that glimpse of truth for which you have forgotten to ask?" [363]), possessed of exceptional vision, it might make more sense to identify this artistry not with Oscar, the playwright, but with Christina. Granted, Oscar writes a fine play, but the play, as mentioned earlier, is wiser than he. Ordinarily, he is quite myopic, and the entire motif having to do with his glasses, sometimes dirtied, sometimes lost, adds to this. But Christina, as Raban points out (5), seems more than anyone else drawn to the pond, to this spot which (like similar scenes in the earlier Gaddis novels, e.g., the El Greco sky in *The Recognitions*, the evening sky in *J R*) represents something like a test of vision, so shiftily do things move in and out of focus. The motif is an important one. At one point, after a discussion about Ilse's sister, who "can hardly see" because of her cataracts, Christina calls Oscar's attention to the squirrel, "[o]ne of Hiawatha's mangy little refugees," outside on the upper lawn: "look. Look, can you see him out there? [. . .] —did you see him? You think maybe he was trying to tell you something?" (322–23). Oscar refuses to look, and turns instead to his book. Meantime, the television offers a documentary on a Scottish loch, with the narrator telling of the way that the lake changed in appearance, "often dramatically," each time he looked back at it. Here, the narrator's attention is almost philosophical: "*At times there is a clarity of detail at great distances when, for example, each branch of a thorn tree on the far bank is minutely sharp to the eye. Instantly it will become a dull strip of grey, and without a cloud in the sky to account for the change. This can produce mild hallucinations as the middle distance advances and recedes*" (324). The description also has a haunting follow-up, with the narrator saying, "*and you can soon begin to feel oppressed by the strange gloom of this lake, with its isolated houses and its wide lawns that slip into the water as if the lake were slowly flooding*" (324).

The passage is, in fact, borrowed from James Fox's *White Mischief*, and has clear thematic importance. It is picked up again, somewhat later, with Oscar

> gazing out over the pond where each branch on the leafless trees standing out sharply on the opposite bank blurred into a dull strip of grey without a cloud in the sky, putting down the pages to steady himself as the whole middle distance seemed to come closer and fall away, abruptly seizing up some pages he'd left on the sill there and bracing himself as though facing an audience intent for the facts not the words, not the sound of the language but its straightforward artless function, —Grant's army ascending the Tennessee River to disembark at Pittsburg Landing where Buell's divisions were to join it, the Confederate army deployed in battle lines near the Shiloh church barely two miles away in the gloom that had descended out there over the pond where the few isolated houses and the wide lawn below seemed to slip into the water as though the pond were flooding [. . .]. (346)

Here, faced with a mystery, Oscar turns to "fact," to language sheared of its aesthetic force. It is a betrayal of sorts, for the pond, in its inexpressible beauty, requires an imaginative response, an effort to reconcile its aporetic power with more quotidian existence. (Cf. Thoreau's "A lake is the landscape's most beautiful and expressive feature. It is earth's eye; looking into which the beholder measures the depth of his own nature.") It even might be said to require musings of a metaphysical sort, the sort that should require a person to seek some kind of reconciliation between one's life and its own most apparent aporia, death.

This is, of course, a novel saturated in death. There are twenty thousand plus ghosts from the battle at Shiloh and a like number from that at Antietam, in addition to other, more approximately identified personages who have crossed the border into death either sometime before or during the course of the narrative. These include Oscar's great-grandmother, Justice Thomas Crease, Winfred Riding, Mrs. Mabel, Elizabeth Booth, Judge Crease, Trish's mother, Harry, Lily's brother Bobbie, Wayne Fickert, and, of course, Spot. It is a veritable ghost story, reminding us of Nietzsche's remark, in *The Gay Science*, that "[t]he living being is only a species of the dead, and a very rare species." This ghost story, meanwhile, begins with Christina referring to the hospitalized Oscar as dressed in "this shroud" and "laid out like a corpse" (19), a description that puts him in a flutter, and recalls the black-suited man seeking out those willing to take "messages to the other side" (20). Throughout there are numerous mentions of things such as "last rites" (349), "sitting [. . .] on the other side" (421), "[l]aying up treasures in heaven" (432), funeral home conversations that search for "some affirmation to deny and obliterate the reality that had brought them together" (461), movies that threaten to snatch "everybody up to meet the Lord in the clouds" (462), Oscar looking "like a schoolboy on his way to a funeral" (486), the law clerk as both "memento mori" and "messenger [. . .] to the other side" (504, 517), the house as "cold as a tomb" (515), suing "from the other side" (551), and chain saws loud "enough to wake the dead" (575). In addition, there are repeated references to the authored work—be it a brief, an opinion, a play—that seeks immortality. Justice Crease's papers, write the historical society women, "properly belonged to the ages" (339); Judge Crease's opinions are also written to be read long past his death (443–44); and Harry's brief in the "Pop and Glow" case is said to be "enough in itself to immortalize him in the annals of First Amendment law" (578). Meanwhile, Oscar's bid for immortality hangs on *Once at Antietam.* When Christina jokingly brings up the possibility that he might have died in the hospital, Oscar has a sudden fright about his play's mortality: "Because my work, it would exist wouldn't it, its only claim to existence would be in this fraudulent counterfeit this, this vulgar distorted forgery and the thing itself, the original immortal thing itself would never be . . ." (421). Rebuked by Christina for discussing his play in terms (i.e., of immortality) that he refuses to use with regard to ordinary people, Oscar goes further in his explanation:

—That's it yes! Sunday mass nailing down their immortality one day a week
so they can waste the rest of it on trash, or the ones who squander it piling up
money like a barrier against death while the artist is working on his immortality every minute, everything he creates, that's what his work is, his immortality
and that's why having it stolen and corrupted and turned into some profane
worthless counterfeit is the most, why it's sacrilege, that's what sacrilege really
is isn't it? Isn't that really why I got into all this? (422)

It is a sad confession. This man who has no real friends to speak of (his
stepsister aside), and who has rightly surmised that there is "nobody around
who seems to care whether I live or I [die]" (254), nevertheless puts all his
hopes in a play that he himself will, in time, judge to be "all sort of stiff and
old fashioned" (489). Later, his third act will be used, by Lily, as kindling,
like Judge Crease's and Harry's papers. This fate seems to cast a gloomy
shadow over the hoped-for immortality of the writer, be it that of the jurist,
lawyer, or playwright. Certainly, there is an innocence in thinking that one's
work will create the possibility of immortality. In fact, we might think that
possibility an impossibility no matter what one does. And yet the impossible
always entails an element of the possible, a truth that Derrida explores in his
own meditation on death and dying, *Aporias*: "Is this [death] an aporia?
Where do we situate it? In the impossibility or in the possibility of an impossibility (which is not necessarily the same thing)? What can the possibility of
an impossibility be? How can we *think* that? How can we *say* it while
respecting logic and meaning? How can we approach that, live, or *exist* it?
How does one *testify* to it?" (68)

Gaddis does not answer these questions, either in *A Frolic of His Own* or
in the earlier novels. He seems desirous of keeping the questions open. This
certainly appears to be the case in *A Frolic of His Own*. I have spoken of the
novel as a meditation on justice, and I think it is this. But it is, I believe, a
meditation that, like Plato's *Republic*, conceives the question as intertwined
with that of our mortality. That is, just as the *Republic* begins its search for
justice with the "apprehensions and concern" expressed by the aged
Cephalus about how he has lived his life and what might be the consequences in the hereafter (Plato, 579; this passage is also quoted in Oscar's
play, 214), the Gaddis novel also begins by linking justice and death:
"Justice? —You get justice in the next world, in this world you have the law"
(11). This formulation helps us only so much. It does not answer our questions so much as postpone them, and gives credence to the sense that our
understanding can take us only so far, and that there is a limit—a
border—beyond which things are shrouded in a fundamental mystery.
Socrates himself said as much. So it is, perhaps, no surprise that at novel's
end there is one final allusion to Socrates, this time to *The Crito*, that same
text that formed the subtext of *Once at Antietam*'s third act. This last allusion

is somewhat veiled, as it needs to be, for it involves an identification of Harry, with his drink and pills, with Socrates and the hemlock (Gaddis uses the word *hemlock* on page 585). If the comparison were to be made too explicit, it would seem ludicrous, but Gaddis offers it in terms of the mildest of hints, and it seems perfectly right. Of course, *The Crito* is about the need to live honorably and rightly within the context of the laws in place. This is what Harry, like Socrates, chooses to do, even when those same laws finally appear too circumscriptive. He dies loyal to the firm, the same firm that has treated him so shabbily and, in short, unjustly.

The novel does not end with Harry's death, however, for there is one more scene, following Lily's burning of Harry's papers. This takes place under the sway of the pond, the pond as it was earlier described with its waters almost flooding, threatening to drown all, and "the far bank gone abruptly in a dull strip of grey" (585). Here, not only does "the middle distance" seem "to advance and recede" (585), but time itself seems to take on a mythic aspect, as the story of Hiawatha once again, as it has throughout the novel whenever attention turned to the pond, intersects with the present moment. That story was addressed to those "Who believe, that in all ages / Every human heart is human, / That in every savage bosom / There are longings, yearning, striv- ings / for the good they comprehend not, / That the feeble hands and help- less, Groping blindly in the darkness, / Touch God's right hand in that darkness / And are lifted up and strengthened" (Longfellow, 4–5). The Gaddis story is addressed to a rather different, much less sentimentally inclined audience. This explains why Gaddis's allusions to the poem appear both serious and comic. Still, the novel does not appear to renounce those "longings" spoken of by Longfellow. How could it, for they are so basic? Instead, these longings appear, as they often appear in Gaddis's work, almost masked, reflective of the author's own deliberate apophaticism. No matter, for the last scene gives, in its way, a clear indication of the intersection of the palpable with the impalpable, with "the whole pond" appearing "to heave as it ebbed from the foot of the lawn in a rising swell toward the other side like some grand seiche coming over it rocked by a catastrophe in the under- world" (585), invoking a world no less magical and mysterious than Hiawatha's own. It is, again, as if we are not so much in a world eclipsed by tragedy as in a ghost story, much like Joyce's "The Dead" to which Gaddis's last line—"Lily! Lily come here quickly I can't, Lily help me!" (586)—seems to make specific allusion. Whatever the case, Christina's girlish laughter, brought on by the boyish tickler (see also 13, 23), concludes the novel in a way that should make the pessimists among Gaddis's critics hesitate.

5

Conclusion

The universal cataract of death
That spends to nothingness—and unresisted,
Save by some strange resistance in itself,
Not just a swerving, but a throwing back,
As if regret were in it and were sacred.
—Robert Frost, "West-Running Brook"

In *Hints and Guesses*, I have not sought to offer a definitive reading of Gaddis's novels. The novels are too encyclopedic and complex to make this a plausible project. Accepting this, I have focused my discussion around the work's element of ethical and social criticism, itself housed within the assumption that a different standard might be imagined. Stanley Cavell, thinking about the discrepancy between what is and what might be, has suggested that we recall the lesson of Kant,

> for whom moral sanity depends on a reasonable hope for future justice, and his necessary positing of the good city as a Realm of Ends—where each of us is legislated for in legislating for all. Unlike Plato's Republic, Kant's good city is essentially unrepresentable by philosophy; if we could represent it we could claim to know it, but that would leave room neither for genuine faith in our effectiveness toward a future nor for genuine knowledge of the present. ("Time after Time," 6)

This is less a dismissal of Plato (an important influence in Gaddis: "From Plato on we try to establish order")[1] than an admission that, in the post-Enlightenment, our greatest beliefs tend to be framed negatively, or apophatically. Still, the sense that we judge the present by a "future today" (Cavell's phrase), leaving us with a powerful intuition that "something's missing" (Brecht's phrase), is an essential characteristic of Gaddis's work. This "something" remains elusive because the good city itself remains elusive, nonrepresentable. Still, if forced to speak of its nature, we might describe it as that which is capable of reconciling society's disparate parts in the light of something larger and more ennobling than cash nexus. Or, if we wish to go further, this "something" might be construed as a numinous or religious order capable not only of holding disparate elements together but also of redeeming them. Redemption, though, is no easy task, for the novels convey a world seriously threatened by disorder, where even the strongest characters cannot altogether escape the mood of belatedness and meaninglessness. (Cf. Wyatt's "It's a question of . . . it's being surrounded by people who don't have any sense of . . . no sense that what they're doing means anything" [R, 144].) Still, Gaddis's novels, so masterfully conceived and executed, are themselves proof that not all is hopeless, for the recognition of disorder entails a conception of order, a sense of how things might be otherwise. That artists figure so centrally in Gaddis's work, and that his own work testifies to the need to collect and compose fragments, shoring them up against his ruin, reflect the author's modernist side. That the artists are so often failed artists, and that Gaddis's own work (an artistry of undisputed power) should meet with such a deaf reception, reflect conditions that, in their manifest indifference to what artists do, might be called postmodern. However, the point is not to claim Gaddis's work for either the modernist or the postmodernist camp, even as respectable arguments can be made either way. Rather, I would prefer to describe Gaddis's work as, at heart, addressing fundamental questions of meaning and purpose alive in any age, the sort that do not presume that the answers have already been given, but rather that demand that we, Thoreau-like, find out for ourselves "whether it [the world] is of the devil or of God," and if it proves "to be mean, why then get . . . the whole and genuine meanness of it, and publish its meanness to the world," or if it proves "sublime, to know it by experience, and [to] be able to give a true account of it."

The mention of Thoreau might, meantime, recall for us how comfortably Gaddis's work fits in with a tradition of American writing that includes not only Thoreau but Emerson, Hawthorne, Melville, Poe, Dickinson, Twain, Henry and William James, Frost, Eliot, Stevens, O'Connor, and others. I myself have not pursued this theme, and leave the task to future scholars. Still, what Frederick Karl says about *J R*—that the "entire world of American writing reverberate[s] through" it (introduction, xi)—can, in fact, be said about all four Gaddis novels. Karl takes note of the way in which

Twain's Huck, Dreiser's Clyde Griffiths, Fitzgerald's Jay Gatsby, Melville's white whale, and Hemingway's "defeated romantics" all find their echoes in *J R*, "creating a continuity with the grand themes of our major fiction, and . . . re-energizing the language in its most colloquial form" (introduction, xi), but we might also extend the bounds beyond fiction, and take note of the importance of Emerson's essays, Thoreau's *Walden*, Holmes's court decisions, Eliot's poetry and prose, and, in an opposing mood, *Cannibals All!* by Fitzhugh, Dale Carnegie's *How to Win Friends and Influence People*, F. W. Taylor's *The Principles of Scientific Management*, and B. F. Skinner's *The Behavior of Organisms*, all brought forward by Gaddis to comment on a nation predicated on the values of cheap labor, efficiency, profits, progress, technology, success, a leveling democracy, and, as Gibbs puts it, "[t]he irrefragable fact" (*J R*, 571). That something is missing from the equation is apparent to certain Gaddis characters, especially among the artists, but it is not a given that either art or theology can fill the vacuum.

The problem, in the cases of art and theology, has to do with the way in which they are coopted by the values in place. The artists, while nominally opposed to the ideal of cash nexus, still tend to mimic what they do not like, especially as their self-imposed exile fosters a mood of separation. They beat a retreat to Greenwich Village, or to the Ninety-Sixth Street apartment, or to Long Island's East End, and by doing so they help to segment off what they do from the larger culture. This is partly a no-win situation, like the way in which the artist's asceticism is, says Weber, at the heart of division-of-labor economics: "The emphasis on the ascetic importance of a fixed calling provided an ethical justification of the modern specialized division of labour" (163). Avoidable or not, Gaddis's fiction portrays artists participating in their own marginalization, to the point that *J R*'s Hyde, in his voice-of-the-people fashion, can with some justice say that "the only time you read about them they're making trouble for somebody, for themselves or somebody else that's the only time you hear about them" (*J R*, 49).

Still, more than other characters, the artist here remains identified with an ethic of resistance. Gaddis himself is a great resister, particularly as he opposes a society gone astray by miming it. Like Adorno, who thinks it should make sense "to study people who have no artistic sensibilities" because "[u]nbeknown to themselves, they represent an extreme form of criticism of art while at the same time showing up art's truth" (177), Gaddis depicts not only struggling artist types but also a host of grotesques recognizable by their embrace of the reality principle and deafness to "the sweet power of music." These people would bring Mozart down to their level rather than seek to rise up to his. For them, the realm of perfection will ever be an irrelevancy, not because it does not exist, but because they choose to live otherwise. And when they do this, they are a reminder to others, caught between two worlds, of what is missing.

What, then, is this something missing? Again, Gaddis does not directly say, unless a reference to the object of the sublime constitutes a description. Mostly, however, this object defies description, and is knowable only through a "negative presentation." The phrase is Kant's (I.127), and it connects to the philosopher's understanding of the sublime object, which he tells us "cannot be contained in any sensuous form" though it "may be excited and called into the mind by the very inadequacy itself which does not admit of sensuous presentation" (I.92). In a sense, then, the sublime (itself an emotion or mood) speaks of a mystery at the heart of things, a mystery that, for Gaddis and the tradition to which he belongs, escapes the net not only of art but of organized religion as well.[2] That is, Gaddis, who speaks of the shaping influence of a New England Protestantism on his life—"the entire Protestant Ethic has been very much in me from my boarding school days on. My mother's family was Quaker. I was brought up pretty much in New England. I was taught that 'This is what you do and you do it right. These are the rules'" (Grove, B 10)—believes, it seems, that this manner of religion has been corrupted by American practices, and that no institution, religious or otherwise, can adequately do justice to a mystery, or a Divinity, that requires a more vigilant openness.

Gaddis's fiction, in fact, suggests that among the things in need of redemption is the Protestant ethic itself. In *J R*, Gibbs pointedly remarks, "God damned Protestant ethic can't escape it have to redeem it" (477). By this and other statements like it, Gibbs argues, à la Weber, that Protestantism, through its celebration of both the individual's one-to-one relation to God and industriousness as a sign of heavenly election, has ironically helped to foster a community that is not less but more secular and individualistic. Protestantism has been, says Gibbs, long intertwined with the ethic of American capitalism and has even influenced the behavior of those citizens whose religious beliefs are quite different: "Protestant ethic have to justify your own existence be a Chinaman like Lin Yutang and make a million dollars, problem now's to justify the Protestant ethic grow up want to be a dry clean[er]" (*J R*, 477). In the United States, the Protestant ethic leads not to the City of God but to General Motors, as suggested by Davidoff's command to a J R Family subordinate that he "dig out some of the President's speeches whole Protestant work ethic head of General Motors on free enterprise whole utilitarian pragmatism angle what works" (*J R*, 530). Meantime, the view that New England Protestantism has been as much in the service of Mammon as of God also strengthens the view—shared by Emerson, Thoreau, Melville, Dickinson, William James, Frost, and Stevens, among others—that no institution, the religious included, can encapsulate truth in its finest and largest and even most spiritual sense. The view has an element of innocence about it, for it protests too much and fails to grant the good that institutions, the religious included, also perform. In any event, traditional religions here are viewed as corporate-like, the loci of bigotry and corruption. Or as William James, in *The Varieties of Religious Experience*, wrote:

> The basenesses so commonly charged to religion's account are thus, almost all of them, not chargeable at all to religion proper, but rather to religion's wicked practical partner, the spirit of corporate dominion. And the bigotries are most of them in their turn chargeable to religion's wicked intellectual partner, the spirit of dogmatic dominion, the passion for laying down the law in the form of an absolutely closed-in theoretic system. The ecclesiastical spirit in general is the sum of these two spirits of dominion; and I beseech you never to confound the phenomena of mere tribal or corporate psychology which it presents with those manifestations of the purely interior life. . . . (338)[3]

In this tradition, Jesus himself is considered but one individual in search of an original relation to the world. Hence Emerson, in "The Over-Soul," writes: "Jesus speaks always from within, and in a degree that transcends all others. In that is the miracle. I believe beforehand that it ought so to be. All men stand continually in the expectation of the appearance of such a teacher. But if a man do not speak from within the veil, where the word is one with that it tells of, let him lowly confess it." Gaddis's fiction also suggests that people spend too much time looking to others to lead them out of the spiritual desert, or as Gibbs notes, "problem everybody running around wants to be told what happens next [. . .], looking for the wise man tell them what am I supposed to do now God damned wise man find out he's doing the same God damned thing walks up the shade and he's gone, rest of us sitting here looking at his footprints think he took it with him and he's gone" (399).

"[G]enius is religious," says Emerson, and while the formulation may, at present, sound too romantic, even anachronistic, Gaddis's fiction also suggests that the pursuit of the religious is largely carried out through an individual's responding to his or her genius, to compulsions that originate as much from within as from without. Not all respond to their genius, of course. In fact, too many live lives that are, by and large, mean, hoping that someone will come and take them by the hand and point the way. They look to Wyatt (who believes that "All our highest goals are inhuman ones" [*R*, 589]), and they, or we, even look to Gaddis, as if he were some modern-day Philoctetes. But the fiction suggests that we need to look less to others than to ourselves—that is, to the extent that the self functions as an opening to an intuition or a genius that is neither personal nor selfish. "No man ever followed his genius till it misled him," Thoreau writes, and Gaddis would probably agree. Certainly, his fiction—written against strong, countervailing pressures—suggests a man remarkably trustful of his genius, of his own inner counsel. Whether this can be read as synonymous with a religious impulse is open to debate, though I am, as this study no doubt suggests, inclined to think so.

In the end, then, I believe that the novels ask us to resist "[t]he universal cataract of death / [t]hat spends to nothingness"; ask us "not to kill the things we love" but to love and to nourish them, something that we shall not likely do unless we understand the importance of conceiving them in the light of a greater good. There can be no small acts of goodness without a recognition of a greater good, and it appears the aim of Gaddis's fiction to remind us of this and to assist us in our own individual acts of recognition. Sometimes, his own faith here wavers and a gruffness enters the voice. But even then, Gaddis never really forgets the urgency of the matter, of how important it is to discern the difference between the things not worth doing and those that are. If "our view of life is misleading" (*J R*, 116), it is, it would seem, because we tend to give too much time to the former and not enough to the latter. But it is the latter, with all their hints of a hidden perfection unknowable to us except through the agencies of our desire and trust, that compel the fiction. So, if "something's missing" has been the dominant mood of Gaddis's fiction, it has always gone hand in hand with the suggestion that anything that is lost stands the chance of being found. Chance, of course, favors the prepared mind, and in Gaddis's work, something quite wonderful is found.

Notes
Works Cited
Index

Notes

Introduction

1. In his dissertation "Splinters from the Yew Tree," Peter Koenig writes, "Gaddis at one point planned to parody every line of T. S. Eliot's *Four Quartets* in *The Recognitions*, and a few such lines do remain. This was, as with all such parodies, to give a humorous sense, but also because he admired Eliot and in parodying him paid tribute to his influence" (67; also quoted in Steven Moore [*RG*, 129-30]). Meanwhile, Moore, having asked Gaddis about the matter, has corrected the Koenig story somewhat, informing me, in the space of our correspondence, that Gaddis's initial intention was to interweave the poem's lines into the novel's text, more out of respect for the poem than for the purposes of "humorous" parody. Then, finally, in the Logan and Mirkowicz interview, Gaddis says of Eliot's influence that he "was very formative in my life and thinking when I was in college and even later, when *Four Quartets* came out. I even wanted to include the whole of it in *The Recognitions*. I think Eliot still has very much to do with my thinking, with my attempts to use language, and so forth."

2. Both passages are borrowing from the *Four Quartets* poem "East Coker." In the first instance, the Eliot lines read:

> Do not let me hear
> Of the wisdom of old men, but rather of their folly,
> Their fear of fear and frenzy, their fear of possession,
> Of belonging to another, or to others, or to God. (II. 93-96)

In the second instance, the lines read:

> There is only the fight to recover what has been lost
> And found and lost again and again: and now, under conditions
> That seem unpropitious. (V. 186-88)

Gaddis also employs the latter quotation in the opening of "Old Foes with New Faces."

3. For a discussion of the encyclopedia in relation to postmodernism, as well as to Gaddis, see Steven Weisenburger, *Fables of Subversion*, 200-10.

4. Tertullian, in fact, wrote, "Certum est quia impossibile est" (It is certain because it is impossible) (*De Carne Christi*).

5. In addition to the Jung and Bultmann definitions of religion, I would also like to add that offered by Giles Gunn: "By religion I . . . mean, first, the predisposition to view all human problems not traceable to natural accidents as reducible to the perfidiousness of human nature; second, the predilection to view the perfidiousness of human nature as unamenable to satisfactory redress by any agencies such as reason, will, or feeling intrinsic to human nature itself; and third, the tendency to view access to any agencies of empowerment transcendent to human nature as possible only through faith rather than works, including the efforts of the human mind to secure through analysis, criticism, or imaginative projection relief from such problems" (*Thinking Across*, 122).

6. De Man writes: "From the organic, still asserted naively in the *Critique of Pure Reason*, to the phenomenological, the rational cognition of incarnate ideas, which the best part of the Kant interpretation in the nineteenth- and twentieth-century will single out, we have reached, in the final analysis, a materialism that, in the tradition of the reception of the *Third Critique*, is seldom or never perceived" ("Phenomenality and Materiality in Kant," 106).

7. Gasché writes:

The true infinite is necessarily characterized by absolute wholeness, in other words, by a wholeness that is also self-inclusive to the extent that it is not in opposition to that of which it is the totality. "The by-itself negative denomination 'infinitude' is," as Manfred Baum has put it, "the name for that which is in opposition to all opposition, to the extent that it is the Other to all limitation which, in conformity with the proposition 'Omnis determinatio est negatio,' lies in mere determinatedness, and which is still thought in the idea of an objective infinitude standing in opposition to a finite subject." True infinity is a unity that cannot be a unity in counter-position to separation. It is not in opposition, but rather beyond and above all opposition. Including itself and its Other, and comprising within itself opposition and separation, the true infinite is a complete whole which, instead of being susceptible to further determination, and hence of a determination of determination, contains this process within itself. (*Inventions*, 133)

The concept of true and spurious infinity is, says Gasché, often identified with Hegel, but is, in fact, a more commonplace philosophical concept than this identification would suggest: "Now, it must be recalled that Hegel's distinction between genuine and spurious infinity is not at all a specifically Hegelian idea" (*Inventions*, 131).

8. Gasché describes Derrida's own notion of infinity as both "syntactic" and "structural": "Based on the developments of 'The Double Session,' one could call Derrida's notion of infinity a *syntactic infinity*, keeping in mind, of course, that the text also sets out to 'systematically outwit and undo the opposition between the syn-

tactic and the semantic.' In the following [discussion], however, I will analyze this type of infinity in terms of *structural infinity*" (*Inventions*, 139).

9. Here I do not see Derrida's deconstruction as a facet of postmodernism, for deconstruction evinces a real skepticism with regard to attempts to periodize, whereas postmodernism is first and foremost a gesture in the direction of periodization. Meanwhile, the postmodernism that I discount here is specifically of the Baudrillardian variety, that which aestheticizes all experience in the direction of the simulacrum.

10. A crucial problem with Johnston's reading of Gaddis is that while he grounds his study in Bakhtin—"Mikhail Bakhtin's theory of the dialogic or polyphonic novel provides the overall theoretical orientation" (4)—his own reading of Bakhtin seems particularly suspect, especially as he transforms Bakhtin into a protopostmodernist:

> According to Bakhtin, reversibility and inversion are the essential strategies of carnivalesque fiction, with inversions of social, physical, and semantic hierarchies (king/clown, face/ass, sacred/profane) generating the most common carnival images and expressions. So far I have concentrated only on a philosophico-aesthetic inversion, which does not mean however that *The Recognitions* does not employ these more familiar carnival inversions. In fact, the energy and spirit of carnival pervade the novel. For in depicting New York in the late 1940s as a world "turned upside down," in which social and aesthetic hierarchies are overturned and the restraints of "good taste" lifted, the novel adopts the "jolly relativity" (Bakhtin) and semiotic riot of carnival as its creative principle. In accord with carnival, it is a world in which the substance of social identity has been dissolved in travesty and masquerade, and everyone mixes in free and overly familiar contact. Not surprisingly, those usually considered to be the socially marginal and the excluded—counterfeiters, drug addicts, homosexuals, schizophrenics, bohemian intellectuals, hack writers, and con men—are here found at the center. The antics and black humor of these characters, like the clowns, jesters, fools, and mimes in carnival performances, invert and mock the normalizing assumptions of modern society. And, in a further carnivalizing reversal, all that is "high" and privileged in the culture is shown to be subject to repetition, perceived now as the degrading mechanism of consumer capitalism and mass culture, which also produces "copies without originals." (42)

It is a very intelligent critique. Yet what Johnston downplays, or even ignores, is that for Bakhtin carnival exists within the logic of a more formal culture, that it constitutes the "temporary suspension" (*Rabelais*, 10) of this world rather than a complete overturning of it. Carnival is licensed by the larger logic, much in the manner that *parodia sacra* was licensed by the church: "We know that men who composed the most unbridled parodies of sacred texts and of cults often sincerely accepted and served religion" (*Rabelais*, 95; also see *Problems of Dostoevsky's Poetics*, 127). Carnival, then, is less a principle of unending reversal than a necessary corrective to a culture that might otherwise be in danger of taking itself too seriously. Its work is, in its own way, utopian: "Let us here stress the special philosophical and utopian character of festive laughter and its orientation toward the highest spheres. The most

ancient rituals of mocking at the deity have here survived [in carnival], acquiring a
new essential meaning. All that was purely cultic and limited has faded away, but the
all-human, universal, and utopian element has been retained" (*Rabelais*, 12). It is also
in this vein that Gaddis himself works. Or as he notes in a letter (to Keith Botsford)
accompanying his "First Notes for a Television Program on Forgery": "The compelling thing about a program on forgery I think is the chance it offers to approach the
arts with a light touch, without the self-conscious overseriousness and frequent condescension that is such a threat to 'cultural' programs" (10 April 1957). It is better, I
think, to read Gaddis's work as something akin to *parodia sacra* than as an "'overthrowing Platonism'" wherein "a logic of the simulacrum and phantasm" rule
(Johnston, 5).

    11. The phrase is Iris Murdoch's, offered in a discussion that seems pertinent to
Gaddis's work: "The written word can fall into the hands of any knave or fool. Only
in certain kinds of personal converse can we thoroughly clarify each other's understanding. The thinker's defence against this may be, like that of Socrates and Christ,
not to write. Or it may be, like that of (for instance) Kierkegaard, Wittgenstein,
Derrida, to employ a careful obscurity" (87). Or it also may be, says Milan Kundera
(thinking of Kafka) to destroy the work before or at one's death: here, "the author still
loves his work and doesn't even think about the future of the world, but having had
his own experiences with the public, he understands the *vanitas vanitatum* of art, the
inevitable incomprehension that is his lot, the incomprehension (not underestimation,
I'm not talking about personal vanity) he has suffered during his lifetime and that he
doesn't want to go on suffering post mortem. (It may incidentally be only the brevity
of life that keeps artists from understanding fully the futility of their labor and making
arrangements in time for the obliteration of both their work and themselves.)" (255-
56). Of course, in Gaddis's novels, there are repeated instances of serious work being
destroyed (think of that of Wyatt in *The Recognitions*, Jack Gibbs and Edward Bast in
J R, McCandless in *Carpenter's Gothic*, and Harry Lutz, Oscar Crease, and Judge
Crease in *A Frolic of His Own*).

    12. In "Old Foes with New Faces," Gaddis has his own fun with the notion that
the text not only anticipates its author but also seems more reflective of its readers'
(rather than its author's) needs, saying that the theory seems a wonderful post hoc
explanation not only for Joseph Smith's *Book of Mormon* but also for the enormous
success of the Church of Jesus Christ of Latter-Day Saints:

> In his extraordinary way, he [Smith] anticipates the modern "scriptor" dear to
> the hearts of the deconstructionists, who is "born simultaneously with the text,
> is in no way equipped with a being preceding or exceeding the writing, is not
> the subject with the book as predicate" described by Roland Barthes in *The
> Death of the Author*. "We know now that a text is not a line of words releasing
> a single 'theological' meaning (the 'message' of the Author-God) but a multi-
> dimensional space in which a variety of writings, none of them original, blend
> and clash," which is one way to explain the continuing worldwide success of
> the Church of Jesus Christ of Latter-day Saints. (7)

    13. I borrow the phrase from Cunningham, who, in *The Reading Gaol*, writes:
"But still, it is my book's continual belief that generalizations about language and its

uses, theoretical generalizations, are only of use to readers, to criticism, if they can be shown to pertain to the literary case, to literary cases. So all the literary criticism, or *Literaturwissenschaft*, that matters and reveals comes down to practical criticism (in the widest sense)" (61).

14. Mindful of the problem, Steven Weisenburger, in *Fables of Subversion: Satire and the American Novel, 1930-1980*, proposes a "degenerative" form of satire, more in keeping with postmodern skepticism. Thus, he

> argues for a mode of "degenerative" satirical writing that stands in crucial opposition to the generative satires of a Pope or Twain. The purpose of satire in the degenerative mode is delegitimizing. Loosely in concord with deconstructionist thought, it functions to subvert hierarchies of value and to reflect suspiciously on all ways of making meaning, including its own. Still more, it suspects that any symbolic practice may entail incursions of power whose logic tends toward either total domination or the final chaos of reciprocal violence. (3)

However, as is here evident, Weisenburger's critique does not escape its own fall into binarism, hierarchization, and totalization, thereby undercutting the vaunted "radicalness" ("Postmodern satire is 'radical' in both of the best senses of that word" [13]) of the project.

15. In *A Theory of Parody*, Linda Hutcheon writes: "For many, the 1960s marked a golden age of satire, but it was a satire that relied very much on parody and therefore shared its variable ethos. In the works of writers like Pynchon and artists like Robert Colescott, there is less of a sense of aiming at what Swift called 'no defect / But what all mortals may correct.' The black humor (as it was labeled) of these years has begun to change our notion of parody" (46).

16. Likewise, Bakhtin writes:

> A particular language in a novel is always a particular way of viewing the world, one that strives for a social significance. It is precisely as ideologemes that discourse becomes the object of representation in the novel, and it is for the same reason novels are never in danger of becoming a mere aimless verbal play. The novel, being a dialogized representation of an ideologically freighted discourse (in most cases actual and really present) is of all verbal genres the one least susceptible to aestheticism as such, to a purely formalistic playing about with words. (*Dialogic Imagination*, 333)

17. In "Old Foes with New Faces," Gaddis juxtaposes a traditional, somewhat Dostoevskian notion of fiction and its contemporary avatar:

> Once upon a time, fiction was a way of getting at some kind of truth: we concocted fictions to get us through the night or, nostalgic for absolutes, we embraced revelation as ultimate Truth. Now fiction is used to bring on the darkest night of all, in which historical reality in its most monstrous epiphany is dismissed as a mischievous, fictive concoction by the so-called Holocaust revisionists, a deceptively mild label for those bent on giving substance to

Hitler's maxim that any lie will pass muster provided it is big enough. This denial, made in the face of all the tangible evidence and witnesses, living and dead, of the systematic murder of six million human beings of different race and religion, is a lie of such enormous proportions that it will live on and reemerge to taint history forever. It offers the worst-case scenario of the willing suspension of disbelief. (15)

The suggestion is that fiction, like truth, cannot protect itself from its opposite, which is not the same thing as saying that it and its opposite are one. Here, the "[o]nce upon a time" should not mislead anyone into thinking that what was once true is true no longer.

18. Here, we might liken Gaddis to Bakhtin's Dostoevsky: "At the level of his religious-utopian world-view Dostoevsky carries dialogue into eternity, conceiving of it as eternal co-rejoicing, co-admiration, con-cord. At the level of the novel, it is presented as the unfinalizability of dialogue, although originally as dialogue's vicious circle" (*Problems of Dostoevsky's Poetics*, 252).

19. In *The Varieties of Metaphysical Poetry*, Eliot writes: "When a subject matter is in its nature vague, clarity should consist, not in making it so clear as to be unrecognisible, but in recognising the vagueness, where it begins and ends and the causes of its necessity, and in checking analysis and division at the prudent point" (60).

20. Louis Auchincloss is a friend of the author, and I somewhat suspect that his remark here testifies to a desire on Gaddis's own part to see criticism of his work reoriented, away from its postmodern slant. In any event, the full quotation, a blurb for *A Frolic of His Own*, used in the Daedalus Books catalogue (Winter 1995), reads: "This brilliant and hilarious satire of America's obsession with law and lawsuits confirms Gaddis's reputation as our most wittily observant, devastating and profound novelist of manners" (8). The Carnegie quotation, meanwhile, is taken from the back cover of the Scribner Paperback Fiction edition of *A Frolic of His Own* (New York, 1995).

21. Again, I think there is a difference between satire and parody, but they also often operate together. Hutcheon writes incisively on the matter:

The grounds upon which other theorists do separate the two genres are sometimes debatable. Winfried Freund claims that satire aims at the restoration of positive values, while parody can only operate negatively. Since her focus is largely on German nineteenth-century literature, parody is said to lack important metaphysical and moral dimensions that satire can demonstrate. But I would argue that the difference between the two forms lies not so much in their perspective on human behavior, as she believes, but in what is being made into a "target." In other words, parody is not extramural in its aim; satire is. Both Northrop Frye and Tuvia Shlonsky have argued this clearly and convincingly in the face of remarks such as "No aspect of society has been safe from the parodist's mocking attention." Yet the obvious reason for the confusion of parody and satire, despite the major difference between them, is the fact that the two genres are often used together. Satire frequently uses parodic art forms for either expository or aggressive purposes, when it desires textual differentiation as its vehicle. Both satire and parody imply critical distancing and therefore value judgments, but satire generally uses that distance to make a negative statement about that which is satirized—"to distort, to belittle, to wound." In modern parody, however, we have found that no such negative judgment is necessarily suggested in the ironic contrasting of texts. Parodic art both deviates from an aesthetic norm and includes that norm within itself as backgrounded material. Any real attack would be self-destructive. (43-44)

22. See Jack Green's castigating review of the reviewers, *Fire the Bastards!*

23. Tanner's praise of the novel, offered in the *New York Times Book Review*, 14 July 1974 (27-28), on the occasion of the book's reprinting in an Avon paperback edition, was, I believe, a turning point in the reception of Gaddis's work, which, at that point, included only the first novel. *J R* came out the following year.

24. In *Forms of Attention*, Kermode writes that canonical texts "share with the sacred at least this quality: that however a particular epoch or a particular community may define a proper mode of attention or a licit area of interests, there will always be something else and something different to say. There is, of course, room for dissent within the agreement that the last word cannot be said, but it is hard to suppose that there can be progress ensured by the testing of hypotheses; all we are sure about is that the inadequacies of earlier exposition become astonishingly obvious to later expositors, that there can be no simple and perpetual consensus as to the proper way to join the shadow of comment to the substance of the play. And this is what it means to call a book canonical" (62).

Chapter 1: *The Recognitions* and Wyatt Gwyon's Role as Artist/Forger/Artist

1. In the spring of 1957, Gaddis, then working at Pfizer International, entered into a correspondence with Keith Botsford, one of the directors of the CBS television show *The Seven Lively Arts*, regarding the possibility of putting together a program on the theme of forgery, a theme closely associated with *The Recognitions*. In fact, Gaddis thought he could use some of the novel's material, though the plan did not involve an adaptation as such: "I'm not proposing an adaptation of that book, incidentally, except to develop by exposition some of the ideas which it investigated in fiction" (10 April 1957). Botsford, though initially intrigued by the plan, ultimately wrote back to reject it:

Now forgive me my sins; I'd rather be honest from the start: some indication of my respect for what you've created. Then, too, you'll take me seriously when I say "get to it." Skip all else. Forget lucre. My God, as though you were wallowing in it!

Please Will, I don't think yr show is going to work. I'll tell you why and why John [Houseman, the executive producer] thinks it won't. It won't work because there isn't enough to show. And far better wd be to do yr book. But how to do it? The real implication of what *you* mean by forgery are things you get across in the novel by implication and *imitation* (the latter particularly)—the way you move out of the frame of reference without ever ceasing yourself, to hold up the mirror of counterfeiting. Yt we cd not do [it] honestly. And what we could do with forgery wd be pale and dishonest. We'd pick some big razzle-dazzle numbers: trials, experts, people dishonoured, etc. and we'd never understand what was at the bottom of it or how this really reflected on *us*. Because boy! are we counterfeits! (8 May 1957)

2. Compare this to the novel's epigraph, "Nihil cavum neque sine signo apud Deum" (In God, nothing is empty), a quotation from Irenaeus, the second-century bishop of Lyons.

3. Of course, of these three, the first two worked outside the realm of Abstract Expressionism, and the third, Rothko, thought of himself almost as working more in the tradition of the Renaissance painter. Dore Ashton, the well-respected art critic, in addition to being a personal friend of Rothko, is very fine on this aspect of Rothko's work, particularly the importance to him of the painter Fra Angelico (the same painter whom Wyatt cannot even imagine trying to imitate [242]): "Fra Angelico was important to Rothko because Rothko understood the context within which he functioned, and because he himself had shifted his sights. His aesthetic was now [1950s-1960s] a renunciation of self-expression in favor of meditation. His innate Platonism triumphed over the tumultuous emotion that had once governed his works" (*About Rothko*, 148; see her chapter 9 for a full discussion).

Ashton, meanwhile, tells of visiting Rothko's studio in February 1969 and finding a painter, much like Wyatt, uncomfortable with the relation of his work to his times:

Many old questions troubled him. . . . Highly nervous, thin, restless, Rothko chainsmoked and talked intermittently. Literature and music, he said, were his base. He was never really "connected" with painting, as he started painting only late. His material is his "inner life," his "inner experience." He has nothing to do with painting today, but rather is a Renaissance painter. (I was reminded that in the 1958 lecture he had firmly declared that in the great artistic epochs "Men with their minds produced a view of the world, transforming our vision of things.") With their minds . . . [, t]his was Rothko's vision of the Renaissance artist; his ideals which, in his isolation after his brush with death, he felt had been abandoned by all the world. The brooding and often harsh character of the many large paintings on paper he showed me that day could only be seen in the light of a man's sinking heart. The dark, he had said with unintentional symbolism, is always at the top. To Stamos, Morton Levine, Bernard Reis, and a few other close friends, he sometimes spoke of his aesthetic despair and the hollowness of his fame. He was convinced that on the whole he had never been properly understood. (*About Rothko*, 188)

I cite this passage at length because, again, I think it points out the elective affinities between Wyatt and Rothko (and one might add between Gaddis and Rothko); and while the connection makes it clear that Wyatt, had he been stronger, might have carved a space for himself in the world of painting, doing so would have been a very difficult matter.

4. In the abbreviated notes sent to Keith Botsford along with the 10 April 1957 letter and television proposal, Gaddis writes, on page 1, "Thesis: Platonism," and on

page 2, "Thesis: the finiteness of man, and the eventual imperfectibility of his creations, aspiring toward the (Platonic) ideal which is ever just beyond reach."

5. On page 463, the phrase "you cannot invent the shape of a stone" is identified as that of Ben Shahn, the social realist painter.

6. The passage from which this is taken involves a contrast between the genius of Mozart and that of Beethoven: "the perfection of Mozart, work of genius without an instant of hesitation or struggle, genius to which argument opposed the heroic struggle constantly rendering the music of Beethoven, struggle never resolved and triumphed until the end" (*R*, 81). The contrast seems analogous to that between Kant's conception of the beautiful and that of the sublime. The beautiful, says Kant, "is the form of *finality* in an object, so far as perceived in it *apart from the representation of an end*" (I.80). By contrast, "the sublime is to be found in an object even devoid of form, so far as it immediately involves, or else by its presence provokes, a representation of *limitlessness*, yet with a super-added thought of its totality" (I.90). Mozart and Beethoven, then, are both joined and separated by their genius.

7. I am mindful that in "Old Foes with New Faces," as well as in an earlier interview, Gaddis speaks contemptuously of Steiner ("sometime critic and failed novelist" [2]). The reason, I believe, has much to do with Steiner's *New Yorker* review of *J R*, which was largely negative. It is not enough of a reason, however, for me to refrain from quoting Steiner when it serves present purposes.

8. In *The Critique of Judgment*, Kant speaks of two kinds of beauty: free and dependent. "The first presupposes no concept of what the object should be; the second does presuppose such a concept and, with it, an answering perfection of the object" (I.72). The first, a "self-subsisting" beauty, includes such things as flowers, plants, and birds, things not dependent on a concept for their determination of beauty. The second, including the beauty of people, horses, and buildings, "presupposes a concept of the end that defines what the thing has to be, and consequently a concept of its perfection" (I.73).

9. The narrator's description of Esme's struggle with her poetry is relevant here:

> It was through this imposed accumulation of chaos that she struggled to move now: beyond it lay simplicity, unmeasurable, residence of perfection, where nothing was created, where originality did not exist: because it was origin; where once she was there work and thought in casual stumbling sequence did not exist, but only transcription: where the poem she knew but could not write existed, ready-formed, awaiting recovery in that moment when the writing down of it was impossible: because she was the poem. (299-300)

10. Not all traditions are the same, of course; and it is not surprising, perhaps, that some modern disciplines should almost wish to dissociate themselves from their earlier incarnations. One instance is modern medicine, whose practitioners tend to look back on the discipline's past with embarrassment, if not horror. To a modern physician Galen's theory of "humors" might, at best, seem humorous, but when one remembers that a healthy George Washington, upon catching a fever and sore throat while out horseback riding in the snow, was insanely bled, by his physician, of five pints of blood, making him so weak that he soon died, the response is likelier to be one of mortification (see Thomas, 9).

258 Notes to Pages 45-49

11. This list is drawn from Ashton's eighth chapter in *The New York School*. Guilbaut writes:

The crisis of the West—the disintegration of modern Western culture exemplified by book-burnings and by exhibitions of degenerate art—was a profound crisis, to be sure, but one that signified not the death of Western culture but rather its rebirth, reinvigoration, and purification by fire, its starting over again in a new place, America. Indeed, New York seemed the only place in the world cosmopolitan enough to replace Paris. Once American artists and intellectuals realized this, it became imperative for them to reconsider their relation to their own national culture as well as the relation of American culture to international culture and to adjust their actions accordingly, so as not to miss this unique opportunity to join the modern movement. (63)

12. In "Old Foes with New Faces," Gaddis returns to the distinction, after having first noted their commonality, writing:

The priest is the guardian of mysteries, the artist is driven to expose them. The manifest difference between them is that the writer is a teller of secrets who grapples with his audience one reader, one page at a time; where the priest engages the collective delusion of his entire congregation all at once. (3)

13. Beginning with the van Eycks, the Flemish painters demonstrated a clear inventiveness in the use of this "new oil technique" (Panofsky, 151), a technique that was most notable for the enhanced luminosity with which it endowed each painting. Panofsky writes:

Rather than inventing entirely new processes, they appear to have perfected the traditional ones and thus to have developed a system of stratification, not unlike that employed in later Limousine enamel work, which permitted them to combine the minuteness of book illumination with the substantiality of tempera painting and the luminosity of *pictura lucida*.
    The whole picture was built up from bottom to top by superimposing "rich" and therefore translucent paint (viz., pigments tempered with a fat medium, mostly, though not exclusively, oil) upon "lean" and therefore more or less opaque paint (viz., pigments tempered with other, aqueous media or, possibly, an emulsion). Lighter and darker tones were produced by applying the translucent colors over an opaque underpainting—significantly called *doodverw*, "dead color," in Dutch and Flemish—which pre-established the light values and, to some extent, the general color; and finer gradation—in certain cases even an optical mixture of two colors—was achieved by applying further films of pigment.
    As a result, the light is not entirely reflected from the top surface of the picture, where opaque pigments appear only in the shape of highlights. Part of the light penetrates the coat or coats of translucent paint to be reflected from the nearest layer of opaque pigment, and this is what endows the pictures of the old masters with their peculiar "depth." Even the darkest tones could never

turn opaque, and ultimately the whole multiple coat of paint would coalesce
into a hard, enamellike, slightly uneven but uniformly luminous substance,
irradiated from below as well as from above, excepting only those sporadic
whites or light yellows which, by their very contrast to the transparent depth of
the surrounding pigments, assume the character of "high lights." (152-53)

14. Dominick LaCapra writes:

The Recognitions might even be taken as the epitome of Mikhail Bakhtin's
notion of the significant novel as the polyphonic orchestration of the heteroge-
neous, fragmentary, often chaotic, at times cacophonous discourses of the
times into a serio-comic, provocatively ambivalent *agon* or carnival of con-
tending "voices" and dissonant possibilities in society and culture. For any
given element—event, character, development—is never simply univocal or
one-sided but generally has two or more valences: it is serious and ironic,
pathos-charged and parodic, apocalyptic and farcial, critical and self-critical.
(35)

15. Max J. Friedländer also writes: "Particularly in the works of Jan that I regard
as early, but also, though less obviously, in his latest works, the basic conditions of
realistic expression remain unfulfilled in the linear perspective and in the proportions
of the figures to the surrounding space, conditions that in a later generation were fulfilled even by bunglers. The unity of lighting is an achievement of genius, centuries
in advance of the time, but Jan never masters linear perspective" (12).

16. William Martin Conway, a key source for Gaddis here, writes:

After giving proof of his abilities to the satisfaction of the appointed officers of
the guild, the workman was now . . . raised to the status of a master of the
craft. He had to take solemn oaths of honesty, and to promise that his work
should be done as in the sight of God. Henceforth he was a man; his status was
fixed. He had a vote along with his fellows for the appointment of the officers
of the guild, and he had his share in the property of the guild. . . . But he was
no more free as a master than he had been before as apprentice or journeyman.
The guild, through its appointed officers, still continued to watch over his
work. He was not allowed to use any except recognized materials and tools. If
bad materials were found by the guild inspectors in his possession, they were
destroyed and he was fined. . . . When an artist bought raw materials he had to
bring them to be approved; when he bought tools he had to bring them to be
marked with the sign of the guild. (*Early Flemish Artists*, 71-72; see also *Van
Eycks*, 93)

17. From Wyatt's initial exchange with Brown, it seems apparent that he thinks of
the Memling canvas as a copy rather than a forgery. Thus, in response to Brown's
query, "You've probably done copies, yourself," Wyatt says, "—Not since I studied.
And who wants them? Who wants copies" (145).
18. Again, Conway, Friedländer, and Panofsky seem unanimous on Memling's value
and on his position as a subordinate talent among the Flemish painters. Conway writes:

Memling was neither passionate like Hugo, nor earnest like Jan van Eyck. He was formed of milder stuff. In his pictures, therefore, no stress is laid upon shadow, neither is he a colourist in the proper sense of the term. The people of his dreams were dwellers in a land where "there is light alike by day and alike by night." (*Early Flemish Artists*, 253)

And Friedländer writes:

Memlinc's narrative flows, in gentle waves, towards the blissful goal of redemption and transfiguration, gliding over that which is fearsome and dwelling on festive events. The slight and shallow stream is not obstructed or dammed by that penetrating observation, that intensive, inward interest in the data of form, that meticulous elaboration of details—in short, by those exertions which invest Netherlandish panels with depth, density, weight and rigidity. Ordered and clean like the people near us, the country greets from afar, parklike, estival, with undulating roads, white horses, quiet bodies of water, swans, cozy and comfortable houses, and blue hills at the horizon—an idyllic homeland where the weather is perpetually fine. Memlinc is neither an explorer like Jan van Eyck nor an inventor like Roger. He lacks both the passion of seeing and the fanaticism of belief. (Panofsky, 348)

And finally Panofsky:

His works give the impression of derivativeness, not because he depended on his forerunners (as even the greatest did and do) but because he failed to penetrate them. The very fact that he, the most placid, serene and suggestible of pupils, fell and remained under the spell of a master as intense, severe and domineering as Roger van der Weyden, precluded both revolt and constructive assimilation. There could be nothing but a submission the very completeness of which prevented understanding. From Roger he appropriated everything except the spirit. From the great Eyckian tradition, the monuments of which surrounded him on all sides, he appropriated only the *agréments*, brocaded cloths of honor and oriental rugs, vistas set off by marble colonnettes, historical capitals, and convex mirrors. And when he undertook a variation on a Goesian "Descent from the Cross" related to the Vienna "Lamentation" and even more trenchant by virtue of its studied fragmentariness, he managed to retain its compositional dissonances but failed—or, rather, did not attempt—to recapture its pathos. (347-48)

At the time of *The Recognitions'* composition, Gaddis would have been aware of all three of these opinions, the last of which, Panofsky's, was delivered in the form of the Charles Eliot Norton Lectures at Harvard during the academic year 1947-48. Nor is there any reason to think that Gaddis's own opinion of Memling might have been different, for the discussion in *The Recognitions* of the several Flemish masters, as of their work in general, seems to echo that found in these specific art historians.

Today, however, critical opinion appears to be, once more, shifting back in favor of Memling. Reviewing the Bruges Groeningemuseum's Hans Memling Exhibition along with Dirk de Vos's favorable treatment of the artist, Jonathan Israel writes:

Since his rediscovery in the Romantic era, Memling has always been popular with the art-loving public; but his reputation among art critics and historians, as one of the greatest of the fifteenth-century Flemish painters, has from time to time been brought into question, and has never been quite so secure as those of Jan Van Eyck (c 1390-1441) and Rogier Van der Weyden (c 1440-64). But now that this exhibition has revealed the full scope and variety, as well as the splendour, of his work, it is hard to believe that his stature as one of the three supreme masters of that school will ever again be in doubt. (18)

19. Or as one of the guests at Esther's Christmas party says, "Mendelssohn Schmendelssohn [. . .] —I'm talking about *music*" (574).

20. Friedländer writes similarly of the Bouts pictures in the Prado: "The observation penetrates lovingly to the details and in certain bits, such as the hands of the oldest king in the *Adoration*, comes startlingly close to nature. The texture—brocades, hair—is rendered with almost Eyckian passion" (27). And so does Panofsky: "His London 'Portrait of a Young Man,' dated 1462, depends on Roger van der Weyden in the arrangement of the figure, especially in the position of the hands, and on Jan van Eyck in the method of illumination, the emphasis on volume rather than line and—all technical differences notwithstanding—the loving attention to surface texture" (316).

21. Parallel to Valentine's remark, Conway writes:

A more emphatic contrast than that between the temperaments of Dirk Bouts and Hugo van der Goes could not easily be cited. The one canny, narrow, painstaking, industrious, slow, definite in aim and aiming only at what he could surely hit; the other bold, fiery, uncertain, passionate, aiming at large, striving for more than he could accomplish, prolific, immensely able, and by nature an artist to the finger-tips. (*Van Eycks*, 173)

22. Conway attributes the invention of this theme to Roger van der Weyden:

Roger's pictures became types. In whatever fashion he represented a subject other artists followed him. His pictures were copied with more or less fidelity by numerous admirers, in a day when plagiarism in art was considered an honest thing. Patrons would contract with a painter for a picture to be like such and such a work by a well-known artist. The most famous of the types to which Roger gave currency was his design for the Descent from the Cross. He repeated the subject himself more than once, and his followers multiplied his picture a hundredfold. (*Early Flemish Artists*, 177)

There is one such work by van der Goes, the *Lamentation*, in the Gemäldegalerie (Vienna). Panofsky believes it an early work, and says of it: "Where the 'Death of the Virgin' and the Berlin 'Nativity' show independent plastic units irrationally manipulated within a space completely mastered, the 'Lamentation' shows a close-knit relief group turned at an angle within a space still to be conquered" (340).

23. This is reminiscent of Stanley's playing of the dissonant devil's interval on the Fenestrula organ (956).

24. Conway, unlike Friedländer and Panofsky, does, in fact, argue that *The Death of the Virgin* is from van der Goes's middle period:

This has generally been considered the latest of his extant works, an assumption which has brought confusion into the deduced sequence of them. The reader should observe that Martin Schongauer in his engraving of the same subject shows knowledge of Hugo's composition, and that Schongauer's engraving was copied by Wenzel von Olmütz in 1481. An interval of nearer ten years than two is likely to have separated the original painting from the engraving at second-hand. For these reasons I venture to place the Bruges Death of the Virgin about the year 1472 rather than 1479, where previous writers have located it. . . . Regarded as an immature transitional work of a tempestuously developing artist, the picture finds a logical position at this moment of Hugo's career, but placed at the end of it would be incongruous. (*Van Eycks*, 180-81)

Conway is Gaddis's most important source when it comes to the Flemish painters, so, more than likely, Wyatt's attributing the *Death of the Virgin* to van der Goes's middle period follows from this fact.

25. However, our concern regarding "aesthetic value" is a rather recent one, as John Guillory persuasively argues in *Cultural Capital: The Problem of Literary Canon Formation*:

the practice of judging works of art need make no reference at all to the concept of value before the emergence of political economy. It was not even the case that a concept of aesthetic value operated *implicitly* in the nascent forms of critical discourse in the early modern period; the point is precisely that the comparison of authors or works to one another need not at that time be expressed as the comparison of their relative "aesthetic values," because neither the concept of the aesthetic, nor the concept of value, are as yet defined in such a way that they can be yoked together. The more surprising fact for us to consider in the context of the present debate about value is that the problem of aesthetic judgment was as essential to the formation of political economy as the problem of political economy was to the formation of aesthetics. (303)

26. About such problems, Gaddis says in the Abádi-Nagy interview, "when ambiguities appear they are deliberate and I've no intention of running after them with explanations" (*PR*, 56).

27. Witness to Gaddis's notes, Koenig makes it clear that Gaddis, while thinking of Wyatt as reborn (see the Abádi-Nagy interview, *PR*, 64), wished to avoid a "trite" ending (*PR*, 25). Or as Gaddis says in one of his notes: "Now, if we've got the reassurance of the preface, that is, that Stephen, as the hero resurrected, comes out all right, that, in a long novel, is far enough behind not to be obvious and conscious. To leave him, then at the moment of his emergence, and go on to the last stages of collapse of all those things he has emerged from, is I think far more effective" (Koenig, 27).

28. In "First Notes for a Television Program on Forgery," Gaddis writes,

why does a man forge? Certainly it is not simply a question of money, nor, as was said of Van Meegeren, bitterness over critical failure. More nearly, forgery reflects the finite state of man, and the eventual imperfectibility of his creations, an aspiring toward a (Platonic) ideal just beyond reach whatever his talents: the creator knows when he fails, the forger obviates this possibility by setting 'perfected' limitations beforehand. (3)

29. Though Wyatt, unlike van Meegeren, does not exploit the matter, there was similar speculation that van der Goes must have, at one point, made a trip to Italy. Panofsky rejects the speculation, however, saying,

> In view of these specific facts, Hugo's hypothetical journey to Italy, supposedly preceding his admission to the guild in 1467, becomes even less probable than it would have been for general considerations. . . . Rather than by a trip before 1467 . . . they can be accounted for by the fresh impact of Hugo's experiences at Bruges where he was intermittently active . . . from the summer of 1468. The houses of the Tani and Canigiani, the Cavalcanti and Tornabuoni, the Frescobaldi and Portinari must have been full of Florentine paintings which could not fail to leave their imprint on a mind developed in the unprejudiced atmosphere of Ghent: images for private worship, *deschi da parto, cassoni*, and, above all, family portraits. (342–43)

30. In the abbreviated notes accompanying his 10 April 1957 letter to Keith Botsford, Gaddis makes two or three references to "Van M[eegeren]'s luck: the critics who said Vermeer had studied in Italy, & c."

31. To sell the painting, van Meegeren used an intermediary, Dr. G. A. Boon, a respected lawyer and former member of the Dutch parliament. He told Boon a "story about a fictitious mistress of his who was a member of an old Dutch family living in Italy" and demanded anonymity (Werness, 30).

32. In recent decades, an interesting reversal has taken place. Too often burned by fakes, art experts have learned to be very hesitant about ascribing authenticity to a painting whose origins are uncertain. Or as Lawrence Jeppson writes,

> the pendulum has swung to the other side and the connoisseur is now unwilling to stick his neck out. It is much easier and safer to deny than to affirm and even easier to commit oneself to no position at all. If one does not accept a picture he avoids any risk of having his reputation tarnished later by someone who disagrees with his judgment. As a result, many fine pictures which deserve better treatment drift in a paternal limbo. (303)

33. Panofsky writes:

> The lettering of these momentous hexameters [of the inscription] is identical with that of the names of the Prophets and Sibyls inscribed below their images in the crowning lunettes, but it differs from that of the numerous inscriptions within the paintings themselves and from the unquestioned legends on the frames of the Adam and Eve panels. This divergence, coupled with the alleged unseasonableness of the chronogram, has given rise to the suspicion that Hubert had in fact no hand in the Ghent altarpiece at all. It has been claimed that his name was associated with it by the Ghent patriots of the Renaissance who wished to match the glory of Jan van Eyck's Bruges and Roger van der

Weyden's Brussels, and that the hexameters were a forgery of the late sixteenth century, committed partly in order to boost Hubert's reputation and partly in order to secure the property rights to the Ghent altarpiece for the collateral descendents of Jodocus Vyd so that it might not be handed over to Queen Elizabeth of England in payment of a debt contracted by the then Protestant municipality of Ghent. (206)

34. To give the reader a greater sense of the obstacles that forging fifteenth-century paintings presents, I offer the following paragraphs from Arnau:

Working materials used by the old masters can be imitated only partially by the forger of today. He can, for instance, attempt to replace the inner sheet of fabric, but only with cloth of much more recent origin. And canvas of more modern date is almost always subject to yellow-brown discoloration by sodium hydrate. Early unbleached fabrics are also distinguishable from those of later manufacture both in thread and weave. The former display no dressing and are innocent of the starch pastes, mineral additives and chemicals which today foster an appearance of better quality. To employ fabric of an alien period, whether as an actual base or as an intermediate textile sheet serving to bind other layers, the forger must first boil it and bleach it in the sun. If he does not boil it sufficiently, lingering traces will be disclosed by chemical analysis. But the more thoroughly he does so the more easily detectable his intervention becomes.

Assuming that the forger has succeeded in procuring old material for coating with gesso and glue, he is now forced to blend starch, sugar and gypsum of modern manufacture, since these substances, unlike glue, can no longer be prepared as they were by the old masters.

After priming and scraping his board, the forger is faced with the difficult task of drying out the now conglomerated surface coating in a structurally correct manner. Violent heat or baking will produce fissures. The only alternative is to use alien binding and siccative agents which are easily detectable. Internal heating with infrared rays achieves no better result.

The more genuine an impression he strives for, the greater the problem a forger has to overcome. In time, his resistance to the temptation of short cuts will weaken. He will make life easier for himself and the detection of his forgery easier for the expert. (59)

Meanwhile, Arnau does allow that Max Doerner, in *The Materials of the Artist and Their Use in Painting*, seems very knowing, and thereby makes credible his contention "that it is possible to match the technique and perfection of the Flemish masters without employing original formulas" (63). Doerner, a Munich professor whose book was first published in 1921 and first translated into English in 1934, offers a seven-stage process for capturing the effects of the Flemish masters. The process is too long to quote, but can be found in the Arnau book (63–64) and in Doerner's own book (335–36). The enveloping chapter in the Doerner book, "The Technique of the van Eycks and of the Old German Masters," is itself very interesting, and will be of interest to those scholars who should wish to pursue further the technical aspect of Wyatt's forgeries.

35. In *The Genuine Article*, Mansfield and Mills offer a half dozen ways in which craquelure can be produced (125).

36. Gaddis's source here is Riccardo Nobili, *The Gentle Art of Faking: A History of the Methods of Producing Imitations & Spurious Works of Art from the Earliest Times up to the Present Day* (London: Seeley, Service, 1922).

37. Mansfield and Mills speak of a technique much like this as being the most successful for producing craquelure:

> But by far the most successful method as far as the forger is concerned, is to put something with the pigment, before he paints, which will, as it dries, crack of its own accord. One of the commonest liquids suitable for this purpose is egg white. The egg needs to be fresh, and after the yolk has been separated from the white it is ground into the pigments chosen, and the combination is painted in the normal way; if left in an ordinary dry atmosphere over two or three days this will dry out and the forger will have a fine and very convincing cracking right through his paint. (125)

38. In the Abádi-Nagy interview, Gaddis says it "is very much the key line to the whole book" (*PR*, 66).

Chapter 2: *J R* and the Question of That Which Is Worth Doing

1. In the Abádi-Nagy interview, Gaddis says, "obviously his name is from Willard Gibbs of the second law of thermodynamics and the concept of entropy" (*PR*, 71). Norbert Wiener argues the revolutionary importance of Gibbs's introduction of probability into modern physics: "[I]t is, I am convinced, Gibbs rather than Einstein or Heisenberg or Planck to whom we must attribute the first great revolution of twentieth-century physics" (17–18).

2. Critics have pointed out that "Eigen" is German for character. It may, in this sense, constitute an allusion to Robert Musil's *Der Mann ohne Eigenschaften*. It is also a name, like "Gibbs," associated with the new physics, as in "eigenvalue," "a scalar for which there exists a nonzero vector such that the scalar times the vector equals the value of the vector under a given linear transformation on a vector space" (*Random House Dictionary*).

3. Much recent theorizing in the humanities has concerned itself with questions of identity and particularly with a critique of what might be spoken of as "the strong [or unitary] concept of identity." It is important to understand, however, that this critique, at least in its most responsible form, has not questioned the concept of identity per se. Or as Rodolphe Gasché, whom I quote, writes:

> it has to be established, and in no uncertain terms, that deconstruction is not a critique of identity in the name of the nonidentical. Undoubtedly, Derrida has, at times, had recourse to the concept of non-identity to describe the limits of identity. In "Before the Law," for example, he speaks of the "non-identity in itself" of the sense or destination of a text such as Kafka's parable, whose "personal identity"—"the identity with itself of a bequeathed corpus"—passes on

nothing but "non-identity with itself." Yet the identity of Kafka's text that "does not tell or describe anything but itself as text" is, Derrida charges, achieved not "within an assured specular reflection of some self-referential transparency—and I must stress this point—but in the unreadability of the text, if one understands by this the impossibility of acceding to its proper significance and its possibly inconsistent content, which it jealously keeps back." Not only, then, is this identity of "Before the Law" not speculatively constituted, but more important . . . , neither is the non-identity that it is said to pronounce and to pass on of speculative origin. (*Inventions*, 218–19)

4. In this chapter, all the Heilbroner citations are to *The Nature and Logic of Capitalism*.

5. Georg Simmel, in his classic text *The Philosophy of Money*, writes,

the role of money is associated with the spatial distance between the individual and his possession. . . . Only if the profit of an enterprise takes a form that can be easily transferred to any other place does it guarantee to property and the owner, through their spatial separation, a high degree of independence or . . . self-mobility. . . . The power of money to bridge distances enables the owner and his possessions to exist so far apart that each of them may follow their own precepts to a greater extent than in the period when the owner and his possessions still stood in a direct mutual relationship, when every economic engagement was also a personal one. (332–33)

6. See Peter Passell's fascinating article "Fast Money." The focus is on Chips, an acronym for the Clearing House Interbank Payments System, responsible for processing, each day, close to a trillion dollars in worldwide electronic money exchanges. Here, says Passell, "money consists of magnetized specks of iron oxide in computer memories and great fortunes move from continent to continent as weightless photons through the electromagnetic ether" (43). It is a system which, through the 1980s and 1990s, has seen a phenomenal growth in its volume. Thus while electronic exchanges currently make up only two percent of all financial transactions, this percentage

is reversed if the count is made in total dollars in transit, rather than by the number of times money changes hands. Cash covers less than 1 percent of the total value of transactions, while money flashed from computer to computer accounts for five out of every six dollars that move in the economy. And while just one transaction in a thousand is made on the two great "wholesale" electronic transfer systems, Chips along with the network run by the Federal Reserve push around a stunning $1.7 trillion a day—80 percent of the total payments made worldwide in dollars.

What's more, the volume of business on these lightning-fast systems has grown at a rate hardly anyone would have imagined possible a few years ago. In 1980, the daily flow of electronic money was roughly 12 times the balances held in accounts at the Federal Reserve—the money that banks use to settle their debts at the end of each day. By 1991, the daily flow had reached 55 times this base of bank reserves. (66)

7. For a more developed discussion of this aspect of *J R*, see O'Donnell's fine chapter, "His Master's Voice: Commodifying Identity in *J R*," in *Echo Chambers*, 154–84.

8. See James, "On a Certain Blindness in Human Beings."

9. In *The Protestant Ethic and the Spirit of Capitalism*, wherein Weber argues that, as an ethic, one of capitalism's principal antecedents is Protestantism, he also fore-shadows Amy's critique of capital's asceticism:

> In fact, the *summum bonum* of this ethic, the earning of more and more money, combined with the strict avoidance of all spontaneous enjoyment of life, is above all completely devoid of any eudaemonistic, not to say hedonistic, admixture. It is thought of so purely as an end in itself, that from the point of view of the happiness of, or utility to, the single individual, it appears entirely transcendental and absolutely irrational. (53)

10. In the United States, the world of business is not the only realm that employs the sport analogy. There are many others, including that of politics, as Gaddis noted in his essay "The Rush for Second Place":

> [Gerald] Ford was, after all, a veteran of the playing fields of Michigan, where he had been voted Most Valuable Player on a college football team that lost every conference game; but these were not the fields where winning mattered less than "how you played the game." They were closer to those of his prede-cessor, lately mired in Watergate while busy on the phone with strategies for the next day's victory by the Washington Redskins. These were not the fields of Eton, where Waterloo was won, but nearer those of the legendary Vince Lombardi, where "winning is not a sometime thing. It is an all time thing. You don't win once in a while, you don't do things right once in a while, you do them right all the time. There's no room for second place. There's only one place, and that's first place." (31)

11. This title refers to a monthly beauty contest, sponsored by the Rheingold Beer company, and advertised mostly via New York City subway placards.

12. Carvel is the Northeast's equivalent of Dairy Queen. Their original ice cream stands were each topped by a large aluminum cone holding an illuminated plastic designed to resemble vanilla ice cream.

13. The study of complexity also goes under the name of chaos theory, which is, in fact, something a little different from what it sounds like. Or as Timothy Ferris, reviewing Murray Gell-Mann's book *The Quark and the Jaguar: Adventures in the Simple and Complex*, writes:

> Complexity theory is related to the better known study of "chaos," a term whose ambiguity has engendered confusion. (As Gell-Mann writes, "The word has been turned into a kind of catchall expression for any sort of real or appar-ent complexity or uncertainty.") The essential point about chaotic systems is that they are "nonlinear." In linear systems, a straightforward cause leads to a straightforward effect. In nonlinear systems, "the outcome of a dynamic pro-

cess is so sensitive to initial conditions that a minuscule change in the situation at the beginning of the process results in a larger difference at the end," as Gell-Mann writes. Consider water flowing out of a faucet. At low velocities the water behaves in linear fashion, flowing out in a predictable way. But if the faucet is opened wide enough, the water becomes highly turbulent and chaotic, spurting in unpredictable directions. The input is not qualitatively different from the input that previously produced a linear result—one just kept opening the faucet, a crack at a time—but the result is suddenly very different. (40)

14. In the Kuchl and Moore interview, Gaddis says that the excerpts from Gibbs's work in progress are actually from one of his own uncompleted manuscripts (6).

15. By 1645, wars with the Dutch purchasers left this same Manhattan tribe almost entirely wiped out.

16. Asked by Abádi-Nagy whether *J R* is about family and an "indictment of the corroding effect that profit-oriented corporate operations exert not only on education and art in particular but also on social values and human relationships in general," Gaddis responds:

It is insofar as it is very much about the absence of the family. We know nothing about his father. All that we know about his mother is that she's a nurse, who keeps odd hours because of her work. He has no past, in other words, and so he's obliged to invent himself, not in the terms of a father, a mother and a family but in terms of what he sees around him. (*PR*, 67)

17. In *J R,* Gaddis uses the word *crèche* often. In addition to its familiar association with small models of the Bethlehem nativity scene, its meaning also entails "a home for foundlings" (*The Random House Dictionary*).

18. In the Abádi-Nagy interview, Gaddis, pointing out the failings of J R's education, says, "all he sees around him—in all the discussions in the principal's office at the school—there is never any mention of actual educational content. They [the administrators and teachers] talk about nothing but paving the parking lot, about buying new teaching machines and teaching equipment and storing what they already have because no one knows how to use it" (*PR*, 67).

19. In his planned 1949 prefatory note to *The Recognitions*, Gaddis writes:

Then, what is sacrelige [*sic*]? If it is nothing more than a rebellion against dogma, it is eventually as meaningless as the dogma it defies, and they are both become hounds ranting in the high grass, never see the boar in the thicket. Only a religious person can perpetrate sacrelige: and if its blasphemy reaches the heart of the question; if it investigates deeply enough to unfold, not the pattern, but the materials of the pattern, and the necessity of a pattern; if it questions so deeply that the doubt it arouses is frightening and cannot be dismissed; then it has done its true sacreligious [*sic*] work, in the service of its adversary: the only service that nihilism can ever perform. (*RG*, 298–99).

Cf. Bakhtin's contention that "Faith lives on the very border of atheism, sees itself there and understands it, and atheism lives on the border of faith and understands it" (*Problems of Dostoyevsky's Poetics*, 176).

20. Mozart writes:

I do entreat you never to allow the thought to cross your mind that I can forget you, for I cannot bear it. My chief purpose was, is and ever shall be to endeavour to bring about our speedy and happy reunion! But we must be patient. You yourself know even better than I do how often things go awry—but they will soon go straight—only do have patience! Let us place our trust in God, Who will never forsake us. I shall not be found wanting. How can you doubt me? (28 February 1778; 498)

21. It is a point also made nicely by Holt:

Intelligent children act as if they thought the universe made some sense. They check their answers against common sense, while other children, not expecting answers to make sense, not knowing what is sense, see no point in checking, no way of checking. Yet the difference may go deeper than this. It seems as if what we call intelligent children feel that the universe can be trusted even when it does not seem to make any sense, that even when you don't understand it you can be fairly sure that it is not going to play dirty tricks on you. (88)

22. In the 1987 spoof "Trickle-Up Economics: J R Goes to Washington," Gaddis has J R employed as a deputy assistant to the director of the White House Office of Management and Budget. J R's duties are enhanced by the fact that his boss has been sentenced to Allenwood Federal Prison, where he can get an early start on his memoirs.

23. In the Abádi-Nagy interview, Gaddis says of J R,

The reason he is eleven is because he is in this prepubescent age where he is amoral, with a clear conscience, dealing with people who are immoral, unscrupulous; they realize what scruples are, but push them aside, whereas his good cheer and greed he considers perfectly normal. He thinks this is what you're supposed to do; he is not going to wait around; he is in a hurry, as you should be in America—get on with it, get going. He is very scrupulous about obeying the *letter* of the law and then (never making the distinction) evading the *spirit* of the law at every possible turn. He *is* in these ways an innocent and is well-meaning, a sincere hypocrite. (*PR*, 68)

24. In the Lloyd Grove interview, Gaddis says of Conrad: "Conrad does it all. He's the marvelous storyteller and his work has depth under depth under depth" (B 10). Meanwhile, in *J R*, Gaddis also notably borrows from *Heart of Darkness*, specifically the scene that has Marlow returning to Belgium to offer a romanticized description of Kurtz's end to his widow. In *J R*, this is parodied in the Tom Eigen-Mrs. Schramm narrative (408, 631).

25. Neil Hertz writes, "Although the moment of blockage [produced by a mass of material that consciousness cannot take in] might have been rendered as one of utter self-loss, it was, even before its recuperation as sublime exaltation, a confirmation of the unitary status of the self" (Budick and Iser, 199).

26. "Psalm 19" is, says Geoffrey Hartman, "the *locus classicus* of all sky poems" (Budick and Iser, 236), opening as it does with the line "The heavens are telling the glory of God," and following this with the suggestion that heaven's choral voice mostly falls on deaf ears: "There is no speech, nor are there words; their voice is not heard; / yet their voice goes out through all the earth, and their words to the end of the earth." In a way, it is much like Heraclitus's "The Oracle at Delphi [that] does not speak, it gives a sign [semainei]," a sign that, as Gerald Brun writes, is not, in fact, a "sign of anything—it is nothing logical, nothing semiotic, nothing that can be diacritically or conceptually determined or put into a statement (made to function semantically). The Heraclitean sign is dark, more word than term; it is, as Heidegger emphasizes every time he takes up Heraclitus, something like a hint (*Wink*). It works not by meaning but by opening" (Budick and Iser, 125). And so work Gaddis's own signs (the night sky included) for all that which, although determinant, remains beyond our comprehension.

27. In his 1993 introduction to *The Recognitions*, William Gass, in fact, calls Gaddis "a romantic," in regard to the reach and the integrity of his artistic ambition (vii). It is, I believe, a sound judgment.

28. In *The Recognitions*, Gaddis has Basil Valentine quote Emerson to the effect that we should "treat other people as though they were real [. . .] because, perhaps they are" (264).

29. In the Abádi-Nagy interview, Gaddis, looking back on the youthful confidence that a big book such as *The Recognitions* required, if it were to be written at all, says: "I think first it was that towering kind of confidence of being quite young, that one can do anything—'All's brave that youth mounts and folly guides,' as we're told in *As You Like It*" (*PR*, 58–59). Gibbs is, unfortunately, past that moment of youthful confidence; but, in *J R*, Bast is not.

> Bast starts with great confidence, . . . that confidence of youth. He's going to write grand opera. And gradually, if you noticed—because of pressures of reality on him and money and so forth—his ambitions shrink. The grand opera becomes a cantata where we have the orchestra and the voices. Then it becomes a piece for orchestra, then a piece for small orchestra, and finally at the end he's writing a piece for unaccompanied cello, his own that is to say, one small voice trying to rescue it all and say, "Yes, there *is* hope." Again, like Wyatt, living it through, and in his adventure with J R having lived through all the nonsense, he will rescue this one small hard gemlike flame, if you like. Because it is that *real* note of hope in *J R* that is very important. (*PR*, 71–72)

In many ways, it is this optimism, this desire to get on with the work, that attracts Gibbs, in his gruff way, to Bast, and helps to explain the offer of the Ninety-Sixth Street apartment, and so on. In a sense, Gibbs sees in Bast what Gaddis, in a reminiscent moment, sees in his own younger self: "I remember Clive Bell looking back on his small fine book, *Art*, thirty-five years after it was published in 1913, and listing *its* faults, finding it too confident and aggressive, even too optimistic—I was never accused of that!—but still feeling, as he said, 'a little envious of the adventurous young man who wrote it'" (*PR*, 59).

30. About the ambitiousness of both *The Recognitions* and *J R*, as well as the pain

that the unfavorable reviews of the first book caused him, Gaddis says in the Grove interview,

> "It was quite painful. It was quite a blow. It took a while to recover. When you're that age, and you spend that much time on that complicated a book, you expect something to happen. And when it doesn't happen, it's very discouraging, to put it mildly. It took a while to recover really. And then I did the same damn thing all over again." He laughs. "Another long, complicated book." (B 10)

31. In the Abádi-Nagy interview, Gaddis says,

> Gibbs is the man who has all of the feelings and the competency but is overcome, overwhelmed by a sense of the futility of doing anything and the consequent question of what is worth doing, which he cannot respond to. And so even though he *could've* done this, he *could've* done this, he *could've* done this, he doesn't *finish* anything because he just thinks it's not worth it, whatever it is. So that finally, when he has been quite a negative figure all the way through, and meets a woman who has great confidence and faith and love for him, and wants him to complete his own work, he tries to go back, but it's too late. (*PR*, 71)

32. I would also include here, though not related to either Amy or Jack, the spoken-of return of James Bast, who is called back (principally by Stella) when his guidance, Philoctetes-like, appears most needed (719).

33. The phrase is Christopher Norris's, commenting upon Ernst Bloch. The full sentence reads, "For Bloch, the only way to transcend such reified notions is by a new kind of listening, one that effectively opens the path towards a state of redeemed utopian promise" (32).

34. In the Abádi-Nagy interview, Gaddis says,

> None of the books has got any interior monologue, easy effects, any of "he wished he could see her that afternoon." I mean he's got to show it, to *tell* someone, "I wish I could see her this afternoon." Authorial absence so that the characters create the situation. I find this much more provocative to me both as a writer when I'm working on it and as a reader. (*PR*, 85)

35. Likewise, regarding his shelved Civil War play, Gaddis mentions, in the Logan and Mirkowicz interview, that a friend said to him: "You don't trust the director, you don't trust the actors and you don't trust the audience."

36. Currently, of course, this equation is made not only by those people who do not really know better, but also by those—i.e., a growing number of academics who while ostensibly interested in the arts esteem them as perfectly commensurable with economic value—who should. It is in rebuttal to the latter view that John Guillory, in *Cultural Capital*, writes:

> Liberal pluralism confronts the absolutist posturing of particular discourses of

value with the philosophical bad news that no metaphysical grounds exist for such posturing. The alternative to the tendential absolutism of value judgments seems obviously to be that all values are "contingent," a condition for which the variability of price in the market provides the most readily available analogy. But the fact remains that the market is the historical *condition* and not merely the proper analogy for the extension of the value-concept to all acts of judgment. The failure to recognize this fact has had the effect of making the economic analogy in recent critiques of aesthetics merely empty, an analogy that erases the history of economic discourse. In the absence of any sense of what has been at stake historically in the emergence of political economy, the critique of value has been conducted as the most arid exercise in philosophical debate, as the choice between the two positions of relativism and absolutism. Hence the relativist critique of the absolutist position congratulates itself for having exposed the groundlessness of "absolute" values, without raising its own discourse of commensuration to the level of historical self-reflection. (324)

37. In the Abádi-Nagy interview, Gaddis admits the connection between his own experience with *The Recognitions* and that of Eigen with his novel:

> The embittered character in *J R*, for instance, who is Eigen, is obviously based in part on my own experience with *The Recognitions*, that it was not a success when it was published and I was obliged to go and work in a pharmaceutical company, which I did not like, but I had a family and had to make a living. (*PR*, 71)

38. The relevant Newman passage in full is as follows:

> Glasenapp tells how in the very last years of his [Wagner's] life he could not work unless surrounded by soft lines and colours and perfumes. His almost morbid sensitivity multiplied enormously the ordinary pleasant or unpleasant sensations of touch and of sight. When in a difficulty with his composition he would stroke the folds of a soft curtain or table-cover till the right mood came. Not only the fabrics but the lines about him had to be melting, indefinite: he could not endure even books in the room he was working in, or bear to let his eyes follow the garden paths; "they suggested the outer world too definitely and prevented concentration." Among scents he particularly loved attar of roses, which he used to get direct from Paris—sent to him, however, under the fictitious name and address of "Mr. Bernard Shnapauf, Ochsengasse, Bayreuth," his barber obtaining delivery of it for him. (135)

In *J R*, the reader might also note that Stella has been reading Newman's book (146, 149).

39. In the Abádi-Nagy interview, Gaddis, like James and Edward Bast, appears to take a practical attitude toward the relation between money and the time it buys wherein one can work:

> When finally [financial] help did come along, recognition as you say, a

Rockefeller Foundation grant, a Guggenheim Fellowship, the National Endowment for the Arts, they came in difficult times and allowed and encouraged me to keep on with the second book and start the third. Without them, I wonder if I might not just have dropped the whole damned business, though God knows what else I might have done, too late even to be any of the things I never wanted to be. There's always the talk about feeding at the public trough, disdaining grants because you've never been given one. I mean we'd all wish to come out with the fierce integrity of Samuel Butler, say, who never wrote simply to publish or published everything he wrote—*The Way of All Flesh* was posthumous after all—and that has been the luxury of the MacArthur. (*PR*, 58)

40. Gadamer, in a late essay on Heidegger ("Being Spirit God") urges this same conception:

Heidegger also described his own thinking-out-ahead [*Vorausdenken*] into that which is as a step back, one attempting to think anew the beginning as a beginning. Thinking-out-ahead is not planning, calculating, estimating, and managing; rather, it is thinking back to the beginning, for the beginning is ultimately the starting point from which even the very last possible step originates, and thus, that last step can be seen as an outcome of the beginning. Thinking is always thinking the beginning. (*Heidegger's Ways*, 194)

41. At novel's end, she makes more emphatic her criticism of what she takes to be Edward's romanticism:

this whole frightened romantic nightmare you'd put me into all of it, all of it! that, that barn out there where these ideas these fantasies these, these obsessions could hide untouched unfinished till you opened the door on them again, on this fear you haven't inherited James' talent so you'll settle for the money that's where it belongs all of it, with your music in the trashbasket all of it! (716)

By this point, however, Edward has better worked out his relation to his work and what it is that he needs to do, namely to pursue it, believing that it is better to risk failure in something that one believes in than to pursue success in other people's projects.

42. In the Grove interview, Gaddis speaks of his interest in—and clearly his identification with—the mythic character of Philoctetes:

There may be something in the notion, and someone has made the rude observation, that every writer writes only one book and writes it over and over again. One's frame of reference is constricted to one's thinking along certain paths, and you realize half way through something that it is a path one has trod before elsewhere.

The myth of Philoctetes for instance. He was the hero with the bow, the great champion of the Greeks, who goes into the sacred garden where he's not supposed to be and is bitten by the snake, and has a festering wound and they

get rid of him, they exile him. Then, when there's trouble and they need him
and his bow, Ulysses and the prince come and say, "Please, come and help us."
And that idea has always fascinated me. (B 10)

43. Here, in support of Bast's notion that there is, somehow, something preferable
in an unfinished work as compared with a finished one, we might refer to Bloch who,
not surprisingly, is very sympathetic to the idea. He for instance does much with the
story of Michelangelo's interest in the unfinished sculpture:

Vasari alerted art history to ponder the small number of Michelangelo's completely finished works and to ponder even more so when one considers that the
huge dimension of the intended goal totally corresponded with the strength and
nature of this genius. But that which corresponded to the huge dimension in
Michelangelo himself, his own understanding of his overpowering nature and
how to overpower a task, resisted the roundness and perfection of art in such a
way that nothing of what had been carried out could become adequate or even
perfect. Thus, perfection is driven so deep into whatever there is that it
becomes a fragment. Such a fragment then is nothing less than an ingredient of
the non-temple-like (*Un-Tempelhaften*), of the nonharmonic cathedral-like
(*Kathedralischen*). It is conscience: the Gothic style still exists *post festum*.
The depth of aesthetic perfection itself sets the unfinished in motion. (152)

44. In *The Critique of Judgment*, Kant writes:

It will be said that this interpretation of aesthetic judgements on the basis of
kinship with our moral feeling has far too studied an appearance to be accepted
as the true construction of the cypher in which nature speaks to us figuratively
in its beautiful forms. But, first of all, this immediate interest in the beauty of
nature is not in fact common. It is peculiar to those whose habits of thought are
already trained to the good or else are eminently susceptible of such training;
. . . In addition to this there is our admiration of nature which in her beautiful
products displays herself as art, not as mere matter of chance, but, as it were,
designedly, according to a law-directed arrangement, and as finality apart from
any end. As we never meet with such an end outside ourselves, we naturally
look for it in ourselves, and, in fact, in that which constitutes the ultimate end
of our existence—the moral side of our being. (I.160)

45. In the Grove interview, Gaddis further comments on the way Americans like
to view—or "humanize"—their artists:

I don't want to be seen in People magazine, romping with my dog. . . . It's the
television influence on America, the tendency to put the man in place of his
work, to think you get more of the writer by seeing him talk nonsense than
from what is in the work on the page, which is really what he has sweated
over, rewritten 90 times. . . .
    I have really tried not to run along and explain—"But what I really meant
was this or that." Eventually there is the book and the reader—and that's all
there is to it. . . . (B 1)

46. Speaking of Eigen and Gibbs, Gaddis refers to

> all the evidence of *their own* appetite for destruction, their frequently eager
> embrace of the forces to be blamed for their failure to pursue the difficult task
> for which their talents have equipped them, failure to pursue their destiny if
> you like, taking art at the center, as you say, as redemption in, and of and from,
> a world of material values, overwhelmed by the material demands it imposes.
> (*PR*, 71)

Chapter 3: *Carpenter's Gothic*'s Bare Ruined Choirs

1. In response to Abádi-Nagy's concern about *Carpenter's Gothic*'s bleakness,
Gaddis responded:

> after all, if our situation—or what I see as our situation—were utterly hopeless,
> why would I have written the book at all? But I will say that this novel proba-
> bly contains the least hope of the three. Because McCandless, who had got it
> all figured out, comes out at the end . . . as hardly the great hero. It is sort of
> *sauve-qui-peut* and she refuses him. (*PR*, 75)

2. It appears that Madame Socrate keeps her appointment the next morning, for
this is when she walks away with the check that Billye Fickert has made out to Paul
(see Paul's telephone conversation with Bobbie Joe [261]). Thus it is Madame
Socrate who first discovers Elizabeth's body, though it is Edie, who arrives later, after
Madame Socrate has departed, who calls the police.

3. Like so many other things in this novel, there is a certain mystery surrounding
this letter. The fragments are found by Elizabeth in the garbage, after McCandless's
first visit, the visit for which Elizabeth herself was not present. Irene has been gone
for two years, and the date of the letter can be only a matter of conjecture. It may be
Irene's farewell letter to McCandless, and thus date from the time of her departure.
More likely, the letter is of recent composition, something that McCandless finds in
the mail pile that has been building up, awaiting his return (15). Certainly, it has not
come from McCandless's closeted papers, for at this point McCandless himself has
yet to gain entry into his room, for the reason of the new lock. If it has, in fact, been
recently received, has it come in "the envelope with the Zaire stamp URGENT
PLEASE FORWARD"(31)? The possibility seems strong, for the letter and the envelope are found in the same garbage, and there is a suggestion that they belong to one
another. If so, does this mean that Irene has written from Zaire? Elizabeth's later fictional musings ruminate on the possibility, imagining first the "wife hidden now in
Marrakech" (93), a suggestion which is soon expanded: "And as though there'd been
no interruption, no two years fallen away in Zaire, Maracaibo, Marrakech" (94).
There is also a suggestion, connected to the friendship with Brian, that Irene might, in
fact, have a certain travel lust (160). At the same time, undercutting Elizabeth's sur-
mises, there is the suspicion that Irene and McCandless never married. This suspicion
is reinforced by Mrs. McCandless's introducing herself to Elizabeth, whom she
believes is Irene, as "Mrs. McCandless" (249), as well as by the fact that when

queried about Mrs. McCandless by Elizabeth, the Haitian cleaning woman, Madame Socrate, professes never to have met her (30), a statement that can be true without meaning that she has never met Irene. In addition to this, there is the very ambiguous response of McCandless himself when Elizabeth speaks of Irene as his wife:

> Oh and wait yes I meant to ask, is her name Irene? your wife I mean . . . ? His nod came less in affirmation than the failure to deny it. (65)

The nod seems to affirm the woman's name but not her status. And yet, Elizabeth has been told by the rental agent that McCandless's "wife" will come to remove the furnishings (22). If her memory and the information are both accurate—a big if—then McCandless has, it would appear, been married twice, for the "first" Mrs. McCandless has clearly no proprietary interest in the furnishings. They are not hers. Meanwhile, another puzzle piece has Lester drawing a connection between the Gwen of McCandless's novel and Irene. Gwen is the protagonist's "wife" (137). Of course, Lester has only a rough knowledge of the details of McCandless's life. He does not, for instance, know that McCandless has a son (145).

In short, Elizabeth's musings about Irene's whereabouts—partly set in motion by the discovery of the discarded letter—are interesting but also suspect. The letter has, it seems, been forwarded, so it is difficult to say whether it originated in Zaire or whether it was passed along from there after its intended recipient, McCandless, was found gone from the scene. The point is that no final determinations can be made here respecting the letter, despite the plethora of clues. The matter of the letter is, of course, that of the novel itself writ large.

4. Lester also exits the house with a similar departing remark, saying to McCandless: "Those drapes, those silk flowers all of it, she's got nice taste hasn't she, the redhead" (148).

5. Steven Moore and Gregory Comnes have noted, respectively, the echoes of Shakespeare's Sonnet 73 and Hopkins's "God's Grandeur" and "The Windhover" in *Carpenter's Gothic*. The echo of the Shakespeare sonnet is hard to miss. For one, there is a specific allusion to the poem on page 167. For another, as Moore does a fine job in showing, there are very close thematic parallels between the poem and the novel (*William Gaddis*, 123–25). The echo of the Hopkins poems is less clear-cut, having more to do, says Comnes, with imagery and an idiosyncratic grammar (Comnes, "Patchwork of Conceits," 22–24). I would say that it also has something to do with the diction, particularly certain patterns of assonance (e.g., "a wing to fling" [1]) and alliteration (e.g., "in where the feathers, mottled? or just mud spattered, still shone . . . ," after Gaddis has used the word *moulting* [in its British variant] also with reference to the dove, a perfect Hopkinesque symbol [24, 1]).

I would also like to call attention to another poetic parallel, and that is to Yeats's "The Second Coming." Gaddis, as Moore has noted (*William Gaddis*, 9), often quotes from Yeats. In *Carpenter's Gothic*, Yeats's "The Second Coming" appears to offer itself as something like a thematic analogue, expressing the fear that the sociopolitical order is unraveling, and that as it is the worst people who seem filled with conviction (McCandless: "talk about their deep religious convictions and that's what they are, they're convicts locked up in some shabby fiction doing life without parole" [186]), the apocalypse cannot be very far off.

6. In *Culture and Imperialism*, Edward Said suggests that the American academic's take on conspiracies might, in fact, entail its own illusions:

> It takes very little for a non-American to accept as a starting point that most, if not all, political assassinations *are* conspiracies, because that is the way the world is. But a chorus of American sages takes acres of print to deny that conspiracies occur in America, since "we" represent a new, and better, and more innocent world. At the same time there is plentiful evidence of official American conspiracies and assassination attempts against the sanctioned "foreign devils" (Castro, Qaddafi, Saddam Hussein, and so on). The connections are not made, and the remainders remain unpronounced. (315)

7. *J R* ends before we know whether Nowunda's replacement will in any way resemble Mobutu Sese Seko, the CIA-backed leader of Zaire (formerly the Congo). In *Carpenter's Gothic*, however, Gaddis picks up the narrative again, and now it is Mobutu's Zaire that seems to shadow the foregrounded events. It is, and is not, Mobutu's Zaire, for he is a surrogate of sorts, or so he was at first. While Mobuto, over time, was able to consolidate his power and to build an extraordinary personal fortune (over five billion dollars, at present), he was in the 1960s and 1970s quite dependent on his United States sponsors. Daniel A. Offiong writes that "[i]n 1967 President Johnson was quick to send in arms to help restore order during an anti-Mobutu mercenary-led coup. In 1977 and 1978, Mobutu had to depend on the U.S. and its Western allies to repel the invasion of exiled Zaireans in Angola" (177). During this period, Mobutu's most important liaison to the West was CIA station chief Lawrence Devlin, a man who bears a rather strong resemblance to Gaddis's Cruikshank, to the point that I would guess he is the model. A striking parallel here is the way that, upon his retirement from the agency in 1974, Devlin went to work for Maurice Tempelsman, a man who bears a strong resemblance to Governor Cates in *J R* and Vorakers and Grimes in *Carpenter's Gothic*, and who was probably the biggest winner in this whole sordid postcolonial narrative. It was, in fact, "a Tempelsman-led consortium" that, in 1970, "gained control of the largest copper seams in the Congo, at Tenke Fungurume" (Gibbs, 194), a prize won through skillful influence peddling.

8. Conrad has, of course, an extraordinary importance for Gaddis. In the Grove interview, he speaks of how "Conrad does it all. He's the marvelous storyteller and his work has depth under depth under depth" (B 10). In *Carpenter's Gothic*, there is the rather touching exchange between McCandless and Elizabeth, who confuses Faulkner's *As I Lay Dying* with *Heart of Darkness*. About the latter, McCandless, surely speaking for Gaddis as well, says, "That's an excellent thing" (158).

9. Urquhart writes:

> The adoption of Marxist-style regimes in the former Portuguese colonies, as well as Soviet, Cuban, and East European support of those regimes, until recently provided South Africa with a pretext for claiming support in the United States for South Africa's alleged resistance to Soviet expansionism, which took the form of backing anti-government movements such as UNITA in Angola and RENAMO in Mozambique. This proved for some time to be a

quite effective policy. The front-line states were kept stabilized, "freedom fighters" in Mozambique and Angola were supported and encouraged, and South Africa played effectively on the United States' fear of Soviet expansionism. For the people of Angola and Mozambique especially, this was catastrophic. (57)

10. In the Abádi-Nagy interview, Gaddis says, "I suppose in all three books I constantly try to call attention to what my mother had told me once at some paranoid moment of mine: 'You must always remember that there is much more stupidity than there is malice in the world'" (*PR*, 86).

11. This statement also appears in Moore, *Reader's Guide* (298). It recalls another passage in Eliot's "East Coker":

> There is, it seems to us,
> At best, only a limited value
> In the knowledge derived from experience.
> The knowledge imposes a pattern, and falsifies,
> For the pattern is new in every moment
> And every moment is a new and shocking
> Valuation of all we have been. (II. 81–87)

12. Early writes,

The architectural revolution engendered by Downing and the other advocates of the picturesque brought a radical change to the shapes and plans of ordinary American houses, the first really profound change since the introduction of classical principles in the last quarter of the seventeenth century. For nearly a hundred and seventy-five years regularity, simplicity, and symmetry had been the ideals of American builders. Now the picturesque taste made geometrical regularity of form an anathema. (67)

13. Maass writes,

The number of full-blown Gothic stone mansions was never large; some have disappeared, others now house private schools. Only wealthy men could afford such homes which required the labors of highly skilled stone carvers. But the costly Gothic style could be translated into wood, and thousands of "Carpenter Gothic" houses still stand. These characteristic Americana have steep gables and pointed windows; sometimes they were sheathed with vertical boarding instead of the familiar horizontal clapboard. This "board and batten" design was considered particularly fitting for a Gothic cottage because of its "upward tendency." (63)

14. In the Abádi-Nagy interview, Gaddis says,

Incidentally, "carpenter" without the apostrophe, "carpenter Gothic" is the correct phrase for this style of architecture, as Lester mentions in the book. So the apostrophe, yes, is a play on the architectural style, and on McCandless, and on the Lord's Father's ramshackle house wherein "are many mansions" and on the author too as "the carpenter." (*PR*, 75)

15. In a somewhat parallel remark, Gaddis, in "Old Foes with New Faces," writes:

[T]he King James version [of the Bible] along with Shakespeare's works are the most glorious achievements in English literature, and the sheer splendor of the English Bible and the images and prophecies of its last book are so formidable that those millions suffused with Jung's numinosum who seek refuge from the clamorous celebration of aporia castigated by Gertrude Himmelfarb embrace its inerrancy against all comers. Their truth is not, perhaps, the pristine, solemn, monistic Truth pursued by Himmelfarb, but it is similarly authoritarian and absolute for all that, subscribing to the same fundamental tenets, differing in little but degree and emphasis, and unleashed broadcast by those twin Pandora's boxes that shape and reshape our world daily, radio and television. (9)

16. Actually, there is a bookcase, standing empty, in an upstairs room (226).

17. This scene is also viewed by Elizabeth on the television (55).

18. Johan Thielmans also argues this. See "Intricacies of Plot: Some Preliminary Remarks to William Gaddis's *Carpenter's Gothic*" (617).

19. In the kitchen there are two near falls, and then her final fall. In the first, she almost falls on the wet floor, which has just been cleaned by Madame Socrate: "When the telephone rang she was standing at the mantel piecing together the china dog. Through the dining room, she almost went down crossing the kitchen floor awash with the woman on hands and knees dipping the green batiste in wide sweeps from the pail" (27). These three falls might tie in with the other suggestions (i.e., she is thirty-three; the dove; her exaltation [245]) that connect her to the Christian narrative, for Christ also falls three times on his way to Golgotha.

20. See Robin Marantz Henig, "Asthma Kills," in the *New York Times Magazine* 28 March 1993, 42+. Henig notes that, between 1979 and 1989, deaths from asthma nearly doubled. One reason for this increase has been the "false sense of security" felt by those asthma sufferers who rely on beta-agonist bronchodilators:

Two recent studies . . . suggest that asthma patients who rely most heavily on inhaled beta-agonist bronchodilators run twice the risk of dying. These observations might simply mean that the sickest people use the most drugs. But they could also be traced directly to the way the medication works. By opening airways that are normally constricted in an asthma attack, beta-agonists might actually expose the lungs to more of the very substances that damage them, hurtling the asthmatic individual down a dangerous spiral. (44)

21. When McCandless gets out of bed, to go downstairs to get a cigarette, Elizabeth tries to delay his trip, yet does not explain why it is imperative that he not smoke in the house:

—But why are you, I mean where are you going.
—Cigarette . . . he had one leg in, —I left things downstairs.
—But no . . . she caught at his shoulder —I mean, you don't have to right now do you? get up I mean?
—Why not.
—Well because you, I mean because we were talking . . . (157–58)

22. Passive smoking's dangers have, of late, received more and more attention, particularly after the Environmental Protection Agency's designation, in January 1993, of secondhand cigarette smoke as a carcinogen. Gaddis himself makes it clear that he understands the danger with Lester's comparison of McCandless's room to Dachau:

It's like Dachau in here, you know that? He struck out to shatter the tranquil column of blue smoke rising between them, —will you put it out? You're not even smoking it, look at it. It's just lying there smoking. You're making me smoke it too, you know that? (133)

The exchange, not surprisingly, is followed by Lester's asking, "When's the red-head due back" (133), drawing a link between passive smoking and Elizabeth. The link is again made a moment later, with Lester bringing the subject of Elizabeth (or more precisely, "the redhead's husband") up just after he says to McCandless, "Go ahead and kill yourself with these things, you don't have to kill us both do you?" (133).

23. In *A Frolic of His Own*, Christina and Trish, ex-classmates of Elizabeth, discuss the death. Trish believes that Paul killed Elizabeth, but Christina tells her, no, the cause of death was a heart attack (382).

24. Creationism was not a monolithic entity, for it too had, and continues to have, its different schools of thought, though it is true that *The Genesis Flood*'s success began to conflate creationism with flood geology in the larger public's mind. In the early 1980s, David A. Young, a proponent of a rival creationist school, for instance, conceded that flood geologists had "come to be known generally as creationists" (Numbers, 299).

25. This is from a summary by Edward Larson (*Trial and Error: The American Controversy over Creation and Evolution* [148]), of Wendell R. Bird's 1978 *Yale Law Journal* essay, wherein he puts forward a strategy for introducing creationism into the public school program.

26. Ronald Reagan, when running for the presidency in 1980, said something similar, that "if evolution is taught in public schools, creation also should be taught" (Numbers, 300).

27. Numbers writes that the plaintiffs "came overwhelmingly from the ranks of religious organizations, while virtually all of the experts testifying in support of creationism possessed graduate degrees in science. The irony prompted the Protestant theologian Langdon Gilkey, who served as a witness for the plaintiffs, to observe that the only 'warfare' in Little Rock found illiberal religion and liberal science on the one side, and absolutist religion and its appropriate 'science' on the other" (xv).

28. Gaddis borrows the name of the Gablers' hometown, "Longview," for the

estate once owned by Elizabeth and Billy's father. The name is meant to be understood ironically, as for instance when Billy speaks of "all that fucking moss hanging off the trees, Longview they call it Longview you can't see ten feet through the . . . " (6). Somewhat similarly, the name of Paul's Vietnam friend, Chick, is also borrowed, this time from Jack T. Chick, the publisher of the fundamentalist comic books often referred to by McCandless. See George Johnson's *Architects of Fear* (87).

29. Gaddis himself, while teaching at Bard College, professed a similar pedagogy. "What I was trying to do," he said at the time, "was raise questions for which there are no distinct answers." Cited in Moore, *William Gaddis*, 112.

30. In the Abádi-Nagy interview, Gaddis himself says:

After all, stupidity—and I don't mean ignorance—is a central issue of our time. In my own case, going back to entropy, I'm most intrigued by its correlation as the loss of available energy in a closed system with stupidity as the corresponding loss of available intelligence in our political establishment especially as regards foreign policy and the economy, its collapse that is to say, where Wiener sees physics' view of the world as it actually exists replaced by one as we observe it, a kind of one way communication. (*PR*, 67)

31. In *The Death of Satan: How Americans Have Lost the Sense of Evil*, Andrew Delbanco also nicely takes up this point (chapter 5.4), taking note of how at the end of the nineteenth and the beginning of the twentieth century, "a new biological theory of evil" (172), working off of Darwinian theory, began to assume prominence, even among intellectuals who imagined themselves progressives (e.g., Oliver Wendell Holmes, Jr., Charles W. Eliot, Beatrice and Sidney Webb, later Harold Laski): "The Darwinian idea behind this movement [i.e., eugenics] for purifying the human race was an immensely powerful explanation for the evolving nature of all living things in a world from which God had departed; and it compelled belief with the force of a religion. If it found an especially hospitable reception in the United States, this was partly because the ideas of eugenics and its various counterparts had been present in dormant form since the outset of the culture and needed only to be resuscitated" (174).

32. By "historical site," I do not mean to sound forgetful that *Carpenter's Gothic* is a fiction, or to claim that Gaddis overtly acknowledges that the Little Rock trial inspires his own. Still, there seem to be enough parallels between the two trials to suggest that the connection is, more or less, warrantable.

33. In the Grove interview, Gaddis speaks of being crushed by the failure of *The Recognitions* to generate a positive response:

It was quite painful. It was quite a blow. It took a while to recover. When you're that age, and you spend that much time on that complicated a book, you expect something to happen. And when it doesn't happen, it's very discouraging, to put it mildly. It took a while to recover really. (B 10)

34. It appears in the *San Francisco Review of Books* (Fall/Winter 1985).

35. The line echoes prior moments in the novel, as when Elizabeth notices first Billy and later McCandless "peering in" through the front door (2, 117); and also as

ncarnated) demands that Pnin, "the water father," hold the drinking fountain button down so that she may quench her thirst.

37. Moore: "The novel struck many reviewers as savagely pessimistic" (*William Gaddis*, 134).

Chapter 4: *A Frolic of His Own:* Whose Law? Whose Justice?

1. "Remembering Auschwitz," *New York Times* editorial, 26 January 1995, A 16 (national ed.). In *The Death of Satan*, Andrew Delbanco, though he agrees that "We live in the most brutal century in human history," is also struck by the fact that while "the work of the devil is everywhere, . . . no one knows where to find him[,]" for "instead of stepping forward to take the credit, he has rendered himself invisible" (9). In short, he writes, "[a] gulf has opened up in our culture between the visibility of evil and the intellectual resources available for coping with it" (3).

2. I quote here from the Gaddis text, but the story is authenticated in several sources, including Francis Biddle's *Justice Holmes, Natural Law, and the Supreme Court* (71) and Gary J. Aichele's *Oliver Wendell Holmes, Jr.: Soldier, Scholar, Judge* (140).

3. Steven Moore tells me that *Once at Antietam* is, in fact, Gaddis's owned shelved play, written in the late 1950s. Oscar's play, however, is said to have been written in the mid-1970s (177). Moore's statement is also confirmed in the Gregory Feeley interview (87). See also Gaddis's mention of the play in a 1962 letter ("a novel begun, rebuilt into an impossibly long play [very rear guard, Socrates in the US Civil War]) quoted by Kuehl and Moore (*In Recognition*, 12). Finally, in the 1984 Logan and Mirkowicz interview, Gaddis says, "But I did write a long play which is perfectly terrible. I take it down and look at it once in a while, and I know there is a play in there, if I could just pull it out. Or a novel, but it doesn't interest me that much, so I put it back and someday it may interest me again."

4. Of course, there is something of Gaddis in all this. Responsibility, or its opposite, is a crucial concern in his work. Asked a question, by Malcolm Bradbury about the matter of responsibility, he offered a long answer, the upshot of which is that things in general seem too much out of control, with no one willing to take responsibility: "I find very much the world we live in as one that is practically out of control, and especially where we're living now—the present administration, and the Pentagon, and what have you—that no one is responsible. It's the party where all the kids are and the parents have left home . . ." (*Writers in Conversation*).

5. "Section 1338 of the Judicial Code defines the jurisdiction of federal district courts over federal intellectual property actions and over certain state claims connected to federal intellectual property actions" (Goldstein, 195).

6. Not to everyone, however. Supreme Court Justice William Douglas, in a 1971 dissenting opinion, wrote that the standard that would apply "novelty" concerns to

patent but not copyright cases was a misstatement of justice: "no reason can be offered why we should depart from the plain import of this grant of congressional power and apply more lenient constitutional standards to copyrights than to patents. . . . To create a monopoly under the copyright power which would not be available under the patent power would be to betray the common birthright of all men at the altar of hollow formalisms" (Goldstein, 580).

7. Goldstein writes:

Of the three national TV networks, one, NBC, currently is receiving 30,000 to 40,000 suggestions of all types every year. These figures include everything from letter outlines to pilot films. One department alone received from 7,000 to 10,000 "approaches" a year. From 2,000 to 3,000 get some serious study. Ten thousand story submissions of all types are offered. The effect of this tremendous influx is obvious. At the present time, the idea-submission lawsuits confronting the networks probably accounts for sixty-five percent of all suits against them in the area of copyright, defamation, right of privacy, and unfair competition. (26–27)

8. This is a rephrasing of Holmes's "The law did not begin with a theory. It has never worked one out" (64).

9. See Steven Weisenburger, *Fables of Subversion* (236–37), for a discussion of misogyny's connectedness to satire, both traditionally and in Gaddis.

Conclusion

1. As recorded, on the occasion of his second National Book Award, by National Public Radio (17 November 1994).

I am aware, of course, that John Johnston's thesis is that Gaddis's work (beginning with *The Recognitions*) represents an overturning of Plato, or as Johnston writes: "Deleuze's concept of the simulacrum and general project of 'overthrowing Platonism' provide the terms for analyzing the dialogic that emerges within *The Recognitions* as the novel's basic thematic and structural opposition between the counterfeit and authentic is eroded and thrown into question, and a logic of the model and copy begins to give way to a logic of the simulacrum and phantasm. It is this 'reversal' . . . that constitutes the novel's central event" (5). However, as noted earlier, while I find the thesis interesting, I ultimately think it an overstatement of the case, entailing an unwarranted reduction of Plato's writings. Or as Gadamer responds to Heidegger's similar bracketing of Plato, "It is far from obvious that this is the only way to read Plato" (*Heidegger's Ways*, 160), a point that Gadamer himself substantially develops in *Dialogue and Dialectic: Eight Hermeneutical Studies on Plato*.

2. I view Gaddis in the tradition of the Melville spoken of by Giles Gunn, whose use of indefinite pronouns works in such a way as to permit him both to appropriate and to dissociate himself from the New England religious tradition. Or as Gunn writes:

While it [the use of indefinite pronouns] permits him to appropriate a sense of evil as a principle of moral and spiritual correction, it enables him at the same time to dissociate this sense from the necessity of any conscious assent to the theological doctrine in which it was first expressed. The cultural utility of the principle continues to engender respect for the tradition which first generated it without requiring that anyone believe in the specific tenets of that tradition itself. Thus Melville and his cultural heirs can remain—and have remained—Puritans at heart while at the same time spurning Puritan dogmas with their mind. (*Thinking Across*, 128)

3. In "Old Foes with New Faces," Gaddis endorses the familiar view that Catholicism and more traditional Protestantism (e.g., Episcopalianism) are corporate in a (more or less) absolutist vein, whereas the ever-enlarging groups of Protestant denominations or sects are quite the opposite: individualistic and centrifugal. He quotes Jung to this effect:

In the religious arena, the distinction is aptly carried over by Jung in examining the Catholic role, "where the Protestant point of view of an individual relationship to God is overpowered by mass organization and correspondingly collective religious feeling." Thus the Catholic "who has turned his back on the church usually develops a secret or manifest inclination toward atheism, whereas the Protestant follows, if possible, a sectarian movement. The absolutism of the Catholic church seems to demand an equally absolute negation, while Protestant relativism permits variations." (4)

He then offers his own embellishment on the opposition initiated

almost five centuries ago [when] simony and flagrant corruption drove Martin Luther to burst the authoritarian grip of the papacy on divine revelation sealed in the blood of Jesus and open the barn door for each individual Christian to have a direct relationship to God and experience the descent of the Holy Ghost and perhaps be born again as a Pentecostal-charismatic, an Evangelical, a Moonie, indeed any one of the fifty million Fundamentalists who range across the country today, each—like Stephen Leacock's Lord Ronald, flinging himself upon his horse and riding madly off in all directions—proclaiming the inerrancy of the Bible, laying hands, speaking in tongues, handling snakes, and converting the Jews to speed up the Second Coming and the end of the world envisioned in the "multi-dimensional space in which a variety of writings, none of them original, blend and clash" in the supreme, ultimate, hair-raising great story detailed in the Revelation of Saint John the Divine Scriptor from his banishment on the barren Aegean island of Patmos in the year 95, enough to drive anyone round the bend. (8–9)

Works Cited

Abádi-Nagy, Zoltán. "The Art of Fiction: An Interview with William Gaddis." *Paris Review* 105 (winter 1987): 56–89.

Adorno, Theodor. *Aesthetic Theory*. New York: Routledge & Kegan Paul, 1984.

Aichele, Gary J. *Oliver Wendell Holmes: Soldier, Scholar, Judge*. Boston: Twayne Publishers, 1989.

Alexandrov, Vladimir E. *Nabokov's Other World*. Princeton: Princeton University Press, 1991.

Arnason, H. H. *Robert Motherwell*. Rev. ed. New York: Harry N. Abrams, 1982.

Arnau, Frank. *The Art of the Faker: Three Thousand Years of Deception*. Trans. J. Maxwell Brownjohn. Boston: Little, Brown, 1961.

Arnheim, Rudolph. "On Duplication." In Dutton, 232–45.

Ashton, Dore. *About Rothko*. New York: Oxford University Press, 1983.

———. *The New York School: A Cultural Reckoning*. Berkeley: University of California Press, 1992.

Attridge, Derek. *Peculiar Language: Literature as Difference from the Renaissance to James Joyce*. Ithaca: Cornell University Press, 1988.

Bakhtin, Mikhail. *The Dialogic Imagination: Four Essays*. Ed. Michael Holquist. Trans. Caryl Emerson and Michael Holquist. Austin: University of Texas Press, 1990.

———. *Problems of Dostoevsky's Poetics*. Ed. and Trans. Caryl Emerson. Minneapolis: University of Minnesota Press, 1993.

———. *Rabelais and His World*. Trans. Hélène Iswolsky. Bloomington: University of Indiana Press, 1984.

Biddle, Francis. *Justice Holmes, Natural Law and the Supreme Court*. New York: Macmillan, 1961.

Bloch, Ernst. *The Utopian Function of Art and Literature: Selected Essays*. Trans. Jack Zipes and Frank Mecklenburg. Cambridge: MIT Press, 1989.

Bradbury, Malcolm. *The Modern American Novel*. New York: Viking, 1993.

———. *Writers in Conversation 13: William Gaddis*. Interview. London: Institute of Contemporary Arts, 1986. Videocassette from the Rowland Collection, Northbrook, Illinois.

Brontë, Charlotte. *Jane Eyre*. Ed. Richard J. Dunn. New York: Norton, 1987.

Broyard, Anatole. *Kafka was the Rage: A Greenwich Village Memoir*. New York: Carol Southern Books, 1993.

Budick, Sanford, and Wolfgang Iser, eds. *Languages of the Unsayable: The Play of Negativity in Literature and Literary Theory*. New York: Columbia University Press, 1989.

Bultmann, Rudolf. *New Testament and Mythology*. Trans. Schubert M. Ogden. Philadelphia: Fortress Press, 1984.

Burke, Kenneth. *The Rhetoric of Religion: Studies in Logology*. Berkeley: University of California Press, 1970.

Campbell, Peter. "To Hell with the Lyrics." Rev. of *The Collected Writings of Robert Motherwell*. *London Review of Books*, 25 March 1993, 19–20.

Cavell, Stanley. *Conditions Handsome and Unhandsome: The Constitution of Emersonian Perfectionism*. Chicago: University of Chicago Press, 1990.

———. "Time after Time." *London Review of Books*, 12 January 1995, 6–8.

Chipp, Herschel B. *Theories of Modern Art: A Source Book by Artists and Critics*. Berkeley: University of California Press, 1984.

Clark, Stephen R. L. "In the Beginning Was What?" Rev. of *The Creationists*, by Ronald L. Numbers. *New York Times Book Review*, 10 January 1993, 24.

Comnes, Gregory. *The Ethics of Indeterminacy in the Novels of William Gaddis*. Gainesville: University Press of Florida, 1994.

———. "A Patchwork of Conceits: Perspective and Perception in *Carpenter's Gothic*." *Critique* 30, no. 1 (fall 1988): 13–26.

Conway, William Martin. *Early Flemish Artists: And Their Predecessors on The Lower Rhine*. New York: Macmillan, 1887.

———. *The Van Eycks and Their Followers*. New York: Dutton, 1921.

Crane, Diana. *The Transformation of the Avant-Garde: The New York Art World, 1940–1985*. Chicago: University of Chicago Press, 1987.

Cunningham, Valentine. *In the Reading Gaol: Postmodernity, Texts, and History*. Oxford UK and Cambridge USA: Blackwell, 1994.

Delbanco, Andrew. *The Death of Satan: How Americans Have Lost the Sense of Evil*. New York: Farrar, Straus, and Giroux, 1995.

de Man, Paul. "Phenomenality and Materiality in Kant." In *The Textual Sublime: Deconstruction and Its Differences*, ed. Hugh J. Silverman and Gary E. Aylesworth. Albany: State University of New York Press, 1990. 87–108.

Derrida, Jacques. *Aporias*. Stanford: Stanford University Press, 1993.

———. *The Gift of Death*. Trans. David Wills. Chicago: University of Chicago Press, 1995.

———. *Given Time: I. Counterfeit Money*. Trans. Peggy Kamuth. Chicago: University of Chicago Press, 1992.

———. *Specters of Marx*. Trans. Peggy Kamuf. New York: Routledge, 1994.

Doerner, Max. *The Materials of the Artist and Their Use in Painting with Notes in the Techniques of the Old Masters*. Trans. Eugen Neuhaus. New York: Harcourt, Brace, 1934.

Doss, Erika. *Benton, Pollock, and the Politics of Modernism: From Regionalism to Abstract Expressionism*. Chicago: University of Chicago Press, 1991.

Dutton, Denis, ed. *The Forger's Art: Forgery and the Philosophy of Art*. Berkeley: University of California Press, 1983.

Early, James. *Romanticism and American Architecture*. New York: A. S. Barnes, 1965.

Eldridge, Richard. *On Moral Personhood: Philosophy, Literature, Criticism, and Self-Understanding*. Chicago: University of Chicago Press, 1989.

Eliot, T. S. *Four Quartets*. San Diego: Harcourt Brace Jovanovich, 1988.

———. *Selected Prose of T. S. Eliot*. Ed. Frank Kermode. New York: Harcourt Brace Jovanovich/Farrar, Straus, and Giroux, 1975.

———. *To Criticize the Critic: Eight Essays on Literature and Education*. New York: Farrar, Straus, and Giroux, 1970.

———. *The Use of Poetry and The Use of Criticism*. Cambridge: Harvard University Press, 1961.

———. *The Varieties of Metaphysical Poetry: The Clark Lectures*. Ed. Ronald Schuchard. New York: Harcourt Brace, 1994

Emerson, Ralph Waldo. *Selected Essays*. New York: Penguin, 1985.

Feeley, Gregory. "An Artist Who Likes to Be Read, Not Heard." Interview with William Gaddis. *Newsday*, 19 January 1994, 55, 87.

Ferris, Timothy. "On the Edge of Chaos." *New York Review of Books*, 21 September 1995, 41–43.

Fish, Stanley. *"Fish v. Fiss."* In *Interpreting Law and Literature: A Hermeneutic Reader*, ed. Sanford Levinson and Steven Mailloux. Evanston: Northwestern University Press, 1988.

Fitzhugh, George. *Cannibals All! or Slaves without Masters*. Cambridge: Harvard University Press, 1960.

Friedländer, Max J. *From Van Eyck to Brueghel*. Ithaca: Cornell University Press, 1981.

Gadamer, Hans-Georg. *Dialogue and Dialectic: Eight Hermeneutical Studies on Plato*. Trans. P. Christopher Smith. New Haven: Yale University Press, 1980.

———. *Heidegger's Ways*. Trans. John W. Stanley. Albany: State University of New York Press, 1994.

———. *Philosophical Hermeneutics*. Trans. David E. Linge. Berkeley: University of California Press, 1976.

———. *The Relevance of the Beautiful and Other Essays*. Trans. Nicholas Walker. Cambridge: Cambridge University Press, 1986.

Gaddis, William. *Carpenter's Gothic*. New York: Viking Penguin, 1985.

———. "Erewhon and the Contract with America: Wealth, Butler Knew, Was Virtue, Bad Luck a Crime." *New York Times Book Review*, 5 March 1995, 3, 26.

———. "First Notes for a Television Program on Forgery." Unpublished three-page proposal. Keith Botsford Papers, Beinecke Library, Yale University.

———. *A Frolic of His Own*. New York: Poseidon Press, 1994.

———. "How Does the State Imagine?" Speech given at the 48th International PEN Congress, New York City, 1986. Unpublished.

———. "An Instinct for the Dangerous Wife." Rev. of *More Die of Heartbreak*, by Saul Bellow. *New York Times Book Review*, 24 May 1987, 1, 16.

———. *J R*. New York: Penguin, 1975.

————. Letters to Keith Botsford. Keith Botsford Papers, Beinecke Library, Yale University.

————. "Old Foes with New Faces." *Yale Review* 83, no. 4 (October 1995): 1–16.

————. *The Recognitions*. New York: Penguin, 1985.

————. "The Rush for Second Place." *Harper's* 262 (April 1981): 31–39.

————. "Trickle-Up Economics: J R Goes to Washington." *New York Times Book Review*, 25 October 1987, 29.

Gasché, Rodolphe. *Inventions of Difference: On Jacques Derrida*. Cambridge: Harvard University Press, 1994.

————. "On Mere Sight: A Response to Paul de Man." In *The Textual Sublime: Deconstruction and Its Differences*, ed. Hugh J. Silverman and Gary A. Aylesworth. Albany: State University of New York Press, 1990. 87–115.

————. *The Tain of the Mirror: Derrida and the Philosophy of Reflection*. Cambridge: Harvard University Press, 1986.

Gass, William. Introduction to *The Recognitions*, by William Gaddis. New York: Penguin, 1993.

Gibbs, David N. *The Political Economy of Third World Intervention: Mines, Money, and U.S. Policy in the Congo Crisis*. Chicago: University of Chicago Press, 1991.

Giddens, Anthony. *The Consequences of Modernity*. Stanford: Stanford University Press, 1991.

Gilligan, Carol. *In a Different Voice*. Cambridge: Harvard University Press, 1982.

Goldstein, Paul. *Copyright, Patent, Trademark and Related State Doctrines of Intellectual Property*. Westbury, N.Y.: Foundation Press, 1993.

Goodrich, David L. *Art Fakes in America*. New York: Viking Press, 1973.

Green, Jack. *Fire the Bastards!* Normal, Ill.: Dalkey Archive Press, 1992.

Greenberg, Clement. *Art and Culture: Critical Essays*. Boston: Beacon Press, 1968.

Grove, Lloyd. "Gaddis and the Cosmic Babble." Interview with William Gaddis. *Washington Post*, 23 August 1985, B 1, B 10.

Gudiol, José. *The Complete Paintings of El Greco*. Trans. Kenneth Lyons. New York: Greenwich House, 1983.

Guilbaut, Serge. *How New York Stole the Idea of Modern Art: Abstract Expressionism, Freedom, and the Cold War*. Trans. Arthur Goldhammer. Chicago: University of Chicago Press, 1983.

Guillory, John. *Cultural Capital: The Problem of Literary Canon Formation*. Chicago: University of Chicago Press, 1993.

Gunn, Giles. *The Culture of Criticism and the Criticism of Culture*. New York: Oxford University Press, 1987.

————. *Thinking across the American Grain: Ideology, Intellect, and the New Pragmatism*. Chicago: University of Chicago Press, 1992.

Hand, Learned. *The Spirit of Liberty: Papers and Addresses of Learned Hand*. Ed. Irving Dilliard. New York: Vintage, 1959.

Harpham, Geoffrey Galt. *Getting It Right*. Chicago: University of Chicago Press, 1992.

Hartman, Geoffrey. *The Fate of Reading*. Chicago: University of Chicago Press, 1975.

Heilbroner, Robert L. *Behind the Veil of Economics: Essays in Worldly Philosophy*. New York: Norton, 1988.

————. *The Nature and Logic of Capitalism*. New York: Norton, 1985.

Henig, Robin Marantz. "Asthma Kills." *New York Times Sunday Magazine*, 28 March 1993, 42+.

Hoff, Lee Ann. *Battered Women as Survivors*. London: Routledge, 1990.

Hofmann, Hans. *Search for the Real and Other Essays*. Ed. Sara T. Weeks and Bartlett H. Hayes, Jr. Cambridge: M.I.T. Press, 1967.

Hofstadter, Richard. *The Paranoid Style in American Politics and Other Essays*. New York: Alfred A. Knopf, 1965.

Holmes, Oliver Wendell. *The Mind and Faith of Justice Holmes: His Speeches, Essays, Letters and Judicial Opinions*. Ed. Max Lerner. Boston: Little, Brown, 1943.

Holt, John. *How Children Fail*. 1964; rev. ed., New York: Delacorte, 1982.

Hope, Charles. *Titian*. New York: Harper and Row, 1980.

Hutcheon, Linda. *A Theory of Parody: The Teachings of Twentieth-Century Art Forms*. New York and London: Methuen, 1985.

Israel, Jonathan. "The Master of Sacred Reality." *Times Literary Supplement*, 25 November 1994, 18–19.

James, William. "On a Certain Blindness in Human Beings." *William James: The Essential Writings*, ed. Bruce W. Wilshire. Albany: SUNY Press, 1984.

————. *The Varieties of Religious Experience*. New York: Penguin, 1985.

Jenkinson, Edward B. *The Schoolbook Protest Movement*. Bloomington: Phi Delta Kappa Educational Foundation, 1986.

Jeppson, Laurence. *The Fabulous Frauds: Fascinating Tales of Great Art Forgeries*. New York: Weybright and Talley, 1970.

Johnson, George. *Architects of Fear: Conspiracy Theory and Paranoia in American Politics*. Los Angeles: Jeremy P. Tarcher, 1983.

Johnston, John. *Carnival of Repetition*. Philadelphia: University of Pennsylvania Press, 1990.

Kant, Immanuel. *The Critique of Judgement*. Trans. James Creed Meredith. Oxford: Oxford University Press, 1986.

Karl, Frederick R. *American Fictions: 1940–1980*. New York: Harper and Row, 1983.

————. Introduction to *J R*, by William Gaddis. New York: Penguin, 1993.

————. "A Tribune of the Fifties." In Kuehl and Moore, *In Recognition*, 174–98.

Kermode, Frank. *An Appetite for Poetry*. Cambridge: Harvard University Press, 1989.

————. *The Art of Telling: Essays on Fiction*. Cambridge: Harvard University Press, 1983.

————. *Forms of Attention*. Chicago: University of Chicago Press, 1987.

————. *The Genesis of Secrecy: On the Interpretation of Narrative*. Cambridge: Harvard University Press, 1979.

————. *History and Value*. Oxford: Clarendon Press, 1989.

Knight, Christopher. "Flemish Art and Wyatt's Quest for Redemption in William Gaddis' *The Recognitions*." In Kuehl and Moore, *In Recognition*, 58–69.

Koenig. Peter W. "'Splinters from the Yew Tree': A Critical Study of William Gaddis' *The Recognitions*." Ph.D. diss., New York University, 1971.

Kuehl, John. *Alternate Worlds: A Study of Postmodern Antirealistic American Fiction*. New York: New York University Press, 1989.

Kuehl, John, and Steven Moore. "An Interview with William Gaddis." *Review of Contemporary Fiction* 2. no. 2 (summer 1982): 4–6.

———, eds. *In Recognition of William Gaddis*. Syracuse: Syracuse University Press, 1984.

Kundera, Milan. *Testaments Betrayed: An Essay in Nine Parts*. Trans. Linda Asher. New York: HarperCollins, 1995.

LaCapra, Dominick. "William Gaddis's *The Recognitions*." *diacritics* 16, no. 4 (winter 1986): 33–47.

Langer, Suzanne. *Feeling and Form*. New York: Charles Scribner's Sons, 1953.

Larson, Edward J. *Trial and Error: The American Controversy over Creation and Evolution*. New York: Oxford University Press, 1985.

LeClair, Thomas. *The Art of Excess: Mastery in Contemporary American Fiction*. Urbana: University of Illinois Press, 1989.

———. "Missing Writers." *Horizon*, October 1981, 48–52.

Lessing, Alfred. "What Is Wrong with a Forgery?" In Dutton, 58–76.

Levinson, Sanford. "Enlivening the Text: Interpreting (or Inventing) the Constitution." In *The United States Constitution: Roots, Rights, and Responsibilities*, ed. A. E. Dick Howard. Washington: Smithsonian Institution Press, 1992. 291–305.

Lipsey, Roger. *An Art of Our Own: The Spiritual in Twentieth-Century Art*. Boston: Shambhala, 1989.

Logan, Marie-Rose and Tomasz Mirkowicz. Interview with William Gaddis. *Literatura na Swiecie* (Warsaw), no. 1: 150 (1984): 178–89. Unpublished, unpaginated translation provided by Julita Wroniak.

Longfellow, Henry Wadsworth. *The Song of Hiawatha*. Chicago: F. G. Ferguson, 1968.

Lyotard, Jean-François. *The Inhuman*. Stanford: Stanford University Press, 1991.

Maass, John. *The Gingerbread Age: A View of Victorian America*. New York: Rinehart, 1957.

Mackie, Alwynne. *Art/Talk: Theory and Practice in Abstract Expressionism*. New York: Columbia University Press, 1989.

Mansfield, John M., and John Fitzmaurice Mills. *The Genuine Article*. London: British Broadcasting Corporation, 1979.

Martin, Del. *Battered Wives*. San Francisco: Volcano Press, 1981.

Marx, Karl. *Capital*. Vol. 1. New York: Penguin, 1990.

Merleau-Ponty, Maurice. *The Primacy of Perception*. Evanston: Northwestern University Press, 1964.

Meyer, Leonard B. "Forgery and the Anthropology of Art." In Dutton, 77–92.

Moore, Donna M., ed. *Battered Women*. Beverly Hills: Sage Publications, 1979.

Moore, Steven. *A Reader's Guide to William Gaddis's The Recognitions*. Lincoln: University of Nebraska Press, 1982.

———. "Reading the Riot Act." Rev. of *A Frolic of His Own*, by William Gaddis. *Nation*, 25 April 1994, 569–71.

———. *William Gaddis*. Boston: Twayne, 1989.

Mozart, Wolfgang Amadeus. *The Letters of Mozart and his Family*. Trans. and Ed. Emily Anderson. New York: Norton, 1985.

Murdoch, Iris. *Metaphysics as a Guide to Morals*. New York: Allen Lane, 1993.

Nabokov, Vladimir. *Pnin*. New York: Vintage, 1985.

————. *Strong Opinions*. New York: McGraw-Hill, 1973.

Nagel, Thomas. *Equality and Partiality*. New York: Oxford University Press, 1991.

————. *The View from Nowhere*. New York: Oxford University Press, 1986.

Nelkin, Dorothy. *The Creation Controversy: Science or Scriptures in the Schools.* New York: W. W. Norton, 1982.

Newman, Ernest. *Wagner: As Man and Artist*. 1924; rpt., New York: Limelight Editions, 1989.

Nietzsche, Friedrich. *The Case of Wagner. The Complete Works*, vol. 8. Trans. J. M. Kennedy. Ed. Dr. Oscar Levy. Edinburgh: T. N. Foulis, 1911.

Norris, Christopher. *Deconstruction and the Interests of Theory*. Norman and London: Oklahoma University Press, 1992.

Numbers, Ronald L. *The Creationists*. New York: Alfred A. Knopf, 1992.

O'Donnell, Patrick. *Echo Chambers: Figuring Voice in Modern Narrative*. Iowa City: University of Iowa Press, 1992.

————. "Engendering Paranoia in Contemporary Narrative." In *National Identities and Post-Americanist Narrative*, ed. Donald E. Pease. Durham: Duke University Press, 1994. 181–204.

————. "The Reader's Frolic." *Profils Americains: William Gaddis* 6 (1994).

Offiong, Daniel A. *Imperialism and Dependency: Obstacles to African Development*. Washington, D.C.: Howard University Press, 1982.

Olson, Walter K. *The Litigation Explosion*. New York: Dutton, 1991.

Ozick, Cynthia. "Fakery and Stony Truths." Rev. of *Carpenter's Gothic*, by William Gaddis. *New York Times Book Review,* 7 July 1985, 1, 18.

Panofsky, Erwin. *Early Netherland Painting: Its Origins and Character*. New York: Harper and Row, 1971.

Parekh, Bhikhu. "Superior People: The Narrowness of Liberalism from Mill to Rawls." *Times Literary Supplement*, 25 February 1994, 11–13.

Passell, Peter "Fast Money." *New York Times Sunday Magazine*, 18 October 1992, 42+.

Pease, Donald E. "Sublime Politics." In *The American Sublime*, ed. Mary Arensburg. Albany: State University of New York Press, 1986. 21–49.

Plante, David. "The Secret of Henry James." *New Yorker,* 28 November 1994, 91–99.

Plato. *Plato: The Collected Dialogues*. Ed. Edith Hamilton and Huntington Cairns. Princeton: Princeton University Press, 1985.

Raban, Jonathan. "At Home in Babel." Rev. of *A Frolic of His Own*, by William Gaddis. *New York Review of Books,* 17 February 1994, 3+.

Rawls, John. *Political Liberalism*. New York: Columbia University Press, 1993.

Rorty, Richard. "In a Flattened Word." *London Review of Books,* 8 April 1993, 3.

Rosenblum, Robert. "Mark Rothko." *Mark Rothko: 1903–1970*. London: Tate Gallery, 1987.

Rousseau, Jean-Jacques. *The Social Contract and Discourse on the Origin of Inequality*. Ed. Lester G. Crocker. New York: Washington Square Press, 1967.

Said, Edward. *Culture and Imperialism*. New York: Alfred A. Knopf, 1993.

Savage, George. *Forgeries, Fakes, and Reproductions: A Handbook for the Art Dealer and Collector*. New York: Fredrick A. Praeger, 1964.

Schumpeter, Joseph A. *The Theory of Economic Development*. Cambridge: Harvard University Press, 1949.

Schwartz, John. "America's Greatest Novelist?" *Washington Post,* 3 February 1994, C 1–2.

Simmel, Georg. *The Philosophy of Money.* Trans. Tom Bottomore and David Frisby. London: Routledge and Kegan Paul, 1978.

Smith, Dinitia. "Gaddis in the Details." *New York Magazine,* 3 January 1994, 34–40.

Smith, Tom. Interview with William Gaddis. "The Public Radio Bookshow with Tom Smith," 21 December 1993. Co-produced by WAMC-FM, Albany, ant the New York Writers Institute.

Sontag, Susan. *A Susan Sontag Reader.* New York: Farrar, Straus, and Giroux, 1982.

Sparshott, Francis. "The Disappointed Art Lover." In Dutton, 246–63.

Steiner, George. "Crossed Lines." Rev. of *J R,* by William Gaddis. *New Yorker,* 26 January 1976, 106–9.

———. *Real Presences.* London: Faber and Faber, 1989.

Strehle, Susan. *Fiction in the Quantum Universe.* Chapel Hill: University of North Carolina Press, 1992.

Tanner, Tony. "After Twenty Years, Recognition." *New York Times Book Review,* 14 July 1974, 27–28.

———. *City of Words: American Fiction 1950–1970.* New York: Harper and Row, 1971.

Taylor, Charles. *The Ethics of Authenticity.* Cambridge: Harvard University Press, 1992.

Thielmans, Johan. "Intricacies of Plot: Some Preliminary Remarks to William Gaddis's *Carpenter's Gothic.*" In *Studies in Honour of René Derolez,* ed. A. M. Simon-Vandenbergen. Ghent: Seminaire voor Engelese en Oud-Germaanse Taalkunde, 1987.

Thomas, Lewis. *The Fragile Species.* New York: Macmillan, 1992.

Thoreau, Henry David. *Walden and Civil Disobedience.* New York: Penguin, 1986.

"'Til Death Do Us Part." *Time,* 18 January 1993, 39–45.

Trilling, Lionel. *The Liberal Imagination.* Garden City, N.Y.: Doubleday-Anchor, 1957.

Urquhart, Brian. *Decolonization and World Peace.* Austin: University of Texas Press, 1989.

Vasari, Giorgio. *The Lives of the Artists.* Trans. Julia Conaway Bondanella and Peter Bondanella. Oxford: Oxford University Press, 1991.

Weber, Max. *The Protestant Ethic and the Spirit of Capitalism.* Trans. Talcott Parsons. New York: Scribner's, 1958.

Weisenburger, Steven. *Fables of Subversion: Satire and the American Novel, 1930–1980.* Athens and London: University of Georgia Press, 1995.

———. "Paper Currencies: Reading William Gaddis." In Kuehl and Moore, *In Recognition,* 147–61.

Werness, Hope B. "*Han van Meegeren* fecit." In Dutton, 1–57.

Wiener, Norbert. *The Human Use of Human Beings: Cybernetics and Society.* New York: Avon Books, 1967.

Wilson, Edmund. *Patriotic Gore: Studies in the Literature of the American Civil War.* New York: Oxford University Press, 1962.

Wilson, Rob. *American Sublime: The Genealogy of a Poetic Genre.* Madison: University of Wisconsin Press, 1991.

Wittgenstein, Ludwig. *Tractatus Logico-Philosophicus.* Trans. C. K. Ogden. 1922; rpt., London: Routledge, 1990.

Wood, James. "Bard in a Black Hole." Rev. of *Meaning in Shakespeare*, by Terence Hawkes. *Times Literary Supplement,* 23 April 1993, 20.

Wood, Michael. "So Sue Me." *London Review of Books*, 12 May 1994, 20–21.

Wren, Michael. "Is, Madam? Nay, Seems!" In Dutton, 188–224.

Index

DATE DUE

MAR 12 1996

UPI   PRINTED IN U.S.A.